Henry Theodore Tuckerman

America and Her Commentators

With a Critical Sketch of Travel in the United States

Henry Theodore Tuckerman

America and Her Commentators
With a Critical Sketch of Travel in the United States

ISBN/EAN: 9783337009755

Printed in Europe, USA, Canada, Australia, Japan

Cover: Foto ©ninafisch / pixelio.de

More available books at **www.hansebooks.com**

AMERICA

AND

HER COMMENTATORS.

WITH A CRITICAL SKETCH OF

TRAVEL IN THE UNITED STATES.

BY

HENRY T. TUCKERMAN.

> Here the free spirit of mankind, at length
>   Throws its last fetters off; and who shall place
> A limit to the giant's unchained strength,
>   Or curb his swiftness in the forward race?
> . . . . .
> For thou, my country, thou shalt never fall,
>   Save with thy children:—
>   —— Who shall then declare
> The date of thy deep-founded strength, or tell
> How happy, in thy lap, the sons of men shall dwell?
> BRYANT: *The Ages.*

NEW YORK:
CHARLES SCRIBNER, 124 GRAND STREET
1864.
LONDON: S. LOW, SON & COMPANY.

PREFACE.

The object of this work is twofold—to present a general view of the traits and transitions of our country, as recorded at different periods and by writers of various nationalities; and to afford those desirous of authentic information in regard to the United States a guide to the sources thereof. Incidental to and naturally growing out of this purpose, is the discussion of the comparative value and interest of the principal critics of our civilization. The present seems a favorable time for such a retrospective review; and the need of popular enlightenment, both at home and abroad, as to the past development and present condition of this Republic, is universally acknowledged. There are special and obvious advantages in reverting to the past and examining the present, through the medium of the literature of American Travel. It affords striking contrasts, offers different points of view, and is the more suggestive because modified by national tastes. We can thus trace physical and social development, normal and casual traits, through personal impressions; and are unconsciously put on the track of honest investigation, made to realize familiar tendencies under new aspects, and, from the variety of evidence, infer true estimates. Moreover, some of these *raconteurs* are interesting characters either in an historical or literary point of view, and form an attractive biographical study. In a work intended to suggest rather than exhaust a subject so extensive, it has been requisite to dismiss briefly many books which, in themselves, deserve special consideration; but whose scope is too identical with other and similar volumes described at length, to need the same full examination. It is not always the specific merits of an author, but the contrast he offers or the circumstances under which he writes, that have induced what might otherwise seem too elaborate a discussion of his claims. In a word, variety of subject and rarity of material have been kept in view, with reference both to the space awarded and the extracts given. The design of the work might, indeed, have been indefinitely extended; but economy and suggestiveness have been chiefly considered.

Many of the works discussed are inaccessible to the general reader; others are prolix, and would not reward a consecutive perusal, though worthy a brief analysis; while not a few are too superficial, and yield amusement only when the grains of wit or wisdom are separated from the predominant chaff. It is for these reasons, and in the hope of vindicating as well as illustrating the claims and character of our outraged nationality, that I have prepared this inadequate, but, I trust, not wholly unsatisfactory critical sketch of Travel in the United States. Those who desire to examine minutely the historical aspects of the prolific theme, will find, in the "Bibliotheca Americana" of Rich, a catalogue of ancient works full of interest to the philosophical student. Another valuable list is contained in "Historical Nuggets," a descriptive account of rare books relating to America, by Henry Stevens (2 vols., London, 1853); and the proposed "American Bibliographer's Manual," a dictionary of all works relating to America, by Joseph

Sabin, of Philadelphia, will, if executed with the care and completeness promised, supersede all other manuals, and prove of great utility. No fact is more indicative of the increased interest in all that relates to our country, than the demand for the earlier records of its life, products, and history;* while the foreign bibliography of the war for the Union, and the American record and discussions thereof, have been already collected or are in process of collection under Government auspices.†

* " If the price of old books anent America, whether native or foreign, should continue to augment in value in the same ratio as they have done for the last thirty years, their prices must become fabulous, or, rather, like the books of the Sibyls, rise above all valuation. In the early part of the present century, the " Bay Hymn Book " (the first book printed in North America), then an exceedingly rare book, no one would have supposed would bring $100; now, a copy was lately sold for nearly $600, and a perfect copy, at this time, would bring $1,000. Eliot's " Grammar of the Indian Tongues " was lately sold for $160—a small tract. The same author's version of the Scriptures into the Indian language could be purchased, fifty years ago, for $50; now it is worth $500. For Cotton Mather's " Magnalia Christi Americana," $6 was then thought a good price; now, $50 is thought cheap for a good copy. Smith's " History of Virginia," $30; now $75. Stith's " History of Virginia," then $5, now $20. Smith's " History of New Jersey," then $2, now $20. Thomas's " History of Printing," then $2, now $15. Denton's " History of New Netherlands," $5, now $50. These are but a few out of many hundreds that could be named, that have risen from trifling to extraordinary prices, in the short space of half a century."—*Western Memorabilia.*

† " The importance of this subject has been more directly brought to our notice in the examination of the foundation of a " Collection of European Opinion upon the War," now before Congress for the use of the members, and to be deposited in the Congress Library. This desirable collection is to comprise the various pamphlets, speeches, debates, and brochures of all kinds that have appeared in reference to the war, from the attack on Fort Sumter to the present day, and to be continued to the end of the struggle. We have the leading editorials, arranged with great care in chronological order, from the most powerful representatives of the public press in England, France, Germany, &c.; also, the correspondence from both armies in the field, of the special agents sent for that purpose. The various opinions expressed by eminent military and naval writers upon our new inventions in the art of war will well deserve study; and the horoscope of the future, not only in our own country, but in its influences upon the welfare of the Old World, should be carefully pondered over by all political economists."—*National Intelligencer.*

Numerous as are the books of travel in and commentaries on America—ranging from the most shallow to the most profound, from the crude to the artistic, from the instructive to the impertinent—so far is the subject from being exhausted, that we seem but now to have a clear view of the materials for judgment, description, and analysis. It required the genius of modern communication, the scientific progress, the humane enterprise, the historical development, and the social inspiration of our own day, to appreciate the problems which events will solve on this continent; to understand the tendencies, record the phenomena, define the influences and traits, and realize the natural, moral, and political character and destiny of America.

NEW YORK, *March*, 1864.

CONTENTS.

	PAGE
INTRODUCTION	1

CHAPTER I.
EARLY DISCOVERERS AND EXPLORERS............................ 13

CHAPTER II.
FRENCH MISSIONARY EXPLORATION.
Hennepin; Menard; Allouez; Marquette; Charlevoix; Marest; etc.... 37

CHAPTER III.
FRENCH TRAVELLERS AND WRITERS.
Chastellux; L'Abbé Robin; Duché; Brissot de Warville; Crevecœur; La Rochefoucauld-Liancourt; Volney; Raynal.................. 58

CHAPTER IV.
FRENCH TRAVELLERS AND WRITERS—*Continued.*
Rochambeau; Talleyrand; Ségur; Chateaubriand; Michaux; Murat; Brillat-Savarin; De Tocqueville; De Beaumont; Ampère; Lafayette; Fisch; De Gasparin; Officers; Laboulaye, etc.................. 110

CHAPTER V.
BRITISH TRAVELLERS AND WRITERS.
Berkeley; McSparran; Mrs. Grant; Burnaby; Rogers; Burke; Douglass; Henry; Eddis; Anbury; Smythe........ 156

CONTENTS.

CHAPTER VI.

BRITISH TRAVELLERS AND WRITERS—*Continued.*

Wansey; Cooper; Wilson; Davis; Ashe; Bristed; Kendall; Weld; Cobbett; Campbell; Byron; Moore; Mrs. Wakefield; Hodgson; Janson; Caswell; Holmes and others; Hall; Fearon; Fiddler; Lyell; Featherstonaugh; Combe; Female Writers; Dickens; Faux; Hamilton; Parkinson; Mrs. Trollope; Grattan; Lord Carlisle; Anthony Trollope; Prentice; Stirling 193

CHAPTER VII.

ENGLISH ABUSE OF AMERICA.. 252

CHAPTER VIII.

NORTHERN EUROPEAN WRITERS.

Kalm; Miss Bremer; Gurowski, and others; German Writers: Saxe-Weimar; Von Raumer; Prince Maximilian Von Wied; Lieber; Schultz. Other German Writers: Grund; Ruppius; Seatsfield; Kohl; Talvi; Schaff.. 293

CHAPTER IX.

ITALIAN TRAVELLERS.

National Relations; Verrazzano; Castiglione; D'Allessandro; Capobianco; Salvatore Abbate e Migliori; Pisani...................... 334

CHAPTER X.

AMERICAN TRAVELLERS AND WRITERS.

John and William Bartram; Madame Knight; Ledyard; Carver; Jefferson; Imlay; Dwight; Coxe; Ingersoll; Walsh; Paulding; Flint; Clinton; Hall; Tudor; Wirt; Cooper; Hoffman; Olmsted; Bryant; Government Explorations; Washington; Mrs. Kirkland; Irving. American Illustrative Literature: Biography; History; Manuals; Oratory; Romance; Poetry. Local Pictures: Everett, Hawthorne, Channing, etc....................................... 371

CHAPTER XI.

CONCLUSION... 438

INDEX.. 451

INTRODUCTION.

La Terre, says Fontenelle, *est une vieille coquette*. While in so many branches of authorship the interest of books is superseded by new discoveries in science and superior art and knowledge, honest and intelligent books of travel preserve their use and charm, because they describe places and people as they were at distinct epochs, and confirm or dissipate subsequent theories. The point of view adopted, the kind of sympathy awakened, the time and the character of the writer—each or all give individuality to such works, when inspired by genuine observation, which renders them attractive as a reference and a memorial, and for purposes of comparison if not of absolute interest. Moreover the early travellers, or rather those who first record their personal experience of a country, naturally describe it in detail, and put on record their impressions with a candor rarely afterward imitated, because of that desire to avoid a beaten path which later writers feel. Hence, the most familiar traits and scenes are apt to be less dwelt upon, the oftener they are described; and, for a complete and *naïve* account, we must revert to primitive travels, whose quaintness and candor often atone for any incongruities of style or old-fashioned prolixity.

A country that is at all suggestive, either through association or intrinsic resources, makes a constant appeal to genius, to science, and to sympathy; and offers, under each of these aspects, an infinite variety. Arthur Young's account of France, just before the Revolution, cannot be superseded; Lady Montagu's account of Turkey is still one of the most complete; and Dr. Moore's Italy is a picture of manners and morals of permanent interest, because of its contrast with the existent state of things. Indeed, that beautiful and unfortunate but regenerated land has long been so congenial a theme for scholars, and so attractive a nucleus for sentiment, that around its monuments and life the gifted and eager souls of all nations, have delighted to throw the expression of their conscious personality, from morbid and melancholy Byron to intellectual and impassioned De Staël, from Hans Andersen, the humane and fanciful Dane, to Hawthorne, the introspective New Englander. What Italy has been and is to the unappropriated sentiment of authors, America has been and is to unorganized political aspirations: if the one country has given birth to unlimited poetical, the other has suggested a vast amount of philosophical speculation. Brissot, Cobbett, and De Tocqueville found in the one country as genial a subject as Goethe, Rogers, and Lady Morgan in the other; and while the latter offers a permanent background of art and antiquity, which forever identifies the scene, however the light and shade of the writer's experience may differ, so Nature, in her wild, vast, and beautiful phases, offers in the former an inspiring and inexhaustible charm, and free institutions an ever-suggestive theme, however variously considered.

The increase of books of this kind can, perhaps, be realized in no more striking way than by comparing the long catalogue of the present day with the materials available to the inquirer half a century ago. When Winterbotham, in 1795, undertook to prepare an "Historical, Geographical, Commercial, and Philosophical View of the United States "*—to meet an acknowledged want in Europe, where so many, contemplating emigration to America, anxiously sought for ac-

* Four vols. 8vo., with a series of maps, plates, portraits, &c., London, 1795. "A valuable record of the state of this continent at the end of the last century, selected from all accessible sources."

curate knowledge, and often for local and political details, and where there existed so much misconception and such visionary ideas in regard to this country—he cited the following writers as his chief resource for facts and principles of history, government, social conditions, and statistics: the Abbé Raynal, Dr. Franklin, Robertson, Clavigero, Jefferson, Belknap, Adams, Catesby, Morse, Buffon, Gordon, Ramsay, Bartram, Cox, Rush, Mitchill, Cutler, Imlay, Filson, Barlow, Brissot, and Edwards. The authenticity of most of these writers made them, indeed, most desirable authorities; but the reader who recalls their respective works will readily perceive how limited was the scope of such, considered as illustrating the entire country. Dr. Belknap wrote of New Hampshire, Jefferson of Virginia, Bartram of Florida and a few other States; Ramsay, Gordon, Adams, and Franklin furnished excellent political information; but Morse's Geography was quite crude and limited, and Brissot's account of America was tinctured with his party views. We need not lose sight of the benefits which our early historical authors and naturalists conferred, while we fully recognize the superior completeness and scientific insight of later and better-equipped authors. Dr. Belknap, it will ever be conceded, stands foremost as a primitive local historian, and benign is his memory as the indefatigable student of venerable records when the steeple of the Old South Church, in Boston, was his study; while, as the founder of the Massachusetts Historical Society, every explorer of New England annals owes him a debt of gratitude: yet his description of the White Mountains is more valuable for its early date than for those scientific and picturesque details which give such interest to the botanical researches of contemporary authors. The data furnished by Catesby and Bartram have still a charm and use for the *savant* who examines the flora and ichthyology of Florida and the Carolinas—notwithstanding the splendid work of Agassiz; and there are temporary aspects of life at the South noted by Paulding, which give emphasis to the more thorough statistics of Olmsted.

To a philosophical reader, indeed, there are few more striking illustrations of character than the diverse trains of thought, sources of interest, and modes of viewing the same subject, which books of travel incidentally reveal: from Herodotus to Humboldt, the disposition and idiosyncrasies of the writers are as apparent as their comparative ability. There is, undoubtedly, great sameness in the numerous journals, letters, and treatises of travellers on America; only a few of them have any claim to originality, or seem animated by vital relations to the subject; a specimen here and there represents an entire class; and to analyze the whole would be wearisome; yet, in all that bear the impress of discrimination and moral sensibility, there is evident the individuality of taste and purpose that belongs to all genuine human work; and in this point of view these writings boast no common variety: each author looks at his theme through the lens to which his vision is habituated; and hence we have results as diverse as the medium and the motive of the respective writers. It accords with Talleyrand's political tastes that the sight of Alexander Hamilton—one of the wisest of the republican legislators—should have been the most memorable incident of his exile in America: equally accordant with Ampère's literary sentiment was it that he should find a Dutch gable as attractive as Broadway, because it revived the genial humor of Irving's facetious History: Wilson and Charles Bonaparte found the birds, French officers the fair Quakers, English commercial travellers the manufactures and tariffs, English farmers the agriculture, Continental economists the prison and educational systems, Lyell the rocks and mines, Michaux the trees, sportsmen the Western plains, and clerical visitors the sects and missions—the chief attraction; and while one pilgrim bestows his most heartfelt reflections upon the associations of Mount Vernon, another has no sympathy for any scene or subject but those connected with slavery: this one is amusing in humorous exaggeration of the Connecticut Blue Laws, and that one extravagant in his republican zeal; tobacco and maple sugar, intemperance and prairie hunting, reptiles and elections, the whale fishery and the Indians, manners and morals, occupy, in most unequal proportions, the attention of different writers; an engineer praises the ingenuity and hardihood, while he deprecates the fragility of the "remarkable wooden bridges in America;" an editor discourses of the influence and abuse of the Press; a horticulturist speculates on the prospects of the vine culture, and an economist on the destruction of the forests and the desultory system of farming. Chambers, accustomed to cater for useful knowledge for the people, describes public establishments and schools; while Kossuth's companion Pulskzy looks sharply at the "white, red, and black" races of the land, and speculates therefrom upon democracy and its results; Lady Stuart Wortley enters into the sentiment of the scenery, and Miss Bremer into the details of domestic economy; the Earl of Carlisle asks first for Allston's studio on landing, and, with the liberality of a scholar and a gentleman, elucidates the country he has partially but candidly observed, in a popular lecture; while the Honorable Augustus Murray had too much rare sport in the West, and formed too happy a conjugal tie in America, not to have his recollections thereof, bright and kindly in the record. In a word, every degree of sympathy and antipathy, of refinement and vulgarity, of philosophical insight and shallow impertinence is to be traced in these books of American travel—from coarse malice to dull good nature, and from genial sense to repulsive bigotry. And while the field may appear to have been well reaped as regards the discussion of manners, government, and industrial resources—recondite inquirers, especially the ethnologists, regard America as still ripe for the harvest.

Years ago, Le Comte Carli* wrote to his cousin: "Je me propose de vous developper mes idées, ou, si vous le voulez,

---

* "Lettres Americaines," 2 vols. 8vo., Paris, 1788. "In the first part, the author describes the manners and customs of the Americans before their country was discovered by Europeans. He also believes that traces of the religious rites of the Church of Rome were found among them, which resembled baptism and the communion of bread and wine."

mes songes, concernant les anciens peuples de l'Amerique que je crois descendus de ces antiques Atlantides si fameux dans l'histoire des premiers temps." And, within a few months, a London critical journal has mercilessly ridiculed the Abbé Em. Domenech, who published his "Seven Years' Residence in the Great American Deserts;" in the introduction to which he remarks: "America is not solely an El Dorado for freebooters and fortune seekers; though few persons have gone thither to gather the fruits of science." He refers to the origin of the Indian tribes and the various theories on the subject, and alludes to the undoubted fact that "numerous emigrations took place at very remote periods;" and adds: "Africa has become known to us, but America has still a vast desert to which missionaries, merchants, and some rare scientific expeditions have alone penetrated. Its history, its geography, and its geology are still wrapped in swaddling clothes. America is now, comparatively speaking, a new country, a virgin land, which contains numerous secrets. The Government of the United States, to its praise be it, have, of late years, sent scientific expeditions into the American Deserts;" and he notes the publications of Schoolcraft, Catlin, and the Smithsonian Institute.

We have first the old voyageurs in the collection of De Bry and his English prototype Ogilby—the quaint, often meagre, but original and authentic records of the first explorers and navigators; then, the diaries, travels, and memoirs of the early Jesuit missionaries; next, the colonial pamphlets and reports, official, speculative, and incidental, including the series of controversial tracts and descriptions relating to New England and Virginia and other settlements; the reports of the Quaker missionaries, the travels of French officers who took part in the Revolutionary War, and the long catalogue of English books—from the colonial to the cockney era; while the lives of the Spanish explorers, of the pioneers, the military adventurers, and the founders of colonies fill up and amplify the versatile chronicle. From Roger Williams's Key to the Indian Languages, to Sir Henry Clinton's annotations of Grahame's History of the American War, from De Vries to De Tocqueville, from Cotton Mather * to Mrs. Trollope, from Harmon's "Free Estate of Virginia," published in 1614, to Dr. Russell's fresh letters thence to the London *Times;* from Champlain's voyage to Dickens's Notes, from Zenger's Trial † to the last report of the Patent Office—the *catalogue raisonnée* of books of American travel, history, and criticism would include every phase of life, manners, creed, custom, development, and character, from the imperfect chart of unknown waters to the glowing photograph of manners in the analytical nineteenth century. We find, in examining the library of American travels, that toleration is the charm that invests her to the heart yet bleeding from the wounds of relentless persecution; and, in the elation of freedom, the page glows with eloquent gratitude even amid the plaints of exile. Mountains, rivers, cataracts, and caves make the child of romance pause and plead; while gigantic fossil or exquisite coral reefs or a superb tree or rare flower win and warm the naturalist: one lingers in the Baltimore cathedral, another at the Moravian settlement at Bethlehem, and a third in a Unitarian chapel at Boston, according to their respective views; while "equality of condition," small taxes, cheap land, or plentiful labor secures the advocacy of the practical; and solecisms in manners or language provoke the sarcasms of the fastidious.

We derive from each and all of these commentators on our country, information, not otherwise obtainable, of the aspect of nature and the condition of the people, at different eras and in various regions: we thus realize the process of national

---

* Cotton Mather's "Magnalia Christi Americana; or, the Ecclesiastical History of New England," 2 vols. 8vo., first American ed., Hartford, 1820.

† "A Brief Narrative of the Case and Trial of John P. Zenger, Printer of the New York 'Weekly Journal,' for a Libel," 4to., pp. 53, New York, 1770. Gouverneur Morris, instead of dating American liberty from the Stamp Act, traced it to the prosecution of Peter Zenger, a printer in the colony of New York, for an alleged libel: because that event revealed the philosophy of freedom, both of thought and speech, as an inborn human right, so nobly set forth in Milton's treatise on unlicensed printing.

development; trace to their origin local peculiarities; behold the present by the light of the past; and, in a manner, identify ourselves with those to whom familiarity had not blunted the impression of scenes native to ourselves, and social traits or political tendencies too near for us to view them in their true moral perspective. It may therefore prove both useful and interesting, suggestive and entertaining, to follow the steps and listen to the comments of these numerous travellers and critics, and so learn better to understand, more justly to appreciate and wisely love the land of our birth, doubly dear since fratricidal hands have desecrated her fame.

After colonial enterprise, republican sympathy, economical zeal, the satirical, the adventurous, and the scientific had thus successively reported to Europe the condition and prospects, the errors and merits of our country, in the height of her material prosperity, broke out the long-matured Rebellion of the Slaveholders; and while a vast and sanguinary civil war tested to the utmost, the moral and physical resources of the nation, it called forth a new, more earnest and significant criticism abroad. To analyze this would be to discuss the entire foreign bibliography of the war for the Union. We can but glance at its most striking features and important phenomena.

The first lesson to be inferred from the most cursory survey of what has been published in Europe on what is there called "the American Question," is the immense and intricate influence and relations which now unite the New to the Old World. Commerce, emigration, political ideas, social interests, literature, science, and religion have, one and all, continued to weave strong mutual ties of dependence and reciprocity between Europe and America, to realize the extent and vital importance of which we have only to compare the issues of the European press for a single week with the sparse and obscure publications whereby the foreigner, a century ago, learned what was going on or likely to be achieved for humanity on the great western continent. This voluminous and impressive testimony as to the essential importance of

America to Europe, is quite as manifest in the abuse as in the admiration, in the repulsion as the sympathy of foreign writers, during the memorable conflict; for selfish fear, interested motives, or base jealousy inspired their bitter comments far more than speculative indifference; while those in a disinterested position, actuated solely by philosophical and humane impulses, elaborately pleaded the cause of our national life and integrity as involved in the essential welfare of the civilized world. Next to this universal acknowledgment of a mutual stake in the vast conflict, perhaps for us the most singular revelation derived from the foreign discussion of our civil and military affairs has been that of the extraordinary ignorance of the country existing abroad. Apart from wilful political and perverse prejudice, this popular ignorance is doubtless the cause and the excuse for much of the patent injustice and animosity exhibited by the press toward the United States. The rebellious government organized a social mission to Europe, whereby they forestalled public opinion and artfully misrepresented facts: so that it has been a slow process to enlighten the leaders of opinion, and counteract the work of mercenary writers in France and England subsidized at the earliest stage of the war.

But with all due allowance for want of knowledge and the assiduity of paid advocates of error, through all the passion, prejudice, and mercenary hardihood which have given birth to so much falsehood, malice, and inhumanity in the foreign literary treatment of our national cause in this stupendous crisis and climax of social and civil life—we can yet distinctly trace the influence and recognize the work of friend and foe in the recent avalanche of new commentators on America: their motives become daily more obvious, their legitimate claims more apparent, and their just influence better appreciated. History has in store for the most eminent an estimate which will counteract any undue importance attached to their dicta by the acute sensibilities of the passing time, so "big with fate." In an intellectual point of view, the course of English writers is already defined and explained

1*

to popular intelligence: the greater part of their insane ill will and perverse misrepresentation being accredited to political jealousy and prejudice, and therefore of no moral value; while the evidence of bribery and corruption robs another large amount of vituperation and false statement of all rational significance; while the more prominent and powerful expositors, as far as position, capacity, and integrity are concerned, are, to say the least, not so unequally divided as to cause any fear that truth and justice lack able and illustrious defenders: in the political arena, Roebuck's vulgar anathemas were more than counterbalanced by the sound and honest reasoning of Cobden and the logical eloquence of Bright; while we could afford to bear the superficial sneers of Carlyle, more of an artist than a philosopher in letters, and the unworthy misrepresentations of Lord Brougham, senilely aristocratic and unsympathetic, while the vigorous thinker and humanely scientific reformer John Stuart Mill so clearly, consistently, and effectively pleaded the claims of our free nationality. And in France, how vain in the retrospect seem the venal lucubrations of pamphleteers and newspaper contributors arrayed against the Government and people of the United States when fighting for national existence and against the perpetuity and canonization of the greatest of human wrongs—when, in the lecture room of the College of France, the gifted and erudite Edouard Laboulaye expounds the grand and rightful basis of our Constitution, and in the *salons* of the same metropolis scatters his wit-kindled pages in vindication of our social privileges and civic growth; and, at the French Academy, Montalembert thus opens his discourse:

"Gentlemen, eighty years have elapsed since M. Montyon confided to the French Academy the mission of crowning not only literary works useful to morals, but virtuous deeds. It was in the year 1782; at the moment when the peace of America commenced to recompense the glorious coöperation which France had lent to the emancipation of the United States and to the birth of a great free people, *whose greatness and whose liberty shall never perish, if it please God, in the formidable trials which it is passing through to-day.* Louis XVI.

showed himself still animated by the wisdom which had called Malesherbes and Turgot to his counsels. The Queen Marie Antoinette had given birth to her firstborn; Madame Elizabeth of France was in her eighteenth year, illuminating Versailles with her virginal graces and her angelic piety—that Elizabeth whose bust you see before you, presented by M. Montyon himself, with the inscription 'To Virtue,' of which she seemed the most perfect and touching type. Liberty then seemed to rise up pure and fruitful in Europe as in America, and our ancient royalty to be steeped in a new fountain of youth, popularity, and virtue.

"How many miscalculations, ruins, and disasters, above all, how many crimes and humiliating failures, since these days of generous illusion, of legitimate enthusiasm and blind confidence! How many cruel lessons inflicted upon the noblest aspirations of the human heart! How many motives for not surrendering themselves to the most reasonable hopes except with a salutary humility, but however, without ever abdicating the indissoluble rights of human liberty or banishing to the land of chimeras the noble ambition of governing men by honor and conscience!"

The new comments on America elicited by the war are threefold: first, political speeches; second, newspaper commentaries; and third, treatises deliberately written and published. Of the first, the greater part are unavoidably ephemeral in their influence, and usually called forth by a special phase of the war in its international relations; the second, especially as regards the leading journal in Great Britain and most famous in the world, have sunk to the lowest conceivable level as a medium of authentic information and a mercenary agency; in the third department alone has anything of a complete and permanent interest been introduced; and there are pages of De Gasparin, Laboulaye, Mill, Cairnes, Newman, Cochin, and Martin, which deserve to be enshrined as literary illustrations of Christian liberalism and eloquent loyalty to truth and humanity in the defence and illustration of American liberty, law, and life, in their magnanimous conflict with injustice, degradation, and cruel sacrilege. When Lafayette, nearly half a century ago, received at the hands of the nation in whose behalf he had fought in his youth, the greatest popular ovation ever granted to a hero, he thus alluded to the

Union in one of his replies to the municipal welcomes that greeted his entrance into every city of the land:

"A Union, so essential, not only to the *fate of each member of the confederacy*, but also to the *general fate of mankind*, that the least breach of it would be hailed with barbarian joy by a universal war-whoop of European aristocracy and despotism."

It was in reply to this base "war whoop" that the writers we have mentioned, so eloquently and seasonably advocated the cause and character of our nation.

One of the most curious and interesting of the countless subjects which the history of our memorable conflict will yield to future philosophical investigation, will be its literary fruit and record—the bibliography of the war—and of this the foreign contributions will afford some remarkable and brilliant specimens. If to ourselves, as a nation, the war for the Union has been a test of extraordinary scope and intensity —developing a military and scientific genius, a sanitary enterprise, an extent of financial resources, a capacity for self-sacrifice and self-reliance undreamed of in our prior experience; if it has tested personal character and modified social estimates, and tried absolutely the comparative worth and latent force of our institutions and national sentiment, not less has it tested the political magnanimity, the press, the prejudices, the social philosophy, and humane instincts of Europe; and if the crisis has evoked much that is mean and mortifying in the spirit of those old communities in their feelings toward our young republic in the bitter hour when the pangs of a second birth are rending her vitals, so also has it called forth memorable, benign, noble words of cheer and challenge from volunteer champions of America abroad, in the foremost ranks of her best and most honest thinkers, lovers of truth, and representatives of humanity.

CHAPTER I.

EARLY DISCOVERERS AND EXPLORERS.

From the time when the existence of this continent was but conjectural to the European mind, and recognized as a fact of nature only in the brain of a poor Genoese mariner, it was looked to, thought of, imagined chiefly in its relation to the Old World, as the completion and resource of her civilization—a new opportunity, a fresh arena. Gold seekers,[*] indeed, were prompted to gaze hither by mere cupidity, and Columbus nearly lost his long-solicited aid from the Spanish sovereigns by insisting on hereditary privileges of rule and possession in case of success; but the idea that warmed the generous purpose of Isabella was the conversion to Christianity of the heathen tribes of America, and the extension of Catholic rule in the world. No candid thinker can look back upon the period of the discovery without tracing a wonderful combination of events and tendencies of humanity, whereof this land seems the foreordained and inevitable goal and consequence. It cannot appear to the least imaginative and philosophical mind as an accident, that the zeal for maritime discovery should have awakened in Europe simultaneously with the access of new social truth, the sudden progress of

---

[*] "Les chercheurs d'or ont commencé, ni voulant qu'or, rien de plus brisant l'homme, Colomb, le meilleur de tous, dans son propre journal, montre cela avec une naïveté terrible, qui d'avance, fait fremir de ce que feront ses successeurs."
—Michelet.

ideas, and the triumph of mechanical genius. With the fifteenth century the "civilization of the sanctuary" overleaped its long exclusive boundaries, and, with the invention of printing, became a normal need and law of humanity; feudalism waned; the Reformation awoke and set free the instinct of faith and moral freedom; and just at this crisis a new world was opened, a fresh sphere afforded. As the idea of "geographical unity"—the conviction that "the globe wanted one of its hemispheres"—was the inspiration of Columbus, so to the eye of the thoughtful observer, an equilibrium of the moral world—a balance to the human universe—was as obvious and imperative a necessity; for the new ideas and the conflict of opinions and interests, and especially the new and absolute self-assertion, incident to the decay of error and the escape from traditional degradation, made it indispensable to the safety of the innovator, the freedom of the thinker, the scope of the dissenter and reformer, to find refuge and audience in a land whose destinies yet lay undeveloped in the wild freedom of nature, and where prowess of mind as well as of animal courage could work into "victorious clearness" the confused problems of an aspiring civilization, and lay the foundation of an eclectic, liberal, and free community of men—"a wider theatre and a new life."

Accordingly, with the progress of time and the accumulation of historical details, with the profound analysis thereof that characterizes modern research—the decline of feudal and ecclesiastical sway in Europe, the Reformation, and the invention of printing are seen to have an intimate relation to and affinity with the discovery of America, in the series of historical events which have resulted in the civilization of the nineteenth century. Nor is this original association of the New and Old World without a vague physical parallel; for it has been a favorite scientific speculation that there was an ancient union or proximity of the two continents—suggested by the fact that the eastern shore of America advances where the opposite shore of Europe recedes. "Firstborn among the continents," says Agassiz, "though so much later in culture and civilization than some of more recent birth, America, as far as her physical history is concerned, has been falsely denominated the *New* World." "America," says Ritter, "although it repeats the contrasts of the Old World, yet the course of its mountain chains is not from east to west, but from north to south. Its sea coast best endowed with harbors and islands is on the eastern side, and so turned toward the civilization of the Old World. The Gulf Stream, which may be called the great commercial highway of nations, brought both of the continents bordering on the North Atlantic into direct connection. North America was, therefore, destined to be discovered by Europeans, and not by Asiatics. Asia could easily have transferred a part of its population to America, in consequence of the proximity of their shores at Behring's Straits. But the sea coast of North America is so richly furnished with harbors and islands, that it readily attracted European civilization. The gentle slopes of the American continent offered a most favorable field to Europeans, allowing, as they did, civilization to penetrate without obstruction every portion of the land. Nature, too, has shown us, by giving to America river systems which run northward to the numerous groups of islands and peninsulas of the Polar Sea, that America was destined even more than Europe to send civilization to the northern portions of the globe." *

The North American continent extends from the twenty-fourth to the forty-ninth degree of north latitude, and from the sixty-sixth to the one hundred and twenty-fourth degree of west longitude: its area is more than five sixths that of Europe, and more than ten times that of Great Britain and France united: there are seven thousand miles of eastern shore line, thirty-four hundred southern and twenty-two hundred western; while the northern lake line is twenty-two hundred miles. Climate, soil, avocation, and productions are, by this affluent space, adapted to the constitution, the character, and the necessity of each European nationality—so that

---

* "Geographical Studies," by Professor Carl Ritter, of Berlin, translated by W. L. Gage.

the German vinedresser, the Italian musician, the Spanish planter, the French modiste—Pole, Russian, Swede, Swiss, and Sicilian—the professor, merchant, man of science, agriculturist, tough rustic, delicate artiste, radical writer, proselyting priest, or cosmopolitan philosopher—with any sagacity, self-respect, or urbanity, can readily find the physical conditions or the social facilities, the climate, business, and community, the scopes, position, and prosperity adapted to his temperament and faculty. The Spanish, French, and colonial history of America—the national epoch with its statistics of navigation, population, taxation, education, public lands, railways, manufactures, patents, canals, telegraphs, legislation, municipal rule, emigration, jurisprudence, trade, and government—and, finally, the causes and significance of the present rebellion—are each and all elements of a vast historical development, wherein a Christian philosopher can easily trace a consecutive significance and Divine superintendence of humanity.

Travellers of ordinary intelligence and observation are not unfrequently lured into vague but rational conjectures as to the history of races by the resemblance so often apparent between the memorials of widely separated and most ancient people. An American familiar with the trophies of an Egyptian museum, who has examined the contents of a Western mound, visited an Etruscan city, like Volterra, Druidical remains in Britain, or compared the porcelain idols of Burmah with those found in South and Central America, will be tempted to follow with credulity the ingenious speculations of antiquarian *savans* who argue from symbolic coincidences that an identical language and worship, in remote ages, linked in a common bond the world's inhabitants; or that similar trophies of faith found in Odin stones and Hindu temples, in Etrurian sepulchres and Mississippi *tumuli*, at least, suggest a more ancient emigration to America than is claimed by the advocates of Norse discoveries. It is but needful to read the history of the serpent symbol and the recent controversies as to unity of races, to find in such ethnological speculations a remarkable basis of fact; whether or not we admit the probability so confidently urged that a Chinese priest and a fifth-century Buddhist missionary visited this continent *via* the Pacific, and reported thereof, ages before Christopher Columbus dreamed of a new world. In fact, the early history and traditions relating to the discovery and casual settlements, is one of the most remarkable chapters in the annals of the world—affording, on the one hand, the greatest scope for imagination, and, on the other, the most suggestive material for philosophical inference and elucidation. How early and in what manner the nearest points of contact between America and the rest of the world, in the far northwest, were first crossed at Behring's Straits, gives room for bold conjecture: ethnologists, archæologists, and antiquarians have broached numerous theories and established curious facts to prove that the "new world" of Columbus was known and partially colonized long before that intrepid navigator heard the thrilling cry of "land!" from the mast head of the Pinta: not only those primitive explorers the Chinese and Japanese, but the ancient Phœnicians, Norman colonists from Greenland, Irish saints, and Russian overland expeditions have been confidently traced and sometimes authenticated. Naturalists have, with subtile knowledge, pointed out how the secret of another continent was whispered by the voice of Nature, seeds borne on the currents of the air, and plants on those of the sea; scholars have culled from old Latin and Italian poets intimations of the existence of a hemisphere unexplored; and ingenious observers have appealed to stone hearths, like those of Denmark, found at Cape Cod, moss-grown clefts in aged trees, brass arrow heads, and copper axes, to evidence a long-lost colony.

The Icelandic navigators are supposed to have made voyages to Vinland, on the southern coast of New England, five centuries before Columbus. The Welsh, too, claim a share in this remote exploration of America. In the preface to his poem of "Madoc," Southey says of the hero, he "abandoned his barbarous country, and sailed away to the west, in search of some better resting place. The land which he discovered pleased him; he left there part of his people, and went back to Wales for a fresh supply of adventurers, with whom he again set sail, and was heard of no more. Strong evidence has been adduced that he reached America, and that his posterity exist there to this day." And a venerable scholar, of our own country, observes that

"Madoc is stated to have been a son of Owen Gwynedd, Prince, or, as he is often styled, King of Wales. His father's death is assigned to the year 1169, and the commencement of his own voyage to the succeeding year. I quote an authority which has apparently been overlooked, in citing Warrington's History of Wales. He writes: 'About this time [1170] Madoc, seeing the contention which agitated the fiery spirit of his brothers, with a courage equal to theirs, but far more liberally directed, gave himself up to the danger and uncertainty of seas hitherto unexplored. He is said to have embarked with a few ships; sailing west, and leaving Ireland to the north, he traversed the ocean till he arrived by accident upon the coast of America. Pleased with its appearance, he left there a great part of his people, and returning for a fresh supply, he was joined by many adventurers, both men and women; who, encouraged by a flattering description of that country, and sick of the disorders which reigned in their own, were desirous of seeking an asylum in the wilds of America.'

"Some, indeed, have regarded the whole subject as unworthy of investigation. But when we perceive it asserted, that individuals have seen in the possession of Indians, as we call them, books or rolls written on parchment, and carefully wrapped up, though they could not be read; and the people who possessed them, though but a fragment of our Indian population, showing a fairer skin than the ordinary tribes, and hair and beard, occasionally, of reddish color—we must think the subject worth some further inquiry; and I cannot but express the hope that the inquiry may be pursued."*

Carl Christian Rafn, a Danish archæologist, in his work on American antiquities, published at Copenhagen in 1837, endeavors to prove that America was not only discovered by the Scandinavians in the tenth, but that during the four succeeding centuries they made frequent voyages thither, and

---

* "Address before the American Antiquarian Society, at their Annual Meeting, October, 1863," by Rev. William Jenks, D. D.

had settlements in what is now Massachusetts and Rhode Island.

Availing himself of these researches, our eminent countryman Henry Wheaton enriched his "History of the Northmen"—a work, like the author's Treatise on International Law, of European reputation—the fruit of studies carried on in the midst of important and admirably fulfilled diplomatic duties.

Alexander von Humboldt, on his way from Mexico *via* Cuba, arrived at Philadelphia in 1804, and was cordially received at Washington by Jefferson; his sojourn in the United States, however, was quite brief: of his views in regard to the ancient memorials found in the American continents the historian Prescott observes: "Humboldt is a true philosopher, divested of local and national prejudices; like most truly learned men, he is cautious and modest in his deductions, and though he assembles very many remarkable coincidences between the Old World and the New, in their institutions, notions, habits, etc., yet he does not infer that the New World was peopled from the Old, much less from one particular nation, as most rash speculators have done." *

From the vague but romantic conjecture of the Egyptian legend which Plato repeated in regard to the island of Atlantis, to the dim traditions which place the wonderful Vinland of the Scandinavian navigators on the shores of Labrador; from the mysterious charm that invested the newly discovered isles of the tropics and found immortal expression in Shakspeare's Tempest, to the curious ethnological speculations which recognize in the ancient mounds of the Mississippi valley relics of a civilization anterior to the American Indians; from the fabulous lures, like the fountain of youth, that attracted Southern Europeans to Florida, to the stern crises of opinion which drove English Puritans to the bleak coast of New England—the earliest descriptions of and associations with the country, now known as the United States of America, are deeply tinctured with visionary legends and traditional fables; to

---

* Ticknor's "Life of Prescott," p. 165.

extricate which from the substratum of truth and fact, is a hopeless attempt. Nor, despite the exploded theories which found in certain rocks and structures evidences of the Northmen's sojourn, and the symbolical science which seems partially to unite the trophies of ancient sepulchres with the Eastern races—are we averse to leave unanalyzed the vast and mysterious region of inquiry outside of authentic history; let it remain in vague extent and dreamy suggestiveness—the domain of limitless possibilities to the philosopher, and of romantic suggestiveness to the poet.

Even the imaginative charm that belongs to this mythical era, yields to one scarcely less attractive, when the American traveller remembers, at St. Malo, that the intrepid Cartier thence sailed to discover the St. Lawrence, or inspects with a deeper feeling than curiosity the letters of Verrazzano, still preserved in the library at Florence, wherein he describes the coast of Carolina and the harbors of New York and Newport in all their virgin solitude; and recalls at Bristol the primitive expeditions of the Cabots.

It is sufficient, indeed, for the inquirer who aims to discern and illustrate the actual resources, development, and prospects of the country, to begin with the first authentic descriptions of the mainland by the old navigators who, in that era of maritime enterprise, visited so many points of the coast toward the close of the fifteenth and the early part of the sixteenth century.

When we consider what geography was in the hands of Strabo and Pliny, and what the literature of travel was when Columbus discovered the West Indies,* Cabot Labrador, and

---

* San Domingo has been well named "the vestibule of American discovery and colonization;" that island having long been the headquarters and rendezvous of Columbus, and the scene of his first success and subsequent misfortunes: it was thither that the animals and plants originally introduced to this country from Europe were brought; there was the first white colony established on this side of the Atlantic; and there, at present, seems to be the most flourishing and promising free negro population. A full and interesting account of this island, whose future is fraught with interest, was recently read before the N. Y. Geographical Society, and is published by G. P. Putnam, of New York.

Vespucci gave a name to this continent—instead of wondering at the meagre details and extravagant generalities of those primitive accounts of the New World, we should rather congratulate ourselves on the amount and kind of authentic material which Navarette collected and arranged and Irving gracefully elaborated in his Life of the Discoverer of America. It is quite an abrupt transition from the glowing fables that immediately precede the first chapter of our regular history, to perceive and admit the fact that " shoals of cod " really established the earliest practical mutual interest between Europe and America; and that the Newfoundland fisheries formed the original nucleus whereby originated the extraordinary emigration which, from that day to the present, has continued to people this hemisphere with the representatives of every race, country, and lineage of Europe. The old navigators were the pioneers—Spanish and Portuguese; in 1512, Ponce de Leon commenced his romantic quest in the Bahamas; eight years later, Magellan finished the demonstration Columbus began, by circumnavigating the globe; in 1524, the Florentine mariner Verrazzano anchored in the bay of New York; in 1528, Narvaez was in Florida; in 1539, De Soto discovered the Mississippi; in 1540, France commenced the colonization of the country around the St. Lawrence, and in 1606 was granted the first charter of Virginia; in 1610, the Dutch began to trade with the aborigines of the Hudson; and in 1620, the "Mayflower" arrived at Plymouth.

For a long period, when the fisheries of Newfoundland were the only attraction and the chief promise to European adventure, the whole country was spoken of and written about by a French appellative signifying codfish; and during another era, Florida, the name given to their southern settlement by the Spaniards, was applied to the whole extent of the coast; while Virginia, whereby the Jamestown colony was called from the Virgin Queen, whose favorite Raleigh was patentee thereof, designated an indefinite extent of country, and on the old maps and in the current parlance stood for America to Englishmen: a German writer laments that one of those names was not retained as national—instead of being confined to a single State; arguing their better adaptation to indicate a flourishing and a virgin land than the vague terms America and the United States. One reason why a citizen of the latter is so often startled at the ignorance of rustics and provincials on the Continent, in confounding North and South America, is that the products of the latter, some of which are in prevalent use in Europe, are known merely as American productions.

The decadence of Spain and the growth of England are intimately associated with the settlement of America. The introduction from the latter country into Europe of the potato, maize, and tobacco, has exerted an influence and produced results far transcending the more obvious economical consequences. Upon maritime enterprise and interests, including both legal and scientific progress, the discovery and settlement of the New World produced effects incalculable. While the priests and the fur traders who explored Canada achieved little beyond the local and often temporary establishment of depots, forts, and chapels, and left in the memory of Champlain a foreign tradition rather than a fresh national development, the colonization of the Atlantic slope embodied and conserved a new political development, and identified the country with progressive industry, religious toleration, free citizenship, educational privileges, and an economical rule. Newfoundland became a school for English seamen; New Belgium preserved and propagated the social enfranchisement and instinct of liberty wrested in the Netherlands from the cruel despotism of Spain; French Protestants found scope and safety in the Carolinas, and English Puritans a bleak but vital realm in New England.

Those formidable-looking folios in old Latin type, and with the imprint of Venice or Amsterdam, dear to antiquarians, wherein the old navigators, through some medieval scholar's pen, registered for the future bibliopole and historian the journal of their American voyages, constitute the first records of travel there, although mainly devoted to descriptions of the coast and adjacent waters. These now rare tomes are curious from their quaint antiquity—the combination of fact and fiction, statements which are confirmed to-day by the measurement of bays and the aspect of nature, and fabulous exaggerations obviously born of honest credulity or superstitious faith—and according, in their obsolete wonderment, with the primitive style and appearance of the venerable books. Very curious also are the illustrations which represent, in stiff and artificial designs, the fields of maize and tobacco and the Indian games and ceremonials which form the marvellous but monotonous features of those first glimpses which the Old World obtained of the New. De Bry's Collection of Voyages and Travels to America, comprised in parts, and printed in folio at Frankfort-on-the-Main in 1590, is the most copious repertory of these ancient records. Florida and Virginia are described as "gardens of the desert," and the heroes of romance cluster around the narrative of their partially explored resources, new products, and mysterious natives.

Most venerable of all, however, is the "Imago Mundi" of Petrus de Alyaco that inspired Columbus, of which Irving says:

"Being at Seville, and making researches in the Bibliotheca Columbina, the library given by Fernando Columbus to the cathedral of the city, I came accidentally upon the above-mentioned copy of the work of Peter Aliaco. It is an old volume in folio, bound in parchment, published soon after the invention of printing, containing a collection in Latin of astronomical and cosmographical tracts of Pedro de Aliaco and of his disciple John Gerson. Aliaco was the author of many works, and one of the most learned and ingenious men of his day. Las Casas is of opinion that his writings had more effect in stimulating Columbus to the enterprise than those of any other author. His work was so familiar to Columbus that he had filled its whole margin with Latin notes, in his handwriting, citing many things which he had read and gathered elsewhere. 'This book, which was very old,' continues Las Casas, 'I had many times in my hands, and I drew some things from it, written in Latin, by the said Admiral Christopher Columbus, to verify certain points appertaining to his history, of which I before was in doubt.'"

Then, among others, there is a "General Description of America," by P. d'Avity (Paris, 1637) ; "News from America" (Rouen, 1678) ; "De Vries's Voyage ;" the famous "Relation of Virginia" (1615), and many other local treatises and more or less authentic accounts written to beguile adventurers, celebrate discoveries, or ventilate controversy respecting the boundless land of promise to military and religious, political and rapacious adventure. Many, and characteristic, too, were these early memorials of New England colonization, tinged with the religious element so largely developed in her primitive annals; as, for instance, "New England Judged by the Spirit of the Lord" (1661) ; "Ill News from New England, by John Clarke, of Rhode Island ;" "The New-England Canaan" (Amsterdam, 1632). The Spanish Voyageurs ; the memorials of Raleigh, De Soto, La Salle—of John Smith, Ponce de Leon, Oglethorpe, Winthrop, Roger Williams, Hendrik Hudson—and, in short, of the pioneers in conquest, colonization, and civilization, whether religious, agricultural, or administrative, furnish a mine of description, more or less curious, whereby the original aspect, indigenous products, and theoretical estimates of America may be learned in part, and inferred from or compared with later and more complete explorations and reports. A vast number of works devoted to this country appeared during the fifteenth and sixteenth centuries ; and they attest the historical development incident to the discovery of America and the reaction of colonization there upon European civilization ; but the legitimate literature of travel, as we understand it, in the New World, was initiated by the French missionaries.

In the venerable records of maritime discovery and exploration, the fabulous and the authentic are curiously blended. One of the earliest collectors of these quaint and valuable data was Richard Hakluyt, an English prebendary, born in London in 1553. His love of nautical science and passion for geographical research made the acquisition of an original journal of one of those adventurous mariners who first visited any part of this continent or other half-explored region of the earth a precious experience. Hakluyt was educated at Westminster school and Oxford; he corresponded with the most famous living geographers of his day—such as Ortelius and Mercator. A residence of five years in Paris as chaplain to the British embassy, gave him excellent opportunities for the prosecution of his favorite studies on the Continent; and these were enlarged on his return to England, when Sir Walter Raleigh appointed him one of the counsellors, assistants, and adventurers to whom he assigned his patent for the prosecution of discoveries in America. To him we owe the preservation of numerous original accounts of English maritime enterprise. Hallam remarks that the best map of the sixteenth century is to be found in a few copies of the first edition of Hakluyt's Voyages. John Locke says of the work that it is "valuable for the good there to be picked out." He was encouraged in his labors by Walsingham and Sidney. Few documentary annalists have rendered better service to our primitive history than Hakluyt; his publications made known the discoveries of his countrymen, and, by disseminating the facts in regard to America, encouraged colonization. He translated from the French, in 1587, "Foure Voyages unto Florida by Captain Londonniere," and an improved edition of Peter Martyr's work, "De Novo Orbe;" but his most celebrated work is "The Principal Navigations, Voyages, Traffiques, and Discoveries of the English Nation, made by sea or over land, within the compass of 1,500 years." The first edition is extremely rare; but an enlarged one appeared in 1598, the third part of which contains a history of expeditions to North America and the West Indies. His papers, at his decease, became the property of Rev. Samuel Purchas, who, in 1613, published that curious work, "Purchas, his Pilgrim," two volumes of which form a continuation of Hakluyt's Voyages. From these sources may be gleaned some of the earliest authentic descriptions of America. In regard to the indigenous products, the geography, and some details of aboriginal character and customs, we recognize the honest intention of the brave pioneer navigators; but their credulity and often their lively imagination are equally apparent, and the style and comments of Purchas sometimes add to the incongruous result. An eminent writer has justly defined these collections of Hakluyt and Purchas as "very curious monuments of the nature of human enterprises, human testimony, and of human affairs. Much more is, indeed, offered to a refined and philosophic observer, though buried amid the unwieldy and unsightly mass, than was ever supposed by its original readers or by its first compilers." *

A very curious relic of these primitive annals of discovery has been renewed to modern readers by Conway Robinson, who so ably prepared for the Virginia Historical Society an "Account of Voyages along the Atlantic Coast of North America, 1520–1573;" and a not less curious antiquarian memorial of old times, in that State, was printed for the Hakluyt Society, "The Historie of Travaile in Virginia Brittanica." Of late years every authentic document emanating from or relating to Columbus, Vespucius, Cabot, Drake, Hudson, La Haye, Champlain, and other discoverers and explorers, has been, by the judicious liberality of historical and antiquarian societies, or by private enterprise, reproduced, collated, and sometimes printed in fac-simile, so that the means of tracing the original ideas and experience of the old navigators have been made accessible to studious comparison and inquiry; and, in addition to such facilities, the jealousy of European Governments in regard to their archives has, with the growth of intelligence and the love of science, become essentially modified, so that charts, journals, commissions, original data of all kinds, relating to early explorations, have been and are freely and sagaciously consulted by geographical and historical scholars.†

---

* "Lectures on Modern History," by Prof. Smythe.

† Among other important collections—besides those of De Bry, Hakluyt, Purchas, and De Vries—may be mentioned that by Murray (Lond. 1839), and Ternaux-Compan's "Voyages, Relations et Memoirs Originaux pour servir à histoire de la découverte de l'Amerique," in ten vols.; and "America, being the latest and most accurate description of the New World, &c.,

There is an absence of details in most of these early chronicles, which indicates but a superficial and limited exploration, such as the dangers and difficulties adequately explain. Yet sufficient is recorded to afford materials for the historian and the naturalist, who aim at fixing the time and indicating the original aspect of those portions of the continent that were first visited by Europeans, and have since become, through the early appreciation of their natural advantages, the centre of prosperous civilization. Thus, in Van der Dock's account of New Netherlands in 1659, he describes the rigors of winter on the coast, the numerous whales that frequented the then lonely waters where is now congregated the shipping of the world, and mentions the fact that two of these leviathans in 1647 grounded forty miles up the river, and infected the air for miles with the effluvia of their decomposition. The abundance and superior quality of the oysters, the wild strawberries, the maize, grapes, hazelnuts, sheephead and sturgeons, are noted with the appreciative emphasis of a Dutch epicure; and that is a memorable picture to the visitor at Albany to-day, which presents to his mind's eye Hendrik Hudson receiving tobacco, beans, and otter and beaver skins from the natives, environed by a dense forest.

Of the primitive reports of colonial explorers and settlers, none has so vivid a personal interest as that of Captain John Smith: the romantic story of Pocahontas alone embalms his name. Sent out by the London Company in 1606, his party landed at Jamestown on the 13th of May of that year; he returned to England in 1609, and five years afterward explored the coast of America from the Penobscot to Cape Cod. In 1615, having commenced another voyage, he was made prisoner by the French, and did not succeed, on regaining his liberty, in securing occupation again in American exploration, although he sought it with earnestness. Captain Smith died in London in 1631. His "True Travels, Adventures, and Observations" was published in 1629. His map, tract on Virginia,

collected from the most authentic authors, and adorned with maps and sculpture, by John Ogilby," folio, London, 1675.

and "Description of New England," attest his claims to a better recompense than he received: "In neither of these two countries," he writes, "have I one foot of land, nor the very house I builded, nor the ground I digged with my own hands, nor any content or satisfaction at all." The original editions of Smith's several works relating to America are very rare: some of them have been reprinted in historical collections. His most extensive work is "The General History of Virginia, New England, and the Summer Isles," prepared at the request of the London Company, and illustrated with portraits and maps. The period described is from 1584 to 1626. These writings are curious rather than satisfactory; valuable as records of pioneer experience and memorials of the early settlements: they were written to inform, and in their day were of great practical value; but, except for aboriginal details and geographical facts, their authority and interest have long been superseded. Yet no American can look upon the old church of St. Sepulchre in London, where Captain John Smith was buried, without recalling that intrepid character, and associating it with the early fortunes of his native land. It is characteristic of this remarkable man that his favorite authors, when a youth, were Macchiavelli's "Art of War," and the Maxims of Antoninus—two books, says the last and best translator of the latter, admirably fitted to form the character of a soldier and a man.* He describes the animals, vegetables, soil, and rivers with quaint and brief eulogium —declaring Virginia "the poor man's best countrie in the world." †

Among these primitive travels is a small quarto in antiquated type, entitled "America Painted to the Life, by Fer-

---

* George Long.
† "The Generall Historie of Virginia, New England, and the Summer Isles, with the names of the Adventurers, Planters, and Governours, from their first beginning, anno 1584, to this present 1626. With the proceedings of those severall Colonies and the accidents that befell them in all their journeys and discoveries. Also the Maps and descriptions of all those countryes, their commodities, people, government, customes, and religion yet knowne. Divided into sixe bookes." Folio, pp. 148, engraved title and one map, London, 1632.

nando Gorges, Esq.," published in London in 1649.* The author says, " all that part of the continent of New England which was allotted by patent to my grandfather, Sir Ferdinand Gorges and his heires, he thought fit to call by the name of the province of Maine," which, we are told, then extended from the Penobscot to the Hudson; and was rented for two shillings per annum the hundred acres. Sir Fernando expended twenty thousand pounds in his American enterprises. The work by his grandson, descriptive thereof, contains the usual details as to products, politics, sects, and Indians: an allusion to a feast of the latter would seem to indicate an early origin for the famous pudding called huckleberry. The occasion was a council, to which the Boston magistrates were invited. "The Indian king, hearing of their coming, gathered together his counsellors and a great number of his subjects to give them entertainment;"—the materials of which are described thus: " boiled chestnuts in their white bread, which is very sweet, as if they were mixed with sugar—and, because they would be extraordinary in the feasting, they strove for variety after the English manner, boyling puddings made of beaten corne, putting therein great store of black berries somewhat like currants." A quaint and compendious account is given of the first settlement of Springfield, in Massachusetts—the few facts related giving a vivid idea of the economical and social condition of that now flourishing town, in 1645. "About this time, one Mr. Pinchin, sometime a magistrate, having, by desire to better his estate, settled him-

* "At the same time, Sir Ferdinand Gorges was gathering information of the native Americans, whom he had received at Weymouth, and whose descriptions of the country, joined to the favorable views which he had already imbibed, filled him with the strongest desire of becoming a proprietary of domains beyond the Atlantic."—BANCROFT's *History of the United States*, vol. i.

When, in 1643, the commissioners from Plymouth, New Haven, Saybrook, &c., assembled at Boston, " being all desirous of union and studious of peace," none of "Sir Ferdinand Gorges, his province beyond Piscataqua, were received nor called into the confederation, because they ran a different course from us, both in their ministry and civil government."—WINTHROP's *Journal*.

self very remote from all the churches of Christ in the Massachusetts Government, upon the river of Conectico, yet under their government, he having some godly persons resorting unto him, they erected a town and church of Christ, calling it Springfield; it lying on this large navigable river, hath the benefit of transporting their goods by water, and also fitly seated for a bever trade with the Indians, till the merchants increased so many, that it became little worth by reason of their outbuying one another, which caused them to live upon husbandry. This town is mostly built along the river side and upon some little rivulets of the same. There hath of late been more than one or two in this town greatly suspected of witchery." Here we have the pious and shrewd motives of the early settlers, the initiation of free trade and their primitive political economy, and superstition quaintly hinted. How curious to compare the picture of that little town and church so "very remote" from others in the colony, the "bever trade with the Indians," and the destructive rivalry therein—the lonely river in the midst of the wilderness, and the godly pioneer who came there "to better his estate," and the "suspicions of witchery"—with the populous, bustling scene of railway travel, manufactures, horse fairs, churches, schools, trade, and rural prosperity, now daily familiar to hundreds of travellers.

It is remarkable how some of these obsolete records link themselves with the interests and the questions of the passing hour. What more appropriate commentary, for instance, upon the provincial egotism of Virginia, can be imagined than the statement of Childs, a man of authority in his day, in England, that while some cavaliers found refuge there, many of the colonists were outcasts, and their emigration the alternative for imprisonment or penal exile?

One of the most suggestive and authentic records whence we derive a true idea of the social tendencies and the natural phenomena amid which the American character was bred in the Eastern States is the journal of John Winthrop. Its very monotony reflects the severe routine of life then and there;

religion enters into and modifies domestic retirement and individual impulse; the rigors of unsubdued nature in a northern climate are painfully manifest: we learn how isolation, strict oversight, and ecclesiastical rule, the necessity of labor and the alternations of extreme temperature disciplined and dwarfed, purified and hardened, elevated and narrowed the associations and instincts of humanity. What a vivid glimpse of life two hundred years ago in New England do the brief notes of the first Governor of Massachusetts afford us, and how easy thence to deduce the characteristics and the history of those remarkable communities, explain their peculiarities, and justify their tenacious traits! Take a few random extracts by way of illustration:

Nov. 15, 1637.—A day of thanksgiving for the victory obtained over the Pequods.

Mar. 7, 1638.—Mrs. Hutchenson, being removed to the Isle of Aquidney, was delivered of a monstrous birth: Mr. Cotton hereupon gathered it might signify her error in denying inherent righteousness.

A woman was judged to be whipped for reproaching the magistrates.

Mar. 1, 1638.—A printing house was begun at Cambridge by one Daye.

―――― charged with taking above sixpence in the shilling profit.

Mar. 10, 1639.—At the General Court an order was made to abolish that vain custom of drinking one to another.

In this winter, in a close calm day, there fell down diverse flakes of snow of this form ✻, very thin, and exactly pointed as art would have cut them in paper.

Sep. 20, 1630.— The wolves killed six calves at Salem.

May 13, 1632.—The French came in a pinnace to Penobscott and rifled a trucking house belonging to Plimouth, carrying away three hundred weight of beaver.

Nov. 5.—The congregation at Watertown discharged elder ―――― for intemperance in speech.

Jan. 17.—A servant of Mr. Skelton lost her way, and was several days in the woods, and half frozen.

June 1, 1633.—A Scotchman by prayer and fasting dispossessed one possessed of the devil.

Droughts, freshets, meteors, intense cold and heat, terrific storms, calm beautiful days, conflagrations, epidemics, Indian massacres, alternate in the record with constant church trials, reprimands and controversies, public whippings and memorable sermons, occasional and long-desired arrivals from England, the establishment of a college and printing press, local emigrations and perilous adventure; wherein bigotry and the highest fortitude, superstitions and acute logic, privation and cheerful toil, social despotism and individual rectitude indicate a rare and rigid school of life and national development.

Among the first colonial tributes of the muse descriptive of the New World was "New England's Prospect," a true, living, and experimental description of that part of America commonly called New England, by William Wood. It was published in London in 1635. The author lived four years in the region he pictures, and states in the preface to his metrical tract his intention to return there. He gives a rhymed account of the colony's situation, and dilates upon the habits of the aborigines. The scene of the poem is Boston and its vicinity, and the versified catalogue of indigenous trees is interesting, as probably the first record of the kind. "Cheerful William Wood" tells us, in delineating the country along the Merrimack, that

> "Trees both in hills and plains in plenty be,
> The long-lived oak and mournful cypris tree,
> Sky-towering pines and chestnuts coated rough,
> The lasting cedar, with the walnut tough :
> The rosin-dropping fir for masts in use;
> The boatman seeks for oares light, neat-growne sprewse;
> The brittle ashe, the ever trembling aspes,
> The broad-spread elm whose concave harbors wasps,
> The water-springie alder, good for nought,"

&c., &c. A more elaborate attempt at a primitive natural history of the same region is "New England's Rarities Discovered," by John Josselyn, published in 1672. The first explorer of the Alleghanies, John Lederer, wrote in Latin an account of "Three several Marches from Virginia to the West of Carolina and other parts of the Continent, begone in March, 1669, and ended in September, 1670." Sir William Talbot made and published an English translation in 1672. The Westover Manuscripts, published by Edmund Ruffin, of Virginia, in

1841, describe expeditions conducted by William Byrd, in 1728, wherein much curious information of Southern life, resources, and manners, at that period, is given.

Governor Bradford, who succeeded Carver as chief magistrate of the Plymouth Colony, left also a poetical description of New England—which, though a fragment, is a singular literary relic of those days—the aspect of the country and "spirit of the Pilgrims." But a better known and more copious as well as quaint memorial of colonial life in the old Bay State, and one which Hawthorne has evidently pondered to advantage, is to be found in the theories of Cotton Mather, illustrated as they are by the facts of his career and the incidental local and personal details of the "Magnalia:" although it appeared in London printed in folio in 1702, not until 1820 was it republished in America. Odd, credulous, learned, speculative, narrow, and anecdotical, this and his other books reflect the times and country.

There lived in Medford, Mass., more than a century ago, a clergyman's daughter and wife, Jane Turrel, who wrote graceful and feeling verses, some of which have been preserved as early specimens of the New England muse. In one of her pieces, called "An Invitation to the Country," she enumerates the fruits and other delicacies with which she proposes to regale the expected guest; and we learn therefrom that one indigenous product of the woods, now only found at a distance from the scene, was then a familiar luxury:

> The blushing peach and glossy plum there lies,
> *And with the mandrake* tempt your hands and eyes.

A class of publications, which belong neither to the department of travels nor memoirs, but which contain many important and specific facts and comments in regard to the original aspect, resources, and character of the country, while yet a colonial territory, remains to be noticed. These are the various publications descriptive, statistical, and controversial, which motives of interest and curiosity elicited from the early emigrants, agents, and official representatives of the different colonies. They are chiefly in the form of tracts: many of them crude and quaint in style, inadequate and desultory; some obviously inspired by the hope of alluring emigration; others suggested by a spirit of rivalry between the different settlements; some are honestly descriptive, others absurdly exaggerated; the theological and political questions of the day, whether local or administrative, gave birth to countless writings; most of them are curious, some valuable from their details and authenticity, and others as unique illustrations of history and manners: passages might be gleaned from not a few of these ancient *brochures*, which would favorably compare with more elaborate works written by educated travellers in America. The greater part of these now rare and costly literary relics of our country at the dawn of and immediately subsequent to its civilization, refer to Virginia and New England; next in number are those devoted to Florida; the tracts which discuss and describe the Carolinas, Maryland, and Pennsylvania being comparatively few; while those that refer to Canada are multifarious. These primitive records of colonization often yield invaluable hints to the philosopher and historian; although a vast proportion of them have lost their significance, and are more attractive to the bibliopole and the antiquarian than the general reader. In the form of letters, appeals, protests, advertisements, picturesque or economical narratives, such incidental records not unfrequently conserve an incident, a law, a fact of nature or government, of natural, political, or social history, that has a permanent interest. Buckminster early called attention to the importance of preserving every publication relating to America, however apparently trivial, as a resource for historians; and societies and individuals have since emulated each other in the purchase and collection of these scattered data.*

As early as 1547 there was printed an account of the

---

* One of the most remarkable private collections is that of John Carter Brown, of Providence, R. I., whose library contains over five thousand publications relating to America, all of a date anterior to 1800, bound, lettered, and classified in the most convenient manner.

"Medical Substances discovered in America;" and a narrative of the deeds and habits of the once formidable buccaneers, who infested the coast (and the traditions regarding whom gave the elder Dana a subject which he treated with effective interest in an elaborate poem), was published in 1685 : ten years later we find a catalogue of American plants; and the query of a native poet in enumerating the subjects of permanent curiosity as yet unsatisfied—"Did Israel's missing tribes find refuge here?"—was partially answered in 1651, by a treatise on "The Jews in America." Numerous publications relating to the fisheries indicate at how early a date that branch of native economy assumed important relations in the eyes of Europeans, while such titles of current tracts as "On the Scheme of Sending Bishops to America," and "The Present Disposition of English, Scots, and Irish to Emigrate" thither, suggest how early the national tendencies of the colonies were regarded as significant of future political results. In 1789, when their character and destiny had grown formidable and definite, more general speculations occupied British writers, and an essay of that year discusses the "Influence of the Discovery of America on the Happiness of Mankind." Indeed, we have but to glance over any catalogue of publications relating to this country to perceive that the theme has afforded a convenient pretext, if not a special motive, to treat of almost every subject connected with political, religious, and social interests: printing, witchcraft, revivals, trade, currency, inoculation, meteors, unitarianism, and agriculture, alternate in the list with tracts on natural history, the fur trade, expeditions, and accounts of Spanish, Dutch, Danish, Swedish, French, and English settlements; until these brief and special gave place to more complex and generalized views, wherein America is "dissected by a divine," "compared with England," and made the subject of "summary views" and "surveys," "sketches," "random shots," "recollections," and criticism of all kinds and degrees of perspicacity and prejudice. It is seldom, even when such works had multiplied incalculably, that the authors write under a *nom de plume;* but there are exceptions, as the Lettres Anonymous of "Rubio," "J. M. B," "A Citizen of Edinburgh," "A Rugbean," "New Englander," "Southron," "Yankee," "Fur Trader," etc.

To no single individual will the seeker for original memorials of American civilization, nationality, and development recognize higher obligations than to the venerable, assiduous, and disinterested Peter Force, of Washington, whose "National Calendar and Annals of the United States" (1820–'36), and whose "Tracts and Papers, Relating to the Origin, Settlement, and Progress of the Colonies in North America, from the Discovery of the Country to the Year 1776" (1836–'46), are a mine of precious and peerless historical materials, as a glance at the contents of the collections and of those not yet published will satisfy the reader. It is true that most of these tracts and documents refer to matters of government, polity, and public events, and can be rarely classed under the literature of travel, yet many of them incidentally include its most desirable features, and some of them are "descriptions," "relations," "narratives," and "accounts," which, in their homely details and quaint sincerity, bring out the life, the manners, and the physical aspect of Georgia and Massachusetts, Maryland and Carolina, Virginia and New England, in the earliest colonial times, quite in the spirit of the old travellers. The enthusiasm and perseverance whereby was realized the great enterprise of collecting and preserving for future generations these inestimable memorials of the Past of America, are unprecedented in this country as an example of intelligent and self-devoted patriotism.*

* Quite an elaborate sketch of the "History of Discovery in America, from Columbus to Franklin," has recently appeared in Germany, from the pen of that intelligent and indefatigable author of valuable books of travel, J. G. Kohl. The work is confessedly incomplete and somewhat desultory, but full of interesting facts and speculations. A translation, by Major R. R. Noel, was published in London early in the present year. "American Archives: consisting of a collection of authentic records, state papers, debates, and letters and other notices of public affairs, the whole forming a Documentary History of the Origin and Progress of the North American Colonies; of the causes and accomplishment of the American Revolution; and of the constitution of government for the United States to the final ratification thereof."

CHAPTER II.

FRENCH MISSIONARY EXPLORATION.

HENNEPIN, MENARD, ALLOUEZ, MARQUETTE, CHARLEVOIX, MAREST.

Long after the Crusades, a spirit of adventure and a love of travel animated men whom religious faith or ecclesiastical influence dedicated to the priesthood. That vocation presented the two extremes of contemplative and active life; and where the temperament and the enthusiasm or intelligent curiosity of the monk made him impatient of routine or a limited sphere, it was easy to become a missionary, and thus combine religious ministrations with the experience of travel. Accordingly, some of the earliest reports of the physical resources of the New World were made to the Old, by Catholic missionaries ostensibly braving its unexplored domain to win the aboriginal inhabitants to Christianity, but now often remembered chiefly as the pioneer writers of American travels. The avidity with which information in regard to this continent was sought in Europe, immediately antecedent and subsequent to its colonization—the interest felt in the natural wonders and possible future of an immense, productive and uncivilized country—the arena it afforded to baffled enterprise, the asylum it promised to the persecuted, the resources it offered the poor—the conquest it invited from regal power and individual prowess—the vague charm with which it inspired the imaginative, and the fresh material it yielded so abundantly to the votaries of knowledge—all tended to make America and descriptions thereof alike attractive to prince and peasant, scholar, soldier, and citizen. Few, indeed, of the early missionaries possessed the requisite qualifications, either scientific or literary, to make what we should now consider desirable writers of books of travel. They either, through a large endowment of what phrenologists call the organ of wonder, exaggerated the natural features of the country, and gave fanciful instead of genuine pictures of what they saw; or, from lack of knowledge and imagination, confined themselves to a literal and limited recital of personal adventure, whence little practical information was to be derived. There is a singular union of extravagance and simplicity, of the fabulous and the true, of the boastful and the heroic, in these narratives. It must have required unusual discrimination on the part of readers in Europe, seeking facts, to disentangle the web of reality and fiction so often confusedly woven in such memoirs of travel. Yet some of them have proved invaluable to the historian of our own day, as the only known repertory of authentic statements as to the early productions, aspects, natives, explorations, and phenomena of parts of this continent: the integrity and patience of some of these missionary authors are apparent in their very style and method; and many of their assertions have been fully proved by subsequent observation and contemporary evidence. Still, there is no class of writings which must be interpreted with more careful reference to the character and motives of the writers, to the state of scientific knowledge at the period, and to the spirit of the age. A certain credulity, the result of superstition, ignorance, and enthusiasm, was characteristic even of the enlightened class of explorers then and there; and, when motives of personal vanity, self-aggrandizement, or national rivalry were added to these normal defects, it is easy to imagine how few of the clerical *raconteurs* are to be considered satisfactory to a philosophic inquirer. On the other hand, the singleness of purpose, the sincere Christian zeal, the pure love of nature and of truth, and a certain heroic conscientiousness of purpose and of practice, make some of these missionary travels in America *naïve*, suggestive, and interesting. As representations of what certain parts of the country were two hundred years ago, of how nature looked, and what life was here and then, they afford us a contrast so vivid and surprising to the scene and the life of the present, that, on this account alone, no imaginative mind can revert to them without realizing anew the mysterious vicissitudes of time and place and the moral wonder involved in the settlement, growth, and present civilization of America.

Among the French missionaries whose travels on this continent attracted much attention in his own day, and, in ours, are regarded at once with curiosity and distrust, was Louis Hennepin, a Franciscan. He was a native of Holland, and born in the year 1640. Quite early in life the instinct of travel asserted itself; for, as one of that privileged mendicant fraternity whom every traveller has encountered in Sicily or Spain, he wandered asking alms through Italy and Germany. It was while thus following the vocation of a pious beggar at Calais and Dunkirk, that Hennepin's wandering passion became infected with that desire to cross the sea, which, sooner or later, seizes upon all instinctive vagabonds. He enlisted as a regimental chaplain, and in that capacity was present at the battle of Senef, between William of Orange and the Prince of Condé, in 1674. He had passed one year as preacher in Belgium; and had been thence sent by his superior to Artois, and subsequently had the charge of a hospital for several months in Holland. Such was the early career of Father Hennepin, previous to entering upon his American mission. He was ordered to Canada in 1675, and embarked at Rochelle, with La Salle. Having preached a while at Quebec, he went, the following year, to the Indian mission at Frontenac; he afterward visited the Five Nations and the Dutch settlement at Albany, and returned to Quebec in 1678. When La Salle prepared to explore the Lakes, and despatched the Chevalier de Tonty and La Motte from Fort Frontenac to Niagara, to construct vessels, Hennepin was attached to the expedition; and, in 1677, passed through Lakes Erie, Huron, and Michigan, to the mouth of the St.

Joseph's, ascended in a canoe to the portage; conveying their slender barks six miles across the country to the Kankaree, they glided down this stream and the Iroquois to the Illinois river, and erected Fort Crévecœur, on the spot where now stands the city of Peoria.

It is said that La Salle's conjectures about the Mississippi river " worked upon him; and that, zealous for the honor of his nation, he designed to signalize the French name." His character has been thus described: " He was a man of regular behaviour, of a large soul, well enough learned, and understanding in the mathematics; designing, bold, undaunted, dexterous, insinuating; not to be discouraged by anything; wonderfully steady in adversity; and well enough versed in several savage languages." Here we have all the requisites for a great explorer; yet few have achieved such fame to endure such misfortunes. "The government of Fort Edward," says his biographer, " which is the place farthest advanced among the savages, was given to him; and he going over to France, in 1675, the king made him proprietor of it; he came home with stories of mines, wild bullocks, forests, &c.; and there grew up a jealousy of him among his countrymen: they thwarted his designs; and after he had picked out forty or fifty of them for a new expedition, and had spent years in going and coming, he was once nearly poisoned; he conciliated the savage inhabitants, and gave her name to Louisiana."

When, after the lapse of a few weeks, La Salle was obliged to return to Frontenac for supplies, he sent Hennepin to explore that mighty river, hitherto only known to Europeans above the mouth of the Wisconsin. The adventurous friar started on this expedition in the month of February, 1680, in his frail canoe, and, tracking the Illinois to its mouth, ascended the Mississippi to the Falls of St. Anthony, which he so named in honor of his patron saint; and was the first European who ever beheld those beautiful rapids in the heart of the wilderness. Having arrived at the mouth of the St. Francis river, in what is now Minnesota, a stream which he thus baptized from the founder of his own religious order, Hennepin again landed, and traversed the country to the distance of one hundred and eighty miles; he sojourned for three months among the Sioux Indians; returned in safety to Quebec, and soon after embarked for France; and in 1683 published his " Descriptions," &c. This work was the most complete account of the first expedition of La Salle, and, as such, was sought for and read with avidity. Had the record of Hennepin's career ended here, his name would have remained honorably associated with those of other European missionaries who, with courage and probity, sought for and proclaimed the wonders of the New World, while planting therein the cross and the faith to whose service he and they were pledged. But, not satisfied with the glory of a pioneer navigator of the Father of Waters, nor with the *prestige* of a faithful *attaché* to a brave but unfortunate chieftain, or that of a self-devoted minister of religion, in 1697, ten years after the death of La Salle, Hennepin audaciously gave to the world his " Nouvelle découverté d'un tres grand pays situé dans l'Amerique entre la Nouveau Mexique et la Mer Glaciale;* claiming therein to have descended the Mississippi and completed, for the first time, its exploration. The mere fact of his extraordinary delay in announcing this remarkable experience is sufficient to make a candid mind distrustful; and the motive thereto seems evident when we remember how immediately this publication followed upon the demise of the only witness its author had reason to fear. Accordingly, Hennepin has been and is regarded as untruthful by our own and European historians, except in regard to topographical and local details confirmed by other testimony and by observation of natural facts. Still his adventures, and the narrative thereof possess an interest derived from their early date; we associate them with the first authentic glimpses of the new continent in its vast Western phase which were attained by Euro-

* " New Discovery of a Vast Country in America, extending above 4,000 Miles, between New France and New Mexico," &c., map and plates, London, 1698.

peans; we cannot but imagine the wonder, hope, and curiosity inspired by such travellers' tales, and look upon the diminutive volumes and obsolete type of the earliest editions with a kind of fond reminiscence; beholding, in fancy, the eagerness and incredulity with which they were originally pondered. And those of us who have sailed along the umbrageous and lofty bluffs of the Upper Mississippi, and gazed from a steamer's deck, in the early summer morning, upon the magnificent solitude—the noble stream, the far reach of woods, the high, castellated limestone rocks—and heard a wild bird's cry, or caught sight of a Sioux, a log hut, a hunter—watched the moving panorama of foliage, prairie, village, fever-stricken settlement and growing city alternating with lonely forest—realizing how Nature's wild seclusion and Humanity's primitive civilization meet, separate, and mingle on the borders of a mighty inland river, flowing deep and far through the West —so fraught with destiny, so recent in the annals of nations, and so ancient in the beauty and grandeur of creation—we, who have thus gazed and mused, when rapidly borne on the wings of steam, where Hennepin's lonely and fragile canoe slowly moved through this scene of virgin and unexplored loveliness and power, cannot refrain from a thrill of sympathy with those emotions of awe and love, of expectancy and danger the roving Franciscan must have felt; and, with all his want of veracity, recognize somewhat of fraternity by virtue of that "touch of nature" which makes us all akin. We accept the memorial of Hennepin, which gives his name to locomotive and steam barge, where he first baptized the waters; we recall him as we stand in the midst of the dashing flood which still murmurs his saintly nomenclature; and, when a prairie flower takes us back to the bosom of nature, or the wind, unchecked on the wide plains, sounds the same eternal anthem that greeted his ears who first invaded their solitude, we feel that, however the face of the land has changed, woods fallen before the settler's axe, and aborigines faded in the path of civilization, and thrift encroached upon sport, agriculture upon the wilderness, Nature still breathes her elemental charms, and preserves not a few of her most significant features. To an imaginative mind there is as much poetry as philosophy in the contrast between the Illinois which Hennepin traversed, and that which to-day holds such a world of life and labor in her bosom. The vast fields of grain, the teeming orchards, the cities and railroads of the present, to the political economist, afford a marvellous parallel to the verdant deserts described in 1680; but not less striking is the coincidence that deserted Mormon temples are there found, and a President of this republic was thence elected to meet the greatest crisis of our national life. One sees the extremes of civilization and the normal physical resources of this Western region, side by side with the distinctive natural features which excited the admiration and fill the chronicles of the missionary explorers. Even a rapid transit brings these associations home to the mind. On one occasion, as our train stopped on the edge of a rolling prairie, whose treeless, undulating surface, for miles, was unbroken save by harvest fields, the early descriptions of the face of the country were realized; and, while specimens of the mineral wealth and fruits of the alluvial soil were passed around, there appeared, pensively walking on the edge of the "garden of the desert," in entire contrast with the solitude and wild fertility of the landscape, an English lady, in the costume of the landed gentry, leading a child— their flaxen hair and high-bred manner suggestive of Saxon lineage: they were evidently of the better class of emigrants, who had sought in the far-away West a sphere, limited and dreary in comparison with their English home, however blessed by nature, but auspicious for the future of children whose native land affords no promising scope either for work or subsistence. The vivacious and brave heralds of the Cross, who, two centuries ago, delighted the Parisians with their accounts of a land of boundless woods and waters in the West, rarely and imperfectly surmised its destiny in the Providential issues of time: it was recognized, indeed, as a new domain for the rule of a French monarch, a new sphere for the triumph of religion, a new arena for military adventure and colonization; but few realized that it was to become a grand scene of political development and a refuge for the baffled nationalities of Europe. Indeed, there is no chapter in the primitive history of the country, which, appreciated in all its relations, picturesque, adventurous, heroic, and religious, that offers such attractive themes for art, romance, and philosophy as these early missions, whereby the Old World first won a foothold in the grandest portions of the New. It was through the vague reports of their aboriginal converts that the pious followers of St. Francis de Xavier, were stimulated to seek now a great lake, and now a mighty river: it was when in search of new tribes as subjects of their missionary zeal, that incidents of romantic interest and scenes of unrivalled beauty became known to them, and, through them, to the civilized world. Ménard, a Huron missionary, planned an expedition in search of the Mississippi in 1660: at the mission on the Saguenay, the Jesuits heard from their wild converts, of a vast lake, that lured them on a voyage of auspicious discovery; while their brethren in New York State witnessed the ceremonious departure of the Iroquois to give battle to an inimical tribe on the shores of the "beautiful river," and, being thus made aware of new links in the magnificent water chain, urged their explorations in the direction of the Ohio. Father Dablon, when superior of the Ottawa mission, established a station among the Illinois, and reached the Wisconsin river after a toilsome voyage: his "Relation" was published in 1670, and contained a map of Lake Superior. But the narrative of Father Claude Allouez, who left France in 1658, contains one of the earliest accounts of an expedition to the Illinois country, which the Indians had described to Father Dablon as intersected by a river "so beautiful that, for more than three hundred leagues from its mouth, it is larger than that which flows by Quebec; and the vast country is nothing but prairies without trees or woods, which oblige the inhabitants of those parts to use turf and dung for fuel, till you come about twenty miles from the sea." Allouez began his journey thither on the ice; one of his companions was killed by a bear; he had seen Father Réne Ménard go forth on his sacred work, to die in the wilderness; but the ardent love of religious enterprise, which made his appointment to this wild and distant land so welcome amid the comforts of home, was not chilled or daunted: one of the first missionaries who reached the Mississippi, his name is associated with that of Marquette in the annals of Western discovery, whom he succeeded in the Illinois mission; in his light canoe he faithfully explored the shores of Michigan, and erected a chapel at Chippewa. The record of strange animals, impressive scenery, savage hospitality and games, alternates curiously, in these narratives, with the observance of saints' days and the rites of Christianity, and the American wilderness with the associations of the Roman Church.

In the Old World, it is a pastime of singular fascination to the cultivated and imaginative American, to haunt an ancient town like Chester, where Roman walls and camp outlines, faded banners won in Cromwell's time, and baronial escutcheons or classic coins identify the site of historic events associated with the distant past. To the native of a land where all is so fresh, active, and changeful, the shadow of the pyramids, the moonlit arches of the Colosseum, and the medieval towers of Florence impart to the landscape a hallowed charm, more impressive from its entire novelty. And yet such experiences are possible at home, if the same retrospective dreamer will but connect the facts of the past, of which there are so few artificial memorials, with the aspect of nature unmodified in her more grand features by the vicissitudes of centuries. Looking forth, in the calm of a summer morning, upon a lonely and wooded reach of Western river or lake, let him recall the story of pioneer, adventurer, or missionary, contrasting it with the tokens of subsequent civilization, and the appeal to wonder is not less emphatic, though more vague. How wild, remote, exuberant must have seemed the Father of Waters to Marquette and Joliet, when they glided out upon its vast and unexplored bosom! On the 13th of May, 1673, with five other Frenchmen, they embarked in two

canoes, provided with a slender stock of Indian corn and
smoked beef; and, guided by such information as they could
gather from the aborigines, left Green Bay, ascended the
Fox river, and, on the 25th of June, entered the Mississippi.
The first *naïve* and quaint record of what they saw, heard,
and did on this primitive expedition, has, by the liberal enterprise of one of our citizens,* been reproduced as it then greeted the eyes of their sympathetic countrymen, with the obsolete type so appropriate to such a *voyageur's* chronicle.
Father Marquette tells us there of the wild rice, grapes, and
plums wherewith they regaled—of the Miamis that assisted
their portage—of the trace of footsteps on the river's bank,
following which they came upon a beautiful prairie—of sojourns in Illinois villages, calumet-smoking with friendly
natives, feverish nights with mosquitos—of the dreary bellow
of herds of buffaloes, and the lowly flights of the startled
quails. Those months of primitive navigation were fraught
with a rare excitement to minds reared amid the highest
existent civilization; but, as if awed by the precarious life
and majestic aspect of primeval nature, the simplicity of the
narrative is only equalled by the unprecedented interest of
the discoveries; and the good priest's memory has long been
hallowed by his death in the midst of scenes forever identified
with his brave and pious character. On the shore of Lake
Michigan, the isolated and picturesque witness of those heroic
toils and that humane ministry, on the 18th of May, 1675, the
canoe of Father Marquette entered a small stream, and he
requested the two men in charge thereof to leave him for
half an hour: on returning, they found him dead. The site
of his grave,† near the bank, is still designated, and the
little river bears his name; but the brief and artless record

* James Lenox, Esq., of New York.

† "Marquette's body was disinterred from its lonely resting place on the
lake shore by the Kiskakon Indians, among whom he had faithfully labored.
Dissecting it, according to custom, they washed the bones and dried them in
the sun, then putting them neatly in a box of birch bark, they set out to bear
them to the house of St. Ignatius, at Michilimakinac."—DABLON'S *Narrative
of Marquette's Expedition.*

of his voyage, a small duodecimo of forty-three pages, is the most characteristic memorial of the man, and one of the most endeared as well as vivid glimpses of that marvellous river and region, as they were first revealed to civilized nations.*

Another French missionary to Canada has left, not only a more ample, but more authentic chronicle, and his name is often invoked with trust and respect by our historical writers. Pierre François Xavier Charlevoix was born in 1682, at St. Quentin, and died in 1761, at Laffèche. His life was devoted to study and travel in behalf of his faith; and few of his order have manifested greater courage, patience, and integrity. His American tour, although now but a pleasant excursion, was formidable and adventurous enough, in his own day, to render him more famous than an African or Arctic traveller of our own. His account of the productions of the wilderness, the extent and character of rivers, woods, and mountains, and especially of the character and customs of the natives, was not only esteemed when the novelty of its details originally won readers, but has continued among the standard books of travel.† Charlevoix carefully and thoroughly, with the means and opportunities at command,

---

* See J. G. Shea's "Discovery and Exploration of the Mississippi Valley, with the Narrative of Marquette, Hennepin, Douay," &c., 8vo., fac-simile and map, New York, 1852; Rev. W. I. Kip's "Early Jesuit Missions in North America, compiled from the letters of the French Jesuits," 1 vol., New York, 1846, and 2 vols. 8vo., London, 1847; and "Relations des Jesuits, contenant ce qui s'est passé de plus remarquable dans les missions des Pères de la Compagnie de Jésus dans la Nouvelle France: ouvrage publié sous les auspices du gouvernement Canadien," 3 vols. royal 8vo., of about 900 pp. each, Quebec, 1858. "This work, of which only a small number were printed, is a complete reprint of all the Jesuit relations concerning the missions in Canada and French North America, from 1611 to 1672, and contains most important matter concerning the Indian tribes, and the early history of Maine, New York, and all the Northwest."

† "Histoire et Description générale de la Nouvelle France," atlas and 6 vols., Paris, 1744.

"Letters to the Duchess of Lesdiguires, giving an account of a voyage to Canada, and travels through that vast country and Louisiana to the Gulf of Mexico," 8vo., London, 1763.

ascended the St. Lawrence, traversed the region called the "country of the Illinois," and descended the Mississippi. A county now bears his name in Michigan. He visited the East and West Indies, and, when at home again, elaborately recorded his extensive travels. They form a valuable work of reference when it is desirable to ascertain the physical and local facts in regard to these countries during the first part of the last century. Among the suggestive historical and personal associations which the rapid march of events, and especially the triumphs of locomotion and intercourse, continually excite in this age and country, few are more impressive than the fact that the two most remote points of Charlevoix's world-wide journeys were, in a manner, brought together when the Japanese embassy visited the United States a few years since. In his wildest dreams the ardent Jesuit could scarcely have imagined that the region of mighty rivers and primeval woods, which he so laboriously explored amid privation, toil, and danger, could, in so brief a period, become accessible, populous, and fused, as it were, into the compass of a recreative tour; and that the natives of that far-away isle in the Indian seas, whose semi-civilization he first reported to Europe, should come hither as ambassadors to a vast republic, and carry their Asian aspect through crowded cities of Anglo-Saxon freemen. Never, perhaps, were stationary and progressive civilization brought so directly in contrast. The Japanese envoys, as well as their distant home, are identical with those Charlevoix so long ago described; while the virgin solitudes of nature, amid which his lonely canoe floated or his solitary camp fire blazed, are superseded by busy towns and peopled with flying caravans of travellers, representing an economy, character, and government full of vitality and of prosperous and original elements.

It is curious to turn to the somewhat monotonous but still instructive pages of Charlevoix, and realize how exclusively, at the time he wrote, the interest of this continent was aboriginal and prospective; for it is with the aspects and resources of nature and the peculiarities of the Indian tribes that his pen is occupied. Whatever of romance tinges his chronicle is Arcadian; the myths and manners of the different tribes, the trees and the reptiles, waterfalls and savannas, are the staple themes. His religious views and mission lend a pensive dignity to his narrative: like most of his countrymen, he develops certain sympathies with, and finds curious interest in, the *sauvages;* he pictures the wild beauty and primitive life of the country when furs were the chief article of traffic—when the convents of Canada, the frontier forts, and the Indian villages were the only places of secure sojourn—when "fire water" had only begun its fascinating destruction among the then *naïve* children of the soil—when rude fields of tobacco, orchards, and maize fields alone gave sign of cultivation, and game and fish supplied the wanderer's subsistence. In Charlevoix we find the germs of colonial romance in America; the primitive maps, the old forts, the early crude botanical nomenclature, with ethnological hints regarding the Hurons, Iroquois, Algonquin, and other tribes. He first elaborately pictured the "lacs"—those wonderful inland seas which constituted so remarkable a feature of the New World to its first visitors, and became the great means of economical development by initiating, under wise statesmanship, the prolific system of communication between the far interior and the broad seacoast.

His letters were commenced in 1720, by order of the King of France. One of the best English translations appeared in 1765. The details are curious now, rather than novel; they are carefully noted, and form the best authority for reference as to the primitive aspect, productions, and aboriginal tribes. The topographical statements are often confirmed by experience at the present day; and the imaginative traveller finds his enjoyment of the scenery enhanced by contemplating it with the record of this venerable guide before him, and contrasting with that early record the scene as modified by the sights and sounds of Anglo-Saxon civilization.

"In New England, and other provinces of America," says Charlevoix, "subject to the British empire, there prevails an opulence of which they seem not to have taken the benefit; and, in New France, a poverty disguised by an air of ease, which does not seem constrained. Commerce and the culture of plantations strengthen the former: the industry of the inhabitants supports the latter; and the taste of the nation diffuses an unbounded agreeableness. The English colonist gathers wealth, and never runs into any superfluous expense; the French enjoys what he has, and often makes a show of what he has not: one labors for his heirs; the other leaves them in the necessity in which he found himself, to shift as well as they can. The English are entirely averse to war, because they have much to lose; they do not regard the savages, because they think they have no occasion for them." In these remarks we have a key, not only to the national characteristics of the two peoples, but one which explains the success of one and the failure of the other in permanent colonization. Our associations with the name of Chicago and of Illinois make it difficult to realize the casual mention of them by Charlevoix as the abode of Indians only: "Fifty years ago," he writes, "the Miamis were settled at the south end of the lake Michigan, in a place called Chicago, which is also the name of a little river that runs into the lake: the Illinois, a savage nation, on the banks of the river Illinois; they burn prisoners, and sing doleful songs." He observes that the "navigation of Lake Michigan requires much care, because the wind comes from the open lake, that is, the west; the waves are the whole length of the lake, and blend with the shock of currents and of rivers running in;"—a primitive description, which comes home to all who have experienced a gale there.

Of the two great rivers of the West, he writes: "The Missouri is far the most rapid, and enters the Misissippi like a conqueror; afterward it gives its color to that river, which it never loses again, but carries quite down to the sea. The natives are obliged to use *pettiaugres* instead of canoes of bark, on account of snags; they are trees made hollow: the natives know the north by the tops of trees, as they lean a little that way; the Mississippi is little known above the Falls of St. Anthony."

Charlevoix was an eminent teacher, both of languages and philosophy, and, for more than twenty years after his return from America, "had a chief share in the *Journal de Trévoux*." His character and learning gave authority to his "Histoire Générale de la Nouvelle France." As we read his accounts of personal observations and experience in Canada and on the Mississippi, of the beavers and cypress trees, the elks and eels, the lakes and falls, the maize and oysters, the snakes and turtles, Indians and missions, we can perceive a directness and honesty of purpose, which is internal evidence of the author's good faith. The simplicity and ingenuousness of his style have always been recognized, though its correctness is not admitted by verbal critics.

With the wild, luxuriant, lonely, remote picture of the Jesuit clear and full to the mind's eye, what a wonderful process of development, relation, and change, does the Illinois region offer to one now familiar with its history and its aspect! The unpeopled desert of the isolated missionary is still in the far West, " a vast prairie dotted with groves and intersected with belts of timber;" but, less remote, its climate is only modified; and the herds of buffalo have disappeared, the wild deer drink no more at the streams; the same millions of fertile acres and a portion of the immense swamp diversify the face of the land; the same limestone bluffs frown imposingly upon the vast river; the same piercing blasts from the Rocky Mountains sweep snow-covered plains; and, away from the settlements, the same blue-bells, wild roses, thistles, sorrels, fragrant herbs, and lofty weeds and hairy-leaved plants, and grassy levels make the summer gorgeous and balmy; the scarlet trumpet blossoms and the golden dandelion, the low box trees, the purple wild grape, and the crimson sumach make brilliant and variegated the meadows; the same gray, mottled, and flying squirrels occasionally cross the wanderer's path; the owl may be heard at night, and the turkey buzzards hover over carrion; the crow, the falcon, the hawk, the vulture, the mocking bird, and the rattlesnake, here and there, attest that old hunters and early naturalists correctly noted the indigenous animal life of the region; but tall maize stalks, and woolly flocks, and fruitful orchards, and herds of cattle have superseded the wilderness where the elk browsed fearlessly and the hares burrowed unharmed. Since the flag of Spain was planted at the mouth of the Mississippi, in 1541—since, a century later, Father Marquette offered the calumet of peace and the Canada fur traders came thither, what vicissitudes and progress have signalized the scenes that Hennepin so long ago described! Bestowed by Louis XIV., in 1712, upon Anthony Crozat, with the entire territory of Louisiana and Wisconsin, the Illinois country became the capital upon which a trading company, managed by John Law, produced financial convulsion which shook the Old World and bred political and social revolution—the only relic and memorial whereof are the poor fragments of Fort Chartres which he erected when at the pinnacle of his audacious success. Wolfe, in 1759, brought to an end the rule of France on this continent; yet many of her children lingered in the Illinois and preserved intact their characteristic modes of life, which have been more or less transmitted. In 1763 the vast domain passed to the British crown; in 1778 its posts there were captured by the Virginia rangers under Roger Clark; in 1809 the country became a separate Territory, in 1818 a State of our Union; and the name of one of her counties preserves the memory of the leader of those who successfully opposed any provision for slavery in her constitution. Her Indian wars, during this period and subsequently, form a remarkable historical episode, which includes the last stand taken by Pontiac, Tecumseh, and Black Hawk for their aboriginal dominion, and the scene of their final sacrifice. But, however romantic, these events are less interesting to the economist than the unprecedented physical development, the vast crops of grain, the coal region, and the lead and copper mines, which have made Illinois so productive. Parallel with these demonstrations of latent wealth and normal fertility, of Indian history and land speculation, social life there has yielded original traits, whereof authors and artists have not inadequately availed themselves. The adventures of missionary, trader, hunter, settler, and traveller have been genially recorded; the descendants of the original three thousand French colonists on the banks of the Mississippi, with their national proclivities, so diverse from the Anglo-Saxon, and manifested in their household economy and vivacious temperament—the primitive manners and costume of the farmers, who long conveyed the products of their farms in flatboats to New Orleans, clad in raccoon-skin caps, buckskin leggings, moccasins, and linsey hunting shirts, with the home-wrought, brightly dyed frocks of the women, and the frank and brave manners and language of this free and thrifty population—have yet a traditional charm : here, too, the terrible justice of Lynch law had full scope—the Missouri ruffians, the *debris* of the Indian tribes, the Western politician, and the robust or ague-stricken emigrant, made up an unique and original population, full of salient points to the eye of a European or visitor from the communities of New England or old Southern States. Cooper, in a novel, and Bryant, in a poem, have graphically described the life and aspect of the Prairie State, which now boasts millions of inhabitants. Kohl, speaking of Illinois, compares it in shape to a grain sack, rent in the middle by its river, and bursting out with grain at both ends. Professor Voelcher, consulting chemist of the Royal Agricultural Society of England, analyzing four samples of prairie soil, said : " The most noticeable feature in the analysis is their very large quantity of nitrogen—nearly twice as much as the most fertile soil of Great Britain ; in each case, taking the soil at an average depth of ten inches, an acre of their prairie soil contains upward of three tons of nitrogen, and as a heavy crop of wheat, with its straw, contains about fifty-two pounds of nitrogen, there is thus a natural store of ammonia in this soil sufficient for more than a hundred wheat crops."

But the most remarkable fact in the economical history of Illinois and its adjacent States, is the effect of locomotive facilities and the genius of communication, in developing the resources and bringing, as it were, to the Atlantic coast and the commercial East, the region Hennepin so laboriously and so long traversed a mighty wilderness to reach. The contrast fully realized of the approach then and now, is one of those modern miracles of practical life to the wonder of which only habit blinds us. Vessels go direct from Liverpool to Chicago, by crossing the Atlantic, entering the St. Lawrence, and surmounting the rapids by means of the Canadian locks and canals, entering Ontario, and, after sailing through that lake, and a descent of three hundred feet of the Niagara River, by the Welland Canal, reach Lake Erie, thence through the straits and lake of St. Clair to Lake Huron and Lake Michigan—in the heart of the American continent. Four thousand seven hundred and thirty-six miles of road terminate there, of which two thousand eight hundred miles are within the State limits. These great highways were built to carry off the surplus of the prairies.*

As an illustration of the cosmopolitan tendency of the population, it was but recently that in this distant inland city, where a blockhouse fort alone stood within the memory of "the oldest inhabitant," sons of the Bishop of London, of Admiral Collingwood, of the novelist Dickens, with German barons and Hungarian officers, were there cheerfully engaged in various vocations.

There is something exciting to the imagination as well as impressive to the mind in the fact that the oldest authentic written memorials of America, after the narratives of mari-

---

* The following table compares the official returns of the population of Chicago:

Year	Population	Year	Population
1830	70	1848	20,023
1840	4,853	1849	23,047
1843	7,580	1850	29,963
1844	10,864	1852	38,734
1845	12,088	1853	60,625
1846	14,169	1860	110,973
1847	16,859	1862	138,835

Thus, in thirty-three years, a colony of seventy persons has grown into a city of nearly 140,000.

time adventurers, are the letters and "relations" of the Jesuit missionaries. Often when a band of hunters or company of early colonists penetrated to a region of the wilderness, as they imagined, unvisited before by any human being except the savage natives, the sight of some relic or token of these religious pioneers brought into immediate contrast the most hallowed associations of the Old World and the virgin wilderness of the New. Sometimes an old aboriginal guide repeated to the astonished strangers what had been whispered in his ear when, as a child, he played around the council fire or the wigwam, of kind and wise men, robed in black, who talked to the children of the forest, of heaven, prayed over their dead, and baptized their maidens. On other occasions, amid the mossy coverings of ancient trees, the curious explorer would find rudely carved the effigies or escutcheon of the French king: here a broken cross, there a respected grave, now a ruined chapel, and again a censer or sacramental cup, even in the heart of the woods revived to the exiles the images, sacrifices, and triumphs of these indomitable members of the Society of Jesus: some of their names are perpetuated in those of towns now flourishing on the site of their apostleship or martyrdom; others are only preserved on a page of history seldom consulted. Poets and novelists, historians and artists have, from time to time, renewed the pious traditions and isolated lives of these remarkable men; but few of the summer tourists who gaze with delight upon the umbrageous islands of the St. Lawrence, or stand entranced amid the foaming rapids of St. Anthony, or watch with rapture the undulating sea of herbage and flowers on a blooming prairie of Illinois or Missouri, associate these characteristic aspects of nature with their first European explorers. Their written memorials, however, aptly consecrate their experience: thereby we learn how cheerfully scholars, soldiers, and courtiers braved the privations and the cruelties incident to such heroic enterprises; we read the artless story of their ministry—how at times they feel rewarded for months of suffering by the saintly development of an Indian virgin, by the acquiescence of a tribe in the rites of Christianity, or by the amelioration in the habits and temper of these fierce children of nature, under the influence of consistent, humane, and holy examples and care. All the correspondence and reports of the Jesuit missionaries are interspersed with local descriptions, sometimes vivid and often so specific as to serve as data for naturalist and historian. The anecdotes of Indian character and of personal adventure also give a quaint zest to the story; and not unfrequently a deep pathos is imparted thereto by the fate of the writer—dying of hunger, at the stake, or by treachery—going forth on their perilous journeys from fort or settlement, conscious they may not hope to return—and yielding up their lives with the same intrepid zeal with which they bore the discouragements, exposure, ingratitude, and lonely struggles of missionary life in the wilderness. Jogues, Du Poisson, Souel, Brebœuf, Lallemand, Senat, La Chaise, Joliet, and Marquette, are names thus endeared and hallowed.

Among other episodes recorded in the letters of the Jesuit missionaries, which combine romantic with historical significance, are the accounts of the Iroquois martyrs, of Catherine, the saint of that tribe, of voyages up the Mississippi, of the massacre by the Natchez, of the mission to the Illinois, and of Montcalm's expedition to Fort George. Some of the letters written by the missionaries to their superiors and brethren in France contain the earliest descriptions of portions of States now constituting the most flourishing region in the West. In his account of a "Journey through Illinois and Michigan, in 1712," Father Marest writes: "Our Illinois dwell in a delightful country. There are great rivers, which water it, and vast and dense forests, with delightful prairies." He descants on the "charming variety" of the scene, speaks of the abundance of game, such as buffaloes, roebucks, hinds, stags, swan, geese, bustards, ducks, and turkeys; he notes the wild oats and the cedar and copal trees, the apple, peach, and pear orchards, and says the flesh of young bears is very delicate, and the native grapes "only moderately good." Of the Indians he remarks that "their physical development is fine—the men being tall, active, and very swift of foot;" he describes their mode of life, their wigwams, corn staple, manitous and medicine men: it is among the women, however, that his mission best succeeds; they, he writes, are "depressed by their daily toil, and are more docile to the truths of the gospel," and are invariably "modestly clothed when they come into the church."

The cheerful temperament and quick observation, as well as the pious zeal of the French Jesuits, made them admirable pioneers and explorers; with enough imagination to enjoy and describe nature, and sympathy adequate to put them in relation with the races they aimed to convert, more or less preliminary study enabled them to note the phenomena and products of the new country, if not with scientific completeness, yet with intelligence and precision. Charlevoix singularly combined the priest and the savan; he tells us, speaking of Christian baptism among the savages, how an *enfant moribund fût guerit par la vertu de ce sacrament;* and, at the same time, his was the first correct estimate of the height of the Falls of Niagara. His "Histoire de la Nouvelle France" is a pleasing memorial of his loyalty and pious self-devotion, whereto he so aptly joined the assiduous observation and careful narrative of an expedition which revealed so many then fresh and valuable facts in regard to the magnificent domain partially colonized, and, as was then hoped, permanently appropriated by France.

3*

CHAPTER III.

FRENCH TRAVELLERS AND WRITERS.

CHASTELLUX; L'ABBÉ ROBIN; DUCHÉ; BRISSOT DE WARVILLE;
CREVECŒUR; LA ROCHEFOUCAULD-LIANCOURT;
VOLNEY; RAYNAL.

AFTER the colonial adventurers and the religious pioneers had made the natural features of America familiar to Europe —after settlements had been made (disputed, declined, and flourished) by representatives of every civilized land, and the English character was the established social influence in the New World—came that memorable struggle for political independence which attracted so many brave and intelligent allies from abroad: some of these have left accounts of their experience and a record of their impressions; they differ from the earlier series of travels in a more detailed report of the manners and customs of the people, in a sympathetic emphasis derived from mutual privations and triumphs, in a speculative interest suggested by the new and vast prospects which then opened before a free people, and in the attractive personal associations which connect these literary memorials with the names of our champions in the War of Independence. Perhaps no one of this class of travels in America is more satisfactory, from the interest of the narrative and the agreeable style, than those of the Marquis de Chastellux.* He vividly

* "Voyages dans l'Amérique Septentrionale dans les années 1780-'81-'82," 2 vols. 8vo., Paris, 1786.

caught the life of America at the time of its most characteristic self-assertion. His amiable manners and intelligent zeal had won him the special regard of Washington. He was one of the forty members of the French Academy, and a major-general of the French army, serving under Count Rochambeau.

François Jean, Marquis de Chastellux, was born in Paris in 1734, and died there in 1788. He was one of those characters almost peculiar to the old *regime*, in France, wherein the *militaire* and the man of letters were gracefully combined with the gentleman. At quite an early age he entered the army, and won distinction in Germany during the Seven Years'. war. His agreeable conversation and urbane manners made him a great favorite when, under Rochambeau, he served in America; in camp and drawing room, at wayside inns and among educated and philosophical men, he was alike pleasant and courteous; and from the commander-in-chief of our army to the shrewd farmer of whose hospitality he partook while travelling, from the stately dowager at Philadelphia to the rustic beauty of an isolated plantation in Virginia, he gained that consideration which high breeding, quick sympathy, and a cultivated mind so naturally win. He acquired no inconsiderable literary reputation by a work that appeared in 1772, *De la Félicité Publique:* the significance of this somewhat ambitious treatise has long since passed away, with the tone of feeling and the state of opinion it once not inadequately represented; still, it is an interesting memorial of an amiable and accomplished champion of the American cause, and a curious illustration of the theories and style once so prevalent in France. The Marquis sympathized with Condorcet's views of the possible and probable progress of humanity, and his work is chiefly inspired with these speculations; but it has no claim to logical order or harmony of plan; it has vigorous thoughts, but they are expressed in too rhetorical a manner to impress deeply a reflective mind; the absence of Christian faith is characteristic of the author's times and country among philosophical writers: yet, notwithstanding the incompleteness and scepticism of the work, its brilliant generalizations so pleased Voltaire that he declared it superior to Montesquieu's famous treatise. As in so many other instances, the fame of the Marquis de Chastellux, as a writer, rests upon the incidental rather than the formal and elaborate achievements of his pen. His *Voyages dans l'Amerique Septentrionale* are the spontaneous comments and descriptions such as fill the letters and journals of an intelligent traveller; they are written in a very pleasant though desultory style, and abound in details of interest not familiar at the time the work appeared. Many important economical, social, and personal facts are gracefully recorded; and the character of the country and of the men who directed the War of Independence and the formation of a free government are described; there are some lively anecdotical episodes, and not a few acute speculations: the work is truly French in the constant alternation of a light vein of remark with serious observation, and warm sentiment with worldly wisdom. The frugal and simple ways, the mental independence, modesty, habits of reading, and political tendencies of the people elicit from the Marquis the most intelligent sympathy; he appreciated the eminent characters to whom the country owed her safety; he notes with accuracy the climate, productions, and habits, with which he comes into contact; but, now and then, a tone of pedantry seems inconsistent with the scene and the sentiment; yet sometimes the associations of both naturally excite classic and romantic memories; he quotes Rabelais and Metastasio, Molière and Guarini; a fair country girl is suggestive of Greuze, and a rural Adonis of Marmontel; he thinks of Buffon among the novel birds and beasts of the wild; and a Connecticut statesman reminds him of a Holland stadtholder; Philadelphia is a modern Capua, and he praises the ladies of that city for skill on the harpsichord; and the fortified Highlands of the Hudson seem a war-girdled Thrace; he contrasts the silent watchfulness of a Quaker meeting with the chanting of the Church of England. The mocking bird and the mountain top, grand old trees and original human beings beguile his fluent pen. As a digest and epitome of his observations in the New World, his discourse on "The Advantages and Disadvantages resulting to Europe from Democracy in America," 1787, is praised by La Harpe as his best work, and seems to have definitely settled the question, as proposed by Raynal, in favor of the advantages. De Chastellux was one of Pope Ganganelli's correspondents; and translated Humphrey's "Campaign." The period of his sojourn in America adds greatly to the interest of his account thereof: the early battle fields of the Revolution were yet fresh, and the momentous conflict was drawing to a glorious end; he saw a fair fugitive from the Wyoming massacre at a New England tavern; and parted with Washington where he took a final leave of his officers, in the "right-hand room" of the old headquarters at Newburgh.

One of the biographers of Chastellux, praising his accomplishments, observes: " *Cette alliance des armes et des lettres, moins rares autrefois, fût doublement glorieux pour lui.*" His "Essay sur l'Union de la Poesie et de la Musique" and his "Vies de quelques grands Capitaines" were highly commended by Buffon, who was president of the Academy when the Marquis was elected a member; the subject of the latter's *discours d'entrance* was *Le Gout :* an appropriate theme for a nobleman whose writings indicate the cultivation of taste in all departments as a mental habit. It has been objected, and justly, to his philosophical writings, that their style is too ambitious; and, in this respect, the simplicity and geniality of his less pretentious Travels give them a more popular tone and scope. They were, notwithstanding their immediate success, bitterly criticized by Brissot de Warville.

An English gentleman, who lived in America at that time, translated the Travels of the Marquis from the French, and added copious notes. Only twenty-four copies of the original had been printed. It is a curious illustration of the period, that "at a time when there was very little hope of any packets reaching Europe but by means of duplicates," the author availed himself of the little printing press on board the squadron at Rhode Island. Only ten out of the twenty-four arrived to the address of those for whom they were destined, and who had been earnestly requested not to take copies; but such was the prevalent desire to know everything possible as to the condition and prospects of America and the remarkable events that had so lately transpired there, that these few impressions were widely circulated; and the translation before alluded to appeared in Dublin and afterward in London, in 1787.* Whoever would compare the present condition of a part of the Southern and most of the New England States with that of eighty years ago, will find few more pleasant authorities than the Marquis de Chastellux. He united, in a singular degree, the gentleman and the scholar, the philosopher and the artist, the man of the world and the good fellow; accordingly he looked upon the primitive life, the original characters, the economical resources, and the natural beauty around him, with curiosity and sympathy; he had the facility of intercourse, the liberal culture, the desire of knowledge so requisite for a traveller; and he was alive to the significance of the present in its relation to the future. His appreciation of the social virtues of the people and his tolerance of their limited means—his interest in their welfare, and his respect for their cause, are evident on every page. No foreigner has manifested a greater admiration of Washington, or more truly described his bearing and principles. Some of his observations are full of interest for those who delight to trace national character and local influence to their sources. Here an anecdote, and there a description; now military details, and again social traits occupy his pen: no phase of domestic economy or statistics of trade and agriculture, no pretty face or shrewd comrade which accident reveals by the way, is allowed to escape him; so that unconsciously he prepared a book of reference whence the philosopher, novelist, and historian may still draw useful hints. It was in the spring of 1782 that the Marquis de Chastellux travelled through Upper Virginia, and,

* "Travels in North America, in the Years 1780, '81, '82," 2 vols. 8vo., maps, London, 1787.

during the ensuing autumn, through Massachusetts, New Hampshire, and part of Pennsylvania. He was accustomed thus to occupy the intervals of professional duty; and, therefore, his journeys were undertaken for the express purpose of acquainting himself with the country and people—a fact indicative of liberal curiosity and a love of travel for its own sake, which is an indispensable requisite for the pleasing report thereof. It is not uninteresting to revert to some of the least uncommon experiences of such a writer, especially when we are familiar with the places described as they appear after nearly a century of prosperous development: we thus obtain veritable glimpses into the life of the past. At the outset of his journal he speaks of having breakfasted at Providence, R. I., " with Colonel Peck. He received me in a small house, where he lived with his wife, who is young also, and has a pleasing countenance, but without anything striking. This little establishment, where comfort and simplicity reign, gave an idea of that sweet and serene state of Happiness which appears to have taken refuge in the New World, after compounding it with Pleasure, to which it has left the Old." His local facts correspond with our experience of the town, which he describes as " pent between two chains of hills, one to the north and the other to the southwest, which causes an insupportable heat in summer; and it is exposed to the northwest wind, which rakes it from one end to the other, and renders it extremely cold in winter. Of the original source of its wealth to the inhabitants, he says they " carry on the Guinea trade—buy slaves and carry them to the West Indies, where they take bills of exchange on old England, for which they receive woollen stuffs and other merchandise." He never fails to note the accommodations at the inns, and is minute in comments on female character and appearance; thus, describing a maiden at a house where he tarried in Rhode Island, he says: " This young person had, like all American women, a very decent, nay, even serious carriage; she had no objection to be looked at, nor to have her beauty commended, nor even to receive a few caresses, provided it was done without an air of familiarity or libertinism. Licentious manners, in fact, are so foreign in America, that freedom itself there bears a character of modesty." He remarks, as a striking circumstance, that in every house he found books which were evidently read; a "town" in America, he observes, means "a few houses grouped round a church and tavern." The obstacles to travelling he finds incessant, having often to cross ferries and to transport provisions and baggage on carts; he alludes to a landlady's expression that she could not *spare* one bed, as a local idiom. The chief man at Hartford, in those days, was Colonel Wadsworth. The Marquis was his guest, and speaks of his honesty as commissary to supply the French troops, and of the high regard in which he was held by Washington and Lafayette. Of Governor Trumbull he says: " He has all the simplicity in his dress, all the importance and even pedantry, becoming the chief magistrate of a small republic. He brought to my mind the burgomasters of Holland in the time of the Barnevelts." He examined manufactures, conversed with intelligent men, noted the "lay of the land," and estimated local resources; he was delighted at the sight of a bluebird, and descants upon the limited nomenclature which designated every water bird as a duck, from the teal to the black duck, distinguishing them only by the term "red," "wood," &c.; and calling cypress, firs, &c., all pine trees. He is impressed with the sight of "mountains covered with woods as old as the creation;" thinks always of Buffon as so many objects of natural history come in view; and experiences a sensation of wonder when, in the midst of "ancient deserts," he comes upon traces of a "settlement;" the process whereof he describes—how the rude hut gives place to the wooden house, the woods to the clearing; and then comes a piece of tilled land, and more trees are girdled and other roofs are raised, at which neighbors "assist" "with no other recompense than a barrel of cider or a gallon of rum." "Such are the means," he adds, "by which North America, only a hundred years ago a vast forest, is peopled with three millions of inhabitants." As illustrative of the equality of condition and personal independence, he speaks of the indifferent reception often met with at the inns, where travellers often give "more trouble than money," and of the custom of the country, when a public house is not at hand, for the traveller to claim and pay for byway hospitality. He compares this conduct with the obsequious manners of innkeepers in France, and accounts for it by the fact that, in this primitive community, "innkeepers are independent of their vocation." He found broken panes common, and glaziers rare; he is enraptured with the scenery of the Housatonic, and the Hudson Highlands. Amid the latter he is saluted with thirteen guns as major-general, by General Heath, then in command there, the echoes whereof are marvellous; the scene of Arnold's treason inspires him with grave thoughts; he describes the batteries, praises the officer in command, and admires the magnificent view. "The guns they fired," he says, "had belonged to Burgoyne's army." Here he is entertained by the officers, enjoys their reminiscences of the war, and talks over the treason of Arnold, then but two years old; he visited Smith's house, and reflects earnestly on this memorable incident: "in this warlike abode," he declares, "one seems transported to the bottom of Thrace, and the dominions of the god Mars;" thence he goes to Lafayette's camp, and notes details as to the state of the army; on seeking his first interview with Washington, he finds him talking with his officers in a farmyard, "a tall man, five feet nine inches high, of a noble and mild countenance;" by the chief he is immediately presented to Knox, Wayne, Hamilton, and others. After three days of delightful intercourse with the leaders of the American army at headquarters, he breakfasts with Lord Stirling, and, upon taking leave of Washington, is presented by him with a horse, of which he stood in much need; and proceeds to New Jersey, where he visits the battle fields of Trenton, Monmouth, and Princeton; at the latter place visiting Dr. Witherspoon, the head of the college; and enjoying the novel carols of a mocking bird. "Addison said," he writes, "in visiting the different monuments of Italy, that he imagined himself on classic ground; all my steps were on *martial* ground; I went, in the same morning, to see two fields of battle." He finds the custom of giving toasts and speeches at table very irksome; and, in allusion to Governor Livingston, of New Jersey, remarks, "I have often had occasion to observe there is more of *ceremony* than of *compliment* in America," a discriminating view of the manners of that time. At Philadelphia, the Marquis notes his intercourse with Reed, whose correspondence with Washington so fully illustrates the anxious perplexities of that immaculate patriot's life during the war; he speaks of a visit to Dr. Franklin's daughter, Mrs. Bache, whom he found "simple in her manners, like her respectable father, and possessed of kindred benevolence of disposition;" Robert Morris he describes as a "large man, very simple in his manners, but his mind is subtile and acute; his head is perfectly well organized, and he is as well versed in public affairs as in his own; a zealous republican and an Epicurean philosopher, he has always played a distinguished part at table and in business." He enjoyed interviews with Rittenhouse and Tom Paine, and had a talk on government with Samuel Adams. Nothing can be imagined more opposite than the social code of a Frenchman and a Quaker, the one having such excessive faith in manner and dealing so fluently in verbal courtesies, and the other repudiating both as inimical to spiritual integrity. Yet there is no trait of the American character, as then exhibited, which won more sincere admiration from this soldier and nobleman than its simplicity; it is the constant theme of his eulogy; but this beautiful quality did not strike him as spontaneous and candid in the Quakers whom he met in the city of brotherly love: "The law," he writes, "observed by this sect, of neither using *you* nor *sir*, is far from giving them a tone of simplicity and candor; they in general assume a smooth and wheedling tone, which is altogether jesuitical." Philadelphia, it would appear from the experience of the Marquis, was as famous then as now for its market and household comfort; for he expresses a fear lest the "pleasures of Capua should make him forget the campaigns of Hannibal;" he therefore determines to leave the luxury of the city, and explore the recent battle fields of Germantown and Brandywine.

The public beneficence of Philadelphia, as indicated by the endowment of hospitals and corrective institutions, had already become a marked feature; but the Marquis comments on a defect, soon after remedied—the absence of a public walk. Milton, Addison, and Richardson he found the authors chiefly read by the young women; and so universal was the interest in and knowledge of civic affairs, that he declares that "all American conversation must finish with politics." His winter journey to Saratoga was a formidable undertaking, or would have been to a gentleman unfamiliar with the hardy discipline of the camp; its principal episodes of interest were the view of Cohoes Falls, and a visit to General Schuyler, just after the marriage of his daughter with Hamilton; he inspected some interesting documents revealing the actual condition of Canada, and expatiates on the novel excitement and exposure of what he calls a "sledge ride." With the present byway scenery of the railroad which intersects the central part of New York State, it is instructive to read his account of that region, through which, by slow stages, he penetrated from town to fort and through a snow-shrouded wilderness. "The country," he tells us, "which lies between Albany and Schenectady, is nothing but an immense forest of pine trees, untouched by the hatchet. They are lofty and robust; and, as nothing grows in their shade, a line of cavalry might traverse the wood without breaking their line or defiling." Schenectady contained then but five hundred houses "within the palisades;" diverging from his road, he visited a Mohawk settlement, a few straggling descendants of which tribe the traveller of to-day still encounters, in that vicinity, among the peddling *habitués* of the railway cars. He also saw, on the way to Fort Edward, the house formerly the home of the unfortunate Jane McRea; startled a bevy of quails, and, at a wayside inn, saw a girl "whom Greuze would have been happy to have taken as a model;" while, on his chamber table, he found an abridgment of Newton's Philosophy, and discovered that his landlord, a surveyor by profession, and incessantly occupied in measuring land, was well versed in Physics. The Marquis, after thus journeying through the northern section of the country, observing its peculiarities, seeking the acquaintance of its leading men, and visiting the scenes of the war, yet fresh in association and destined to become memorably historical, rejoined the French army then stationed at Newport, R. I., whence, after a brief interval, he started on a Southern expedition.

The Marquis thus records his method of setting out on a journey into Virginia, eighty-four years ago : " On the eighth of the month I set out with Mr. Lynch, then my aide-de-camp and adjutant, now general; Mr. Frank Dillon, my second aide, and Mons. la Chevalier d'Oyrè, of the engineers, six servants, and a led horse composed our train ; so that our little caravan consisted of four masters, six servants, and eleven horses." At the very outset of the expedition he notes that capricious state of the climate which in our country so often blends the aspect of different seasons ; writing of the month of April, he says : " I regretted to find summer in the heavens, while the earth afforded not the smallest appearance of spring ; " the devastations of war were yet fresh ; he sojourned at a house which " had been pillaged by the English ; they had taken the very boots off the owner's legs." On this journey he first made acquaintance with a mocking bird, and gives a lively description of its performance : " Apparently delighted at having an auditor, it kept hopping from branch to branch, and imitated the jay, lapwing, raven, cardinal, &c." He finds " a garden in the English style ; " court houses usually in the centre of counties ; daughters of the isolated planters, " pretty nymphs, more timid and wild than Diana ; " and, approaching the South, observes a different kind of popular amusement and of traffic than prevailed in New England, especialy cock fighting and horse trading ; he is struck with the conjugal epithet of his landlord, who calls his wife " honey," which he regards as synonymous with the French term of endearment—*mon petit cœur;* with him the transition from gallant to economical details is easy, and, traversing the then sparsely inhabited region comprised within and around the State of Virginia, he observes the frequent instances, among the inhabitants, of "patriarchal agriculture, which consists in producing only what is sufficient for their own consumption;" and remarks that "nails are the articles most wanted in these new colonies; for the axe and saw can supply every other want." He visits Monticello, a name signifying little mountain, though he finds it a big one, and the house of Jefferson "in the Italian style, and more architectural than any in the country;" while the master thereof elicits all his enthusiasm: "Let me describe," he writes, "a man not yet forty—tall, and with a mild and pleasant countenance; but whose mind and understanding are ample substitutes for every exterior grace; an American who, without ever having quitted his own country, is at once a musician, skilled in drawing, a natural philosopher, legislator, and statesman. Before I had been two hours with him, we were as intimate as if we had passed our whole lives together; walking, books, but, above all, conversation always varied and interesting, made four days pass away like so many minutes." The twain grew eloquent about Ossian over a bowl of punch, and speculated upon the genus of American deer, which Jefferson fed with Indian corn, and the Marquis describes as half roebuck and half English deer. They also engaged in a meteorological discussion, and expatiated on the advantages for observations in this then embryo science, afforded by the extent and variety of the American climate. Jefferson stated some interesting results of his observations as to the effect of woods in breaking clouds and absorbing exhalations. Political and social questions were not forgotten by the two philosophers: "A Virginian," writes the Marquis, "never resembles a European peasant; he is always a freeman, participates in the government, and has the command of a few negroes, so that, uniting in himself the two qualities of citizen and master, he perfectly resembles the bulk of individuals who formed what were called the 'people' in the ancient republics." He also expresses the conviction that "the dignity of man is relative;" and is struck with the superior riflemen of the Virginia militia; he finds novel sport in shooting a wood hen, and discovers quite an ideal rustic in the person of a handsome miller: "He was a young man, twenty-two years of age, whose charming face, fine teeth, red lips, and rosy checks recalled to mind the pleasant portrait which Marmontel gives of Lubin." The alternation of pastoral, patriarchal, and aristocratic manners, the aboriginal traditions, the grand economical resources observed, and frequent personal discomfort experienced, offered to his thoughtful, susceptible, and adventurous mind constant subjects of interest—a vivid contrast with the society and condition of the Old World, a freshness and freedom combined with hardihood and privation, an originality of character and vast promise for humanity; the primitive and the cultivated elements of life were brought into frequent contact; and the urbane and intelligent French officer seems to have had an eye and a heart for all around him suggestive of the past or prophetic of the future. By a most toilsome and perplexing access, he visited the Natural Bridge of Virginia; delighted with this wonderful structure, he measured its dimensions with care, and speculated upon its formation with curiosity; it excited in his mind a kind of "melancholy admiration."

Another characteristic scene which impressed him was a conflagration in the woods—a feature of the landscape which, to his European vision, was ever fraught with interest; he records his appreciation of the "strong, robust oaks and immense pines, sufficient for all the fleets of Europe," which "here grow old and perish on their native soil." He is much struck with the cheerful spirit with which emigration goes on in the New World, when he encounters, in the lonely wild, a buoyant adventurer "with only a horse, saddle bags, cash to buy land, and a young wife;" of the latter he observes: "I saw, not without astonishment, that her natural charms were even embellished by the serenity of her mind." The importance to a traveller of a love of nature and an eye for character, is signally manifest in the American travels of Chastellux. To one destitute of these resources the journey thus described would have been irksome, through its monotony and discomfort. But the vivacious and amiable French officer found novelty in the wild creatures, the vegetation, and the people he encountered; he was constantly alive to the fact that he was traversing a new country, and therefore bound to observe all its phases; it is surprising how much he discovered to awaken pleasant memories of his studies and experience in Europe; how the charms of nature suggested reminiscences of art, and the individuality of character recalled the celebrities of other eras and climes. A vulgar mind, an ignorant man, would have hastened through the rude domain, and sought amusement only in the more settled and populous districts; but the resources and character of the country, the eminent among its inhabitants, their sacred struggle for freedom, and the vast possibilities incident to such an extent of territory and to a great political experiment, quickened the sympathies and enlisted the careful observation of the cultivated soldier. The rabbit that runs across his woodland path, the delicate pink blossoms of the peach trees in a settler's orchard, the novel sight of a marmoset caught by the way, a fat and original landlord, tobacco "as a circulating medium," and the magnificent prospect from the summit of the Blue Ridge, suffice to occupy and interest. A fair Virginian recalls to his mind "those beautiful Virgins of Raphael;" he is agreeably surprised at the opportunity of practising Italian with a cook of that nation he finds in a Richmond inn, and is eloquent in describing the humming bird, and precise in delineating the sturgeon; repeats the story of Pocahontas amid the local traditions that endear her memory, and thinks one "must be fatigued with hearing the name of Randolph while travelling in Virginia." It would appear that "young America" was as real then as now: "The youth of both sexes," he says, "are more forward and ripe than with us; and our maturity is more prolonged." Still he finds special charms in the Old Dominion, and thinks the inhabitants of Virginia best situated of all the colonists under the English Government. "The Government," he adds, "may become democratic at the present moment; but the national character, the spirit of the Government itself, will always be aristocratic; it was originally a 'company' composed of the men most distinguished for their rank and birth." He appreciates the diversity of political origin and local character in the different sections of the country; observing that New England was settled "to escape arbitrary power"—New York and the Jerseys by necessitous Dutchmen, "who occupied themselves more about domestic economy than the public government;" that of Pennsylvania he considers a "government of property—feudal, or, if you will, patriarchal." He describes the domestic luxury of the Virginians as consisting in "furniture, linen, and plate, in which they resemble our ancestors, who had neither cabinets nor wardrobes in their castles, but contented themselves with a well-stored cellar and a handsome *buffet*." In analyzing their domestic life, he makes the just and suggestive remark, "they are very fond of their *infants*, but care little for their *children*," which trait, in a measure, explains the facility with which families disperse, and the early separation of households, wherein our civilization is so different from that of the Old World. It is both curious and instructive, at this moment, when her soil has been stained and furrowed by contending armies, which rebellious slaveholders evoked by violence because of an indirect and legitimate interference with "property in man," to note the calm statement of this disinterested traveller, after free intercourse with all classes of Virginians, eighty years ago: "They seem afflicted," he writes, "to have any slavery, and are constantly talking of abolishing it, and of contriving some other means of cultivating their estates;" the motives thereto, he says, are various—young men being thus disposed from "justice and the rights of humanity," while "fathers complain that the maintenance of their negroes is very expensive."

The Marquis, in a subsequent journey, after visiting Concord, made a careful observation of Dorchester and Bunker Hill; and, in reference to the battle at the latter place, he remarks that "without the protection of the shipping, the British could not have embarked to return from Bunker Hill; the little army in Boston would, in that case, have been almost totally destroyed, and the town must, of course, have been evacuated. But what would have been the result of this? Independence was not then declared, and the road to negotiation was still open; an accommodation might have taken place between the colonies and the mother country, and animosities might have subsided." While at Portsmouth, N. H., on Sunday, he attended church, and heard the father of one of Boston's most endeared young divines; his comment on the discourse is characteristic both of the writer and of the times: "The audience was not numerous, on account of the severe cold; but I saw some handsome women, elegantly dressed. Mr. Buckminster, a young minister, spoke with a great deal of grace, and reasonably enough for a preacher. I could not help admiring the address with which he introduced politics into his sermon." One of those old-fashioned brick dwellings, with front yard, wide portal, and broad staircase, wherein of yore abode the colonial aristocracy of New England, still stands, with its venerable trees, in this pleasant town; and is still the abode of genial hospitality; there our traveller "drank tea at Mr. Langdon's;" and, impressed with the prosperous situation and evident wealth of the place, he declares "there is every appearance of its becoming to New England what the other Portsmouth is to old." To those familiar with the old localities and associations of Boston, it is not uninteresting to know, from the journal of the Marquis, that, when, in 1782, he visited the metropolis of New England, he first "alighted at Mr. Brackett's, the Cromwell's Head inn; and, after dinner, went to the lodgings proposed for me, at Mr. Colson's, a glover, in the Main street." In the evening he attended the "association ball," which, he tells us, "was opened by the Marquis de Vaudreuil with Mrs. Temple; and

4

that "the prettiest of the women dancers were Mrs. Jarvis, her sister Mrs. Betsy Broom, and Mrs. Whitmore." He calls on Hancock, who is too ill with the gout to see him; but is more fortunate in finding Dr. Willard, president of Cambridge University; he meets Mrs. Tudor, Mrs. Morton, and Mrs. Swan at a party; drinks tea with Mrs. Bowdoin, and finds the younger lady of that name "has a mild and agreeable countenance, and a character corresponding with her appearance;" he dines with Mr. Breck; of Mrs. Temple he writes: "Her figure is so distinguished as to make it necessary to pronounce her truly beautiful;" and describes a girl of twelve he meets at the house of one of his Boston acquaintance as "neither a handsome child nor a pretty woman, but rather an angel;" he notes "feather beds" as a local peculiarity; and praises the skill of Dr. Jarvis, and the wisdom of Dr. Cooper.

The Marquis of Chastellux, as we have seen, took leave of Washington at Newburgh, in the "parlor on the right" as you enter the low-roofed stone farmhouse, now preserved there as national property, and consecrated as the "headquarters" of our peerless chief; "it is not difficult," writes the French officer, "to imagine the pain this separation gave me; but I have too much pleasure in recollecting the real tenderness with which it affected him, not to take a pride in mentioning it." If an ardent yet judicious appreciation of his character merited such regrets at parting, few of his foreign friends deserved it more than Chastellux, whose written portrait of the American leader was the most elaborate and discriminating of contemporary delineations; familiar as it is, we cannot better take leave of the courteous and intelligent nobleman and soldier than by quoting it:

"Here would be the proper place to give the portrait of General Washington; but what can my testimony add to the idea already formed of him? The continent of North America, from Boston to Charleston, is a great volume, every page of which presents his eulogium. I know that having had the opportunity of a near inspection, and of closely observing him, some more particular details may be expected from me; but the strongest characteristic of this respected man is the perfect union which reigns between the physical and moral qualities which compose the individual: one alone will enable you to judge of all the rest. If you are presented with medals of Cæsar, of Trajan, or Alexander, on examining their features you will be led to ask what was their stature and the form of their persons: but, if you discover in a heap of ruins the head or the limb of an antique Apollo, be not anxious about the other parts, but rest assured that they were all conformable to those of a god. Let not this comparison be attributed to enthusiasm. I wish only to express the impression General Washington has left on my mind; the idea of a perfect whole—which cannot be the product of enthusiasm, but would rather reject it, since the effect of proportion is to diminish the idea of greatness. Brave without temerity, laborious without ambition, generous without prodigality, noble without pride, virtuous without severity—he seems always to have confined himself within those limits where the virtues, by clothing themselves in more lively but less changeable and doubtful colors, may be mistaken for faults. This is the seventh year that he has commanded the army, and that he has obeyed the Congress; more need not be said, especially in America, where they know how to appreciate all the merit contained in this simple fact. Let it be repeated that Condé was intrepid, Turenne prudent, Eugène adroit, Catinat disinterested. It is not thus that Washington will be characterized. It will be said of him, at the end of a long civil war, he had nothing with which he could reproach himself. If anything can be more marvellous than such a character it is the unanimity of the public suffrages in his favor. Soldier, magistrate, people—all love and admire him; all speak of him in terms of tenderness and veneration. Does there then exist a virtue capable of restraining the injustice of mankind, or a glory and happiness too recently established in America for Envy to have deigned to pass the seas?

"In speaking of this perfect whole, of which General Washington furnishes the idea, I have not excluded exterior form. His stature is noble and lofty; he is well made and exactly proportioned; his physiognomy mild and agreeable, but such as to render it impossible to speak particularly of any of his features, so that, in quitting him, you have only the recollection of a fine face. He has neither a grave nor a familiar air; his brow is sometimes marked with thought, but never with inquietude; in inspiring respect, he inspires confidence, and his smile is always the smile of benevolence."

Nor did the Marquis fail to remember his American friends and advocate their country when returned to his own. He translated the Address to the American Armies, written in heroic verse, in 1782, by Colonel Humphreys; and, in a letter to Franklin, dated at Paris, June 21st, 1786, he says: "When you were in France there was no need praising the Americans; for we had only to say, 'Look, here is their representative.' But, however worthily your place may have since been filled, it is not unreasonable to arouse anew the interest of a kind-hearted but thoughtless nation. Such has been my motive in translating Colonel Humphrey's poem. My success has fully equalled and even surpassed my expectations. Not only has the public received the work with favor, but it has succeeded perfectly at court, especially with the king and queen, who have praised it highly."

L'Abbé Robin was a chaplain in the Count Rochambeau's army. He writes in the same genial strain as most of his countrymen, with the peculiar kind of observation and tone of sentiment which marks almost all French travels. He was touched and repelled, at the same time, by the domestic life of New England—its religious teachings and exemplary dutifulness; while he laments the fragile beauty of her daughters, and speaks of rum as the commodity which served as a connecting link between Yankeeland and the French colonies. Sunday in the Puritan capital, impresses him strongly, and he discovers, by the dates on the tombstones, that the women there are short lived; the following letter, dated Boston, 14th June, 1781, is a fair specimen of the Abbé's manner of viewing things, while it is a curious picture of the "hub of the universe" eighty years ago:

"At last, after two more days of anxiety and peril, and of sickness to me, a favorable breeze sprang up and brought us safely into the roadstead of Boston. In this roadstead, studded with pleasant islands, we saw, over the trees on the west, the houses rising amphitheatre-like, and forming along the hillsides a semicircle of nearly half a league; this was the town of Boston.

"The high regular buildings, intermingled with steeples, appeared to us more like a long-established town of the continent than that of a recent colony. The view of its interior did not dissipate the opinion which was formed at first sight. A fine mole or pier projects into the harbor about two thousand feet, and shops and warehouses line its whole length. It communicates at right angles with the principal street of the town, which is long and wide, curving round toward the water; on this street are many fine houses of *two and three stories*. The appearance of the buildings seems strange to European eyes; being built entirely of wood, they have not the dull and heavy appearance which belongs to those of our continental cities; they are regular and well lighted, with frames well joined, and the outside covered with slight, thinly-planed boards, overlapping each other somewhat like the tiles upon our roofs. The exterior is generally painted of a grayish color, which gives an agreeable aspect to the view.

"The furniture is simple; sometimes of costly wood, after the English fashion; the rich covering their floors with woollen carpets or rush matting, and others with fine sand.

"The town contains about six thousand houses, or nearly thirty thousand inhabitants, with nineteen churches of all denominations. Some of the churches are very fine, especially those of the Presbyterian and Episcopal societies. They are generally oblong, ornamented with a gallery and furnished with pews throughout, so that the poor as well as the rich may hear the gospel with much comfort.

"The Sabbath is here observed with much rigor. All kinds of business, however important, cease; and even the most innocent pleasures are not allowed. The town, so full of life and bustle during the week days, becomes silent like the desert on that day. If one walks the streets, he scarcely meets a person; and if perchance he does, he will hardly dare to stop and speak.

"A countryman of mine, lodging at the same inn with me, took it into his head one Sunday to play a little upon his flute; but the neighborhood became so incensed that our landlord was obliged to acquaint him with their uneasiness.

"If you enter a house, you will generally find each member of the household engaged in reading the Bible; and it is a very interesting and touching sight to see a parent, surrounded by his family, reading and explaining the sublime truths of the sacred volume.

"If you enter a temple of worship, you find a perfect stillness reigns, and an order and behavior which are not found generally in our Catholic churches.

"The singing of the Psalms is slow and solemn, and the words of the hymns being in their native tongue, serves to increase the interest and engage the attention of the worshippers. The churches are without ornament of any kind; nothing there speaks to the mind or heart; nothing to recall to man why he comes there, or what shall be his hope of the future. Sculpture and painting trace no sacred events there to remind him of his duties or awaken his gratitude."

His *Nouveau Voyage dans l'Amérique Septentrionale en l'année* 1781, consists of thirteen letters, which were published in Paris in 1782. Of Boston trade at the period he says:

"The commerce of the Bostonians embraced many objects, and was very extensive before the war. They furnished Great Britain with masts and yards for the royal navy. They constructed by commission, or on their account, a great number of merchant vessels, renowned for their superior speed. In short, their construction is so light that it is not necessary to be a great connoisseur to distinguish their vessels in the midst of those of other nations. Those which they freighted at their own expense were loaded, for the American islands or for Europe, with timber, clapboards, pitch, tar, turpentine, rosin, cattle and swine, and some peltry. But their principal article of commerce was the codfish which they found near their coast, and particularly in the Bay of Massachusetts. This fishery amounted to fifty thousand quintals, which they exported to the other New England provinces, and even to Spain, Italy, and the Mediterranean. Those of the poorest quality were destined for the negroes of the islands. They employ a large number of men, who make excellent mariners. The province of Massachusetts, which has a poor soil, will always be powerful, owing to this branch of commerce; and if one day this new continent spreads its formidable forces upon the sea, it is Boston that will first advance. In exchange for this merchandise, they bring back the wines of Madeira, Malaga, and Oporto, which they prefer to ours, on account of their mildness, and perhaps also from the effect of habit. They take from the islands a good quantity of sugar, which they use for their tea, which the Americans drink at least twice a day; they also bring from there a greater quantity of molasses, which they distil into rum, their ordinary beverage. The importation was so considerable, that before the war it was only worth two shillings a gallon.

"Their fishery, their commerce, and the great number of vessels which they build, have made them the coasters of all the Northern colonies.

"It is estimated that in 1748 five hundred vessels cleared at this port for a foreign trade, and four hundred and thirty entered it; and about one thousand vessels were employed in the coasting trade. It appears, however, from the statement of an Englishman, that their commerce has declined. In 1738, they constructed in Boston forty-one ships, making a total of 6,324 tons; in 1743, thirty-eight were built; in 1746, twenty; in 1749, fifteen, making in total 2,450 tons. This diminution of the commerce of Boston arises, probably, from the new settlements formed along the coast, which attract to themselves the different branches that their situation may render most favorable.

"The great consumption of rum by the Americans induced them to establish commercial relations with the French colonies; our wines and brandy rendering this liquor little used by us, they flattered themselves with bringing the molasses to a better use. This speculation resulted beyond their expectations; they had only to give in exchange wood and salt provisions."

The following observations indicate the feeling and relations between our countrymen and their Gallic allies:

"It is difficult to imagine the opinion that the Americans entertained of the French before the war. They regarded them as enslaved under the yoke of despotism, delivered up to prejudices and superstitions, almost idolaters in their worship, incapable of firmness and stability, and occupied only with curling their hair and painting their faces; unfeeling, faithless—not even respecting the most sacred duties. The English were eager to spread and strengthen these prejudices. Presbyterianism [Congregationalism], an implacable enemy of Catholicism, has made the Bostonians, where this sect is dominant, still more disposed to this opinion.

"All seemed, at the commencement of the war, to confirm these views. Most of the Frenchmen who first came to America at the rumor of revolution, were men involved in debts and ruined in reputation, who announced themselves with titles and fictitious names, obtained great distinction in the American army, received considerable advance money, and suddenly disappeared.

"The simplicity of the Americans and their inexperience rendered these impositions easy. Many of these adventurers even committed crimes worthy of the scaffold. The first merchandise that the Bostonians received from France contributed again to support them in these notions, so unfavorable to our honesty and industry. Even at the present time, French goods are sold, for this reason, at a much lower price than English goods of the same quality.

"On the arrival of M. le Count d'Estaing, the people were very much astonished not to see frail and deformed men. They believed that these had been expressly chosen to give them a more advantageous idea of the nation. Some with over-florid faces, whose toilet was careless, convinced them that we made use of rouge.

"Notwithstanding my being a Frenchman and Catholic priest, I receive daily new civilities in many good families of this city. But the people still retain their first prejudices. I have lately seen a proof of this in an event which has at the same time served to make me better acquainted with their character. The house where I lodged took fire; it belonged to a Frenchman. One can imagine what emotion this sight would produce in a city built of wood. The people ran thither in crowds, but when they arrived there, they remained only spectators of the scene. I caused the doors to be closed, in order to arrest the currents of air, and sealed the chimney, whence the fire was, hermetically with a wet cloth, causing water to be poured upon it without intermission, that it might retain its dampness. The women of the house were enraged at the sight of their flooded and dirty floor. If I had not made myself the master, they would have preferred to let the danger increase.

"The arrival of the army of M. le Count de Rochambeau at Rhode Island spread terror there. The country was deserted, and those whom curiosity led to Newport found the streets empty. All felt the importance of dissipating these prejudices, and exercising self-respect has contributed to this. The superior officers established the strictest discipline; the other officers employed that politeness and amenity which has always characterized the French nobility; the private soldier, even, has become gentle and circumspect, and in a year's sojourn here, not one complaint has been made.

"The French at Newport are no longer a trifling, presumptuous, noisy, and ostentatious people; they are quiet and retiring, limiting their society to that of their guests or visitors, that they may become daily more dear to them. These young noblemen, whose fortune, birth, and court life would naturally lead them to dissipation, luxury, and extravagance, have given the first example of simplicity and frugality; they have shown themselves as affable and familiar as if they had lived entirely among similar people. This elevated conduct has brought about an entire revolution in the minds of people. Even the Tories cannot help loving the French, while blaming the cause which they uphold, and their departure afflicts a thousand times more than their arrival alarms."

An interesting evidence of the vast promise, social and economical, with which the extent, resources, and political prospects of America inspired thoughtful and enthusiastic observers at this period, may be found in the characteristic expressions of a clergyman, born in Philadelphia, but of

Huguenot origin, whose rhetoric and writing were much admired in his own day, and whose name is not wholly unfamiliar in our own, from the circumstance that, at the suggestion of Samuel Adams, he opened the old Continental Congress of 1774 with prayer. Three years previously, while assistant minister of Christ Church, Philadelphia, were published the Letters of Tamoc Caspipina, in which Jacob Duché thus speaks of the country, just before the Revolution : " My attachment to America, I am apt to think, proceeds from the prospects of its growing greatness. In Europe, architecture, gardening, agriculture, mechanics are at a stand ; the eye is weary with perpetual sameness ; after roaming over the magnificence of churches and palaces, we are glad to fix our gaze awhile upon a simple farmhouse or straw-built cottage ; we feel a particular delight in tracing the windings of a beautiful river. The objects of Art, as well as those of Nature, in this New World, are, at present, in such a state as affords the highest entertainment ; here and there, in the midst of venerable woods, scarce a century ago the haunts of roaming savages, are fields of corn and meadows. Within the compass of a mile we behold Nature in her original rusticity and Art rising by rapid advances. I see learning stripped of all scholastic pedantry and religion restored to gospel purity." The transition state, the strong contrasts, the process of development, and the opportunity of going back to first and true principles in civil and social life, hinted at in such views, constituted the great attraction which the New World offered to philosophical and benevolent minds. This it was that urged Berkeley's prophetic muse and gracious enterprise, and, a century before, the " Church Militant " declared George Herbert's " Prophecy," in the " Country Parson," realized in America.

Duché's reputation, however, has a less amiable and honorable side ; of him it has been written : " He, whose sublime prayer as chaplain of the Continental Congress, melted the hearts of his audience every time he bent to repeat it, fell away from his loyalty, and enjoys the sole infamy of having sought to corrupt Washington. While the wretch was praying to Almighty God for the success of the Revolution, his heart was black with treason."

One of those extraordinary children of the time who, without any remarkable endowments or adaptation for the career of politics, were whirled into that sphere of thought and action by the tides of the French Revolution, came to America in 1788, and, like Ceracchi, the sculptor, not only derived new ideas and enthusiasm from his visit, but became a martyr to his convictions and the circumstances of his native land. We find the record * of his observations in the New World quoted with deference by his contemporaries; it was translated more than once into English, † and seems to have been more permanently attractive than any other of the several political treatises from the same pen; one of Brissot's biographers calls him an *écrivain mediòcre et un dissateur monotone et verbeux;* yet, with all his speculative hardihood and French sentiment, many of his remarks on our country at the time are characteristic and noteworthy. Born in 1754, at the village of Ouarville, near Chartres, he subsequently modified his local appellation into Warville, for the prestige of an English name while under surveillance; placed in the Bastile for the *hardiesse de ses écrits contre l'inégalité des rangs,* he was liberated through the influence of the Duke of Orleans, whose sympathy in his behalf had been excited by Madame de Genlis; and the association thus induced led to his marriage with one of the ladies of the Duchess and to his embassy to England on a secret mission as lieutenant of police. Having vainly sought to advance his fortunes in that country, he crossed the ocean early in 1788; and, in the following year, left our shores on account of the terrible political and social crisis which convulsed his own country. He soon became

---

* Nouveau Voyage dans les Etats Unis de l'Amerique Septentrionale, fait en 1788, 3 vols., Paris, 1791.

† Brissot de Warville's New Travels in the United States of America, performed in 1788, 8vo., London, 1792.

Brissot's Travels in the United States in 1788, with Observations on the Genius of the People and Government, &c., 8vo., 1794.

prominent as a journalist in Paris, was bold and unscrupulous as an advocate of revolution, and soon drew upon himself the bitter attacks of rivals and opponents, one of whom, Morande, issued a pamphlet charging Brissot with the basest conduct while in England, and proposing to make *Brissoter* the synonyme of *Voler*. Undaunted by scandal, he took an active part in forwarding the petition of the *Champs du Mars*, whereby he alienated Lafayette, with whom he ostensibly and ardently sympathized; chosen a deputy, and, on account of his foreign travels, placed on the diplomatic committee, Brissot advocated war with Europe, attached himself to Delessart, then at the head of foreign affairs, and, with the disgrace of the latter, became the object of invective from Camille Desmoulins and of persecution from Robespierre. Brissot reverted to his original theories, denounced those who were attached to the king, was accused of federalism, which he had defended as the true principle of the American Government, and of conspiracy against the French republic. He drafted the declaration of war against England and Holland; and never ceased, with tongue and pen, to attack the colonial proprietors and plead for their slaves; so that he was considered a prime instigator of the St. Domingo insurrection: proscribed on the last of May, 1795, he was soon after arrested at Moulins, and perished, by the guillotine, during the following October. There was something anomalous in his character; of feeble constitution, he was energetic and pertinacious; an adventurer, he failed to seize opportunities for advancing his own interest; without being a man of pleasure, he neglected his wife and children, leaving them without the means of subsistence; of this he sincerely repented at last, and died bravely. He accomplished little practical good, while convinced he could regenerate his country. His *Voyage aux Etats Unis* was first published at Paris in 1791.

Brissot expatiates on the religious tolerance he found prevailing in Boston in 1788. "Music," he writes, "which was proscribed by their divines as a diabolical art, begins to form a part of their education; you hear, in some rich houses, the pianoforte." He notes the absence of *cafés* in that city, and the existence of clubs "not held at taverns, but at each other's houses." "A favorite amusement," he adds, "is to visit the country in parties, and drink tea, spruce beer, and cider;" he notes the "distilleries of rum at Watertown, destined for the coast of Guinea," and declares that "two maladies afflict the State—emigration west and manufactures." He exults in the sight of his native authors in the library of Harvard College: "The heart of a Frenchman palpitates," he writes, "to find Racine, Montesquieu, and the Encyclopédie, where, a hundred and fifty years ago, smoked the calumet of the savage." Hancock was then Governor, Jarvis the leading physician, and Willard president of Harvard College, each of whom Brissot seems to have appreciated; and he compliments as leaders in Boston society, Wigglesworth, Sullivan, Lloyd, Dexter, and Wendall; he explores Bunker Hill, and visits John Adams, whom he compares to Epaminondas. He suggests the establishment of diligences in Massachusetts; and describing his journey from Boston to New York, commends the white sheets of Spenser and the cheap breakfast at Brookfield. He is vexed at the tolls; sees Colonel Wadsworth at Hartford, and remembers that Silas Dean is a native of Weathersfield, where the immense fields of onions duly impress him. New Haven interests him as having "produced the celebrated poet Trumbull, author of the immortal McFingal;" at Fairfield, "the pleasures of the *voyage* ended," and thenceforth there was "a constant struggle with rocks and precipices." At New Rochelle he sees Mr. Jay, and at Rye finds an excellent inn. He witnessed Fitch's steamboat experiment on the Delaware; and was interested in the "places fortified by the English," as he approached New York. The market, the blacks, and the Quakers of Philadelphia are subjects of curious observation; the calmness and the costume of the latter fascinated him to such a degree that, for a while, he abjured the use of hair powder and other luxuries of the toilet; and describes with interest a Quaker farm, meeting, and funeral. Of the social characteristics of the people, especially in the Eastern States, he thus speaks: "La propreté sans luxe est une des caractères physiognomonique de cette pureté morale; et cette propreté se retrouve par-tout a Boston, dans l'habillement, dans les maisons, dans les eglises; rien de plus charmant que le coup d'œil d'un eglise ou d'un *meeting*. Je ne me rappellerai jamais sans emotion le plaisir que je rassentis, en entendant un fois le respectable ministre Clarke qui a succéde docteur Cooper." But, like most of his countrymen who then visited and described the young republic, his warmest admiration was reserved for "the Father of his Country," whom he visited, and thus describes as only a Frenchman would: "This celebrated general is nothing more at present than a good farmer. His eye bespeaks great goodness of heart; manly sense marks all his answers, and he is sometimes animated in conversation; but *he has no characteristic feelings which render it difficult to seize him*. He announces a profound discretion and a great diffidence in himself; but, at the same time, an unshaken firmness, when once he has made a decision. *His modesty is astonishing to a Frenchman*. He speaks of the American war and of his victories as of things in which he had no direction. He spoke to me of Lafayette with the greatest tenderness." Brissot passed three days at Mount Vernon, and, according to his own statement, was "loaded with kindness." The after career and melancholy fate of Brissot lends a peculiar interest to his narrative; inconsistently combined and imperfectly manifested in his life and nature, we find the philosopher and the republican (wherein he declared Priestley and Price were his models), the philanthropist, the man of letters, the editor, and the politician. He criticized Chastellux—defended America; according to his opponents, "fled with a lie," and yet, by undisputed testimony, died with courage. He thought our lawyers superior; and calls Isaiah Thomas the Didot of America: associating with Franklin, Madison, Hamilton, and other eminent citizens, he learned highly to estimate the influence of free institutions upon human character. Among other pleasant sojourns in New England he delighted to remember the "Laurels," where he was entertained by Dr. Dalton, while on his way from Newburyport up the Merrimac. In his apostrophe to this beautiful stream, Whittier gracefully alludes to Brissot's enjoyment thereof:

> "Its pines above, its waves below,
>   The west wind down it blowing,
> As fair as when the young Brissot
>   Beheld it seaward flowing,—
> And bore its memory o'er the deep
>   To soothe a martyr's sadness,
> And fresco, in his troubled sleep,
>   His prison walls with gladness."

Brissot, seeking to unite economical with social philosophy, devotes no inconsiderable portion of his work to the commerce and commodities of the New World; like other sojourners of that era, he is beguiled into speculative remarks as to the maple tree as a substitute for the sugar cane; coincident with his visit was the initial movement in behalf of the negroes, which then enlisted the best sympathies of the new republic; anti-slavery societies had just then been established in various parts of the country, and their object was freely discussed in regions where, in our day, law and social tyranny barred all expression thereon. Brissot rejoiced in Washington's views and purposes in this regard: "It is a task," he writes, "worthy of a soul so elevated, so pure, and so disinterested, to begin the revolution in Virginia, to prepare the way for the emancipation of the slaves." He was not always a true prophet, as for instance, when he remarks: "Albany will soon yield in prosperity to a town called Hudson." The spectator of two, and the actor and victim in one revolution, there is a certain pensive charm in his earnest appreciation of the political and social advantages of America: "The United States," he declares, "have demonstrated that the less active and powerful the Government, the more active and powerful the people"—a moral fact eminently illustrated by the recent history of the nation. He appreciated the essential influence of personal character to attain civic prosperity: "There can be no durable revolution," he observes, " but where reflection marks the operation and matures the ideas: it is among such men of principles that you find the true heroes of humanity—the Howards, Fothergills, Penns, Franklins, Washingtons, Sidneys, and Ludlows." He invokes his erratic countrymen who wish for " valuable instruction " to ponder his record: " Study the Americans of the present day, and see to what degree of prosperity the blessings of freedom can elevate the industry of man; how they dignify his nature and dispose him to universal fraternity; by what means liberty is preserved; and that the great secret of its duration is good morals."

Thus enthusiastic as a republican, and recognizing so warmly the simplicity of rural and the intrepidity of working life in America, Brissot looked with suspicion upon the encroachments of fashion and wealth upon manners and tastes. It is amusing to read his account of New York and find so many coincidences at the present day in her social tendencies, and to compare the limited indulgences then practicable with the boundless extravagance now so apparent. Thus he wrote of the commercial metropolis of the New World in 1788:

" The presence of Congress, with the diplomatic body and the concourse of strangers, contributes much to extend here the ravages of luxury. The inhabitants are far from complaining of it; they prefer the splendor of wealth and the show of enjoyment to the simplicity of manners and the pure pleasures which result from it. If there is a town on the American continent where the English luxury displays its follies, it is New York. You will find here the English fashions: in the dress of the women you will see the most brilliant silks, gauzes, hats, and borrowed hair; equipages are rare, but they are elegant: the men have more simplicity in their dress; they disdain gewgaws, but they take their revenge in the luxury of the table; luxury forms already a class of men very dangerous to society; I mean bachelors; the expense of women causes matrimony to be dreaded by men. Tea forms, as in England, the basis of parties of pleasure: many things are dearer here than in France; a hairdresser asks twenty shillings a month; washing costs four shillings the dozen."

Lafayette, in his letter introducing Brissot to Washington,

writes: "He is very clever, and wishes to write the history of America." It is a singular coincidence that while he praises the inns of the country, which were so generally complained of by English travellers, he expresses a national repugnance to a habit now so prevalent among his countrymen as, in the view of some of the late critics, to have essentially modified their disposition of mind, if not of bodily temperament. "The habit of smoking," observes Brissot, in his account of New York, "has not disappeared with the other customs of their fathers—the Dutch. They use cigars. These are leaves of tobacco rolled in the form of a tube six inches long, and are smoked without the aid of any instrument. This usage is revolting to the French, but it has one advantage—it favors meditation and prevents loquacity." It is characteristic of this writer's political prepossessions that, while he found "decency, neatness, and dignity" in the taverns, when dining with General Hamilton he recognized in his host the "countenance of a determined republican."

Much ridicule has been expended upon that artificial rural enthusiasm which once formed a curious phase of French literature, wherein the futile attempt was made to graft the ancient Arcadian on the modern rustic enjoyment of nature. This incongruous experiment originated in Italy, and found its best development in the pastoral verse of Guarini and Sannazzaro; but when the Parisian pleasure-seekers affected the crook and simplicity of shepherd life—when box was trimmed into the shape of animals and fountains, grottos and bowers, in the midst of fashionable gardens, and the scent of musk blended with that of pines and roses—the want of genuine love of and sympathy with nature became ludicrously apparent; the manners and talk of the *salon* were absurd in the grove, and the costume and coquetry of the ballroom were reproached by the freedom and calm beauty of woods and waters. The hearty love of country life which is an instinct of the English, and has found such true and memorable expression in the poetry of Great Britain, finds an indifferent parallel in the rhymes of Gallic bards or the rural life of the gentry of France. But there is a vein of rural taste and feeling, of a more practical kind, native to the French heart—a combination of philosophic content and romance—a love of the free, independent life of the wilderness, a capacity of adaptation to new conditions, and a facility in deriving satisfaction from inartificial pleasures, which, when united to the poetical instinct, makes nature and agricultural life a singularly genial sphere to a Frenchman. The sentiment of this experience has been eloquently uttered by St. Pierre, Chateaubriand, and Lamartine; its practical realization was long evident in the urbane, cheerful, and tasteful colonists of Canada and of the West and South of the United States; and the writings of French travellers there and in the East, abound in its graceful commemoration. The literature of American travel is not without memorable illustrations thereof; and one of the best is a book, which, although the production of a Frenchman, was originally written in English under the title of " Letters of an American Farmer." * It is a most pleasing report of the possible resources and charms of that vocation, when it was far more isolated and exclusively rural than at present, when town habits had not encroached upon its simplicity or fashion marred its independence. Somewhat like a prose idyl is this record; Hazlitt delighted in its *naive* enthusiasm, and commended it to Charles Lamb as well as in the Quarterly, as giving " an idea how American scenery and manners may be treated with a lively poetic interest." " The pictures," he adds, " are somewhat highly colored, but they are vivid and strikingly characteristic. He gives not only the objects but the feelings of a new country." The author of this work, Hector St. John Crevecœur, was of noble birth, a native of Normandy, born in 1731; he was sent to England when but sixteen years old, which is the cause of his early and complete mastery of our language. In 1754 he came to New York, and settled on a farm in the adjacent region.

---

* "Letters from an American Farmer, conveying some Idea of the Late and Present Interior Circumstances of the British Colonies in North America," by J. H. St. John Crevecœur, 8vo., London, 1782.

The British troops repeatedly crossed over and lingered upon his estate during the war of the Revolution, much to his annoyance and its detriment. His affairs obliged him to return to France in 1780, and he was allowed to pass through the enemy's lines in order to embark with one of his family; but the vessel was intercepted by the French fleet then off the coast, and Crevecœur was detained several months under suspicion of being a spy. After his release he reëmbarked for Europe, and reached his paternal home safely, after an absence of twenty-seven years. In 1783 he returned to New York to find his dwelling burned to the ground, his wife dead, and his children in the care of friends.

He brought with him, on his return to America, a commission as French consul at New York—a situation which he honorably filled for ten years, when, once more returning to his native land, he resided at his country seat near Rouen, and subsequently at Sarcelles, where he died in 1813. All accounts agree in describing him as a man of the highest probity, the most benevolent disposition, rare intelligence, and engaging manners. Washington esteemed him; he made a journey in Pennsylvania with Franklin, on the occasion of the latter's visit to Lancaster to lay the corner stone of the German college. The account of the incidents and conversation during this trip recorded by Crevecœur, are among the most characteristic reminiscences of the American philosopher extant. His "Letters of an American Farmer" were published in London in 1782. He translated them into his native tongue.* They have a winsome flavor, and picture so delectably the independence, the resources, and the peace of an agricultural life, just before and after the Revolution, in the more settled States of America, that the reader of the present day cannot feel surprised that he beguiled many an emigrant from the Old World to the banks of the Ohio and the Delaware. But this charm originated in the temper and mind of the writer, who was admirably constituted to appreciate and

---

* "Lettres d'un Cultivateur Americain, traduites de l'Anglois," 2 vols., 8vo., Paris, 1784.

improve the advantages of such an experience. He found on his beautiful farm and among his kindly neighbors, the same attractions which Mrs. Grant remembered so fondly of her girlhood's home at Albany. Among the best of his letters are those extolling the pleasures and feelings of a farmer's life in a new country, and those descriptive of Nantucket, Martha's Vineyard, and Charleston, the notice of Bartram the naturalist, and the account of the Humming Bird. Nor was this the author's only contribution to the literature of American travel. In 1801, the fruit of his leisure after his final return to Normandy, appeared in the shape of a work in the publication of which he indulged in a curious literary *ruse*. It was entitled " Voyage dans la haute Pennsylvania et dans l'Etat de New York, par un Membre Adoptif de la nation Oneida, traduit par l'Auteur des Lettres d'un Cultivateur Americain." It needed not this association of his first popular venture with this new book of travels in the same country, to pierce the thin disguise whereby he announced the latter as printed from MSS. found in a wreck on the Elbe; for the author enjoyed the eclat of success in the Paris *salons*, while elsewhere his kindliness and wisdom made him a great favorite. These two works have the merit and the interest of being more deliberate literary productions than any that preceded them. There is a freshness and an ardor in the tone, which is often magnetic; and in the material, a curious mixture of statistics and romance, matter of fact and sentiment, reminding the reader at one moment of Marmontel, and at another of Adam Smith; for it deals about equally in stories and economical details: many of the most remarkable Indian massacres and border adventures, since wrought into history, dramas, and novels, are narrated in these volumes fresh from current traditions or recent knowledge. The author was on intimate terms with the savages, and had been made an honorary member of the Oneida tribe. He gives a clear and probably, at the time, a novel account of the different States, their productions, condition, &c.

Keenly appreciating the relation of landed property to citizenship, exulting in the independence of an agricultural life in a free country, and alive to all the duties and delights of domestic seclusion, his letters breathe a wise and grateful sense of the privileges he enjoys as an American farmer:

"The instant I enter on my own land," he writes, "the bright idea of property, of exclusive right, of independence, exalts my mind. Precious soil, I say to myself, by what singular custom of law is it that thou wast made to constitute the riches of the freeholder? What should we American farmers be without the distinct possession of that soil? It feeds, it clothes us; from it we draw our great exuberancy, our best meat, our richest drink—the very honey of our bees comes from this privileged spot. No wonder we should thus cherish its possession—no wonder that so many Europeans, who have never been able to say that such a portion of land was theirs, cross the Atlantic to realize that happiness. This formerly rude soil has been converted by my father into a pleasant farm, and in return it has established all our rights; on it is founded our rank, our freedom, our power as citizens, our importance as inhabitants of such a district. These images, I must confess, I always behold with pleasure, and extend them as far as my imagination can reach; for this is what may be called the true and only philosophy of the American farmer. Often when I plough my low ground, I place my little boy on a chair which screws to the beam of the plough; its motion and that of the horses please him; he is perfectly happy, and begins to chat. As I lean over the handle, various are the thoughts which crowd into my mind. I am now doing for him, I say, what my father formerly did for me: may God enable him to live, that he may perform the same operations for the same purposes, when I am worn out and old. I release his mother of some trouble while I have him with me; the odoriferous furrow exhilarates his spirits and seems to do the child a great deal of good, for he looks more blooming since I have adopted the practice: can more pleasure, more dignity be added to that primary occupation? The father, thus ploughing with his child and to feed his family, is inferior only to the emperor of China, ploughing as an example to his kingdom."

Very loving and observant are his comments on the aspect, habits, and notes of birds; they remind us of the spirit without the science of our endeared ornithologists, Audubon and Wilson. "I generally rise from bed," writes Crevecœur, "about that indistinct interval, which, properly speaking, is neither night nor day; for this is the moment of the most universal vocal choir. Who can listen unmoved to the sweet love tales of our robins, told from tree to tree; or to the shrill catbird? The sublime accents of the thrush from on high, always retard my steps that I may listen to the delicious music." A long discussion with Dr. Franklin during their memorable journey in 1787, as to the origin of the aboriginal tribes and the mounds of the West, which of late years have so interested ethnologists, is reported at length by this assiduous writer; we thence learn that this new and extended interest was foreseen by the venerable philosopher, who remarked to his companion: "When the population of the United States shall have spread over every part of that vast and beautiful region, our posterity, aided by new discoveries, may then, perhaps, form more satisfactory conjectures."

The religion and politics of the country are defined in these epistles. The Quakers, the weather, the aspect of the land, excursions, speculations, anecdotes, and poetical episodes are the versatile subjects of his chronicle: several old-fashioned engraved illustrations give a quaint charm to the earlier editions; domestic *fêtes, ma fille Fanny*, and the transplanting of a sassafras tree, alternate in the record with reflections on the war of the Revolution, the "Histoire de Rachel Bird," and "La Père Infortuné!" There is a *naïve* ardor and the genial egotism of a Gallic raconteur and philosopher, in the work—which survives the want of novelty in its economical details and local descriptions.

During Crevecœur's visit to Normandy, five American sailors were shipwrecked on that coast, and he befriended them in their great need and peril, with a humane zeal that did credit to his benevolent heart. A gentleman of Boston in New England was so impressed with this kindness to his unfortunate countrymen, that, hearing of the destruction of the generous Frenchman's homestead far away, he made a long and hazardous journey in search of the deserted children, discovered, and cherished them till the father's arrival enabled him to restore them in health and safety. The ardent style of Crevecœur's writings, and that tendency to exaggeration incident to his temperament, caused his books to be criticized with some severity as incorrect, highy colored, and prolix; yet the vital charm and ingenuous sentiment of the enthusiast, combined with his tact as a *raconteur*, and his love of nature and freedom, made these now neglected works popular at the time and long subsequent to their original publication.

One of the most striking instances of the historical value of authentic and detailed records of travel, is the use which philosophical annalists, like De Tocqueville, have made of Arthur Young's observations in France. This intelligent and enthusiastic agricultural writer chronicled, as a tourist, the practical workings of the old *régime* in regard to the peasantry and rural districts, so as to demonstrate the vital necessity of a revolution on economical and social principles alone. A disciple of this writer, whose integrity and patriotism as well as painstaking research make up in no small degree for his limited scientific knowledge and want of originality, prepared a large and well-considered work from a careful survey of the American States and their statistics in 1795. The Duke de La Rochefoucault-Liancourt commanded at Rouen, when the Constituent Assembly, of which he was a member, dissolved; subsequently he passed many months in England, and then visited this country. His "Voyage dans les Etats Unis," and his efficiency in establishing the use of vaccination in France, cause him to be remembered as a man of letters and benevolence; he reached a venerable age, and won the highest respect, although long subject to the unjust aspersions of partisan opponents whom his liberal nature failed to conciliate. There is little of novel information to an American reader in his voluminous work, except the record of local features and social facts, which are now altogether things of the past; yet the fairness and minute knowledge displayed, account for the value and interest attached to this work for many years after its appearance. It is evident that the Duke de La Rochefoucault travelled as much to beguile himself of the *ennui* of exile and the disappointments of a baffled patriot, as on account of his inquiring turn of mind. He occupied himself chiefly with economical investigations, especially those connected with agriculture; the process whereby vast swamps and forests were gradually reduced to tilled and habitable domains, interested him in all its stages and results. He describes each town, port, and region with care and candor; and it is a peculiarity of his Travels that they contain many elaborate accounts of certain farms and estates in different sections, whence we derive a very accurate notion of the methods and the resources of rural life in America soon after the Revolution. The Duke was a philosophical traveller, content to journey on horseback, making himself as much at home with the laborer at the wayside as with the gentleman of the manor; and seeking information with frankness and patience wherever and however it could be properly acquired. The lakes, bays, roads, the markets, manufactures, and seats he examines, in a business-like way; complains of all crude arrangements, and bears the hardships then inseparable from travel here, like a soldier: Indians and rattlesnakes, corn and tobacco, the Hessian fly, pines, maples, negroes, rice plantations, orchards, all the traits of rural economy and indigenous life, are duly registered and speculated upon.

He visited, with evident satisfaction, the battle grounds of the Revolution, and complacently dwells on Yorktown, the grave of Ternay at Newport, and the grateful estimation in which Lafayette was held. He seems to have well appreciated our leading men in public life and society; Jefferson, Marshall, Jay, Hamilton, Adams, and Burr figure in his political tableaux, and he was the guest of General Knox, in Maine. He sums up the character of the Virginians as a people noted for dissipation, hospitality, and *attachment to the Union;* of the special characteristics of the different States he was singularly cognizant; and notes the slow adoption of vaccination, the adaptation of soils, and the existence of wild hemp on the shores of Ontario.

Apart from the specific information contained in his

"Voyage dans les Etats Unis d'Amérique," the Paris edition of which, printed in 1800, consists of eight volumes, 8vo., there is little to attract the reader of warm sympathies or decided tastes. An English translation was published in quarto.* Although the work is the chief source of the Duke de La Rochefoucault's literary reputation, it is justly characterized, by an intelligent French critic, as a *froide* compilation, *sans imagination et sans l'esprit d'artiste*. Both this writer, Chastellux, and other of their countrymen, gave satisfactory facts in regard to American military and political leaders, who can be most fairly estimated by competent foreign critics: the former describes Stirling, and the latter Simcoe, Knox, and others.

The Duke sums up, in the last chapter of his voluminous work, his impressions and convictions: like Brissot, he praises the Quakers for their civic virtues; he notes what he calls the "prejudice" among the men against "domestic servitude," a feeling in which the women then did not share; of the freedom of action accorded the latter, he speaks with a Frenchman's national surprise, and adds that, when married, "they love their husband because he is their husband;" he expatiates on the need of a more thorough educational system; physically, however, he thinks the Americans had the advantage of Europeans in their habits of sporting and use of the rifle, and deems the liberty enjoyed by children the best method of teaching them self-reliance; he describes the prevalent manners as essentially the same as those which exist in the provincial towns of England; he praises the hospitality and benevolence of the people; and says that drunkenness is "their most common vice," and "the desire of riches their ruling passion;" "the traits of character common to all," he adds, "are ardor for enterprise, courage, greediness, and an advantageous opinion of themselves." Such are some of the opinions formed by this noble but somewhat prosaic traveller

---

* "Liancourt's (Duke de La Rochefoucault) Travels through the United States, the Country of the Iroquois, &c., in the years 1795, '96 and '97," 2 vols. 4to., large folding maps, London, 1799.

immediately after the Revolutionary war, when, as he observes, the Americans " having for the most part made their fortunes by their own industry, labor had not become repugnant to them." He ends his work with the most benign wishes for the prosperity and integrity of the nation.

That gifted and solitary pioneer of American fiction, Charles Brockden Brown, among his numerous and ill-rewarded but most creditable literary labors, made a translation of Volney's once noted book on America.* The career and the character of this writer must be understood in order to estimate aright his writings, and especially those that belong to the sphere of political and social speculation. Born in one of the provinces of France, just before the commencement of that memorable chaos of thought and action which ushered in the Revolution, of a studious and independent habit, he early manifested that boldness of aim and originality of conviction which marked the adventurous and the philosophic men of his day. Changing his name, and accustoming himself to hardships, he aspired to an individuality of life and a freedom from conventionalities, somewhat akin to the motive that made Byron a wanderer and Lady Stanhope a contented sojourner in the desert. The passion for travel early possessed him, and he equipped himself therefor by adopting a stoical *régime*, and acquiring the historical and philological knowledge so essential to satisfactory observation in foreign countries. An invalid from birth, his sequestered habits and sensitive temper gave a misanthropic tinge to his disposition, while his limited means induced a remarkable frugality; the result of which circumstances and traits was to make Volney a morbid man, but a speculative thinker and a social nonconformist. Like Bentham and Godwin, but with less geniality, he professed to disdain the tyranny of custom, and to seek the good of humanity and the truth of life, in the neglected and superseded elements of society, so hopelessly

---

* "View of the Soil and Climate of the United States of America," translated by Charles Brockden Brown, with maps and plates, 8vo., Philadelphia, 1804.

overlaid by blind habit and unreasoning acquiescence. Like all Frenchmen, in carrying out this programme as a written theory, he is rhetorical, and, in practice, more or less grotesque; yet with enough of ability and original method to excite the curious, and suggest new ideas to less adventurous minds, however more sound judgment and holier faith might repudiate his principles. Professedly a social reformer, and at war with the life and law around him, he, like so many other civilized malcontents, turned ardently to the East.

A Breton and a peer of France, there is much in Volney to remind us of Chateaubriand—the same passion for knowledge, love of travel, political enthusiasm, romantic egotism, vague and vaunted sentiment; but there the parallel ends: for Chateaubriand's conservatism, social relations, and opinions, literary, political, and religious, separate him widely from Volney, although their experience of vicissitude was similar. The genius of the author of Atala was pervasive, and is still influential and endeared; while the writings of Volney are comparatively neglected. He was born in 1755, and known, in youth, as Constantine Francois Count de Chasseboeuf—a name he not unwisely discarded when seeking the honors of authorship. After his early education was completed, he converted his little patrimony into money, and travelled through Egypt and Syria, lived for months in the Maronite convent on Mount Lebanon, to acquire the Oriental languages, studied Arabic with the Druses, and sojourned in an Arab tent. Not the least remarkable fact of his three years of Eastern life, was that the sum of a thousand dollars defrayed the entire expense thereof—a result he attributes to his simple habits and hardihood, and his facile self-adaptation to the modes of life prevalent among those with whom he became domesticated.

Volney's Travels in the East, based, as they were, on such unusual opportunities for observation, and written *con amore*, as indicative of his opinions not less than his adventures, proved eminently successful, and drew attention to his claims as a scholar and thinker, and indirectly led to his appointment to an official station in Corsica, where he knew Bonaparte. Volney's ambition, however, seems to have originally tended to philosophical eminence rather than political distinction. He was a profound hater of tyranny, and too independent and fastidious, as well as physically sensitive, to engage heartily in the struggles of party: he loved rather to speculate freely, and to wander, observe, theorize, protest, and portray. Having established himself at Auteuil, near Paris, he became intimate with the literary men of the day, embraced the Liberal cause, and, as deputy from Anjou, in 1789, proved an effective speaker. In 1791 he published "Les Ruines; or, Meditations on the Revolutions of Empires"—the work that embodies at once his scepticism, sentiment, historical speculations, and humanitarian ideas; a work whose rhetoric and vaguely sad but eloquent tone won the imaginative as it repelled the religious. It was regarded as among the most dangerous of the many sceptical works of the day. The remarks on sects and religion excited Joseph Priestley to a vigorous protest. Volney declined the proposed controversy; and there is something absurd to the English reader (who, if candid and intelligent, must know that a more honest and humane philosopher than Priestley never lived) in the assertion of the author's biographer, that the malevolence of a rival writer's jealousy, and not a love of truth, led to the original challenge. Volney was a radical, and a victim of the Revolution. He accompanied Pozzo di Borgo to Corsica, and endeavored to establish sugar cultivation there. Failing therein, he returned to Paris, to suffer persecution in the reign of terror; and, on the fall of Robespierre, regained his liberty, after ten months' imprisonment. In 1794 he was appointed professor of history in the Normal School, on the philosophy of which subject he ably lectured; and, in 1795, embarked at Havre, "with that disgust and indifference which the sight and experience of injustice and persecution impart," intending to settle in the United States. He tells us that the prospect that allured him thither was certain facts in regard to that country wherein he considered it surpassed altogether the rest of the civilized world as a home for the man of independent mind, brave individuality, enterprise, and misfortune. These were, first, an immense territory to be peopled; second, the facility of acquiring landed property; and third, personal freedom. Although Volney found these privileges extant and established, neither his antecedents nor his disposition were auspicious to their realization. In his famous Treatise, he had traced the fall of empires, and speculated on the origin of government and laws; the prejudices and errors of mankind he considers the cause of social evil, and advocates a return to normal principles, recognizing, however, no basis of faith as the foundation of social prosperity. Montesquieu and Montaigne, Rousseau and Godwin, have made the essential truths of social reform patent; the question of their practical organization remains an unsolved problem, except, as regards individual fealty. Combe and Spurzheim showed that the violation of the natural laws was the root of human misery. Buckle illustrates the historical influence of superstition upon society; and Emerson throws aphoristic shells at fortified popular errors, or what he considers such, that explode and sparkle, but fail to destroy: all and each of these and other kindred theorists expose evil far better than they propose good; repudiate, but do not create; and this vital defect underlies the philosophy of Volney, which is destitute of the conservate elements of more benign and receptive minds. It eloquently depicts wrong, ingeniously accounts for error, but offers no positive conviction or practical ameliorations whereon the social edifice can firmly rise in new and more grand proportions.* His Utopian anticipations of a political millennium in America were disappointed; and per-

---

* "The conclusion to which Volney makes his interlocutor come, is, that nothing can be true, nothing can be a ground of peace and union which is not visible to the senses. Truth is in conformity with sensations. The book is interesting as a work of art; but its analysis of Christianity is so shocking that its absurdity alone prevents its becoming dangerous."—*Critical History of Free Thought*, by A. S. FARRAR, M. A.

sonal resentment, imprudence, and egotism aggravated this result. His visit was abruptly closed; and the record thereof became, for these reasons, incomplete, and warped by prejudice, yet not without special merit, and a peculiar interest and value.

Volney's difficulties as an emigrant were complicated by political excitement incident to the troubles in France, the arrogant encroachments of Genet, and the partisan strife thus engendered. In the words of his biographer, "the epidemic animosity against the French breaking out, compelled him to withdraw"—a course rendered more imperative, according to the same authority, "by the attacks of a person who was then all powerful." He was charged with being a secret agent of his Government, conspiring to deliver Louisiana to the Directory; and we are gravely told that "the world would be astonished at the animosity of John Adams," who, Volney declares, "had no motive but the rancor of an author, on account of my opinion of his book on the Constitution of the United States." In these statements, those cognizant of the attempted interference of foreigners, sustained by party zeal, and the just indignation and firm conduct of Washington, at that memorable crisis, can easily understand why Volney found it expedient to relinquish his purpose to settle in America. On returning to France, he was a senator during the consulship of Napoleon; and, in 1814, a member of the Chamber of Peers. He died in Paris in 1820. The following year his works were collected and published in eight handsome volumes. "I am of opinion," he writes, "that Travels belong to history, and not to romance. I have, therefore, not described countries as more beautiful than they appeared to me; I have not represented their inhabitants more virtuous nor more wicked than I have found them."

Volney made the reflections, historic and speculative, induced by the contemplations of "solitary ruins, holy sepulchres, and silent walls," the nucleus and inspiration for the utterance of his theories of life and man. He apostrophizes them as witnesses of the past, and evokes phantoms of buried empires to attest the causes of their decline, and the means and method of human regeneration. There is a novelty in this manner of treating great questions; and this, combined with rhetorical language, a philosophical tone, and no inconsiderable knowledge, explains the interest his work excited. Stripped of glowing epithets and conventional terms, there is, however, little originality in his deductions, and much sophistry in his reasonings. Like Rousseau, he reverts to the primitive wants and rights of humanity; like Godwin, he advocates a return to the normal principles of political justice as the only legitimate basis of social organization; and, like the enthusiasts of the first French Revolution, he claims liberty and equality for man as the only true conditions of progress; while he ascribes to ignorance and cupidity the evils of his lot and the fall of nations. In common, however, with so many speculative reformers of that and subsequent periods, his practical suggestions are altogether disproportioned to his eloquent protest; and his estimate of Christianity fails to recognize its inherent authority as verified by the highest and most pure moral intuitions, and confirmed by the absolute evidence manifest in the character, influence, and truths made patent and pervasive by its Founder. As a traveller, Volney wrote with remarkable intelligence; as a student of history, his expositions were often comprehensive and original; as a moralist, he grasped the *rationale* of natural laws and duties; and as a linguist, his attainments were remarkable. There is more pique than candor in his reply to Priestley's letter controverting his atheistical views. His labors as professor in the Normal School of Paris, as administrator in Corsica, as a political representative, and an economical writer, indicate rare assiduity, insight, and progressive zeal. His biographer claims that from his "earliest youth he devoted himself to the search after truth;" extols "the accuracy of his views and the justness of his observations"—his moral courage, and the originality of his system "of applying to the study of the idioms of Asia a part of the grammatical notions we possess concerning the languages of Europe "—and of his doctrine " that a state is so much the more powerful as it includes a greater number of proprietors—that is, a greater division of property." Erudite, austere, a lover of freedom, and a seeker for truth, whatever might be the speculative tendencies of Volney, his information and his philosophic aspirations won him friends and honor at home and abroad; but his sceptical generalizations repel as much as his adventurous individuality attracts. His visit to this country is thus alluded to by his biographer: " Disgusted with the scenes he had witnessed in his native land, he felt that passion revive within him, which, in his youth, had led him to visit Africa and Asia. Then, in the prime of life, he joyfully bade adieu to a land where peace and plenty reigned, to travel among barbarians; now, in mature years, but dismayed at the spectacle of injustice and persecutions, it was with diffidence, as we learn from himself, that he went to implore from a free people an asylum for a sincere friend of that liberty that had been so profaned."

Although imbittered by personal difficulties and acrimonious controversy, the sojourn of Volney in the United States was not given to superficial observation, but to scientific inquiry. In this respect, his example was worthy of a philosopher; and it is a characteristic evidence of his assiduity, that he improved his acquaintance with the famous Miami chief, Little Turtle, when the latter visited Philadelphia, in 1797, on treaty business, to make a vocabulary of the language of that aboriginal tribe.

His work[*] on this country, published in England with additions, is less rhetorical, on account of the subjects discussed, than his other writings; singularly devoid of personal anecdote, and, but for the description of Niagara Falls, and the bite of a rattlesnake, comparatively unpicturesque

[*] Volney's (C. F.) " View of the Climate and Soil of the United States, &c., and Vocabulary of the Miami Language," 8vo, maps and plates, London, 1804.

and unadventurous as a narrative. It anticipates somewhat the later labors of *savans* and economists, and sets forth with acumen many of the physical features, resources, and characteristics of the country. It possesses an extrinsic interest quite unique, from the antecedents and literary reputation of the author; and it is in the latter character that he is remembered, as identified with the progress of infidelity—but original, philosophic, and liberal. Catharine of Russia recognized his merit; Holbach introduced him to Franklin; and he solaced his wounded pride, after leaving this country, by reverting to the consideration manifested for him by Washington. He is the first foreign writer of eminence who made the climate of North America a subject of study and scientific report; and his views and facts have been and are still often referred to as authoritative, notwithstanding their limited application. His description of the action and influence of winds is highly picturesque, and his observations on rain and electricity noteworthy.

When Volney, in his preface, advises Frenchmen not to emigrate to America, because the laws, language, and manners are uncongenial, though better adapted to the English, Scotch, and Dutch, he adds: "I say with regret, my experience did not lead me to find *ces dispositions fraternelles* I had looked for." The political exigencies at the time of his visit, and personal disappointment, evidently warped the philosopher's candid judgment; and he confesses feeling obliged thereby to give scientific rather than social commentaries on America. His analysis and description of the soil and climate are brief. He begins with the geographical situation, discusses the marine, sandy, calcareous, granite, mountain, and other regions, the Atlantic coast, and the Mississipi basin. Subsequent geological researches, the progress of meteorological and ethnological science since his day, combine to render Volney's *tableaux* more curious than satisfactory or complete. He has specific remarks on New Hampshire, based on a then current history of that State by Samuel Williams, many facts and speculations in regard to the aborigines, and interesting notes respecting the French colonists.

Volney's visit was long remembered by our older citizens. A Knickerbocker reminiscent, in describing the local associations of " Richmond Hill," in the city of New York—a domain now marked by the junction of Varick and Vandam streets—speaks of the Lispenard meadows once flanking the spot, and of the adjacent forest trees, where the echo of the sportsman's gun often resounded; and, in allusion to the mansion itself, notes the curious fact that the first opera house was built upon its site; that the elder Adams resided there when Congress met in New York; and that the dwelling became the home of the notorious Aaron Burr, among whose guests he mentions Volney, " whose portly form gave outward tokens of his tremendous vitality, while the Syrian traveller descanted on theogony, the races of the red men, and Niagara." *

We have a curious glimpse of Volney during his tour in this country, from another venerable reminiscent: " Some thirty or more years ago, at the close of a summer's day, a stranger entered Warrentown. He was alone and on foot, and his appearance was anything but prepossessing; his garments coarse and dust-covered, like an individual in the humbler walks. From a cane resting across his shoulder was suspended a handkerchief containing his clothing. Stopping in front of Turner's tavern, he took from his hat a paper, and handed it to a gentleman standing on the steps. It read as follows: 'The celebrated historian and naturalist, Volney, needs no recommendation from G. Washington.'"

It is said that the idea of his celebrated work on the Ruins of Empires was first suggested in the cabinet of Franklin. Herein he elaborately proclaims and precisely defines the law of decay as the condition of humanity in her most magnificent social development; and states, with the eloquence of scientific logic, the right, necessity, and duty of

---

* " Old New York," by Dr. Francis.

toleration—then a doctrine but casually recognized as a philosophical necessity. It was objected to this work, in addition to its sceptical generalization, that, in describing sects, he misrepresented their creed and practice. A merit, however, claimed for Volney, and with reason, is his freedom from egotism when writing as a philosopher. There is a remarkable absence of personal anecdote and adventures both in his work on the East and his American travels. One of his biographers claims that the topographical descriptions in the latter are written in a masterly style, and that his remarks on the course and currents of the winds denote original insight and observation. The same writer, however, states that his character, which was naturally serious, became morose as he advanced in life.

It was his original purpose to treat of America as a political essayist and social philosopher. He intended to trace "the stock, the history, language, laws, and customs; to expose the error of the romantic colonists, who gave the name of a virgin people to their descendants—a combination of the inhabitants of old Europe—Dutch, Germans, Spaniards, and English from three kingdoms; to indicate the differences of opinions and of interests which divide the New England and Southern country—the region of the Atlantic and that of the Mississippi; to define republicanism and federalism," &c. A profound admirer of the liberty of the press and of opinion, he would have explained the antagonism between the followers of Adams and of Jefferson. In a word, the scope of his work, as at first projected, resembled that so ably achieved by his more consistent and judicious countryman, De Tocqueville. Instead of this, Volney wrote in a scientific vein. He treats of the winds, temperature, qualities of soil, local diseases; and writes as a naturalist and physiologist, instead of making the great theme subservient to his political theories. There is much condensed knowledge and remarkable scientific description; interesting accounts of Florida, the French colony on the Scioto, and others in Canada, with curious remarks on the aborigines. The style and thought as well as scope of the work, although thus partial in its design, are superior to most of those which preceded it.

Another Frenchman, who enjoyed considerable literary renown in his day, was instrumental, though not in the character of a traveller, in making America and her political claims known in Europe. Born at St. Geniez, Guienne, in 1711, and dying at Paris in 1796, the life of the Abbé Raynal includes a period fraught with extreme vicissitudes of government and religion, whereof he largely partook in opinion and fortune. Bred a Jesuit, he went to Paris, and, from some elocutionary defects, failed as a preacher at St. Sulpice, became intimate with Voltaire, Diderot, and D'Alembert, and abandoned theology for philosophy. Familiar with the writings of Bayle, Montaigne, and Rousseau, he became an ardent liberal and active *litterateur*; first compiling memoirs of Ninon de L'Enclos, then writing " L'Histoire du Stathoudérat"—a branch of the noble theme since so memorably unfolded by our countryman Motley; the "Histoire du Parlement d'Angleterre;" articles in the "Cyclopædia;" literary anecdotes, &c. But the work which for a time gave him most celebrity, was written in conjunction with Diderot— " Histoire philosophique et politique des Etablissements et du commerce des Européens dans les Indes." The first edition appeared in 1770. In the second, ten years after, his direct attacks upon the existing government and religion caused the work to be prohibited, and its author condemned to imprisonment; which latter penalty he escaped by flight. In 1781 appeared his " Tableau et Revolutions des Colonies Anglaises dans l'Amérique Septentrionale,"* whose many errors of fact were indicated in a pamphlet by Tom Paine. Elected a deputy, his renunciation of some of his obnoxious opinions failed to conciliate his adversaries; and, despoiled by the Revolution, he died in poverty, at the age of eighty-four. Incorrect and desultory as are the Abbé Raynal's writings,

* " The Abbé Raynal on the Revolution in America," 12mo., Dublin, 1781.

and neglected as they now are, his advocacy of the American cause, and description of the country, drawn apparently from inadequate yet sometimes authentic sources, on account of a certain philosophical tone and agreeability of style, were for some years read and admired. As we recur to them in the ninth volume of the latest edition of his chief work, wherein they are now included, we obtain a vivid idea of the kind of research and rhetoric then in vogue, and can imagine how to foreign minds must then have appeared the problem of our nascent civilization.

The Abbé's biographer claims that he was personally very agreeable, and possessed of a fine figure; that the vivacious discussions and literary fellowship of the Paris *salons* enlivened and enlarged the acquisitions of this *eleve* of the cloister who "succeeded in the world," and, though he did not understand the science of politics, and often contradicted himself, was, notwithstanding, an ardent and capable defender of human rights, and a true lover of his race. It is a curious fact, that he was a warm admirer and eloquent eulogist of Sterne's fair friend, Eliza Draper; and a more interesting one, that he was among the very earliest to protest against the cruelties then practised against the negro race. He draws a parallel, at the close of his history, between the actual results of European conquests in America, and their imagined benefits. The new empire multiplied metals, and made a grand movement in the world; but, says the Abbé, "le mouvement ne'st pas le bonheur," and the Western empire "donné naissance au plus infame, au plus atroce de tous les commerces, celui des esclaves." Chiefly occupied with the West India Islands, what is said of North America is discursive. He describes the process of civilization in brief; the Puritan, Dutch, and Catholic leaders; Penn, and Lord Baltimore; the settlement of Georgia and Carolina; the trees, grain, birds, tobacco, and other indigenous products; notes the imported domestic animals, and the exported wood and metals; discusses the probable success of silk and vine culture in the southern and middle regions, and gives statistics of the population, and partial accounts of the laws, currency, municipal and colonial systems, &c., of the several States; and then, in outline, describes the Revolution. A love of freedom, and a speculative hardihood and interest in human progress and prosperity, imbue his narratives and reasonings, though the former are often incorrect, and the latter inadequate.

According to the habit of French authors of those days, the Abbé occasionally turns from disquisition to oratory; and it is amusing to read here and now the oracular counsel he gave our fathers: addressing the "peuples de l'Amérique Septentrionale," in 1781: "Craignez," he says, "l'affluence de l'or qui apporte avec le luxe la corruption des mœurs, le mepris des lois; craignez une trop inégale repartition des richesses; garantissez-vous de l'esprit de conquête; cherchez l'aisance et la santé dans le travail, la prosperité dans la culture des terres et les ateliers de l'industrie, la force dans les bonnes mœurs et dans la vertu; faites prosperer les sciences et les artes; veillez à l'education de vos enfans; n'établissez aucune preference légale entre les cultes. Après avoir vu dans le début de cet ouvrage, en quel état de misère et de tenèbres était l'Europe à la naissance de l'Amérique, voyons en quel état le conquête d'un monde a conduit et poussé le monde conquerante." He laments the fanaticism of Massachusetts; tells the story of Salem witchcraft, and the perpetuation in the New of the cruel laws of the Old World; says epidemics like the small pox acquire new virulence in America; praises the Long Wharf of Boston, and compares the dwellings and furniture of that city to those of London.

CHAPTER IV.

FRENCH TRAVELLERS AND WRITERS CONTINUED.

ROCHAMBEAU ; TALLEYRAND ; SÉGUR; CHATEAUBRIAND ; MICHAUX ; MURAT; BRILLAT-SAVARIN ; DE TOCQUEVILLE ; DE BEAUMONT; AMPÈRE, AND OTHERS ; LAFAYETTE ; FISCH ; DE GASPARIN ; OFFICERS ; LABOULAYE, ETC.

SOME of the most pleasing and piquant descriptions of America, and life there, at the period of and subsequent to the Revolutionary War, are to be found in the memoirs and correspondence of French allies and *emigrés*. In some instances, as we have seen in the case of Chastellux, Brissot, the Abbé Robin, and others, instead of an episode, our Gallic visitors have expanded their observations into separate volumes; but even the casual mention of places and persons, character and customs that are interwoven in the biography and journals of some of the French officers, are noteworthy as illustrations of the times, especially in a social point of view. We find them in the memoirs of De Lauzun, De Segur, De Broglie, and other of the gallant beaux who made themselves so agreeable to the pretty Quakers at Newport, where they were so long quartered ; and left, as in the case of Vosmencul, traditions of wit, love, and dancing—the evanescent record whereof still survives in the initials cut on the little window panes of the gable-roofed houses with their diamond rings, and were long rehearsed by venerable ladies of Philadelphia and Boston. Among these incidental glimpses of America as her scenes and people impressed a noble *militaire*, are many passages in the Memoirs of Count Rochambeau, who is so prominently represented beside Washington in the picture of the surrender of Yorktown, at Versailles. Born in 1725, and soon distinguished as a soldier, in 1780 he was sent as the commander-general of six thousand troops, to assist our Revolutionary struggle. He landed at Newport, R. I., and acted in concert with Washington against Clinton in New York, and against Cornwallis at Yorktown. On his return to France, he was made marshal, and commander of the Army of the North, by Louis XVI. He was gradually superseded by more energetic officers, became the object of calumny to the journalists, and vindicated himself in a speech before the Assembly, who passed a decree approving his conduct. He retired to his estate at Vendome, resolved to abandon public affairs. He was arrested, and narrowly escaped death under Robespierre—like so many of his eminent countrymen who had become well known on this side of the ocean. In 1803 he was presented to Bonaparte, who conferred on him the cross of the Legion of Honor. He died in 1807, and, two years after, his " Mémoires " were published.

Count Rochambeau describes at length the military operations of which he was a witness in America, and looks at the country, for the most part, with the eyes of a soldier. He repudiates all idea of writing in the character of a professed author, and both the style and substance of his autobiography are those of a military memoir. Still he records many significant facts, geographical and economical. He notes the agricultural resources of those parts of the country he visited, describes the houses, ports, and climate, and gives an interesting account of Arnold's treason—first revealed to Washington in connection with a journey undertaken by the latter to meet him; and of many of the subsequents events connected therewith he was a witness. But the most attractive feature of Rochambeau's American reminiscences is his cordial recognition of the popular mind and heart. He appreciated, better than many more superficial observers, the domestic discipline, the religious toleration, and the genuine independence of character which then formed our noble distinction in the view of liberal Europeans. He remarks the unequal interest in the war in different localities: "En distinguant d'abord les commerçans des agricoles, les habitudes des grandes villes maritimes de ceux des petites villes ou des habitans de l'intérieur, ou ne doit pas être étonné que les commerçans et ceux qui, dans ces ports, avaient une relation ou des intérêts directs avec le gouvernement Anglais, aient témoigné moins de zéle pour la révolution que les agricoles." Boston was an exception; and the Northern States seconded the Revolution which the violence of the British and Hessians precipitated. The equal fortunes of the North favored democracy, while the large proprietors of the South formed an aristocracy. He says of American women: "Les filles y sont libres jusqu'à leur mariage. Leur première question est de savoir si vous êtes marié; et, si vous l'êtes, leur conversation tombe tout à plat." Sometimes in youth, though going to church with parents, "elles n'aient pas encore fait choix d'une religion; elles disent qu'elles seront de la religion de leur maris." They observe, he says, "une grande propriété." He describes a settlement "par mettre le feu à la foret (to clear). Il seme en suite, entre les souches, toutes sortes de grains, qui croissant avec la plus grande abondance, sous une couche de feuilles, pourries et réduites en terreau vegetal formé pendant un très-grand nombre d'années. Il batit son habitation avec les rameaux de ces arbres placés l'un sur l'autre, soutenus par des piquets. Au bout de vingt ou trente ans, lorsqu'il est parvenu à desancher et à rendre la terre ameublie, il songe à construire une maison plus propre"—and later one of brick; "on y fait au moins quatre repas, interrompu par un travail modéré, et le petit négre est continuellement occupé à défaire et à remettre le couvert."

"Dans les grands villes," he adds, "le luxe a fait plus de progrès. Le pays circonscrit sous le nom des États Unis, avec les arrondissemens qu'ont cédés les Anglais, par la paix de 1783, pourra comporter un jour plus de trente millions d'habitans sans à gener."

He recognizes the complete division of church and state in our democratic system: " Par ces precautions, la religion n'entra pour rien dans les délibérations politiques; chacun professa son culte avec exactitude; la sanctification du dimanche s'y observoit avec exactitude;" and, like so many other sojourners of that period, he attests that "l'hospitalité est la vertu la plus généralement observée."

An incident related by his companion, illustrates the popular respect for law: " At the moment of our quitting the camp," writes Count Ségur, " as M. de Rochambeau was proceeding at the head of his columns, and surrounded by his brilliant staff, an American approached him, tapped him slightly on the shoulder, and, showing him a paper he held in his hand, said: ' In the name of the law I arrest you.' Several young officers were indignant at this insult offered to their general; but he restrained their impatience by a sign, smiled, and said to the American, ' Take me away with you, if you can.' ' No,' replied he; ' I have done my duty, and your excellency may proceed on your march, if you wish to put justice at defiance. Some soldiers of the division of Soissonnais have cut down several trees, and burnt them to light their fires. The owner of them claims an indemnity, and has obtained a warrant against you, which I have come to execute.' "

Rochambeau was much impressed with the state of religion in America, and especially the voluntary deference to the clergy, coexistent with self-respect and self-reliance in matters of faith, so manifest at the era of the Revolution. " They reserve," he writes, " for the minister the first place at public banquets; he invokes a blessing thereon; but his prerogatives, as far as society is concerned, extend no farther; and this position," he adds, obviously in view of clerical corruption in Europe, " should lead naturally to simple and pure manners."

Another anecdote, illustrative of the times and people, is

related with much zest: "Je hasarde," he says, "d'interrompre ici l'attention du lecteur, par le recit d'une historiette qui ni laisse pas de caracteriser parfaitement les mœurs des bons republicans du Connecticut." He then states that, being on his way to Hartford, to confer with Washington, and accompanied by the Count de Ternay, who was an invalid, the carriage broke down, and his aide was sent to find a blacksmith to repair it. The only one in the vicinity, being ill with fever and ague, refused, and declared a hat full of guineas would not induce him to undertake the job; but when the Count explained to the resolute Vulcan, that if his vehicle was not repaired, he could not keep his appointment with Washington, "I am at the public service. You shall have your carriage at six to-morrow morning," said the blacksmith, "for you are good people." Such instances of disinterested patriotism, and superiority to the blandishments of rank and money, among the mechanics and farmers, struck Rochambeau and his companions as memorable evidences of the effect of free institutions and popular education upon national character.

Another famous Frenchman, at a later period, received quite a different impression—finding in the isolated materialism of American border life a hopeless dearth of sentiment and civilized enjoyment, which, in his view, though habituated to the sight of starving millions and effeminate courtiers, more than counterbalanced the independence and prospective comfort of the masses thus bravely secured. When Talleyrand was a temporary exile in the United States, he visited a colony of his countrymen, and wrote thus of the American backwoodsman: "He is interested in nothing. Every sentimental idea is banished from him. Those branches so elegantly thrown by nature—a fine foliage, a brilliant hue which marks one part of the forest, a deeper green which darkens another—all these are nothing in his eye. He has no recollections associated with anything around him. His only thought is the number of strokes which are necessary to level this or that tree. He has never planted;

he is a stranger to the pleasure of that process. Were he to plant a tree, it never could become an object of gratification to him, because he could not live to cut it down. He lives only to destroy. He is surrounded by destruction. He does not watch the destiny of what he produces. He does not love the field where he has expended his labor, because his labor is merely fatigue, and has no pleasurable sentiment attached to it."

Few men born in the Eastern States, especially if they have visited Europe, can fail to realize a certain forlorn remoteness in the sensation experienced, when surrounded by the sparsely inhabited woods and prairies, akin to what Talleyrand describes. The back country of the Upper Mississippi seems more oppressively lonely to such a traveller than the interior of Sicily. The want of that vital and vivid connection between the past and present; the painful sense of newness; the savage triumph, as it were, of nature, however beautiful, over humanity, whose eager steps have only invaded, not ameliorated her domain—seem, for the moment, to leave us in desolate individuality and barren self-dependence. But the experience Talleyrand compassionated was and is but a transition state—a brief overture to a future social prosperity, where sentiment as well as enterprise has ample verge.

Count Ségur, the French ambassador to Russia and Prussia, was born in 1753, and his first youth was educated under that *chevalresque* social luxury that marked the reign of Louis XV. Of noble birth, and commencing life as a courtier, he experienced to an unusual extent, the vicissitudes, the discipline, and the distinction incident to his age and country. He was an accomplished military officer and diplomatist, an author, a politician, a *voyageur*, and a peer; and, withal, seems to have been an amiable, liberal, and brave gentleman. He came to America in 1783, with despatches to Rochambeau, to whom he was appointed aide, with the rank of colonel; and, after various and provoking delays and privations, joined the French camp and his own regiment on the Hudson River.

The circumstances of his landing were such as to predispose a less heroic and gracious nature to take an unfavorable view of the New World; for battle, shipwreck, the loss of his effects, great discomfort, and a series of annoyances and mishaps attended him from the moment his battered ship ran aground in the Delaware, within sight of the enemy's fleet, until he reached his commander's quarters, after a wearisome and exposed journey. Yet few of his gallant countrymen looked upon the novelties of life, manners, and scenery around him with such partial and sympathetic eyes. Perhaps it was by virtue of contrast that the young courtier of Louis conceived a strong attachment for the Quakers of Philadelphia; and this feeling received a fresh and fond impulse from the charms of the beautiful Polly Lawton, of Newport.

The sight of the American forests inspired him; and the independent character, probity, and frugal contentment of the people was the constant theme of his admiration. "I experienced," he writes, "two opposite impressions—one produced by the spectacle of the beauties of a wild and savage nature, and the other by the fertility and variety of industrious cultivation of a civilized world. Indigence and brutality were nowhere to be seen; fertility, comfort, and kindness were everywhere to be found; and every individual displayed the modest and tranquil pride of an independent man, who feels that he has nothing above him but the laws, and who is a stranger alike to the vanity, to the prejudices, and to the servility of European society. No useful profession is ever ridiculed or despised. Indolence alone would be a subject of reproach."

He was, at first, astonished to find men of all vocations with military titles. The "wild and savage" prospect around West Point delighted him. He dined with Washington, and describes the toasts and the company with much zest. He enjoyed a week's furlough at Newport, and, with his brother officers, gave a ball there. Quartered with a family at Providence, he learned to love the simplicity of domestic life in America. One of his general observations on the country has now a prophetic significance :

"The only dangers which can menace, in the future, this happy republic, consisting in 1780 of three millions, and now (1825) numbering more than ten millions of citizens, is the excessive wealth which is promised by its commerce, and the corrupting luxury which may follow it. Its Southern provinces should foresee and avoid another peril. In the South are to be found a very large class of poor whites, and another of enormously wealthy proprietors; the fortunes of this latter class are created and sustained by the labor of a population of blacks, slaves, which increases largely every year, and who may and must be frequently driven to despair and revolt by the contrast of their servitude with the entire liberty enjoyed by men of the same color in other States of the Union. In a word, this difference of manners and situation between the North and South; does it not lead us to apprehend in times to come a separation which would enfeeble and perhaps break this happy confederation, which can preserve its power only in being firmly locked and united together? Such was the sad thought which ended my last conversation with the Chevalier de Chastellux, on the eve of his departure from the army." *

Like so many other visitors, he was struck with the resemblance of Boston to an English town, with the beauty of its women, and with the preaching of Dr. Cooper. In a letter written on embarking for the West Indies, he expresses keen regret at leaving America, dwells with much feeling upon the kindness he had received and the opportunities he had enjoyed there, and descants upon the purity of manners, equality of condition, and manly self-reliance which, combined with the natural advantages of the country and the freedom of its institutions, made America to him a subject of the most interesting speculation and affectionate interest.

Another Frenchman, whose name and fame are far more illustriously identified with the political vicissitudes and influential literature of his times, saw somewhat of America, and

* "Mémoires," &c., par M. le Comte de Ségur, tom. i, pp. 412, 413, Paris, 1825.

reported his impressions with characteristic latitude and sentiment. The scene of his best romance is laid in one of the Southern States; but the description of nature and perception of Indian character are far removed from scientific precision. Yet over all that Chateaubriand wrote, however warped by egotism or rendered melodramatic by exaggeration, there breathes an atmosphere of sentiment, whereby a certain humanity and eloquence make significant what would otherwise often seem unreal and meretricious. He loved nature, and, by virtue of a vivid imagination and intense consciousness, connected all he saw with his own life and thought. His visit to our shores forms an interesting episode in his "Mémoires d'outre Tombe." After crossing the Atlantic, he was becalmed off the shores of Maryland and Virginia, and had leisure to appreciate the beautiful skies; imprudently bathed in waters infested with sharks; traversed woods of balsam trees and cedars, where he observed with infinite pleasure the cardinal and mocking birds, the gray squirrels, and a "negro girl of extraordinary beauty." The contrast between these wild charms and the cities was most uncongenial to the poetical *emigré*. He "felt the architectural deformity" of the latter, and declares, sadly, that "nothing is old in America excepting the woods." But his chief disappointment consisted in the discovery that the modes of life and tone of manners were so far removed from what he had fondly imagined of the ideal republic. "A man," he writes in 1791, "landing, like myself, in the United States, full of enthusiasm for the ancients—a Cato, seeking, wherever he goes, the austerity of the primitive manners of Rome—must be exceedingly scandalized to find everywhere elegance in dress, luxury in equipages, frivolity in conversation, inequality of fortunes, the immorality of gaming houses, and the noise of balls and theatres. In Philadelphia I could have fancied myself in an English town. There was nothing to indicate that I had passed from a monarchy to a republic." Reasoning from historical facts and analogy, one would imagine that a foreign visitor could only expect to find Anglo-Saxon traits, local and social, in those American communities directly founded by English emigrants. Yet Dickens expressed the same disappointment in Boston, at the similarity of the place and people to what was familiar to him at home, that Chateaubriand confesses, half a century previous, in the city of Brotherly Love. The allusion to Roman names and manners, so common with French writers in their political criticisms, would strike us as extremely artificial, were it not that the drama and the academic talk in France, at that time, continually adopted the characters and history of Greece and Rome as the standard and nomenclature of an era in every respect essentially different—a pedantic tendency akin to the Arcadian terms and tastes which so long formalized the degenerate muse in Italy. It is not, indeed, surprising that the republican enthusiasts of the Old World should have been disenchanted in the New, when they found what is called "society" but a tame reflection of that from which they had fled as the result of an effete civilization. But the complaint was as unreasonable as unjust; for, in all large and prosperous communities, an identical social, conventional system prevails. In America, however, this sphere was very limited, and, at the dawn of the republic, embraced remarkable exceptions to the usual hollowness and vapid display; while, in the vast domain beyond, the rights, the abilities, and the self-respect of human beings found an expression and a scope which, however different from Roman development, and however unsatisfactory to a modern Cato, offered a most refreshing contrast to and auspicious innovation upon the crushing, hopeless routine of European feudalism. The political disappointment of the author of Atala induced him to write against the Quakers. He found Washington was "not Cincinnatus, for he passed in a coach and four;" but when he called on the President with a letter of introduction, he recognized in his surroundings "the simplicity of an old Roman—no guards, not even a footman." Chateaubriand's object was to promote an expedition, set on foot in his own country, for the discovery of the long-sought and much-desired "Northwest Passage." It appears that Washington rather discouraged the enterprise; upon which the complimentary instinct was aroused in his guest, who, with the usual misapprehension of foreigners as to the character of our Revolution, and of our matchless chief's relation thereto, replied, "It is less difficult to discover the Northwest Passage than to create a nation, as you have done." And we can easily imagine the amused and urbane "Well, well, young man," with which Washington dismissed the subject. He showed Chateaubriand the key of the Bastile. In describing their interview, the French author compares him with Bonaparte; and, in allusion to his own feelings on the memorable occasion, significantly declares, "I was not agitated." A startling experience in his subsequent journey, was encountering, in the wilderness of New York State, a dancing master of his country teaching the Iroquois to caper scientifically. Indeed, the great pleasure derived from his visit was that afforded by the salient contrast of a nascent civilization with the wild beauty of nature. He was awestruck when, in the heart of the lonely woods, the distant roar of Niagara struck his ear; and few have approached that shrine of wonder and grace with more reverence and delight. The great lakes of the interior, the coast fisheries, the isolated sugar camp in the maple groves, and the aspect, rites, and traits of the aboriginal tribes, excited the earnest curiosity and gratified the adventurous sentiment which afterward found such copious inspiration in a pilgrimage to Jerusalem, a sojourn in Rome, exile in England, and a conservative and pathetic plea for outraged Christianity in his native land. "It is impossible," he writes, "to conceive the feelings and the delight experienced on seeing the spire of a new steeple rising from the bosom of an ancient American forest."

The transition from the political essayist to the natural historian is refreshing. The zest with which Michaux describes some of the arborescent wonders of the West is as pleasant as his intelligent discussion of economical facts and

Puritan domesticity in the East. Dr. Michaux, in the year 1802, visited the country westward of the Alleghanies and the Carolinas, under the auspices of the Minister of the Interior. He found delightful companions in the trees, and charming hospitality among the flowers; and, contrasting the vegetation of the Southern with that of the Western States, gave to his countrymen a correct and impressive idea of the products and promise of the New World, as an arena for botanical investigation, and a home for the enterprising and unfortunate.* He describes new species of rhododendron and azalea; expatiates on the varieties of oak and walnut; gives statistics of size, grouping, and diversities in the native forests; points out indigenous medicinal and floral products, and discourses genially of the cones of the magnolia, the fish and shells of the Ohio, the salt licks of Kentucky, and bear hunting in the Alleghanies. In a word, his brief and discursive journal illustrates that delightful series of Travels, whose inspiration is the love of nature, and whose object is the exposition of her laws and productions, with which Nuttall, Wilson, Audubon, Lyell, and Agassiz have so enriched scientific literature on this continent. And while it is interesting to compare the more copious and special narratives of these endeared writers with that of Michaux, and realize the advancement of knowledge and scientific zeal since he wrote, it is no less cheering to witness the social progress of the West—especially the effects of the temperance reform and the success of the grape culture—and revert therefrom to the earnest protest of this amiable writer, who, as a Frenchman and a naturalist, was revolted at the perversion of nature's best gifts which the current habits of the population evinced. "The taverns, and especially that in which we lodged," writes Michaux of the valley of the Ohio, fifty years ago, "were filled with drunkards, who made a frightful uproar, and yielded to excesses so horrible as to be

---

* "Travels to the Westward of the Alleghany Mountains in Ohio, Kentucky and Tennessee," &c., by Dr. F. A. Michaux, translated by Lambert, 8vo., 1805.

scarcely conceived. The rooms, the stairs, the yard were covered with men dead drunk; and those who were still able to get their teeth separated, uttered only the accents of fury and rage. An inordinate desire for spirituous liquors is one of the characteristics of the country in the interior of the United States. This passion is so powerful, that they quit their habitations, from time to time, to go and get drunk at the taverns. They do not relish cider, which they think too mild. Their distaste for this salutary and agreeable beverage is the more extraordinary, since they might easily procure it at little expense, for apple trees of every kind succeed wonderfully in this country." It has been charged against Michaux, that he accepted a commission from Genet to raise troops in Kentucky and Louisiana.

Among the political refugees who found safety and comfort in the United States after the fall of Napoleon, were two sons of the dashing and brave but superficial and unfortunate Murat. One dwelt many years in New Jersey, where Joseph Bonaparte, with benign philosophy, enjoyed the elegant seclusion of a private gentleman so much more than he had the cares and honors of royalty; and, among the extraordinary vicissitudes that mark the history of individuals associated with European politics in our day, the marvellous restoration of Murat to fortune in France, under the imperial success of Louis Napoleon, is to the people of that little town in New Jersey "stranger than fiction;" for the refugee was a boon companion and needy adventurer among them; for years supported by his accomplished wife and daughter, who kept a most creditable school, and maintained their self-respect with dignity and tact. The other brother, Achille, found a home and a wife, with slaves and a plantation, near Tallahassee, Fla., and seems to have enjoyed his adopted country with the zest of a sportsman and the adventurous spirit of his race, and easily to have reconciled himself to the incongruities of such a lot. Nine years of residence made him familiar with the country; and, when an honorary colonel in the Belgian army, he presented to a comrade the manuscript wherein, to inform a friend in Europe, he had written at length his impressions and convictions in regard to the United States. After his death, it was translated and published in this country.* The distinction of the work is, that it is written by a foreigner whose experience of the country and whose sympathies are almost as exclusively Southern, as if he was a bigoted native instead of a stranger in the land. He considers agriculture the primal and pervasive interest; he advocates slavery both on practical and metaphysical grounds; he considers Charleston, S. C., the centre of all that is polished and superior in American society; he shares and repeats the obsolete prejudices about "Yankees," founded upon the days of blue laws and peddling; he prophesies the political ascendency of the Southern States, and deems the "spirit of calculation" elsewhere "marvellously connected with the observance of the Sabbath." Yet he is enthusiastic in his admiration of and firm in his trust in the "principles of liberty" and the system of government. He is proud and happy in his American citizenship, grateful for the prosperous home and independent life here enjoyed, and throughout his observations there is a singular combination of the political enthusiast and the man of the world, the *militaire* and the advocate, the lover of pleasure and the devotee of freedom. There is little said about the beauties of nature, few criticisms on manners; but the processes whereby the Indians are dispossessed, the forest occupied, the hunter superseded by the squatter, the latter by the settler, and the Territory made a State, are given with the details only obtainable through long personal observation. One chapter is devoted to the history of parties; another to the administration of justice; one to religion, and one to finance. Our national means of defence, the Indians, and the new settlements are described and discussed; and thus a large amount

* Murat's (Achille) "Moral and Political Sketch of the United States of America," 8vo., London, 1833.
"America and the Americans," by the late Achille Murat, New York, 1849.

of correct and valuable information is given. But it is evident the writer is acquainted intimately with only one section of the country; that the new, and not the old communities, have been the chief scene of his observation; and, while there is much both fair and fresh in his comments, they refer in no small degree to local and temporary facts. Murat writes, however, with acute and sympathetic intelligence, from a material point of view; and it is interesting to contrast his speculations of thirty-seven years ago with the events of the hour. "The English minister," he writes in 1827, "wishing to stop emigration to the United States, descended so far as to induce mercenary writers to travel, and promulgate, through the press, false statements against our people and Government. In all these works, which had an extensive circulation with John Bull, and thereby influenced his mind, the subject of slavery has been the avowed and principal topic." On which subject he thus argues: "A man meets a lion, and has the indubitable right to appropriate the skin of the animal to his own particular purpose; while, on the other hand, the lion has an equal right to the flesh of the man. The difference is, one defends his skin, the other his flesh; hence it follows that the spontaneous *objection* in each becomes an obstacle to the other, and which either has the right to destroy. By an individual right we are by no means to understand a natural right. A man has undoubtedly no claim to the possession of another man in relation to that man, but possesses this claim in relation to society. If I mistake not, public opinion in the Southern States is, that slavery is *necessary*, but *an evil*. I, however, am far from considering the question in this point of view. On the contrary, I am led to consider it, in certain periods of the history or existence of nations, as a good."

His pro-slavery argument, when at all original, is undisguised sophistry, and compares absurdly with his recognition of the principles of civil liberty and self-government; while no foreigner has more cordially entered into the redeeming spirit of individual self-reliance and a controlling public opinion, as means and methods of social progress and safety. The plan and scope of the work are such as to render it useful and interesting to educated Europeans who contemplate emigration. Its economical details and political philosophy are comparatively unauthoritative now, facilities of travel and more comprehensive and elevated criticism having made the questions and facts clear and familiar. The "America and Americans" of Achille Murat is, therefore, a work more interesting from the circumstances and history of its author, than from its intrinsic novelty or value.

In that ingenious work wherein the *rationale* of luxury is so genially expounded—the "Physiologie du Gout"—there is an episode, wherein the same kindly and cordial estimate of republican manners and economy characteristic of French travellers in America,—is naively apparent. The author, though chiefly known by a work which associates his name with the pleasures of the table, was, in fact, a philosopher whose cast of mind was judicial rather than fanciful; and who, in his most popular book, under the guise of epicurean zest, grapples with and illustrates profound truths. An indefatigable student, a keen sportsman, and a conscientious official, Brillat-Savarin, from the moment his early education was completed, filled important situations, such as deputy, mayor, president of the civil tribunals, and judge of the bureau of cassation, in his native province; with the exception of three years of exile during the Revolution, which he passed in this country, and chiefly in New York, gaining a subsistence by teaching his native language and regulating a theatrical orchestra. He alludes to his sojourn as an era of pleasant experiences. He made numerous friends in America, and attributes this to his facility in adopting the habits and manners of the country, and his knowledge of the language; although his quotations are often amusingly incorrect. A scholar, musician, man of the world, and jurist, his culture and his endowments were such as to make him an appreciative observer of life and institutions here; for he united rare powers of observation and reflection with adequate sensibility to the beautiful and the true. He was so tall, that his brother judges called him the drum major of the court of cassation. He was an *habitué* of Madame Recamier's charming *salon*. Balzac expressed the opinion that no writer, except La Bruyère and La Rochefoucauld, ever gave to French phrases such vigorous relief. Since the death of Brillat-Savarin, science has thrown new light upon many subjects connected with those so agreeably discussed in the "Physiologie du Gout;" still the scope and style of the work give it prominence. The application of science to gastronomy, of taste and wisdom to the art of human nutrition, was thus initiated in a most attractive manner, and the incidental relations of the subject shown to be identical with the best interests of society. The author varies his disquisition by logical, anecdotical, and eloquent alternations. His personal experience is often made to illustrate his speculative opinions. In the chapter devoted to "Coq d'Inde," or "Dindon," after describing the turkey as the most beautiful gift which the New World has made to the Old, treating as paradoxical the tradition that it was known to the ancients, describing its introduction to Europe by the Jesuits, discussing its natural history, its financial importance, and its gastronomic value, he thus describes an *exploit du professeur:*

"During my residence at Hartford, in Connecticut, I had the pleasure of shooting a wild turkey. This exploit deserves to be transmitted to posterity, and I record it with the more complaisance, inasmuch as I was the hero. A venerable American farmer had invited me to sport on his domain; he lived near the least-settled portion of the State; he promised me excellent game, and authorized me to bring a friend. Mr. King, my companion, was a remarkable sportsman; he was passionately fond of the exercise, but, after having killed his bird, he regarded himself as a murderer, and made the victim's fate the subject of moral reflections and interminable elegies. On a beautiful morning in October, 1794, we left Hartford on hired horses, hoping to reach our destination, five mortal leagues distant, before the evening. Although the route was scarcely indicated by travel, we arrived without accident, and were received with that cordial and unpretending hospitality which is expressed in actions rather than words: in short, we were immediately made to feel comfortable and at home—men, horses, and dogs—according to their respective wants and convenience. Two hours were spent in examining the farm and its dependencies; I would describe all this in detail, but I prefer to introduce to the reader the four beautiful daughters of Monsieur Bulow, to whom our visit was an important incident. Their ages ranged from sixteen to twenty; they were radiant with the freshness of health, and they possessed that simplicity, ease, and frankness which the most common actions develop into a thousand charms. Soon after our return from the walk, we were seated at a table abundantly provided;—a superb piece of corned beef, a fine stew, a magnificent leg of mutton, plenty of vegetables, and, at each end of the table, enormous jars of excellent cider, with which I could not be satiated. When we had proved to our host that we were genuine sportsmen, at least in regard to appetite, the conversation turned upon the object of our visit. He pointed out the best places for game, the landmarks whereby we could find our way back, and the farmhouses at which we could procure refreshments. During this discussion the ladies had prepared some excellent tea, of which we drank several cups; after which, ascending to a double-bedded room, we enjoyed the delicious sleep induced by exercise and good cheer. The next morning, after partaking of refreshment ordered to be in readiness by Monsieur Bulow, we started for a day's sport, and I found myself, for the first time, in a virgin forest. I wandered there with delight, observing the effects of time, both productive and destructive; and amused myself by following the different periods in the life of an oak, from the moment it breaks through the mould with two little leaves, until all that remains of it is a long black trace—the dust of its heart. Mr. King reproached me for these abstract musings; and we began the sport in earnest; shooting numerous small but fat and tender partridges: we bagged six or seven gray squirrels, which are much esteemed here; and, at last, my happy star brought us into the midst of a flock of wild turkeys. They followed, at short intervals, one after the other, with rapid, brief flights, and uttering loud cries. Mr. King shot first, and ran on; most of the flock were soon out of range, but the largest bird rose ten paces before me; I fired instantly, and he fell dead. One must be a sportsman to conceive the delight which this beautiful shot occasioned me. I seized the superb fowl, and a quarter of an hour afterward heard Mr. King calling for aid; hastening toward him, I found that the assistance he craved was help in finding a turkey which he pretended to have shot, but which had mysteriously disappeared. I put my dog on the trace; but he only led us among thickets and brambles, which a man could hardly penetrate; it was necessary to abandon the pursuit, which my companion did in a fit of ill humor that lasted all the rest of the day.

The remainder of our sport does not merit description. In returning, we became confused in the woods, and ran no small risk of passing the night there; but the silvery voices of the ladies Bulow and the shouts of their father, who had the kindness to seek us, guided us back. The four sisters were in full dress: fresh robes, new girdles, beautiful bonnets, and bright shoes, proclaimed that they had made a toilette in our honor; and I had, on my side, equal intention to make myself agreeable to these ladies, one of whom accepted my arm with as much candor and propriety as if she had been my wife. On reaching the house we found a supper already served; but, before partaking of it, we seated ourselves an instant near a bright fire, which had been kindled, although the weather did not make it indispensable; we found it, however, most welcome. This custom is, doubtless, adopted from the aborigines, who always have a fire on their hearth; perhaps thence came the tradition of Francis de Sales, who said a fire was desirable twelve months in the year. We ate as if half famished, and finished the evening with an enormous bowl of punch; and a conversation, wherein our host was more free than the previous evening, occupied us far into the night. We talked of the War of Independence, in which Monsieur Bulow had served as a superior officer; of La Fayette, who grows continually in the grateful appreciation of the Americans, and whom they always designate by his title—the Marquis; of agriculture, which then was enriching the United States, and finally of that dear France which I love all the more since I was obliged to quit her shores. To vary the conversation, M. Bulow, from time to time, said to his oldest daughter: 'Maria, give us a song;' and she sang, without being urged, and with an embarrassment that was charming, the national song, the complaint of Queen Mary, and trial of Major André, which are very popular in this country. Maria had taken a few lessons, and, in this isolated region, passed for an adept; but her singing derived all its merit from the quality of her voice, at once sweet, fresh, and emphatic. The next day we left, notwithstanding the most friendly remonstrances; for I had indispensable duties to fulfil. While the horses were preparing, Monsieur Bulow took me aside and said, 'You see in me, my dear sir, a happy man, if there is one on earth: all that you see around and within is mine. These stockings my daughters knit; my shoes and garments are provided by my flocks and herds; they contribute, also, with my garden and fields, to furnish a simple and substantial nourishment; and, what is the best eulogy upon our Government, is the fact, that thousands of Connecticut farmers are not less content than myself; whose doors, too, like my own, are without locks. The taxes here are not large; and, when they are paid, we can sleep in peace. Congress favors our industry with all its power; manufacturers are eager to take whatever surplus produce we have to sell; and I have money laid up, and am about to dispose of grain at twenty-four dollars a ton, which usually sells for eight. All this comes from the liberty we have conquered and founded upon good laws. I am master in my own domain; and it will surprise you to know that I never hear the sound of a drum, except on the Fourth of July, the glorious anniversary of our independence, and never see uniforms, soldiers, or bayonets.' During the whole period of return I was absorbed in profound reflections; and you may well believe that these last words of Monsieur Bulow occupied my mind. At last I had another subject of meditation: I thought how it was best to have my turkey cooked and served. I was not without perplexity, as I feared it would be difficult to find at Hartford all the requisite means; for I wished to dispose of my trophy in the most effective and brilliant manner. I make a painful sacrifice in suppressing the details of profound study—the aim whereof was to treat in a distinguished manner the American guests whom I had engaged for the banquet. Suffice it to say that the wings of the partridges were served *au papillote*, and the gray squirrels *cour bouillonnés au vin de Madère*. As to the turkey, which constituted our only plate of roast, it was charming to behold, fragrant to inhale, and delicious to the taste: so much so that, until the last morsel had disappeared, we heard from all sides of the table the exclamations: *Très-bon, extremement bon! O, mon cher monsieur, quel glorieux morceau!*"

From a region of vast promise, the United States had become one of accomplished destiny, so far as the establishment of a novel and extensive free government is concerned; and the results, economical, political, and social, in full development. Accordingly, the exploration of the agriculturist and manufacturer, the comments of the practical emigrant, and the social gossip, began to give way to the speculations of the philosopher; science investigated what curiosity had originally observed; and our country won the earnest thought of the humanitarian analyst, intent upon tracing laws of civil life and popular growth under the extraordinary physical, moral, and social influences of the New World. A young Frenchman who came to America as commissioner, to report upon our system of prison discipline, in 1830, subsequently published a work on the United States quite different in scope and aim from those we have before noted. Whatever may be thought of Alexis de Tocqueville's views of "Democracy in America," that treatise began a new era in the literature of American travel.* It seriously grasped the problems of human life, destiny, and progress involved in an Anglo-Saxon republic on the immense scale of these United States. The peculiar claim and character of De Tocqueville's work is, that, ignoring, in a great measure, the superficial aspects and casual traits of the country and people, he has patiently and profoundly examined and reported the elementary civic life thereof, with a view to ascertain and demonstrate absolute political and social truth. A brief analysis, or even a running commentary on such a treatise, would do it no justice; and a more elaborate discussion is inconsistent with the limits of a volume like this. The necessity for either course is obviated by the fact that De Tocqueville's work is so familiar to all thinkers, and so accessible to all readers. To indicate the scope and motives of the author, we have but to recur to his own introductory statement:

"It is not merely to satisfy a legitimate curiosity that I have examined America. My wish has been to find instruction by which we may ourselves profit. Whoever should imagine that I have intended to write a panegyric, would be strangely mistaken, and, on reading this work, he will perceive that such is not my design. Nor has it been my object to advocate any form of government in particular; for I am of opinion that absolute excellence is rarely to be found in any legislation. I have not even affected to discuss whether the social revolution, which I believe to be irresistible, is advantageous or prejudicial to mankind. I have acknowledged this revolution as a fact already accomplished, or on the eve of accomplishment; and I have selected the nation from

---

* "De la Démocratie en Amérique," par A. de Tocqueville, 4 vols., 8vo., Paris, 1835–'41.

De Tocqueville's "Democracy in America," translated by Henry Reeve, Esq.; edited, with notes, the translation revised and in great part rewritten, and the additions made to the recent Paris editions now first translated, by Francis Bowen, Alford Professor of Moral Philosophy in Harvard University; 2 vols., post 8vo.

among those who have undergone it, in which its development has been the most peaceful and the most complete, in order to discern its natural consequences, and, if it be possible, to distinguish the means by which it may be rendered profitable. I confess that in America I saw more than America; I *sought* the image of democracy itself, with its inclinations, its character, its prejudices, and its passions, in order to learn what we have to fear or to hope from its progress."

Thus it is universal principles, and not special traits, that M. de Tocqueville discusses. It is because of the identity of American development with human destiny, and not as a fragmentary phenomenon and a peculiar nationality, that he deemed it worthy of his conscientious study. In the first part of his work, he shows "the tendency given to the laws by the democracy of America;" in the second, "the influence which the equality of conditions and the rule of democracy exercise on civil society." The mere mention of such texts indicates at once the vastly superior aim and higher motives of De Tocqueville, when compared with so many other commentators on America. Not as a social critic, a naturalist, a complacent vagabond, a pedantic *raconteur*, or a vivacious gossip, but as a humane philosopher, does he approach the problem of American life, institutions, and destiny. Hence the permanent value and present significance of his work, than which no abstract political treatise was ever so frequently quoted and referred to in the current discussions of the hour. The prophetic wisdom of his work proves how justly he declared: " I have undertaken not to see differently, but to look farther than parties ; and, while they are busied for the morrow, I have turned my thoughts to the future."

The mature and wholesome fruit of such conscientious intelligence has long been recognized both at home and abroad. "M. de Tocqueville," writes Vericour, "has revealed to Europe the spirit of the American laws, deduced from a comprehensive survey of usages and institutions. He has decomposed, with a firm and skilful hand, the curious mechanism of this new government. In a calm and dispassionate spirit he investigates its action, effects, impulses, and destinies, gradually leading his reader to a profound knowledge of America; while, upon manifold questions of the gravest interest to Europe, affecting its future progress and welfare, he throws unexpected streams of light." With the fondness for broad generalization from inadequate premises, and for specific inferences from casual facts, which makes so many of his countrymen philosophize charmingly, but at random, De Tocqueville yet seized upon some vital principles of our national life, clearly and truly illustrated some normal tendencies and traits of our civil and social character, and initiated a method of observation and discussion more thoughtful, authentic, and wise than any one of his more superficial predecessors. No one can read his work without finding it full of valuable suggestions, and often profoundly significant. He looked upon the country with the eye of a philosopher; and, however the prejudices of his own country and culture may have exaggerated some and obscured other perceptions, the spirit of his survey was comprehensive, humane, and acute. The geographical peculiarities of the country, the origin of her Anglo-American colonists, and their different national elements, are briefly considered. The "advanced theory of legislation" of the first laws enacted; the Puritan as distinguished from the English character of the colonists; the system of townships in New England; the predominance of popular will; the ideas of honor, of equality, administration, prerogative, suffrage, law; the allegiance to education and religion, trial by jury, the Federal Constitution—each distinctive form and feature of our political system is described and considered; and then the reflex influence of these upon manners, language, labor, family life, letters, art, and individual character, is more or less truly indicated — our restlessness of temper, monotonous social experience, devotion to physical well-being, absorption in the immediate, unchastened style of speech and writing, materialism, subservience to public opinion. The unique privileges and peculiar dangers born of our political condition, are defined and delineated, not, indeed, with strict accuracy, but often with salutary wisdom and rare perspicacity.

Alexis de Tocqueville was born at Paris, in 1805. He studied for some time at the College of Metz; travelled with one of his brothers in Italy and Sicily; was attached, after his return, to the court of justice at Versailles, where his father, the Count de Tocqueville, was prefect. While performing the duties of *Juge-Auditeur*, he found time to engage with ardor in political studies. After the Revolution of 1830, he obtained from the Ministry of the Interior a mission to America, for the purpose of examining our system of prison discipline. In 1831 he came to the United States with his friend M. de Beaumont, and, after a year's residence, returned to Paris, and soon after published the first two volumes of his "Democracy in America"—a work that established his reputation as an original and systematic thinker on political questions and social science. He married an English lady; became a member of the Chamber of Deputies, being reëlected from Valognes for nine successive years. Meantime he was chosen a member of the Institute, received an academy prize, and published the additional volumes of his work on America. Eminently conscientious and useful in public, and happy in domestic life, De Tocqueville continued to think, write, and speak on subjects of vital social interest, until the failure of his health enforced a life of retirement, which was peculiarly congenial to his studious habits and elevated sympathies. "There ever seemed to stand before his imagination," says a recent critic, "two great moral figures, sufficient to occupy his entire being, ever correlative, continually intermingled: the one, France, her Revolution and its consequences; the other, England, her constitutional liberty and its gigantic democratic development in the United States of America." With all his recognition of democracy as the inevitable political tendency and test of humanity, he thoroughly understood how few were able to conceive or enjoy the legitimate fruits of liberty as an inspiration of character. "It enters," he writes, "into the large hearts God has prepared to receive it; it fills them, it enraptures them: but to the meaner minds which have never felt it, it is past finding out."

He was one of the deputies arrested on the 2d of December, 1851, at the time of Napoleon III.'s *coup d'état*, and was confined for a time at Vincennes. "Here," writes his friend and biographer, De Beaumont, "ended his political life. It ended with liberty in France." We have the same authority for a beautiful and harmonious estimate of his character both as a writer and a man. He died at the age of fifty-four, in 1859.

"I have said," remarks his intimate companion and faithful biographer, "that he had many friends; but he experienced a still greater happiness—that of never losing one of them. He had also another happiness: it was the knowing how to love them all so well, that none ever complained of the share he received, even while seeing that of the others. He was as ingenious as he was sincere in his attachments; and never, perhaps, did example prove better than his, 'combien l'esprit ajoute de charmes à la bonté.'"

"Good as he was, he aspired without ceasing to become better; and it is certain that each day he drew nearer to that moral perfection which seemed to him the only end worthy of man. . . . . He was more patient, more laborious, more watchful to lose nothing of that life which he loved so well, and which he had the right to find beautiful—he who made of it so noble a use! Finally, it may be said to his honor, that at an epoch in which each man tends to concentrate his regard upon himself, he had no other aim than that of seeking for truths useful to his fellows, no other passion than that of increasing their well-being and their dignity."

An episode of De Tocqueville's American tour, published after his death, evinces a sensibility to nature and a power of observation in her sphere, which are rarely combined with such logical tendencies as his political disquisitions manifest.

It is a remarkable fact, that a visit to one of the oldest seats of civilization, in his youth, inspired him with that love of economical and humane studies which led, in his prime, to the sojourn in and the examination of the United States. His biographer tells us that, during De Tocqueville's tour in Sicily, "witnessing the misery inflicted on the people by a detestable Government, he was led to reflect on the primary conditions on which depends the decay or the prosperity of nations." We learn, from the same authority, that his mission to the United States was a pretext for, not the cause of, investigations there. The secret of his liberal and earnest spirit of inquiry, whereby his work attained permanent significance and philosophic value, is to be found not less in the character than the mind of De Tocqueville; for his intimate friend and the companion of his travels assures us, that "the great problem of the destiny of man impressed him with daily increasing awe and reverence." It is this sentiment, so deep and prevailing, which enabled him, as a social and political critic, to rise "above the narrow views of party and the passions of the moment;" for it was his noble distinction as a writer, a citizen, and a man, "in a selfish age, to aim only at the pursuit of truths useful to his fellow creatures." De Tocqueville was surprised and attracted by the "admirable and unusual good sense of the Americans." He entered with singular zest into the freshness and adventure of border life, enjoyed a bivouac in the forests of Tennessee, and a "fortnight in the wilderness," where he saw the Indian, the pioneer, and the different classes of *emigrés;* noting the sensations and the sentiment of this experience, with as much accuracy and relish as breathe from his speculations on the institutions and the destiny of the New World. He found "mosquitoes the curse of the American woods," yet realized therein the "soft melancholy, the vague aversion to civilized life, and the sort of savage instinct" which so many poetical and adventurous minds, from Boone to Chateaubriand, have acknowledged under the same influences. His analysis of the French, American, half-caste, and

Indian inhabitants of the new settlements is discriminating; and he was keenly alive to the contrast of this new life and its primitive conditions to that he had known in Europe. "Here," he writes, "man still seems to steal into life." The uniform tone of character, and the similarity of aspect incident to the fact that the dwellers in the woods of America are, with few exceptions, emigrants from civilized communities, struck De Tocqueville forcibly, accustomed as he was to a peasant class, and those diversities of character which spring from feudal distinctions. His remarks on this subject are true and suggestive:

"In America, more even than in Europe, there is but one society, whether rich or poor, high or low, commercial or agricultural; it is everywhere composed of the same elements. It has all been raised or reduced to the same level of civilization. The man whom you left in the streets of New York, you find again in the solitude of the far West; the same dress, the same tone of mind, the same language, the same habits, the same amusements. No rustic simplicity, nothing characteristic of the wilderness, nothing even like our villages. This peculiarity may be easily explained. The portions of territory first and most fully peopled have reached a high degree of civilization. Education has been prodigally bestowed; the spirit of equality has tinged with singular uniformity the domestic habits. Now, it is remarkable that the men thus educated are those who every year migrate to the desert. In Europe, a man lives and dies where he was born. In America, you do not see the representatives of a race grown and multiplied in retirement, having long lived unknown to the world, and left to its own efforts. The inhabitants of an isolated region arrived yesterday, bring with them the habits, ideas, and wants of civilization. They adopt only so much of savage life as is absolutely forced upon them; hence you see the strangest contrasts. You step from the wilderness into the streets of a city, from the wildest scenes to the most smiling pictures of civilized life. If night does not surprise you, and force you to sleep under a tree, you may reach a village where you will find everything, even French fashions and caricatures from Paris. The shops of Buffalo or Detroit are as well supplied with all these things as those of New York. The looms of Lyons work for both alike. You leave the high road; you plunge into paths scarcely marked out; you come at length upon a ploughed field, a hut built of rough logs, lighted by a single narrow window; you think that you have at last reached the abode of an American peasant; you are wrong. You enter this hut, which looks the abode of misery; the master is dressed as you are; his language is that of the towns. On his rude table are books and newspapers; he takes you hurriedly aside to be informed of what is going on in Europe, and asks you what has most struck you in his country. He will trace on paper for you the plan of a campaign in Belgium, and will teach you gravely what remains to be done for the prosperity of France. You might take him for a rich proprietor, come to spend a few nights in a shooting box. And, in fact, the log hut is only a halting place for the American—a temporary submission to necessity. As soon as the surrounding fields are thoroughly cultivated, and their owner has time to occupy himself with superfluities, a more spacious dwelling will succeed the log hut, and become the home of a large family of children, who, in their turn, will some day build themselves a dwelling in the wilderness."

As was inevitable, De Tocqueville, in describing and discussing our governmental institutions, made some mistakes. Looking at the organization of the central and State Governments in the abstract, he could not perceive any guarantee for the supremacy of the former in case of serious dissatisfaction on the part of a State. To one familiar with the military and administrative system of Europe, it is not surprising that the national power should appear inadequate and unsanctioned in such a contingency; but farther consideration would have modified this scepticism, had the sagacious and honest critic been more practically acquainted with the latent agencies at work. The fact is to be found in the history of the Constitution itself, wherein it is made apparent that the surrender of State sovereignty to national law was regarded as absolute, and not experimental. The hesitation of some States, the arguments for and against union, so able, deliberate, and earnest, and the entire tone and tactics of the peerless Convention which, at last, gave authority to that great instrument of republican rule, all show that the compact was a vital and permanent inauguration of popular sentiment and embodiment of popular will. Less binding affiliations had been tried under the old Confederacy, and the independent coexistence of the several States had brought the country to the verge of ruin, before the wise and patriotic instincts of the people led them to merge the life of States, so flickering and fugitive, into that of a nation so self-subsistent and powerful; and to the maintenance thereof the people thus became forever pledged, and hence prepared to defend and enforce what they had calmly and voluntarily decreed. Hence the resources of all the States became pledged to the integrity of the nation; precisely as, in so many instances, in the history of other Governments, the will of the majority has made the law, the system, the form, and the foundation, thenceforth the object of loyal support, protection, and faith. Recent events have, indeed, proved the fallacy of De Tocqueville's remark, that "if one of the States desires to withdraw its name from the compact, it would be difficult to disprove its right of doing so, and the Federal Government would have no means of maintaining its claims either by force or right." Even this experiment has never yet been tried, no legitimate and free expression of the desire "to withdraw its name from the compact" ever yet having been made by the constitutional voice of any State. The "secession" of 1861 was effected by as flagrant violation of State as of Federal law.

The prescience and wisdom of De Tocqueville are emphatic in what he says of the dangers attending our institutions. Herein, instead of seeking in the form of government itself the only causes for vigilance, and finding sophistical arguments to decry republican manners and culture, after the prejudiced style of most English writers, he notes the local and incidental influences, the facts of nature and of history peculiar to America, as threatening to the integrity of the republic—especially the disproportionate increase of certain States; the jealousy of the slaveholders and their economical theories; the conflict between free and slave labor, and the consequences thereof; the sudden growth of population; universal suffrage without equal or adequate education; the frequency of elections—and utters thereon many philosophical arguments full of insight and sympathy. "There are, at the present time," he observes, "two great nations in the world, which seem to tend toward the same end, although they started from different points: I allude to the Russians and the Americans. The world learned their existence and their greatness at almost the same time. The Anglo-American relies upon personal interest to acomplish his ends, and gives free scope to the unguided exertions and common sense of the citizens; the Russian centres all the authority of society in a single arm. The principal instrument of the former is freedom; of the latter, servitude. Their starting point is different, and their courses are not the same; yet each of them seems to be marked out by the will of Heaven to sway the destinies of half the globe."

"It was my intention," observes De Tocqueville, "to depict, in another work, the influence which the equality of condition and the rule of democracy exercise upon the civil society, the habits, and the manners of the Americans. I begin, however, to feel less ardor for the accomplishment of this object since the excellent work of my friend and travelling companion, M. de Beaumont, has been given to the world.*

The grave statistical work with which the name of De Beaumont was identified, made his advent as a romance writer a surprise. But he aspired to no such title. His "Marie" deals with historical and social facts under a very thin disguise of fiction, adopted rather to give free scope to speculation in the form of imaginary conversations, than to subserve dramatic effect. The thread of the story is evolved from what the author found to be a prevalent and permanent social prejudice. He relates an incident which occurred in a Northern city during his sojourn in America, which made a great impression upon his mind. A gentleman of dark complexion, and regarded as a mulatto, was forcibly ejected from the theatre, simply and only because of his color. M. de Beaumont sought to trace the extent and ascertain the force of this " barrière placé entre les deux races par un préjugé

---

* "Marie, ou L'Esclavage aux États Unis, Tableau de Mœurs Américaines," par Gustave de Beaumont, Bruxelles, 1825.

sociale;" and this forms the inspiration of his story, wherein the course of true love does not run smooth because of a difference, not of character, refinement, or position, but of chemical proportions in the blood of the lovers. Much romantic emotion and no little social and moral philosophy are ingeniously deduced from this circumstance. If there are few startling incidents, there is a charming tone and grace of style. If the "situations" are not dramatic, they are often picturesque. Extreme statements occur in the discussions, but they are modified by explanations given in the copious notes appended to the story. While antipathies of race and the problem of slavery constitute the serious and pervading themes, manners and customs in general are illustrated and considered with reference to the institutions of the United States. There is little originality in these topics or their treatment. They have long been staple texts for theoretical and practical criticism by the pulpit and the press. M. de Beaumont, or rather his imaginary characters, comment on the materialism, the devotion to gain, the absence of taste, the nomadic habits, the unimaginative spirit, and the monotonous routine of American life. Elections, emeutes, Sundays, sects, domestic and social tendencies and traits, are delineated often in a partial or exaggerated way, yet, on the whole, with candor, and in much more pleasing and finished language than we often find in books of travel. Our sociable arrangements are attributed in part to our comparative equality of condition, which is also justly declared to promote marriage, whereas rank, in France, discourages it. The total separation of church and state, and the consequent multiplicity of sects, however favorable to religious convictions, are described as wholly opposed to the development of art. An industrial career being the destiny of the American, he is soon in the way of gaining at least subsistence, and a home and family of his own is the natural consequence; so that one of the rare things in America, according to this observer, is "an old boy of twenty-five"—in other words, a young bachelor.

From Baltimore the reader is transported to *un forêt vierge*, and refreshed with some delicious landscapes; for De Beaumont, as well as his friend and companion De Tocqueville, had a keen eye for nature in the New World, and describes her wild and characteristic features with vivid truth and feeling. Few modern books of travel in America give a more complete, authentic, and interesting sketch of the condition of the different Indian tribes. They and the ne groes occupy a large space in the descriptions and discussions of this work, and obviously enlist the warmest and most intelligent sympathies of the author. His comments on the lack of artistic enthusiasm, of *bon gout* and *tact fin et subtil* in literature, and on the intensely practical tone of mind, the pride and jealousy of which money is the motive and object, the want of time for sentiment and gallantry, the partisan ferocity, and the dearth of romance and repose, are sometimes extravagant, but often piquant and just, and not unfrequently amusing from their partial recognition of latent facts and feelings whereby their power and prevalence are essentially modified. We are told there is no *heureuse pauvreté* in America, and no small theatres, and—as consequent upon the latter defect—a lamentable want of dramatic talent and taste; and that, while love is wholly in abeyance to interest, our charitable institutions are original and effective. The extreme " facilité de s'enricher et d'arriver au sacerdoce," it is declared, produces serious and often sinister social results. As with all Frenchmen, the different relative positions of the sexes, and the character and career of women in America and in France, excite frequent comment. " Les femmes Americaines," we are told, " ont, en général, un esprit orné mais peu d'imagination et plus de raison que de sensibilité; pour toute fille qui a plus de seize ans la mariage est la grand intérêt de la vie. En France elle le désire; en Amérique elle le cherche: chez nous la coquetterie est une passion; en Amérique un calcul." He is touched with the fragility of constitution which makes the beauty of our women so proverbially transient, and observes that their girlish days are the most free and happy; for while, in France, marriage brings a liberty to the wife unknown to the maiden, in America it ends the irresponsible gayety, and initiates "les devoirs austères au foyer domestique." There is much truth and wisdom in many of the generalizations in M. de Beaumont's graceful supplement to M. de Tocqueville's stern analysis of facts. But, while the reasoning and principles of the latter are quite as, if not more significant to-day than when they were written, many of the former's comments have lost their special application, and may now be quite as justly appropriated by his own countrymen as by Americans —so completely, in a quarter of a century, has chivalric France become material, and money overpowered rank, subsidized political aspirations, and made uniform, luxurious, and mercenary the standard tone and traits of social life; while, in America, new and momentous practical issues have succeeded the speculative phase of slavery, and a direct physical and moral conflict between its champions and those of free constitutional government, has developed unimagined resources of character and results of democratic rule, which may yet purify and exalt the national ideal and the social traits, so as to make wholly traditional many of the worse "blots on the escutcheon" so emphatically designated by this and other humane and enlightened commentators on America.

Another of De Tocqueville's most congenial friends was J. J. Ampère, so long the amiable and accomplished professor of belles lettres in the College of France, and the biographer of the author of "Democracy in America" judiciously refers to Ampère's "Promenade en Amérique"* as an excellent illustration of his friend's philosophical work, giving the facts and impressions which confirm and explain it. Not only did community of opinion and mutual affection suggest this relation between the two authors, diverse in plan and power as are their respective books on this country; but it

* "Promenade en Amérique," par J. J. Ampère, de l'Académie Française, Paris, 1855.

was when reading De Tocqueville's "Democracy," during a trip up the Rhine, that Ampère conceived the desire and purpose to visit the United States. Looking up from the thoughtful page to some ruined tower or memorable scene, he had the relics of feudalism before his eyes, while his mind was occupied with the modern development of humanity in the most free and fraternal civic institutions. He had travelled in Greece, Italy, and the East, and brought a scholar's wisdom and a poet's sympathy to the illustration of that experience; and now, under the inspiration of his friend's treatise on the condition and prospects of the Western republic, he felt a strong interest in the experiment whereby he could compare the New with the Old World, and observe the most intense life of the present as he had explored the calm monuments of the past. Ampère's record of his American tour is singularly unpretending. It resembles, in tone and method, the best conversation. The style is pure and animated, and the thoughts naturally suggested. He describes what he sees with candor and geniality, criticizes without the slightest acrimony, and commends with graceful zeal. And yet, simple and unambitious as the narrative is, it affords a most agreeable, authentic, and suggestive illustration of De Tocqueville's theories. "Toujours," he exclaims, "la negligence Américaine!" in noting a shower of ignited cinders falling upon cotton bales on the deck of a crowded steamboat; and, in describing the substitute for bells in the hotel at New Orleans, he remarks: "Les sonnettes sont remplacées par un appareil électro-magnetique. En ce pays, non-seulement la science est appliqué à l'industrie, mais on l'emploie aux offices les plus vulgaires. Au lieu de tirer le cordon d'une sonnette on fait jouer une pile de Volta."

The arrival of Kossuth gave Ampère an excellent opportunity to note the phases of popular feeling in America. He has that catholic taste and temper so essential to a good traveller. He takes an interest in whatever relates to humanity, and his extensive reading and cosmopolitan experience place him *en rapport* with people and things, historical associations, and speculative opinions, with the greatest facility. While devoting attention to those subjects which have always occupied intelligent travellers in America, he sought and enjoyed, to an uncommon extent, the companionship of men of letters and of science, and, when practicable, secured them as *ciceroni*. On this account his work gives more exact and full information in regard to the intellectual condition and scientific enterprises of the country than any similar record of the same date. His intellectual appetite is eager, his social affinities strong, and his love of nature instinctive: hence the variety and vividness of his observations. He describes a sunset and a political *fête*, analyzes a sermon as well as a theory, can feel the meditative charm of Gray's Elegy while roaming, on an autumn afternoon, through Mount Auburn, and patiently investigate the results of the penitentiary system in a model prison. Observatories, ornithological museums, the maps of the Coast Survey, the trophies of the Patent Office, private libraries and characters, the antiquities of the West and the social privileges of the East, schools, sects, botanical specimens, machines, the physiognomy of cities and the aspects of primeval nature, embryo settlements and the process of an election, an opera or a waterfall—are each and all described and discussed with intelligence and sympathy. He recalled Irving's humorous description of New York at the sight of a Dutch mansion; examined the process of the sugar manufacture in Louisiana, discussed glaciers and geology with Agassiz, jurisprudence with Kent, Mississippi mounds with Davis, and the Alhambra with Irving. He contrasts the German and New England character in Ohio, traces the history of parties and the character of statesmen at Washington, and utters his calm but earnest protest against slavery while describing the hospitality of Carolina. He portrays with care and feeling the representative characters of the land, and is picturesque in his scenic descriptions, drawing felicitous comparisons from his experience in Italy and the East. He calls Agassiz a veritable *enfant des Alpes*, and Sparks the American Plutarch; recognizes the military instinct of the nation, since so remarkably manifest, and aptly refers to Volney, Chateaubriand, and other French travellers. Sometimes his distinctions are fanciful: as when he attributes the different aspects under which he saw Longfellow and Bryant—the one in his pleasant country house, and the other at his editorial desk—to political instead of professional causes; but, usually, his insight is as sagacious as his observation is candid. He writes always like a scholar and a gentleman, and, as such, is justly revolted by the indifference exhibited toward travellers in this country, on the part of those in charge of public conveyances. He truly declares the absence of indications and information in this regard a disgrace to our civilization, and gives some striking examples of personal inconvenience, discomfort, and hazard thus incurred. Indeed, when we remember that Ampère, during his sojourn among us, was more or less of an invalid, his good nature and charitable spirit are magnanimous, when left to wander in wet and darkness from one car to another, obliged to pass sleepless nights on board of steamers recklessly propelled and overloaded, robbed of his purse at a Presidential *levée*, and subjected to so many other vexations. He was much interested in discovering what he calls a *veine européenne* pervading the educated classes, and was agreeably surprised to find so often an identity of culture between his old friends in Europe and new ones in America, which made him feel at home and at ease. He protests against the bombastic appellatives to which the Americans are prone. He was gratified to find his illustrious father's scientific labors recognized by a professor at the Smithsonian Institute, and his own archæological research by a lecturer at New Orleans. The sound of the bell saluting Mount Vernon, as he glided down the Potomac, touched him as did the "tintement de l'Angelus dans la campagne Romaine." He felt, like most of his countrymen, the "tristesse du dimanche" in America, but, unlike them, found congenial employment in a critical examination of the hymns, the homilies, and the character of the various denominations of Prot-

7

estant Christians. Amused at the universality of the term "lady" applied to the female sex in America, he yet soon learned to recognize, in this deference, a secret of the social order where no rank organizes and restrains. Quakers and Mormons, cotton and architecture, aqueducts and Indians, Niagara and the prairies, a slave auction and a congressional debate, are with equal justice and sensibility considered in this pleasant "Promenade en Amérique," which extends from Canada to Cuba and Mexico, and abounds in evidences of the humane sympathies, the literary accomplishment, and the social philosophy of the author.

One of the most deservedly popular French economical works on the United States is that of Michael Chevalier. It contains valuable and comparatively recent statistical information, and is written with care, and, in general, with liberality and discrimination. The "Voyage dans l'Intérieure des États Unis," by M. Bayard (Paris, 1779); Godfrey de Vigny's "Six Months in America" (London, 1833); the "Essais Historiques et Politiques sur les Anglo-Américaines," by M. Hilliard d'Ubertail (Brussels, 1781), and the "Recherches" on the same subject, by "un citoyen de Virginie" (Mazzei), as well as the account of the United States furnished "L'Univers, ou Histoire et Descriptions des Tous les Peuples"—a work of valuable reference, by M. Roux, who was formerly French Minister in this country, of which he gives a copious though condensed account—are among the many works more or less superseded as authorities, yet all containing some salient points of observation or suggestive reasoning. "La Spectateur Américaine," of Mandrillon, Cartier's "Nouvelle France," Bonnet's "États Unis à la fin du 18me Centurie," Beaujour's "Aperçu des États Unis," Gentry's "Influence of the Discovery of America," and Grasset's "Encyclopédie des Voyages," afford many suggestive and some original facts and speculations. Lavasseur's "Lafayette in America,"[*] and Count O'Mahony's "Lettres

---

[*] "Lafayette in America in 1824–'25; or, A Journal of a Voyage to the United States," by A. Lavasseur, Secretary to General Lafayette, 2 vols., 12mo., Philadelphia, 1829

sur les États Unis," contain some curious details and useful material. To these may be added, as more or less worthy of attention, of the earlier records, the "Memoires de Baron La Honton,"* and later, the "Observations upon Florida," by Vignoles,† and the volumes of Clavière, Soutel, Engle, Franchère, Palessier, Bossu, Hariot, Chabert, Bouchet, Hurt-Binet, &c.

Besides the more formal records of tours in America, and episodes of military memoirs devoted thereto, the incidental personal references in the correspondence of the gallant officers and noblemen of France who mingled in our best local society, at the Revolutionary era, afford vivid glimpses of manners and character, such as an ingenious modern novelist would find admirable and authentic *materiel*. It was a period when republican simplicity coalesced with the refinements of education and the prestige of old-school manners, and therefore afforded the most salient traits. Some of the most ardent tributes to American women of that date were written from Newport, in Rhode Island, by their Gallic admirers; and in these spontaneous descriptions, when stripped of rhetorical exaggeration, we discern a state of society and a phase of character endeared to all lovers of humanity, and trace both, in no small degree, to the institutions and local influences of the country. The Duc de Lauzun, when sent into Berkshire County, because his knowledge of English made his services as an envoy more available than those of his brother officers, seems to regard the errand as little better than exile, and says, "Lebanon can only be compared to Siberia." Attached to the society of Newport, and domesticated with the Hunter family, he is never weary of expatiating upon the sweetness, purity, and grace of the women of "that charming spot regretted by all the army."

* La Honton's (Baron) "Mémoires de l'Amérique Septentrionale, ou la Suite des Voyages, avec un petit Dictionnaire de la Langue du Pais," 2 tomes, 12mo., map and plates, Amsterdam, 1705.

† Vignoles' (Charles) "Observations upon the Floridas," 8vo., New York, 1823.

And when De Vauban there introduced the Prince de Broglie to a pretty Quakeress, the former writes that he "suddenly beheld the goddess of grace and beauty—Minerva in person." It is a striking illustration of the social instinct of the French, that manners, character, and personal appearance occupy so large a space in their commentaries on America.

"Other parts of America," says another officer, "were only beautiful by anticipation; but the prosperity of Rhode Island was already complete. Newport, well and regularly built, contained a numerous population. It offered delightful circles, composed of enlightened men and modest and handsome women, whose talents heightened their personal attractions." This was in 1782, ere the commercial importance of the port had been superseded, and when the belles of the town were the tôast and the triumph of every circle. La Rochefoucault and other French tourists, at a later period, found the prosperity of the town on the wane, and the social distinction modified; yet none the less attractive and valuable are the fresh and fanciful but sincere testimonies to genuine and superior human graces and gifts, of the French memoirs.

But such casual illustrations of the candid and kindly observation of our gallant allies, fade before the consistent and intelligent tributes of Lafayette, whose relation to America is one of the most beautiful historical episodes of modern times. After his youthful championship in the field, and his mature counsels, intercessions, and triumphant advocacy of our cause in France (for, "during the period," says Mr. Everett, "which intervened, from the peace of '83 to the organization of the Federal Government, Lafayette performed, in substance, the functions of our Minister"), when forty years had elapsed, he revisited the land for which he had fought in youth, to witness the physical and social, the moral and intellectual fruits of "liberty protected by law." And during this whole period, and to the time of his death, he was in correspondence, first with Washington and the leading men of the Revolution, and later with various personal friends. In his letters from and to America, there is constant indirect testimony to and illustration of the character of the people, the tendencies of opinion, the means and methods of life and government, founded on observation, intercourse, and sympathy, and endeared and made emphatic by his devotion to our spotless chief, his sacrifices for our cause, and his unswerving devotion to our political principles; in a word, by his vigilant and faithful love of America.

In 1824, De Pradt, formerly archbishop of Malines, and deputy to the Constituent Assembly from Normandy, a voluminous political writer, published "L'Europe et l'Amérique," in two volumes, the third of his works on this subject, "in which he gives an historical view of the principles of government in the Old and New Worlds." Judicious critics pronounce his style verbose and incorrect, and his views partial and shallow. His motto is, "Le genre humain est en marche et rien ne le fera rétrograder."

Several of the French Protestant clergy have visited the United States within the last few years, and some of them have put on record their impressions, chiefly with regard to the actual state of religion. In many instances, however, the important facts on this subject have been drawn from the copious and authentic American work of Dr. Baird.* Among books of this class, are "L'Amérique Protestante," par M. Rey, and the sketches of M. Grandpierre and M. Fisch. The latter's observations on Religion in America, originally appeared in the "Revue Chretien," but were subsequently embodied in a small volume, which includes observations on other themes.†

The latter work, though limited in scope, and the fruit of a brief visit, has an interest derived from the circumstance that the worthy *pasteur* arrived just before the fall of Sumter, and was an eyewitness and a conscientious though terse reporter of the aspects of that memorable period. He recog-

---

* "Religion in America," by Robert Baird, D. D.
† "Les États Unis en 1861," par Georges Fisch, Paris, 1862.

nizes in the Americans "un peuple qui n'avait d'autre force publique que celle des idées;" and deprecates the hasty judgment and perverse ignorance so prevalent in Europe in regard to "une grande lutte où se debattant les intérêts les plus élevés de la morale et de la religion;" and justly affirms that it is, in fact, "le choc de deux civilizations et de deux religions." M. Fisch, however, disclaims all intention of a complete analysis of national character. His book is mainly devoted to an account of the religious organization, condition, and prospects of America, especially as seen from his own point of view. Many of the details on this subject are not only correct, but suggestive. He writes in a liberal and conscientious spirit. His sympathies are Christian, and he descants on education and faith in the United States with intelligent and candid zeal. Indeed, he was long at a loss to understand what provision existed in society to check and calm the irresponsible and exuberant energy, the heterogeneous elements, and the self-reliance around him, until convinced that the latent force of these great conservative principles of human society were the guarantee of order and pledge of self-control. There is no people, he observes, who have been judged in so superficial a manner. America he regards as having all the petulance of youth, all the *naïveté* of inexperience: all there is incomplete—in the process of achievement. This was his earliest impression on landing at New York, the scene whereof was "un bizarre melange de sauvagerie et de civilization." But, after his patience had been nearly exhausted, he entered the city, emerging with agreeable surprise from muddy and noisome streets into Broadway, to find palaces of six or seven stories devoted to commerce, and to admire "les figures fines et gracieuses, la démarche légère et libre des femmes, les allures vives de toute la population." The frank hospitality with which he was received, and the interesting study of his *specialité* as a traveller, soon enlarged and deepened his impressions. He has a chapter on "La lutte présidentielle" which resulted in Lincoln's election, the phenomena whereof he briefly describes.

Then we have a sketch entitled "Statistique religieuse des États Unis;" followed by judicious comments on the "Unité de l'Église Américaine, son esprit et son influence." He considers Henry Ward Beecher an improvisatore—"mais c'est l'improvisation du génie;" and says, "L'on va entendre M. Beecher comme on irait a théâtre." He describes succinctly the system of public instruction; alludes to the progress of art and letters; expatiates on *l'energie* and *l'audace* of the Americans; is anecdotical and descriptive; praises the landscapes of Church and the sculpture of Crawford, Powers, and Palmer; gives a chapter to the "Caractère national," and another to "L'esclavage aux États Unis;" closing with hopeful auguries for the future of the country under "le réveil de la conscience;" wherein he sees the cause and scope of "la crise actuelle;" declaring that "la vie puissante de l'Amérique reprendra son paisible cours. Elle pourra se réprendre avec une puissance incomparable sur une terre renouvelée, et le monde apprendra une fois de plus que l'Evangile est la salut des nations, comme il est celui des individus."

Brochures innumerable, devoted to special phases of American life, facts of individual experience, and themes of social speculation, swell the *catalogue raisonnée* of French writings in this department, and, if not of great value, often furnish salient anecdotes or remarks; as, for instance, M. August Carlier's amusing little treatise on "La Mariage aux États Unis," the statement of one *voyageur* who happened to behold for the first time a dish of currie, that the Americans eat their rice with mustard, and the disgust natural to one accustomed to the rigorous municipal *régime* of Paris, expressed by Maurice Sand, at the exposure, for three days, of a dead horse in the streets of New York. Xavier Eyma's "Vie dans le Nouveau Monde" (Paris, 1861) is one of the most recent elaborate works, of which a judicious critical authority observes:

"He has given two goodly octavos to a solid criticism and description of American 'men and institutions;' two more octavos to a history of the States and Territories; one volume to the 'Black-Skins,' in which he sketches with admirable fidelity the peculiarities and the iniquities of slave life in the South; and one volume to the 'Red-Skins,' in which he shows the Indian tribes as they are. Besides these, he has told of the islands of the West Indies, of their corsairs and buccaneers, and of the social life of the various classes in America, native and immigrant, and has devoted one amusing volume to 'American Eccentricities.' In such a mass of material there must of course be repetition; nor are any of the views especially profound. M. Eymɑ is in no sense a philosopher. He loves story-telling better than disquisition, and arranges his materials rather for romantic effect than for scientific accuracy."

Finally, we have the prolific emanations of the Paris press on the war for the Union; pamphlets evoked by venality, abounding in sophistical arguments, gross misstatements, and prejudice; editorials written in the interest of partisans, and a mass of crude and unauthentic writing destined to speedy oblivion. A valuable contribution to the national cause was made, of late, by our able and loyally assiduous consul at Paris,* in a volume of facts, economical, political, and scientific, drawn from the latest and best authorities, published in the French language, and affording candid inquirers in Europe precisely the kind of information about America they need, to counteract the falsehood and malignity of the advocates of the slaveholders' rebellion. Army critics and correspondents from France, some of them illustrious and others of ephemeral claims, have visited our shores, and reported the momentous crisis through which the nation is now passing. The Prince de Joinville has given his experience and observation of the battles of the Chickahominy; and several pleasant but superficial writers have described some of the curious phases of life which here caught their attention, during a hasty visit at this transition epoch. Apart from virulent and mercenary writers, it is remarkable that the tone of French comment and criticism on the present rebellion in America has been far more intelligent, candid, and sympathetic than across the Channel. Eminent publicists and professors of France have recognized and vindicated the truth,

* John Bigelow, Esq.

and sent words of faith and cheer across the sea. In his lectures, and extravagant but piquant and suggestive "Paris dans l'Amérique," Laboulaye has signally promoted that better understanding and more just appreciation of the struggle, and the motives and end thereof, which now begin to prevail abroad. De Gasparin's "Uprising of a Great People" fell on American hearts, at the darkest hour of the strife, like the clarion note of a reënforcement of the heroes of humanity. Cochin, Henri Martin, and others less eminent but equally honest and humane, have echoed the earnest protest and appeal; which contrasts singularly with the indifference, disingenuousness, and perversity of so many distinguished writers and journals in England. Herein we perceive the same diversity of feeling which marks the earliest commentators of the respective nations on America, and the subsequent feelings manifested toward our prosperous republic. Mrs. Kemble, in a recent article on the "Stage," observes that the theatrical instinct of the Americans creates with them an affinity for the French, in which the English, hating exhibitions of emotion and self-display, do not share. With all due deference to her opinion, it seems to us her reasoning is quite too limited. The affinity of which she speaks, partial as it is, is based on the more sympathetic temperament of these two races compared with the English. The social character, the more versatile experience of American life, assimilate it in a degree, and externally, with that of France, and the climate of America develops nervous sensibility; while the exigencies of life foster an adaptive facility, which brings the Anglo-American into more intelligent relations with the Gallic nature than is possible for a people so egotistic and stolid as the English to realize. But this partial sympathy does not altogether account for the French understanding America better: that is owing to a more liberal, a less prejudiced, a more chivalric spirit; to quicker sympathies, to more scientific proclivities, to greater candor and humanity among her thinkers. They are far enough removed in life and character to catch the true moral perspective; and they have few, if any, wounds of self-love to impede their sense of justice in regard to a country wherewith their own history is often congenially and honorably associated.

Yet anomalous and sad will it seem, in the retrospect, that to a nation alien in blood and language, we are indebted for the earliest and most kindly greeting in our hour of stern and sacrificial duty and of national sorrow, instead of receiving it (with rare exceptions) from a people from whom we inherit laws, language, and literature, and to whom we are united by so many ties of lineage, culture, and material interests.

Humane, just, and authoritative, indeed, is the language of those eminent Frenchmen, Agenor de Gasparin, Augustin Cochin, Edouard Laboulaye, and Henri Martin, addressed to a committee of loyal Americans, in response to their grateful recognition of such distinguished advocacy of our national cause; and we cannot better close this notice of French writers on America, than with their noble words:

"Courage! You have before you one of the most noble works, the most sublime which can be accomplished here below—a work in the success of which we are as interested as yourselves—a work the success of which will be the honor and the consolation of our time.

"This generation will have seen nothing more grand than the abolition of slavery (in destroying it with you, you destroy it everywhere), and the energetic uprising of a people which in the midst of its growing prosperity was visibly sinking under the weight of the tyranny of the South, the complicity of the North, odious laws and compromises.

"Now, at the cost of immense sacrifices, you have stood up against the evil; you have chosen rather to pour out your blood and your dollars than to descend further the slope of degradation, where rich, united, powerful, you were sure to lose that which is far nobler than wealth, or union, or power.

"Well, Europe begins to understand, willingly or unwillingly, what you have done. In France, in England, everywhere your cause gains ground, and be it said for the honor of the nineteenth century, the obstacle which our ill will and our evil passions could not overcome, the obstacle which the intrigues of the South could not surmount, is an idea, a principle. Hatred of slavery has been your champion in the Old World. A poor champion seemingly. Laughed at, scorned, it seems weak and lonely. But what matters it; ere the account be closed, principles will stand for something, and conscience, in all human affairs, will have the last word.

"This, gentlemen, is what we would say to you in the name of all who with us, and better than ourselves, defend your cause in Europe. Your words have cheered us; may ours in turn cheer you! You have yet to cross many a dark valley. More than once the impossibility of success will be demonstrated to you; more than once, in the face of some military check or political difficulty, the cry will be raised that all is lost. What matters it to you? Strengthen your cause daily by daily making it more just, and fear not; there is a God above.

"We love to contemplate in hope the noble future which seems to stretch itself before you. The day you emerge at last from the anguish of civil war—and you will surely come out freed from the odious institution which corrupted your public manners and degraded your domestic as well as your foreign policy—that day your whole country, South as well as North, and the South perhaps more fully than the North, will enter upon a wholly new prosperity. European emigration will hasten toward your ports, and will learn the road to those whom until now it has feared to approach. Cultivation, now abandoned, will renew its yield. Liberty—for these are her miracles—will revivify by her touch the soil which slavery had rendered barren.

"Then there will be born unto you a greatness nobler and more stable than the old, for in this greatness there will be no sacrifice of justice."

CHAPTER V.

BRITISH TRAVELLERS AND WRITERS.

BERKELEY; McSPARRAN; MRS. GRANT; BURNABY; ROGERS; BURKE; DOUGLASS; HENRY; EDDIS; ANBURY; SMYTHE.

"THERE* are more imposing monuments in the venerable precincts of Oxford, recalling the genius which hallows our ancestral literature, but at the tomb of Berkeley we linger with affectionate reverence, as we associate the gifts of his mind and the graces of his spirit with his disinterested and memorable visit to our country.

In 1725, Berkeley published his proposals in explanation of this long-cherished purpose; at the same time he offered to resign his livings, and to consecrate the remainder of his days to this Christian undertaking. So magnetic were his appeal and example, that three of his brother fellows at Oxford decided to unite with him in the expedition. Many eminent and wealthy persons were induced to contribute their influence and money to the cause. But he did not trust wholly to such means. Having ascertained the worth of a portion of the St. Christopher's lands, ceded by France to Great Britain by the treaty of Utrecht, and about to be disposed of for public advantage, he undertook to realize from them larger proceeds than had been anticipated, and sug-

---

* From the author's "Essays, Biographical and Critical."

gested that a certain amount of these funds should be devoted to his college. Availing himself of the friendly intervention of a Venetian gentleman whom he had known in Italy, he submitted the plan to George I., who directed Sir Robert Walpole to carry it through Parliament. He obtained a charter for 'erecting a college, by name St. Paul's, in Bermuda, with a president and nine fellows, to maintain and educate Indian scholars, at the rate of ten pounds a year, George Berkeley to be the first president, and his companions from Trinity College the fellows.' His commission was voted May 11th, 1726. To the promised amount of twenty thousand pounds, to be derived from the land sale, many sums were added from individual donation. The letters of Berkeley to his friends, at this period, are filled with the discussion of his scheme; it absorbed his time, taxed his ingenuity, filled his heart, and drew forth the warm sympathy and earnest coöperation of his many admirers, though regret at the prospect of losing his society constantly finds expression. Swift, in a note to the Lord Lieutenant of Ireland, says: 'I do humbly entreat your excellency either to use such persuasions as will keep one of the first men of the kingdom for learning and genius at home, or assist him by your credit to compass his romantic design.' 'I have obtained reports,' says one of his own letters, 'from the Bishop of London, the board of trade and plantations, and the attorney and solicitor-general;' 'yesterday the charter passed the privy seal;' 'the lord chancellor is not a busier man than myself;' and elsewhere, 'I have had more opposition from the governors and traders to America than from any one else; but, God be praised, there is an end of all their narrow and mercantile views and endeavors, as well as of the jealousies and suspicions of others, some of whom were very great men, who apprehended this college may produce an independency in America, or at least lessen her dependency on England.'

Freneau's ballad of the 'Indian Boy,' who ran back to the woods from the halls of learning, was written subsequently, or it might have discouraged Berkeley in his idea of

the capacity of the American savages for education; but
more positive obstacles thwarted his generous aims. The
king died before affixing his seal to the charter, which delayed the whole proceedings. Walpole, efficient as he was as
a financier and a servant of the house of Brunswick, was a
thorough utilitarian, and too practical and worldly wise to
share in the disinterested enthusiasm of Berkeley. In his
answer to Bishop Gibson, whose diocese included the West
Indies, when he applied for the funds so long withheld, he
says: 'If you put the question to me as a minister, I must
assure you that the money shall most undoubtedly be paid as
soon as suits with public convenience; but if you ask me as a
friend whether Dean Berkeley should continue in America,
expecting the payment of twenty thousand pounds, I advise
him by all means to return to Europe.' To the project, thus
rendered unattainable, Berkeley had devoted seven years of
his life, and the greater part of his fortune. The amount
realized by the sale of confiscated lands was about ninety
thousand pounds, of which eighty thousand were devoted to
the marriage portion of the princess royal, about to espouse
the Prince of Orange; and the remainder, through the influence of Oglethorpe, was secured to pay for the transportation of emigrants to his Georgia colony. Berkeley's scheme
was more deliberate and well-considered than is commonly
believed. Horace Walpole calls it ' uncertain and amusing;'
but a writer of deeper sympathies declares it 'too grand and
pure for the powers that were.' His nature craved the united
opportunities of usefulness and of self-culture. He felt the
obligation to devote himself to benevolent enterprise, and at
the same time earnestly desired both the leisure and the retirement needful for the pursuit of abstract studies. The
prospect he contemplated promised to realize all these
objects. He possessed a heart to feel the infinite wants,
intellectual and religious, of the new continent, and had the
imagination to conceive the grand destinies awaiting its
growth. Those who fancy that his views were limited to
the plan of a doubtful missionary experiment, do great injus-

tice to the broad and elevated hopes he cherished. He knew that a recognized seat of learning open to the poor and uncivilized, and the varied moral exigencies of a new country, would insure ample scope for the exercise of all his erudition and his talents. He felt that his mind would be a kingdom wherever his lot was cast; and he was inspired by a noble interest in the progress of America, and a faith in the new field there open for the advancement of truth, as is evident from the celebrated verses in which these feelings found expression :

> ' The Muse, disgusted at an age and clime
>   Barren of every glorious theme,
> In distant lands now waits a better time,
>   Producing subjects worthy fame.
>
> ' In happy climes, when from the genial sun
>   And virgin earth such scenes ensue,
> The force of art by nature seems outdone,
>   And fancied beauties by the true ;
>
> ' In happy climes, the seat of innocence,
>   Where nature guides and virtue rules ;
> Where men shall not impose for truth and sense
>   The pedantry of schools ;
>
> ' Then shall we see again the golden age,
>   The rise of empire and of arts,
> The good and great inspiring epic rage,
>   The wisest heads and noblest hearts ;'
>
> ' Not such as Europe breeds in her decay ;
>   Such as she bred when fresh and young,
> When heavenly flame did animate her clay,
>   By future poets shall be sung.
>
> ' Westward the course of empire takes its way ;
>   The four first acts already past,
> A fifth shall end the drama with the day ;
>   Time's noblest offspring is the last.'

In August, 1728, Berkeley married a daughter of the Honorable John Foster, speaker of the Irish House of Commons, and, soon after, embarked for America. His companions were, his wife and her friend, Miss Hancock; two gentlemen of fortune, James and Dalton; and Smibert the painter. In a picture by the latter, now in the Trumbull gallery at New Haven, are preserved the portraits of this group, with that of the dean's infant son, Henry, in his mother's arms. It was painted for a gentleman of Boston, of whom it was purchased, in 1808, by Isaac Lothrop, Esq., and presented to Yale College. This visit of Smibert associates Berkeley's name with the dawn of art in America. They had travelled together in Italy, and the dean induced him to join the expedition partly from friendship, and also to enlist his services as instructor in drawing and architecture, in the proposed college. Smibert was born in Edinburgh, about the year 1684, and served an apprenticeship there to a house painter. He went to London, and, from painting coaches, rose to copying old pictures for the dealers. He then gave three years to the study of his art in Italy.

'Smibert,' says Horace Walpole, ' was a silent and modest man, who abhorred the *finesse* of some of his profession, and was enchanted with a plan that he thought promised tranquillity and an honest subsistence in a healthy and elysian climate, and, in spite of remonstrances, engaged with the dean, whose zeal had ranged the favor of the court on his side. The king's death dispelled the vision. One may conceive how a man so devoted to his art must have been animated, when the dean's enthusiasm and eloquence painted to his imagination a new theatre of prospects, rich, warm, and glowing with scenery which no pencil had yet made common.' *

Smibert was the first educated artist who visited our shores, and the picture referred to, the first of more than a single figure executed in the country. To his pencil New England is indebted for portraits of many of her early statesmen and clergy. Among others, he painted for a Scotch

* "Anecdotes of Painting," vol. iii.

gentleman the only authentic likeness of Jonathan Edwards. He married a lady of fortune in Boston, and left her a widow with two children, in 1751. A high eulogium on his abilities and character appeared in the *London Courant*. From two letters addressed to him by Berkeley, when residing at Cloyne, published in the *Gentleman's Magazine*, it would appear that his friendship for the artist continued after their separation, as the bishop urges the painter to recross the sea and establish himself in his neighborhood.

A considerable sum of money, and a large and choice collection of books, designed as a foundation for the library of St. Paul's College, were the most important items of the dean's outfit. In these days of rapid transit across the Atlantic, it is not easy to realize the discomforts and perils of such a voyage. Brave and philanthropic, indeed, must have been the heart of an English church dignitary, to whom the road of preferment was open, who was a favorite companion of the genial Steele, the classic Addison, and the brilliant Pope, who basked in the smile of royalty, was beloved of the Church, revered by the poor, the idol of society, and the peer of scholars; yet could shake off the allurements of such a position, to endure a tedious voyage, a long exile, and the deprivations attendant on a crude state of society and a new civilization, in order to achieve an object which, however excellent and generous in itself, was of doubtful issue, and beset with obstacles. Confiding in the pledges of those in authority, that the parliamentary grant would be paid when the lands had been selected, and full of the most sanguine anticipations, the noble pioneer of religion and letters approached the shores of the New World.

It seems doubtful to some of his biographers whether Berkeley designed to make a preliminary visit to Rhode Island, in order to purchase lands there, the income of which would sustain his Bermuda institution. The vicinity of that part of the New England coast to the West Indies may have induced such a course; but it is declared by more than one, that his arrival at Newport was quite accidental. This conjecture, however, is erroneous, as in one of his letters, dated September 5th, 1728, he says: 'To-morrow, with God's blessing, I set sail for Rhode Island.' The captain of the ship which conveyed him from England, it is said, was unable to discover the Island of Bermuda, and at length abandoned the attempt, and steered in a northerly direction. They made land which they could not identify, and supposed it inhabited only by Indians. It proved, however, to be Block Island, and two fishermen came off and informed them of the vicinity of Newport harbor. Under the pilotage of these men, the vessel, in consequence of an unfavorable wind, entered what is called the West Passage, and anchored. The fishermen were sent ashore with a letter from the dean to Rev. James Honyman. They landed at Canonicut Island, and sought the dwellings of two parishioners of that gentleman, who immediately conveyed the letter to their pastor. For nearly half a century this faithful clergyman had labored in that region. He first established himself at Newport, in 1704. Besides the care of his own church, he made frequent visits to the neighboring towns on the mainland. In a letter to the secretary of the Episcopal mission in America, in 1709, he says: 'You can neither believe, nor I express, what excellent services for the cause of religion a bishop would do in these parts; these infant settlements would become beautiful nurseries, which now seem to languish for want of a father to oversee and bless them;' and in a memorial to Governor Nicholson on the religious condition of Rhode Island, in 1714, he observes: 'The people are divided among Quakers, Anabaptists, Independents, Gortonians, and infidels, with a remnant of true Churchmen.'* It is characteristic of the times and region, that with a broad circuit and isolated churches as the sphere of his labors, the vicinity of Indians, and the variety of sects, he was employed for two months, in 1723, in daily attending a large number of pirates who had

---

* Hawkins's "Historical Notices of the Missions of the Church of England in the North American Colonies," p. 173.

been captured, and were subsequently executed—one of the murderous bands which then infested the coast, whose extraordinary career has been illustrated by Cooper, in one of his popular nautical romances.

When Berkeley's missive reached this worthy pastor, he was in his pulpit, it being a holiday. He immediately read the letter to his congregation, and dismissed them. Nearly all accompanied him to the ferry wharf, which they reached but a few moments before the arrival of the dean and his fellow voyagers. A letter from Newport, dated January 24th, 1729, that appeared in the *New England Journal*, published at Boston, thus notices the event: 'Yesterday arrived here Dean Berkeley, of Londonderry, in a pretty large ship. He is a gentleman of middle stature, and of an agreeable, pleasant, and erect aspect. He was ushered into the town by a great number of gentlemen, to whom he behaved himself after a very complaisant manner. 'Tis said he purposes to tarry here about three months.'

We can easily imagine the delightful surprise which Berkeley acknowledges at first view of that lovely bay and the adjacent country. The water tinted, in the clear autumn air, like the Mediterranean; the fields adorned with symmetrical haystacks and golden maize, and bounded by a lucid horizon, against which rose picturesque windmills and the clustered dwellings of the town, and the noble trees which then covered the island; the bracing yet tempered atmosphere, all greeted the senses of those weary voyagers, and kindled the grateful admiration of their romantic leader. He soon resolved upon a longer sojourn, and purchased a farm of a hundred acres at the foot of the hill whereon stood the dwelling of Honyman, and which still bears his name.*

There he erected a modest homestead, with philosophic taste choosing the valley, in order to enjoy the fine view from

---

* The conveyance from Joseph Whipple and wife to Berkeley, of the land in Newport, is dated February 18th, 1729.

the summit occasionally, rather than lose its charm by familiarity. At a sufficient distance from the town to insure immunity from idle visitors; within a few minutes' walk of the sea, and girdled by a fertile vale, the student, dreamer, and missionary pitched his humble tent where nature offered her boundless refreshment, and seclusion her contemplative peace. His first vivid impressions of the situation, and of the difficulties and consolations of his position, are described in the few letters, dated at Newport, which his biographer cites. At this distance of time, and in view of the subsequent changes of that region, it is both curious and interesting to revert to these incidental data of Berkeley's visit.

'NEWPORT, IN RHODE ISLAND, April 24, 1729.

'I can by this time say something to you, from my own experience, of this place and its people. The inhabitants are of a mixed kind, consisting of many sects and subdivisions of sects. Here are four sorts of Anabaptists, besides Presbyterians, Quakers, Independents, and many of no profession at all. Notwithstanding so many differences, here are fewer quarrels about religion than elsewhere, the people living peacefully with their neighbors of whatever persuasion. They all agree in one point—that the Church of England is the second best. The climate is like that of Italy, and not at all colder in the winter than I have known everywhere north of Rome. The spring is late, but, to make amends, they assure me the autumns are the finest and the longest in the world; and the summers are much pleasanter than those of Italy by all accounts, forasmuch as the grass continues green, which it does not there. This island is pleasantly laid out in hills and vales and rising ground, hath plenty of excellent springs and fine rivulets, and many delightful rocks, and promontories, and adjacent lands. The provisions are very good; so are the fruits, which are quite neglected, though vines sprout of themselves of an extraordinary size, and seem as natural to this soil as any I ever saw. The town of Newport contains about six thousand souls, and is the most thriving place in all America for its bigness. I was never more agreeably surprised than at the first sight of the town and its harbor.'

'*June* 12, 1729.—I find it hath been reported in Ireland that we intend settling here. I must desire you to discountenance any such report. The truth is, if the king's bounty were paid in, and the charter could be removed hither, I should like it better than Bermuda. But if this were questioned before the payment of said money, it might perhaps hinder it and defeat all our designs. I snatch this moment to write, and have time only to add that I have got a son, who, I thank God, is likely to live.'

'*May* 7.—This week I received a package from you *via* Philadelphia, the postage of which amounted to above four pounds sterling of this country money. I am worried to death by creditors, and am at an end of patience, and almost out of my wits. Our little son is a great joy to us: we are such fools as to think him the most perfect thing of the kind we ever saw.'

To the poet, scenery of picturesque beauty and grandeur is desirable, but to the philosopher general effects are more congenial. High mountains, forests, and waterfalls appeal more emphatically to the former, and luxuries of climate and atmosphere to the latter. Accordingly, the soft marine air and the beautiful skies of summer and autumn, in the region of Berkeley's American home, with the vicinity of the seacoast, became to him a perpetual delight. He alludes, with grateful sensibility, to the 'pleasant fields,' and 'walks on the beach,' to 'the expanse of ocean studded with fishing boats and lighters,' and the 'plane trees,' that daily cheered his sight, as awakening 'that sort of joyful instinct which a rural scene and fine weather inspire.' He calls Newport 'the Montpelier of America,' and appears to have communed with nature and inhaled the salubrious breeze, while pursuing his meditations, with all the zest of a healthy organization and a susceptible and observant mind. A few ravines finely wooded, and with fresh streams purling over rocky beds, vary the alternate uplands; from elevated points a charming distribution of water enlivens the prospect; and the shore is indented with high cliffs, or rounded into graceful curves. The sunsets are remarkable for a display of gorgeous and radiant clouds; the wide sweep of pasture is only broken by low ranges of stone wall, clumps of sycamores, orchards, haystacks, and mill towers; and over luxuriant clover beds, tasselled maize, or fallow acres, plays, for two thirds of the year, a southwestern breeze, chastened and moistened by the Gulf Stream.

Intercourse with Boston was then the chief means on the island of acquiring political and domestic news. A brisk trade was carried on between the town and the West Indies, France, England, and the Low Countries, curious memorials of which are still visible, in some of the old mansions, in the shape of china and glass ware, of obsolete patterns, and faded specimens of rich brocade. A sturdy breed of Narraganset ponies carried fair equestrians from one to another of the many hospitable dwellings scattered over the fields, on which browsed sheep and cackled geese, still famous in epicurean reminiscence; while tropical fruits were constantly imported, and an abundance and variety of fish and fowl rewarded the most careless sportsman. Thus blessed by nature, the accidental home of the philosophic dean soon won his affection. Intelligent members of all denominations united in admiration of his society and attendance upon his preaching. With one neighbor he dined every Sunday, to the child of another he became godfather, and with a third took counsel for the establishment of the literary club which founded the Redwood Library. It was usual then to see the broad brim of the Quakers in the aisles of Trinity Church; and, as an instance of his emphatic yet tolerant style, it is related that he once observed, in a sermon, 'Give the devil his due: John Calvin was a great man.'* We find him, at one time, writing a letter of encouragement to a Huguenot preacher of Providence, and, at another, visiting Narraganset with Smibert to examine the aboriginal inhabitants. His own opinion of the race was given in the discourse on 'The Propagation of the Gospel in Foreign Parts,' delivered in London on his return. To the ethnologist it may be interesting, in reference to this subject, to revert to the anecdote of the portrait painter cited by Dr. Barton. He had been employed by the Grand Duke of Tuscany to paint two or three Siberian Tartars, presented to that prince by the Czar of Russia; and, on first landing in Narraganset with Berkeley, he instantly recognized the In-

---

* Updike's "History of the Narraganset Church."

dians there as the same race as the Siberian Tartars—an opinion confirmed by Wolff, the celebrated Eastern traveller.

During his residence at Newport, Berkeley became acquainted with the Rev. Jared Elliot, one of the trustees of Yale College, and with the Rev. Samuel Johnson, an Episcopal minister of Stratford, Conn., who informed him of the condition, prospects, and wants of that institution. He afterward opened a correspondence on the subject with Rector Williams, and was thus led, after the failure of his own college scheme, to make his generous donations to a seminary already established. He had previously presented the college with a copy of his writings. In 1732, he sent from England a deed of his farm in Rhode Island, and, the conditions and descriptions not being satisfactory, he sent, the ensuing year, another deed, by which it was provided that the rents of his lands should be devoted to the education of three young men, the best classical scholars; the candidates to be examined annually, on the 6th of May; in case of disagreement among the examiners, the competitors to decide by lot; and all surplus funds to be used for the purchase of classical books. Berkeley also gave to the library a thousand volumes, which cost over four hundred pounds—the most valuable collection of books then brought together in America. They were chiefly his own purchase, but in part contributed by his friends. One of the graduates of Yale, educated under the Berkeley scholarship, was Dr. Buckminster, of Portsmouth, N. H. Unfortunately, the income of the property at Newport is rendered much less than it might be by the terms of a long lease. This liberality of the Bishop of Cloyne was enhanced by the absence of sectarian prejudice in his choice for the stewardship of his bounty of a collegiate institution where different tenets are inculcated from those he professed. That he was personally desirous of increasing his own denomination in America, is sufficiently evinced by the letter in which he directs the secretary of the Episcopal mission there to appropriate a balance originally contributed to the Bermuda scheme. This sum had remained at his banker's for many years unclaimed, and he suggests that part of it should be devoted to a gift of books for Harvard University, 'as a proper means to inform their judgment, and dispose them to think better of our church.' His interest in classical education on this side of the water is also manifested in a letter advocating the preëminence of those studies in Columbia College.*

It is a remarkable coincidence that Berkeley should have taken up his abode in Rhode Island, and thus completed the representative character of the most tolerant religious community in New England, by the presence of an eminent Episcopal dignitary. A principal reason of the variety, the freedom, and the peace of religious opinion there, to which he alludes, is the fact that, through the liberal wisdom and foresight of Roger Williams, that State had become an asylum for the persecuted of all denominations from the neighboring provinces; but another cause may be found in the prevalence of the Quakers, whose amiable tenets and gentle spirit subdued the rancor and bigotry of fanaticism. Several hundred Jews, still commemorated by their cemetery and synagogue, allured by the prosperous trade and the tolerant genius of the place, added still another feature to the varied population. The lenity of Penn toward the aborigines, and the fame of Fox, had given dignity to the denomination of Friends, and their domestic culture was refined as well as morally superior. Enterprise in the men who, in a neighboring State, originated the whale fishery, and beauty among the women of that sect, are traditional in Rhode Island. We were reminded of Berkeley's observations in regard to the natural productions of the country, during a recent visit to the old farmhouse where he resided. An enormous wild grapevine had completely veiled what formed the original

---

* "I am glad to find a spirit toward learning prevails in these parts, particularly in New York, where, you say, a college is projected, which has my best wishes. Let the Greek and Latin classics be well taught; be this the first care as to learning."—BERKELEY's *Letter to Johnson*.—MOORE's *Sketch of Columbia College, New York*, 1846.

entrance to the humble dwelling; and several ancient apple trees in the orchard, with boughs mossy with time, and gnarled by the ocean gales, showed, in their sparse fruit and matted twigs, the utter absence of the pruning knife. The dwelling itself is built, after the manner common to farmhouses a century ago, entirely of wood, with low ceilings, broad fireplace, and red cornice. The only traces of the old country were a few remaining tiles, with obsolete designs, around the chimney piece. But the deep and crystal azure of the sea gleamed beyond corn field and sloping pasture; sheep grazed in the meadows, hoary rocks bounded the prospect, and the mellow crimson of sunset lay warm on grass slope and paddock, as when the kindly philosopher mused by the shore with Plato in hand, or noted a metaphysical dialogue in the quiet and ungarnished room which overlooks the rude garden. Though, as he declares, 'for every private reason' he preferred 'Derry to New England,' pleasant was the abode, and grateful is the memory of Berkeley, in this rural seclusion. A succession of green breastworks along the brow of the hill beneath which his domicile nestles, by reminding the visitor of the retreat of the American forces under General Sullivan, brings vividly to his mind the Revolution, and its incalculable influence upon the destinies of a land which so early won the intelligent sympathy of Berkeley; while the name of Whitehall, which he gave to this peaceful domain, commemorates that other revolution in his own country, wherein the loyalty of his grandfather drove his family into exile. But historical soon yield to personal recollections, when we consider the memorials of his sojourn. We associate this landscape with his studies and his benevolence; and, when the scene was no longer blessed with his presence, his gifts remained to consecrate his memory. In old Trinity, the organ he bestowed peals over the grave of his firstborn in the adjoining burial ground. A town in Massachusetts bears his name. Not long since, a presentation copy of his 'Minute Philosopher' was kept on the table of an old lady of Newport, with reverential care. In one family, his gift

of a richly wrought silver coffee pot, and, in another, that of
a diamond ring, are cherished heirlooms. His rare and costly
books were distributed at his departure, among the resident
clergy. His scholarship at New Haven annually furnishes
recruits to our church, bar, or medical faculty. In an adjacent parish, the sacramental cup was his donative. His leg-
acy of ingenious thoughts and benign sentiment is associated
with hanging rocks that are the seaward boundary of his
farm; his Christian ministry with the ancient church, and
his verse with the progress of America."

A brave clerical resident of South Kingston, R. I., where
he died in 1757, wrote a brief but useful and interesting
account of the English settlements in America. He describes, in a series of letters, the Bermudas, Georgia, and the
northern dominions of the crown as far as Newfoundland.
As one of the founders of the Episcopal Church in America,
an intimate friend of Berkeley, and a respected and efficient
minister of Narraganset, the Rev. James McSparren's "Historical Tract" has a special authority and attraction.

One of the most pleasing and *naive* memorials of social
life in the province of New York in her palmy colonial days, is
to be found in the reminiscences of Mrs. Grant, a daughter of
Duncan McVickar, an officer of the British army, who came
to America on duty in 1757. This estimable lady, in the
freshness of her youth, resided in Albany, and was intimate
with Madam Schuyler, widow of Colonel Philip Schuyler, and
aunt to the general of the same name so prominent in the
war of the Revolution. The four years which Mrs. Grant
passed in America, made an indelible and charming impression on her mind. She married the Rev. James Grant, of
Laggan, Invernesshire, and, in 1801, was left a widow with
eight children. Nine years after, she removed to Edinburgh,
where she became the centre of a literary and friendly circle,
often graced by the presence of Sir Walter Scott and other
celebrities. He secured her a pension of a hundred pounds.
Mrs. Grant's conversation was of unusual interest, owing to
her long experience, and, for that period, varied reading.

She was ambitious of literary distinction. Her "Letters from the Mountains," for their descriptive ability and independent tone, won no inconsiderable popularity. Jeffrey remarks that her "poetry is not very good;" while Moir pays her the somewhat equivocal compliment of declaring that she "respectably assisted in sustaining the honors of the Scottish Muse." But she is chiefly remembered as a writer by her "Memoirs," and they have served many novelists, historians, and biographers as a little treasury of facts wherewith to delineate the life and the scenery of those days, not elsewhere obtainable. Notwithstanding his moderate estimate of her other literary efforts, Jeffrey gave Mrs. Grant credit, in the *Edinburgh Review*, for this autobiography, as "a very animated picture of that sort of simple, tranquil, patriarchal life, which was common enough within these hundred years in the central parts of England, but of which we are rather inclined to think there is no specimen left in the world." It was not, however, merely the reproduction of this attractive and primitive kind of life that lent a charm to these Memoirs. Many of the features of that Albany community, its habits, exigencies, and aspects, were novel and curious; and the lively record thereof from the vivid impressions of such a woman, at her susceptible age, gives us a remarkably clear though perhaps somewhat romantic idea of what the manorial and colonial life of the State of New York was, and wherein it differed from that of Virginia and New England.

In her day, the amiable and intelligent author of the "Memoirs of an American Lady" enjoyed no little social consideration from her literary efforts—unusual as such a distinction was with her sex at that period—and from her kindly and dignified character. De Quincey, when quite a youth, met her in a stage coach, and cherished very agreeable recollections of her manners. "I retain the impression," he writes, "of the benignity which she, an established wit, and just then receiving incense from all quarters, showed, in her manners, to me, a person utterly unknown."

According to Mrs. Grant,

"The summer amusements of the young were simple, healthful, and joyous. Their principal pleasure consisted in what we now call picnics, enjoyed either upon the beautiful islands in the river near Albany, which were then covered with grass and shrubbery, tall trees and clustering vines, or in the forests on the hills. When the warm days of spring and early summer appeared, a company of young men and maidens would set out at sunrise in a canoe for the islands, or in light wagons for 'the bush,' where they would frequently meet a similar party on the same delightful errand. Each maiden, taught from early childhood to be industrious, would take her work basket with her, and a supply of tea, sugar, coffee, and other materials for a frugal breakfast, while the young men carried some rum and dried fruit to make a light, cool punch for a midday beverage. But no previous preparations were made for dinner, except bread and cold pastry, it being expected that the young men would bring an ample supply of game and fish from the woods and the waters, provision having been made by the girls of apparatus for cooking, the use of which was familiar to them all. After dinner, the company would pair off in couples, according to attachments and affinities, sometimes brothers and sisters together, and sometimes warm friends or ardent lovers, and stroll in all directions, gathering wild strawberries or other fruit in summer, and plucking the abundant flowers, to be arranged into bouquets to adorn their little parlors and give much pleasure to their parents. Sometimes they would remain abroad until sunset, and take tea in the open air; or they would call upon some friend on their way home, and partake of a light evening meal. In all this there appeared no conventional restraints upon the innocent inclinations of nature. The day was always remembered as one of pure enjoyment, without the passage of a single cloud of regret."

In 1759–'60, a kindly and cultivated minister of the Church of England made a tour of intelligent observation in the Middle States; and fifteen years after, when the alienation of the colonies from Great Britain had passed from a speculative to a practical fact, this amiable divine gave to the public the narrative of his Amerian journey. There is a pleasant tone, a wise and educated spirit in this record, which make ample amends for the obvious influences of the writer's religious and political views upon his impressions of the country and the people. The Rev. Andrew Burnaby was a native of Lancashire, an *élève* of Westminster School, and a graduate of Queen's College, Cambridge. He became vicar of Greenwich in 1769, and obtained credit as an author by a volume of sermons, and an account of a visit to Corsica. His book on America was "praised and valued" as a fair and agreeable report of "the state of the colonies" then called the "Middle Settlements." The author states, in his preface, that its appearance during "the present difficulties" may expose him to misrepresentation; but he asserts the candor of his motives, and frankly declares that, while his "first attachment" is for his native country, his second is to America.

Burnaby landed from Chesapeake Bay, and his book (a thin quarto) opens with a description of Virginia, where he sojourned with Colonel Washington. He is struck with the efficiency of lightning rods, and the efficacy of snakeroot, and with the abundance of peaches, which are given as food to the hogs. He describes the variety of squirrels, the indigenous plants and birds, the ores and crops of the Old Dominion. The women there, he says, "are immoderately fond of dancing, and seldom read or endeavor to improve their minds." He notes the "prodigious tracts of land" belonging to individuals, and then a wilderness, and, like so many other travellers there, is impressed with the comparative improvident habits of the people. "The Virginians," he says, "are content to live from hand to mouth. Tobacco is their chief staple, and they cultivate enough to pay their merchants in London for supplying those wants which their plantations do not directly satisfy." On the other hand, he celebrates the virtuous contentment of the German settlers on the low grounds of the Shenandoah. Their freedom, tranquillity, and "few vices" atone, in his estimation, for the absence of elegance. He attended a theatre in a "tobacco house" at Marlborough, and enjoyed a sixteen hours' sail along the Chesapeake to Frederickstown. "Never," he writes, "in my life, have I spent a day more agreeably or with higher entertainment." Much of this zest is to be ascribed to the good clergyman's enjoyment of scenery, fresh air, and fine weather. The streams, the woods, and the mountains of the New World elicit his constant admiration. A salient trait of his journal is the positive character he confidently assigns to the inhabitants of the different colonies. Sometimes it is evident that their respective religious and political tendencies enlist or repel his sympathies, and therefore modify his judgment, but, at other times, his opinion seems to be the result of candid observation; and it is interesting to compare what he says on this subject, with later estimates and present local reputations. Of Philadelphia he remarks: "There is a public market held twice a week, almost equal to Leadenhall. The people there are quiet, and intent on money getting, and the women are decidedly handsome." He notes the stocking manufacture of the Germans, and the linen made by the Irish in Pennsylvania. He thinks the New Jersey people "of a more liberal turn than these neighbors of theirs," and is enthusiastic about the Falls of the Passaic. He recognizes but two *churches* in New York—Trinity and St. George's—and declares the women there "more reserved" than those of the colony of Penn. He speaks of a memorable social custom of New York— "turtle feasts," held at houses on the East River, where, also, ladies and gentlemen, to the number of thirty or forty, were in the habit of meeting "to drink tea in the afternoon," and return to town "in Italian chaises," one gentleman and one lady in each. The good doctor evidently is charmed with these snug arrangements for a legitimate *tête-à-tête*, and mentions, in connection therewith, a practice not accordant with the greater reserve he elsewhere attributes to the New York belles. "In the way" (from these turtle feasts and tea drinkings), "about three miles from New York, there is a bridge, which you pass over as you return, called the Kissing Bridge, where it is part of the etiquette to salute the lady who has put herself under your protection."

Like most Englishmen, Burnaby finds a rare combination of scenery, climate, and resources on Long Island, and makes especial mention of one feature. "About sixteen miles from the west end of it there opens a large plain, between twenty and thirty miles long and four or five miles broad. There is not a tree growing upon it, and it is asserted there never was. Strangers are always carried to see this plain, as a great curiosity, and the only one of the kind in North America." What would he have thought of a Western prairie?

He is reminded in Hellgate of Scylla and Charybdis; and the aspect and climate of Newport, R. I., charm him. "There is a public library here," he writes, "built in the form of a Grecian temple, and by no means inelegant." The Quakers, the Jews, and the fortified islands are duly noted; but the multiplicity of sects in the Providence Plantations evidently does not conciliate the doctor's favorable opinion. He speaks of the buttonwood trees, then so numerous and flourishing on the island; "spruce pines," and the beer made from their "tender twigs;" of the abundant and excellent fish, and hardy sheep, as well as of the superior butter and cheese. Of Newport commerce then, he says: "They import from Holland, money; from Great Britain, drygoods; from Africa, slaves; from the West Indies, sugar, coffee, and molasses; and from the neighboring colonies, lumber and provisions." Of manufactures he observes, "they distil rum, and make spermaceti candles." The people of Rhode Island, he declares, "are cunning, deceitful, and selfish, and live by unfair and illicit trading. The magistrates are partial and corrupt, and wink at abuses." All this he ascribes to their form of government; for "men in power entirely depend on the people, and it has happened more than once that a person has had influence to procure a fresh emission of paper money solely to defraud his creditors." It is obvious that the Churchman leans toward the Proprietary form of rule then existent in Maryland, and the manorial state of society farther south; but he concludes his severe criticism of the Rhode Islanders with a candid qualification: "I have said so much to the disadvantage of this colony, that I should be guilty of great injustice were I not to declare that there are many worthy gentlemen in it." Although forty years had elapsed since the benevolent and ingenious Bishop of Cloyne had left Newport, the beneficent traces of his presence and the anecdotical traditions of his character still prevailed among the people. Burnaby thus alludes to the subject: "About three miles from town is an indifferent wooden house, built by Dean Berkeley when he was in these parts. The situation is low, but commands a fine view of the ocean, and of some wild, rugged rocks that are on the left hand of it. They relate here several strange stories of the dean's wild and chimerical notions, which, as they are characteristic of that extraordinary man, deserve to be taken notice of. One in particular I must beg the reader's indulgence to allow me to repeat to him. The dean had formed the plan of building a town upon the rocks which I have just taken note of, and of cutting a road through a sandy beach which lies a little below it, in order that ships might come up and be sheltered in bad weather. He was so full of this project, as one day to say to Smibert, a designer whom he had brought over with him from Europe, on the latter's asking him some ludicrous question concerning the future importance of the place, 'Truly you have little foresight; for, in fifty years, every foot of land in this place will be as valuable as land in Cheapside.' The dean's house," continues Burnaby, "notwithstanding his prediction, is at present nothing more than a farmhouse, and his library is converted into a dairy. When he left America, he gave it to the college in New Haven, Connecticut, which have let it to a family on a long lease. His books he divided between this college and that of Massachusetts. The dean is said to have written the 'Minute Philosopher' in this place."

Conservative Dr. Burnaby was not so perspicacious as he thought, when he thus reasoned of Berkeley's views of the growth in value of the region he loved. However mistaken as regards the specific locality and period, he was essentially right as to the spirit of his prophecy—as the price of desirable "lots" and the value of landed property in Newport now evidence. Herein, as in that more comprehensive prediction which foretold the westward course of empire, the good and gifted dean exhibited the prescience of a benignant genius.

Burnaby, like countless other visitors, was delighted with the country around Boston. He notes the two "batteries of sixteen and twenty guns built by Mr. Shirley," and is struck, in 1770—as was Dickens, eighty years after—with the resemblance between the New England capital and the "best country towns in England." Indeed, natives of the former recognize in Worcester, Eng., many of the familiar local traits of Boston, U. S. Our clerical traveller has an eye for the picturesque, and expatiates on the "unsurpassed prospect" from Beacon Hill. He thus enumerates the public edifices then there: "The Governor's palace, fourteen meeting houses, the Court House, Faneuil's Hall, the linen manufactory, the workhouse, the Bridewell, the public granary, and a very fine wharf at least a mile long." In architecture he gives the palm to King's Chapel, but significantly records the building of an Episcopal church near the neighboring university, that was long a beautiful exception to the "wooden lanterns" which constituted, in colonial times, the shrines of New England faith. "A church has been lately erected at Cambridge, within sight of the college, which has greatly alarmed the Congregationalists, who consider it the most fatal stroke that could possibly be levelled at their religion. The building is elegant, and the minister of it—the Rev. Mr. Apthorp—is a very amiable young gentleman, of shining parts, great learning, and engaging manners." Well considered, the details of this statement singularly illustrate the ecclesiastical prestige and prejudice of the day. Burnaby recognizes quite a different style of manners and mode of action in the Puritan metropolis from those which characterized the Cavalier, the Quaker, or the Dutch colony before visited. "The character of this province is much improved in comparison with what it was; but Puritanism and a spirit of persecution are not yet totally extinguished. The gentry of both sexes are hospitable and good-natured: there is an air of civility in their behavior, but it is constrained by formality and preciseness. Even the women, though easiness of carriage is peculiarly characteristic of their nature, appear here with more stiffness and reserve than in the other colonies. They are formed with symmetry, are handsome, and have fair and delicate complexions, but are said universally, and even proverbially, to have very indifferent teeth. The lower orders are impertinently curious and inquisitive." He records some singular, obsolete, and scarcely credible customs, which, with other of his observations, are confirmed by Anbury, and other writers, who visited New England a few years later. The strict if not superstitious observance of the Sabbath in New England has been often made the theme of foreign visitors; but Burnaby gives us a curious illustration both of the custom and its results. He says that a captain of a merchant vessel, having reached the wharf at Boston on Sunday, was there met and affectionately greeted by his wife; which human behavior, on Sunday, so outraged the "moral sense of the community," that the captain was arrested, tried, and publicly whipped for the offence. Apparently acquiescing in the justice of his punishment, he continued on pleasant terms with his numerous acquaintances after its infliction, and, when quite prepared to sail, invited them to a *fête* on board; and, when they were cheerfully taking leave, had the whole party seized, stripped to the waist, and forty lashes bestowed on each by the boatswain's cat-o'-nine-tails, amid the acclamations of his crew; after which summary act of retaliation he dismissed his smarting guests, and instantly set sail.

At the close of his book,* the Rev. Andrew Burnaby, D. D., Vicar of Greenwich, expresses some general opinions in regard to the colonies, which are noteworthy as the honest impressions of a candid scholar and amiable divine, received nearly a century ago, while traversing a region wherein an unparalleled development, social, political, and economical,

* "Travels through the Middle Settlements of North America, 1759–'60," 4to., London, 1775.

has since occurred. "America," he declares, "is formed for happiness, but not for empire." The average prosperity of the people made a deep impression. "In a course of twelve hundred miles," he writes, "I did not see a single object that solicited charity." He was convinced that the latent elements of discord and division already existed. "Our colonies," he remarks, "may be distinguished into Southern and Northern, separated by the Susquehanna and that imaginary line which divides Maryland from Pennsylvania. The Southern colonies have so many inherent causes of weakness, that they never can possess any real strength. The climate operates very powerfully upon them, and renders them indolent, inactive, and unenterprising. I myself have been a spectator of a man, in the vigor of life, lying upon a couch, and a female slave standing over him, wafting off the flies, and fanning him. These Southern colonies will never be thickly settled, except Maryland. Industrial occupation militates with their position, being considered as the inheritance and badge of slavery." The worthy author also seriously doubts if "it will be possible to keep in due order and government so wide and extended an empire." He dwells upon the "difficulties of intercourse, communication, and correspondence." He thinks "a voluntary coalition almost difficult to be supposed." "Fire and water," he declares, "are not more heterogeneous than the different colonies of America." It is curious to note wherein these diversities were then thought to lie. Dr. Burnaby tells us that Pennsylvania and New York were mutually jealous of the trade of New Jersey; that Massachusetts and Rhode Island were equally contentious for that of Connecticut; that the commerce of the West Indies was "a common subject of emulation," and that the "bounds of each colony were a constant source of litigation." He expatiates upon the inherent differences of manners, religion, character, and interests, as an adequate cause of civil war, if the colonies were left to themselves; in which case he predicts that both the Indian and the negro race would "watch their chance to exterminate all." Against external foes he is of opinion that maritime power is the exclusive available defence. "Suppose," he writes, "them (the colonies) capable of maintaining one hundred thousand men constantly in arms (a supposition in the highest degree extravagant), half a dozen frigates could ravage the whole country;" for it is "so intersected with rivers of such magnitude as to render it impossible to build bridges over them, and all communication is thus cut off." The greater part of America's wealth, when Burnaby wrote, according to his observations, "depended upon the fisheries, and commerce with the West Indies." He considered England's best policy "to enlarge the present, not to make new colonies; for, to suppose interior colonies to be of use to the mother country by being a check upon those already settled, is to suppose what is contrary to experience—that men removed beyond the reach of power, will be subordinate to it." From speculations like these, founded, as they are, in good sense, and suggested by the facts of the hour, we may infer how great and vital have been the progressive change and the assimilative process whereby enlarged commercial relations have doomed to oblivion petty local rivalries, mutual and comprehensive interests fused widely-separated communities, and the application of steam to locomotion brought together regions which once appeared too widely severed ever to own a common object of pursuit or sentiment of nationality. The Revolutionary War, the naval triumphs, the system of internal improvements and communication, the agricultural, commercial, and manufacturing growth of the United States, in eighty years, are best realized when the present is compared with such authentic records of the past as honest Dr. Burnaby has left us. Yet the events of the passing hour not less emphatically suggest how truly he indicated the essential difficulties of the social and civic problem to be solved on this continent, when he described the antagonism of the systems of labor prevalent in the North and South.

"A Concise View of North America,"[*] by Major Robert

[*] "A Concise Account of North America, and the British Colonies, Indian Tribes, &c.," by Major Robert Rogers, 8vo., 1765.

Rogers, published in London in 1765, contains some general information; chiefly, however, but a meagre outline, which subsequent writers have filled up. The unhealthiness and mosquitos of the Carolinas seem to have annoyed him physically, and the intolerance of the "New Haven Colony" morally. He finds much in the natural resources, but little in the actual life of the country to extol; and gives the following sombre picture of Rhode Island, which forms an entire contrast to the more genial impression which Bishop Berkeley recorded of his sojourn there:

" There are in this colony men of almost every persuasion in the world. The greater number are Quakers, and many have no religion at all, or, at least, profess none; on which account no questions are asked, each man being left pretty much to think and act for himself—of which neither the laws nor his neighbors take much cognizance: so greatly is their liberty degenerated into licentiousness. This province is infested with a rascally set of Jews, who fail not to take advantage of the great liberty here granted to men of all professions and religions, and are a pest not only to this, but to the neighboring provinces. There is not a free school in the whole colony, and the education of children is generally shamefully neglected."

Two works on America appeared in London in 1760-'61, which indicate that special information in regard to this country was, then and there, sufficiently a desideratum to afford a desirable theme for a bookseller's job. The first of these was edited by no less a personage than Edmund Burke;* and somewhat of the interest he afterward manifested in the rights and prospects of our country, may be traced to the research incident to this publication, which was issued under the title of "European Settlements in America." It was one of those casual tasks undertaken by Burke before he had risen to fame: like all compilations executed with a view to emolument rather than inspired by personal taste, these two respectable but somewhat dull volumes seem to have made little impression upon the public. They succinctly describe

* "Account of the European Settlements in America," by Edmund Burke, 2 vols., 8vo. maps, London, 1757.

the West India Islands, the Mississippi and Ohio rivers, the colonies of Louisiana, and the French, Dutch, and English settlements, the rise and progress of Puritanism, and the persecution and emigration of its votaries. With reference to the latter, considerable statistical information is given in regard to New England, and the colonial history of Pennsylvania, Virginia, Maryland, and the Carolinas sketched. Trade, laws, natural history, political views, productions, &c., are dwelt upon; and, as a book of reference at the time, the work doubtless proved useful. It appeared anonymously, with the imprint of Dodsley, who issued a fourth edition in 1766.

"The affairs of America," says Burke, in his preface, "have lately engaged a great deal of public attention. Before the present hour there were very few who made the history of that quarter of the world any part of their study. The history of a country which, though vast in itself, is the property of only four nations, and which, though peopled probably for a series of ages, is only known to the rest of the world for about two centuries, does not naturally afford matter for many volumes." He adds, that, to gain the knowledge thus brought together, "a great deal of reading has been found requisite." He remarks, also, that "whatever is written by the English settlers in our colonies is to be read with great caution," because of the "bias of interest for a particular province." He found most of these records "dry and disgusting reading, and loaded with a lumber of matter;" yet observes that "the matter is very curious in itself, and extremely interesting to us as a trading people." Although irksome, he seems to have fulfilled his task with conscientious care, "comparing printed accounts with the best private information;" but calls attention to the fact that "in some-places the subject refuses all ornament." He acknowledges his obligation to Harris's "Voyages."

It is interesting, after having glanced at this early compendium of American resources, history, and local traits—the work of a young and obscure but highly gifted Irish *letterateur*—to turn to the same man's plea, in the days of his oratorical renown and parliamentary eminence, for that distant but rapidly growing country. "England, sir," said Burke, in the House of Commons, in 1775, in his speech on conciliation with America, "England is a nation which still, I hope, respects, and formerly adored her freedom. The colonists emigrated from you when this part of your character was most predominant; and they took this bias and direction the moment they parted from your hands. They are, therefore, not only devoted to liberty, but to liberty according to English ideas, and on English principles;"—and, in allusion to the whale fishery, "neither the perseverance of Holland, nor the activity of France, nor the dexterity and firm sagacity of English enterprise, ever carried this most perilous mode of hardy industry to the extent to which it has been pushed by this recent people—a people who are still in the gristle, not yet hardened into the bone of manhood."

The other current book of reference, although of somewhat earlier date, was the combined result of personal observation and research, and, in the first respect, had the advantage of Burke's compilation. It is curious to remember, as we examine its now neglected pages, that when "Rasselas" and the "Vicar of Wakefield" were new novels, and the "Traveller" the fresh poem of the day, the cotemporaries of Johnson, Goldsmith, and Burke, as they dropped in at Dodsley's, in Pall Mall, found there, as the most full and recent account of North America, the "Summary, Historical and Political, of the First Planting, Progressive Improvements, and Present State of the British Settlements in North America, by William Douglass, M. D." * There is much information, especially historical, in these two volumes, although most of it has long since been elaborated in more finished annals. Here is the story of the Dutch East India trade; of the Scots' Darien Company, which forms so graphic an episode of Macaulay's posthumous volume; of the Spanish dis-

---

* "Summary, Historical and Political, of the First planting, Progressive Improvement, and Present State of the British Settlements in America," by Dr. William Douglass 2 vols. 8vo., London, 1755.

coveries and settlements, and of the Hudson's Bay Company.
The voyages of Cabot, Frobisher, Gilbert, Davis, Hudson,
Middleton, Dobbs, Button, James, Baffin, and Fox, are briefly
sketched. On the subject of the whale and cod fisheries,
numerous details, both historical and statistical, are given.
The "Mississippi Bubble" is described, and the Canadian expedition under Sir William Phipps, in 1690, as well as the
reduction of Port Royal in 1710. Each State of New England is delineated, as well as New York, Pennsylvania, New
Jersey, and Virginia; and what is said of the Indians, of
sects, of boundaries, polity, witchcraft, currency, colleges,
scenery, and products, though either without significance or
too familiar to interest the reader of to-day, must have
proved seasonable knowledge to Englishmen then meditating
emigration to America. The author of this "Summary"
was a Scotchman by birth, who long practised his profession
in Boston. He seems to have attained no small degree of
professional eminence. He published a treatise on small
pox in 1722, and one on epidemic fever in 1736. The most
original remarks in his work relate to local diseases, and his
medical digressions are frequent. He remarks, in stating the
diverse condition of the people of old and New England,
that the children of the latter " are more forward and precocious; their longevity is more rare, and their fecundity identical." He enumerates the causes of chronic distempers in
America, independent of constitutional defects, as being bad
air and soil, indolence, and intemperance. The worthy doctor, though an industrious seeker after knowledge, appears to
have indulged in strong prejudices and partialities according
to the tendency of an eager temperament; so that it is often
requisite to make allowance for his personal inferences. He
was warmly attached to his adopted country, and naively
admits, in the preface to his work, that, in one instance, his
statements must be reconsidered, having been expressed
with a "somewhat passionate warmth and indiscretion"
merely in affection to Boston and the country of New
England, his *altera patria*. Dr. Douglass died in 1752.

His work on the "British Settlements in North America" was originally published in numbers, at Boston, between January and May, 1749, forming the first volume; the second in 1753; and both first appeared in London in 1755. The work was left incomplete at the author's death. An improved edition was issued by Dodsley in 1760. Adam Smith calls him "the honest and downright Dr. Douglass;" but adds that, in "his history of the American colonies he is often incorrect; and it was his foible to measure the worth of men by his personal friendship for them."

Chancellor Kent, in a *catalogue raisonné* he kindly drew up for the use of a Young Men's Association, commended to their attention the "Travels and Adventures of Alexander Henry,"* a fur trader, and a native of New Jersey, who, between the years 1760 and 1776, travelled in the northwest part of America, and, in 1809, published an account of this long and remarkable experience. Confessedly "a premature attempt to share in the fur trade of Canada directly on the conquest of the country, led him into situations of some danger and singularity"—quite a modest way of stating a series of hazards, artifices, privations, and successes, enough to furnish material for a more complacent writer to excite the wonder and sympathy of a larger audience than he strove to win. In the year 1760 he accompanied General Amherst's expedition, which, after the conquest of Quebec, descended from Oswego to Fort Levi, on Lake Ontario. They lost three boats and their cargoes, and nearly lost their lives, in the rapids. Much curious information in regard to the Indians, the risks and method of the fur trade, and the adventurous phases of border life in the northwest, may be found in this ingenious narrative. Henry's "enterprise, intrepidity, and perils," says Kent, "excite the deepest interest."

Forty letters,† written between 1769 and 1777, by William

---

* "Travels and Adventures in Canada and the Indian Territory, between the Years 1760 and 1776," New York, 1809.

† "Letters from America, Historical and Descriptive, comprising Occurrences from 1769 to 1777, inclusive," by William Eddis, 8vo., 1792.

Eddis, and published in London in 1792, contain numerous statistical and historical facts not elsewhere obtainable. The author's position as surveyor of the customs at Annapolis, in Maryland, gave him singular advantages as an observer; and his letters are justly considered as the "best account we have of the rise of Revolutionary principles in Maryland," and have been repeatedly commended to historical students by British and American critics, although their details are so unfavorable to the former, and so full of political promise to the latter. The writer discusses trade, government, manners, and climate, and traces the progress of the civil dissensions which ended in the separation of the colonies from the mother country.

If from an urbane French officer and ally we turn to the record of an English *militaire*, whose views of men and things we naturally expect to be warped by political animosity and the fact that many of his letters were written while he was a prisoner of war, it is an agreeable surprise to find, with occasional asperity, much candid intelligence and interesting local information. Thomas Anbury was an officer in Burgoyne's army, and his "Travels in the Interior of America" was published in London in 1789. He tells us that the lower classes of the New Englanders are impertinently curious and inquisitive; that a "live lord" excited the wonderment of the country people, and disappointed their expectations then as now. He complains of Congress as "ready to grasp at any pretence, however weak, to evade the terms of the convention;" but, at the same time, he commends the absence of any unmanly exultation on the part of the Americans at Burgoyne's surrender. "After we had piled our arms," he writes, "and our march was settled, as we passed the American army, I did not observe the least disrespect, or even a taunting look; all was mute astonishment and pity." He sympathizes with the sorrowful gratification of a bereaved mother, to whom one of his brother officers restored her son's watch, which the British soldiers had purloined from his body on the battle field. He writes of the bright plumage of the hummingbird, and the musical cry of the whippoorwill; the grandeur of the Hudson, and the grace of the Passaic Falls. He notes some curious and now obsolete New England customs, and describes the process of cider making, and the topography of Boston; in which vicinity he experienced all the rigor of an old-fashioned winter in that latitude, the dreariness of which, however, seems to have been essentially relieved by the frolicking sleigh rides of the young people. In one of his letters, dated Cambridge, where he was quartered for many weeks, he thus speaks of that academic spot as it appeared during the Revolution:

"The town of Cambridge is about six miles from Boston, and was the country residence of the gentry of that city. There are a number of fine houses in it going to decay, belonging to the Loyalists. The town must have been extremely pleasant; but its beauty is much defaced, being now only an arsenal for military stores: and you may suppose it is no agreeable circumstance, every time we walk out, to be reminded of our situation, in beholding the artillery and ammunition wagons that were taken with our army. The character of the inhabitants of this province is improved beyond the description that our uncle B—— gave us of them, when he quitted the country, thirty years ago; but Puritanism and the spirit of persecution are not yet totally extinguished. The gentry of both sexes are hospitable and good-natured, with an air of civility, but constrained by formality and preciseness. The women are stiff and reserved, symmetrical, and have delicate complexions; the men are tall, thin, and generally long-visaged. Both sexes have universally bad teeth, which must probably be occasioned by their eating so much molasses."

Although a more genial social atmosphere now pervades the comparatively populous city, since endeared by so many gifted and gracious names identified with literature and science, the "stiffness" of Cambridge parties was long proverbial; and an artist who attended one, after years of sojourn in Southern Europe, declared his fair partner in a solemn quadrille touched his hand, in "crossing over," with a reticence so instinctively cautious as to remind him of "a boy feeling for cucumbers in the dark." The defective teeth then so characteristic of Americans, which Anbury attributes to the use of molasses, was noticed by other foreign visitors, and more justly ascribed to the climate, and its effect upon the whole constitution. It is owing, perhaps, to the greater need of superior dental science on this side of the water, that it subsequently attained such perfection, and that the most skilful American practitioners thereof not only abound at home, but are preferred in Europe. A Virginian, to whom this writer complained of the inquisitiveness and exacting local pride of the people, advised him to avoid it by an anticipatory address to every new set of acquaintance, as follows: "Ladies and gentlemen, I am named Thomas Anbury. It is no little mortification that I cannot visit Boston, for it is the second city of America, and the grand emporium of rebellion; but our parole excludes us from it."

Despite an occasional sleigh ride along the Mystic and the Charles, some interesting phases of nature that beguiled his observant mind, and the hospitable treatment he frequently received, we cannot wonder that he found renewing his "pass" every month, and the monotonous limits of his winter quarters, irksome; so that every morning, with his comrades, he eagerly gazed "from their barracks to the mouth of Boston harbor, hoping to catch sight of the fleet of transports that was to convey them to England."

A striking illustration of the influence of Tory prejudice and disappointment, immediately after the successful termination of the War of Independence, may be found in the Travels of J. F. D. Smythe.* The work was published by subscription, and among the list of patrons are many names of the nobility and officers of the British army. The writer professes to be actuated by a desire to gratify public curiosity about a country which has just passed through an "extraordinary revolution." He declares it a painful task "to mention the hardships and severities" he had undergone in the cause of loyalty and the pursuit of knowledge. He disclaims ill will, having "no resentments to indulge, no revenge

* "A Tour in the United States of America," by J. F. D. Smythe, Esq., London, 1784.

to pursue;" and adds, "The few instances I have met with of kind and generous treatment, have afforded me infinite gratification." The occasion and motive of his publication are thus stated: "Having lately arrived from America, where I had made extensive journeys, and fatiguing, perilous expeditions, prompted by unbounded curiosity and an insatiable enthusiasm for knowledge, during a residence in that country for a considerable length of time, I had become perfectly reconciled and habituated to the manners, customs, dispositions, and sentiments of the inhabitants." He conceived himself peculiarly fitted to describe and discuss the new republic. Moreover, he was dissatisfied with all that had been published on the subject. "I eagerly sought out and pursued," he observes, "with a degree of avidity rarely felt, every treatise and publication relating to America, from the first discovery by the immortal Columbus to Carver's late travels therein, and even the 'Pennsylvania Farmer's Letters,' by Mr. Hector St. John, if, indeed, such a person ever existed; but always had the extreme mortification to meet with disappointment in my expectations, every one grasping at and enlarging on the greater objects, and not a single author descending to the minutiæ, which compose as well the true perspective as the real intercourse and commerce of life." He bespeaks the kindly judgment of his readers for a work "written without ornament or elegance, and perhaps, in some respects, not perfectly accurate, being composed under peculiarly disadvantageous circumstances." The latter excuse is the best. Baffled and chagrined in his personal aspirations, and having suffered capture, imprisonment, and, according to his own account, some wanton cruelty; remembering the privations and dangers of travel in a new, and exposure in an inimical country, shattered by illness, and, above all, mortified at the ignominious failure of the Royal cause, he writes with bitter prejudice and exaggerated antipathy, despite the show of candor exhibited in the preface. Nor can we find in his work, as a literary or scientific performance, any just reason for his depreciation of his predecessors. He may note a few circumstances overlooked by them, but, on the score of accurate and fresh information, there is little value in the physical details he gives; while the political and social are so obviously jaundiced by partisan spite as to be of limited significance. Indeed, there is cause to suspect that Mr. Smythe was not infrequently quizzed by his informants; and his best reports are of agricultural and topographical facts. His "Travels in America," therefore, are now more curious than valuable: they give us a vivid idea of the perverse and prejudiced commentaries in vogue at the period among the least magnanimous of the Tory faction. He, like others of his class, was struck with the "want of subordination among the people." He descants on the "breed of running horses" in Virginia. The bullfrogs, mosquitos, flying squirrels, fossil remains, and lofty timber; the wheat, corn, sugar, cotton, and other crops; the characteristics of different Indian tribes; the clearings, the new settlements, the hospitality, splendid landscapes, and "severe treatment of the negroes;" the handsome women, the "accommodations not suited to an epicure," the modes of farming, the habits of planters and riflemen, the extent and character of the large rivers, the capacity of soils, and the behavior of different classes, &c., form his favorite topics of description and discussion, varied by inklings of adventure and severe experiences as a fugitive and a prisoner. He tells us of the "harems of beautiful slaves" belonging to the Jesuit establishment in Maryland; of being "attacked by an itinerant preacher;" of the "painful sensation of restraint" experienced from the "gloom of the woods;" of his horse "refusing to eat bacon;" and of the "formal circumlocution" of a wayside acquaintance, evidently better endowed with humor than himself. In these and similar themes his record assimilates with many others written at the time; but what give it peculiar emphasis, are the political comments and prophecies —very curious to recall now, in the light of subsequent events and historical verdicts. "I have no wish to widen the breach," he says; "but the illiberal and vindictive principles of the prevailing party" in America, seem to him fatal to any hearty reconciliation between the mother country and her wayward and enfranchised offspring. So absolutely is his moral perception obscured, that he deliberately maligns a character whose immaculate purity even enemies then recognized with delight. "It was at Alexandria," he writes, "that George Washington first stepped forth as the public patron and leader of sedition, having subscribed fifty pounds where others subscribed only five, and having accepted the command of the first company of armed associates against the British Government." So far we have only the statement of a political antagonist; but when, in the retrospect of his career as military chieftain and civic leader, he thus estimates the man whose disinterestedness had already become proverbial, we recognize the absolute perversity of this professedly candid writer:

"Mr. Washington has uniformly cherished and steadfastly pursued an apparently mild, steady, but aspiring line of conduct, and views of the highest ambition, under the most specious of all cloaks —that of moderation, which he invariably appeared to possess. His total want of generous sentiments, and even of common humanity, has appeared notoriously in many instances, and in none more than in his sacrifice of the meritorious but unfortunate Major André. Nor during his life has he ever performed a single action that could entitle him to the least show of merit, much less of glory; but as a politician he has certainly distinguished himself, having, by his political manœuvres, and his cautious, plausible management, raised himself to a degree of eminence in his own country unrivalled, and of considerable stability. In his private character he has always been respectable."

As a specimen of Tory literature, this portrait forms a singular and suggestive contrast with those sketched of the same illustrious subject by Chastellux, Guizot, Erskine, Brougham, Everett, and so many other brilliant writers. It is easy to imagine what discouraging views of the new republic such a man would take, after this evidence of his moral perspicacity and mental discrimination. Yet Mr. Smythe was of a sentimental turn. There are verses in his

American Travels, "written in solitude," not, indeed, equal to Shelley's; and, when incarcerated, he inscribed rhymes with charcoal on his prison wall. We must make due allowance for the wounded sensibilities of a man who had been the victim of a "brutal Dutch guard," a "robber of the mountain," and a "barbarous jailer," when he tells us that the "fatal termination of the war," and the "consequences of separation from Great Britain and alliance with France," are "inauspicious for both countries." According to Mr. Smythe, the Americans were "corrupted by French gold," and entered into an "affected amity with that artful, perfidious, and gaudy people." He prophesies that "when the intoxication of success is over, they will repent their error." Meantime, he pleads earnestly for the Loyalists, declares America rapidly becoming depopulated on account of its "unsettled government" and the check of emigration, and, altogether, an "unfit place of residence."

CHAPTER VI.

BRITISH TRAVELLERS AND WRITERS CONTINUED.

WANSEY; COOPER; WILSON; DAVIS; ASHE; BRISTED; KENDALL; WELD; COBBETT; CAMPBELL; BYRON; MOORE; MRS. WAKEFIELD; HODGSON; JANSEN; CASWELL; HOLMES, AND OTHERS; HALL; FEARON; FIDDLER; LYELL; FEATHERSTONAUGH; COMBE; FEMALE WRITERS; DICKENS; FAUX; HAMILTON; PARKINSON; MRS. TROLLOPE; GRATTAN; LORD CARLISLE; ANTHONY TROLLOPE; PRENTICE; STIRLING.

If, in early colonial times, North America was sought as a refuge from persecution and a scene of adventurous exploration, and, during the French and Revolutionary wars, became an arena for valorous enterprise; when peace smiled upon the newly organized Government of the United States, they allured quite another class of visitors—those who sought to ascertain, by personal observation, the actual facilities which the New World offered, whereby the unfortunate could redeem and the intrepid and dexterous advance their position and resources. Hence intelligent reporters of industrial and social opportunities were welcomed in Europe, and especially among the manufacturers, agriculturists, and traders of Britain; and these later records differ from the earlier in more specific data and better statistical information. To the American reader of the present day they are chiefly attractive as affording facts and figures whereby the development of the country can be distinctly traced from the adoption of the Federal Constitution to the present time, and a salient contrast afforded between the modes of life and the aspect of places sixty years ago and to-day. The vocation, social rank, and personal objects of these writers so modify their observations, that, in almost every instance, allowance must be made for the partialities and prejudices, the limited knowledge or the self-love of the journalist and letter writer; yet, as their aim usually is to impart such information as will be of practical benefit to those who contemplate emigration, curious and interesting details, economical and social, may often be gleaned from their pages. One of these books, which was quite popular in its day, and is still occasionally quoted, is that of Wansey, which was published in 1794, and subsequently reprinted here.* His voyage across the Atlantic was far from agreeable, and not without serious privations. Indeed, nothing more remarkably indicates the progress of comfort and luxury within the last half century, than the speed and plentiful resources wherewith the visitor to America now makes the transit. Wansey, as was the custom then, furnished his own napkins, bedding, and extras for the voyage; his account of which closes with the remark, that "there does not exist a more sordid, penurious race than the captains of passage and merchant vessels." Yet a nobler class of men than the American packet captains of a subsequent era never adorned the merchant service of any nation.

Henry Wansey, F. S. A., was an English manufacturer, and his visit to America had special reference to his vocation. He notes our then very limited enterprise in this sphere, and examined the quality and cost of wool in several of the States. On the 8th of June, 1794, he breakfasted with Washington at Philadelphia. "I confess," he writes, "I was struck with awe and veneration. The President seemed very thoughtful, and was slow in delivering himself, which in-

---

* "An Excursion to the United States, in the Summer of 1794," by Henry Wansey; with a curious profile portrait of Washington, and a view of the State House in Philadelphia, 12mo., pp. 280, Salisbury, 1798.

duced some to believe him reserved; but it was rather, I apprehend, the result of much reflection; for he had, to me, the appearance of affability and accommodation. He was, at this time, in his sixty-third year, but had very little the appearance of age, having been all his life exceedingly temperate. There was a certain anxiety visible in his countenance, with marks of extreme sensibility."

Wansey, like most visitors at that period, was struck with the great average of health, intelligence, and contentment among the people. "In these States," he writes, "you behold a certain plainness and simplicity of manners, equality of condition, and a sober use of the faculties of the mind. It is seldom you hear of a madman or a blind man in any of the States; seldom of a *felo de se*, or a man afflicted with the gout or palsy. There is, indeed, at Philadelphia, a hospital for lunatics. I went over it, but found there very few, if any, that were natives. They were chiefly Irish, and mostly women." What an illustration of our present eagerness for wealth and office—of the encroachments of prosperity upon simple habits and chastened feelings—is the fact that now insanity is so prevalent as to be characteristic, and that a "sober use of the faculties of the mind" is the exception, not the rule, of American life!

To those curious in byway economics, it may be pleasant to know, that Wansey, in the year '94, found the "Bunch of Grapes" the best house of entertainment in Boston; that it was kept by Colonel Colman, and that, though "pestered with bugs," his guest paid "five shillings a day, including a pint of Madeira." He records, as memorable, the circumstance that he "took a walk to Bunker Hill with an officer who had been on the spot in the battle;" and that they returned "over the new bridge from Cambridge," which Wansey—not having lived to see the Suspension Bridge at Niagara, the Victoria at Montreal, nor the Waterloo in London—observes is "a most prodigious work for so infant a country —worthy of the Roman empire." Boston then boasted "forty hackney coaches, which carry one to any part of the town for a quarter of a dollar." The pillar on Beacon Hill, and Long Wharf, were to him the chief local objects of interest. He visited the "famous geographer," Jedediah Morse, at Charlestown, read the *Columbian Centinel*, and attended "the only Unitarian chapel yet opened in America, and heard Mr. Freeman." Springfield, in Massachusetts, put him in mind of Winbourn, in Dorsetshire; the coffee there was "ill made," and the "butter rank," while the best article of food he found was "fried fish." He was charmed with the abundance of robins and swallows, and saw "a salmon caught in a seine in the Connecticut River," and "a schoolhouse by the roadside in almost every parish." He attended a meeting of the Legislature in Hartford, and heard a debate as to how "to provide for the poor and sick negroes who had been freed from slavery—the question being whether it was incumbent on the former masters, or the State, to subsist them. Like all strangers then and there, he was hospitably received by Mr. Wadsworth. He mentions, as a noteworthy facility for travellers, that "three or four packets sail every week from New Haven to New York." Of New England commodities which he records for their novelty or prevalence, are sugar from the maple tree, soft soap, and cider. Like all foreigners, he complains of the bad bread, and enumerates, as a curious phenomenon, that there is "no tax on candles;" that thunder storms are frequent, and lightning conductors on all the houses; that woodpeckers, flycatchers, and kingbirds abound; that the dwellings are built exclusively of timber, and that "women and children, in most of the country places, go without caps, stockings, and shoes." The well poles of New Jersey, and her domestic flax spinners, cherry trees, and fireflies impress him as characteristic; and he is disappointed in the quality of the wool produced there. In New York, Mr. Wansey lodged at the Tontine Coffee House, near the Battery, where he met Citizen Genet and Joseph Priestley, breakfasted with General Gates, and received a call from Chancellor Livingston. He "makes a note" of the then "public buildings"—viz., the Governor's house, the Exchange, the Society Library, the Literary Coffee House, Columbia College, the hospital, and workhouse. He found some "good paintings by Trumbull" at Federal Hall, was interested in Montgomery's monument, went with a party to see "Dickson Colton's manufactory at Hellgate," and Hodgkinson in "A Bold Stroke for a Husband" at the theatre. He encountered John Adams, then Vice-President, at Burling Slip, "on board the packet just sailing for Boston," and describes him as "a stout, hale, well-looking man, of grave deportment, and quite plain in dress and person." He dined with Comfort Sands; and Mr. Jay, "brother to the ambassador," took him to "the Belvidere—an elegant tea-drinking house, with delightful views of the harbor;" also to "the Indian Queen, on the Boston road, filled with Frenchmen and tri-color cockades." In Philadelphia, he saw Washington at the play, which was one of Mrs. Inchbald's; dined with Mr. Bingham, and heard all about the ravages of the yellow fever of the preceding year.

How suggestive are even such meagre notices of personal experience, reviving to our minds the primitive housewifery, the political vicissitudes, and the social tastes which mark the history of the land sixty years ago: when the first President of the republic had been recently inaugurated; when the mischievous "French alliance" was creating such bitter partisan feeling; when a Unitarian philosopher fled from a Birmingham mob to the wilds of Pennsylvania; when the abolition of slavery was a familiar fact in our social life; when good Mrs. Inchbald's dramas were favorites, and Brockden Brown was writing his graphic story of the pestilence that laid waste his native city; when Trumbull was the artist, Hodgkinson the actor, Genet the demagogue, Livingston the lawyer, and Washington the glory of the land!

Among the economical writers on our country, Thomas Cooper was at one time much quoted.* His remarks were, however, the fruits of quite a brief survey, as he left Eng-

---

* "Some Information respecting America," London, 1794.

land late in the summer of 1793, and embarked on his return the ensuing winter. He found "land cheap and labor dear;" praises the fertility of the Genesee Valley, then attracting emigrants from New England, as its subsequent inhabitants were lured by the same causes to the still farther western plains of Ohio and Illinois. Cooper indicates, as serious objections to New York State, the intermittent fevers, and the unsatisfactory land tenure—both of which obstacles have gradually disappeared or been auspiciously modified, as the civilization of the interior has advanced, and its vast resources been made available by the genius of communication. This writer also declares that the climate of Pennsylvania is more dry. The existence of slavery he considers a vital objection to the Southern sections of the country for the British emigrant. He remarks of Rhode Island, that it is "in point of climate as well as appearance the most similar to Great Britain of any State in the Union"—a remark confirmed often since by foreign visitors and native travellers. It is to be observed, however, that most of those who explored the States, when the facilities for travel were meagre and inadequate, for the purpose of obtaining economical information, usually confined their experience to special regions, where convenience or accident induced them to linger; and thus they naturally give the preference to different places. Brissot recommends the Shenandoah Valley, and Imlay, Kentucky. Cooper thought "the prospect in the professions unprofitable." He states that literary men, as a class, did not exist, though the names of Franklin, Rittenhouse, Jefferson, Paine, and Barlow were distinguished. The number of articles he mentions as indispensable "to bring over," in 1793, gives one a startling idea of the deficiencies of the country. He asserts, however, that the "culinary vegetables of America are superior to those of England;" but, on the other hand, was disappointed in the trees, as, "although the masses of wood are large and grand," yet the arborescent specimens individually "fell much short of his expectations;" which does not surprise those of his readers who have seen the noble and impressive trees which stand forth in such magnificent relief in some of the parks and manor grounds of England. The details of a new settlement given by this writer, are more or less identical with those which have since become so familiar to us, from the vivid pictures of life in the West; but we can easily imagine how interesting they must have been to those contemplating emigration, or with kindred who had lately found a new home on this continent. More, however, of the Puritan element mingled with and marked the life of the settlers in what was then "the West"—and tinctured the then nascent tide of civilization. Somewhat of the simplicity noticed by writers during colonial times, yet lingered; and the social lesson with which Cooper ends his narrative is benign and philosophical: "By the almost general mediocrity of fortune," he writes, "that prevails in America, obliging its people to follow some business for subsistence, those vices that arise usually from idleness are in a great measure prevented. Atheism is unknown; and the Divine Being seems to have manifested His approbation of the mutual forbearance and kindness with which the different sects treat each other, by the remarkable prosperity with which He has been pleased to crown the whole country."

Alexander Wilson, the ornithologist, the Paisley weaver and poet, after enduring political persecution and great privations at home, landed at Newcastle, in Delaware, July 14th, 1794, and, having shot a red-headed woodpecker, was inspired with an ornithological enthusiasm which decided his career. He became a schoolmaster, an ardent politician, and, through intimacy with Bartram, a confirmed naturalist. He wrote for Brockden Brown's magazine, made a pedestrian tour to Niagara, was the author of "The Foresters"—an elaborate poem in the *Portfolio*, and fixed his home on the banks of the Susquehanna: meantime, and subsequently, toiling, in spite of every obstacle and with beautiful zeal, upon his "American Ornithology;" and in this and other writings, in verse and prose, giving the most vivid local descriptions of life and nature in America as revealed to the eye of science and of song.*

Travel here, as elsewhere, brings out the idiosyncrasies, and proves a test of character. A certain earnestness of purpose and definite sympathy lend more or less dignity to the narratives of missionary, soldier, and *savant;* but these were soon succeeded by a class of men whom accident or necessity brought hither. The welcome accorded some of them, when "stranger was a holy name" among us, and the greater social consideration experienced in a less conventional state of society than that to which they had been accustomed, sometimes induced an amusing self-complacency and oracular tone. With the less need of the heroic, more superficial traits of human nature found scope; and a fastidious taste and critical standard were too often exhibited by writers, whose previous history formed an incongruous parallel with the newborn pretensions warmed into life by the republican atmosphere of this young land. A visitor whose narrow means obliged him often to travel on foot and rely on casual hospitality, and whose acquirements enabled him to subsist as a tutor in a Southern family, for several months, would challenge our respect for his independence and self-reliance, were it not for an egotistical claim to the rank of a practical and philosophical traveller, which obtrudes itself on every page of his journal. Some descriptive sketches, however, atone for the amiable weakness of John Davis,† whose record includes the period between 1798 and 1802, during which he roamed over many sections of the country, and observed various phases of American life. "I have entered," he says, "with equal interest, the mud hut of the negro and

---

* "American Ornithology; or, The Natural History of the Birds of the United States," with plates from original drawings taken from nature, 9 vols., folio, Philadelphia, 1808–'14.

"The Foresters, a Poem descriptive of a Pedestrian Journey to the Falls of Niagara," 12mo., Paisley, 1825.

† "Travels of Four Years and a Half in the United States, during the years 1798 to 1802," by John Davis, dedicated to President Jefferson, 8vo., London, 1803.

the log house of the planter; I have likewise communed with the slave who wields the hoe and the taskmaster who imposes the labor." Pope, Addison, and Johnson were his oracles, and the style of the latter obviously won his sympathy. Burr fascinated him; Dennie praised his verses, and he saw Brockden Brown. His volume abounds with byway anecdotes. He records the details of his experience with the zest of one whose self-esteem exalts whatever befalls and surrounds him. To-night he is kept awake by the howls of a mastiff, to-morrow he dines on venison; now he writes an elegy, and now engages in literary discussion with a planter. His odes to a cricket, a mockingbird, to Ashley River, etc., evidence the Shenstone taste and rhyme then so much in vogue. He "contemplated with reverence the portrait of James Logan," and draws from an Irish clergyman new anecdotes of Goldsmith. He disputes Franklin's originality in the form of an amusing dialogue between a Virginian and a New Englander, tracing the philosopher's famous parable to Bishop Taylor, and his not less famous epitaph to a Latin author. He praises Phillis Wheatley, and notes, with evident pleasure, the trees, grains, reptiles, birds, and animals. Great is his dread of the rattlesnake. Anecdotes and verses, philosophical reflections and natural history items, with numerous personal confessions and impressions, make up a characteristic *mélange*, in which the vanity of a bard and the speculations of a traveller sometimes grotesquely blend, but with so much good nature and harmless pedantry, that the result is diverting, and sometimes instructive. "My long residence," he writes, "in a community 'where honor and shame from no condition rise,' has placed me above the ridiculous pride of disowning the situation of a tutor." In this vocation he certainly enjoyed an excellent opportunity to observe that unprecedented blending of the extremes of high civilization and rude economics which forms one of the most salient aspects of our early history. The English tutor, when domesticated in a Southern family, was sheltered by a log house while he shared the pleasures of a sumptuous table;

and, when surrounded by the crude accommodations of a
new plantation, witnessed the highest refinement of manners,
and listened to the most intellectual conversation. If, during
his wanderings, he was annoyed, one night, by a short bed,
he was amused, the next, by a travelling menagerie. If, in
tutoring, his patience was tried by seeing people " strive to
exceed each other in the vanities of life," he was compensated, in the woods, by shooting wild turkeys with his pupil.
He quotes Shakspeare, and observes nature with great relish;
and the cotton plant, the autumn wind, the wild deer, eagles,
hummingbirds, whippoorwills, bog plant, and flycatchers,
with occasional flirtations with a mellifluous muse, beguile
the time; and he boasts, in the retrospect of his four years'
sojourn, and the written digest thereof, that he "scorns complaints of mosquitos and bugs," that he "eschews magnificent epithets," "makes no drawings," and "has not joined
the crew of deists"—which negative merits, we infer, were
rare in travellers' tales half a century ago. The republican
ideas, inquiring turn of mind, or extreme deference of this
writer, seems to have won him the favorable regard of Jefferson, upon whom and Burr he lavishes ardent praise: and
the former seems to recognize not only a political admirer,
but a brother author, in Davis; for, in reply to his request
to dedicate his Travels to the apostle of American democracy, Jefferson, after accepting graciously the compliment,
writes: " Should you, in your journeyings, have been led to
remark on the same objects on which I gave crude notes
some years ago, I shall be happy to see them confirmed or
corrected by so accurate an observer." His work is entitled,
"Travels of Four and a Half Years in the United States,
1799–1802," London, 1817. " With more sincerity," says
Rich's *Bibliotheca Americana*, " than is usual among travellers, he states that he made the tour on foot, because he
could not afford the expense of a horse."

In 1806, Thomas Ashe visited North America, with the
intention of examining the Western rivers, in order to learn,
from personal inspection, the products of their vicinage, and

the actual state of the adjacent country. The Mississippi, Ohio, Monongahela, and Alleghany were the special objects of his exploration. His "Travels in America"* is a curious mixture of critical disparagement, quite too general to be accurate, and of romantic and extravagant episodes, which diminish the reliance that might otherwise be placed on the more practical statements. The work appeared in London in 1808.

The natural appetite for the marvellous, and the desire to obtain a knowledge of facts, at that time, in regard to the particular region visited, being prevalent, this now rarely consulted volume was much read. From Pittsburg he writes: "The Atlantic States, through which I have passed, are unworthy of your observation. The climate has two extremes." The Middle States "are less contemptible; the national features not strong;" and, from this circumstance, he thinks it difficult to conjecture what national character will arise. At Carlisle, Pa., he "did not meet a man of decent literature." He seeks consolation, therefore, in the picturesque scenes around him, which are often described in rhetorical terms, and in a recognition of the fairer portion of the community. Thomson's "Seasons" is evidently a favorite book; and he presents a copy to a "young lady among the emigrants," on the blank leaf of which, he tells us, he wrote a "romantic but just compliment." Education, sects, manufactures, and provisions are commented on; but the tone of his remarks, except where he praises the face of nature or the manners of a woman, is discouraging to those who contemplate settling in the western part of the country—which he continually brings into severe comparison with the more developed communities of the Old World. Indeed, he repudiates the flattering accounts of previous travellers; and it is evident that the reaction from his own extravagant expec-

* "Travels in America, performed in 1806," by Captain Thomas Ashe, 3 vols. 12mo., London, 1808.

"His account of the Atlantic States forms the most comprehensive piece of national abuse we ever recollect to have read."—*Rich.*

tations leads him to picture the dark side with earnestness. Personal disappointment is expressed in all his generalizations, although certain focal beauties and exceptional individuals modify the strain of complaint, which, though sometimes well founded, is often unreasonable. He describes the hardships and privations incident to emigration, and illustrates them by melancholy examples. The "vicious taste in building," the formidable catalogue of snakes, the want of literary culture, the discomfort, and the coarse manners quite eclipse the charms of landscape and the natural advantages of the vast region which, since his journey, has become so populous, enterprising, and productive. He "reports" a boxing match, horse race, ball and supper in Virginia; hears a debate in Congress, and retires "full of contempt;" swindlers and impostors intrude on his privacy at a tavern. He says, with truth, that "no people live with less regard to regimen;" and, as we read, beautiful scenes seem to be counterbalanced by bad food, grand rivers by uncultured minds, cheap land by narrow social resources; in a word, the usual conditions of a new country, where nature is exuberant and civilization incomplete, are described as such anomalies would be by a man with a fluent and ambitious style, tastes and self-love easily offended, and to whom the "law of a production," which Goethe deemed so essential to wise criticism in letters, is scarcely applied, though still more requisite to a traveller's estimate. Ashe put on record some really useful information, and stated many disenchanting truths about the New World, and life there; but the rhetorical extravagance and personal vanity herewith ventilated, detract not a little from his authority as a reference and his tact as a romancer. The gentler portion of creation alone escape reproach. "I assure you," he writes, "that when I expressed the supreme disgust excited in me by the people of the United States, the ladies were by no means included in the general censure."

When we remember that such books, half a century ago, were the current sources of information in Great Britain in regard to America, and that a writer so limited in scope, indiscriminate in abuse, and superficial in thought, was regarded as an authority, it is easy to perceive how the inimical feeling toward this country was fostered. One fact alone indicates the shallowness of Ashe: he dates none of his complacent epistles from the Northern States, and gives, as a reason therefor, that they are "unworthy of observation." He thinks the social destiny of Pittsburg redeemed by a few Irish families settled there, who "hindered the vicious propensities of the genuine American character from establishing here the horrid dominion which they have assumed over the Atlantic States." He finds the men deteriorated on account of their "political doctrines," which, he considers, tend "to make men turbulent citizens, abandoned Christians, inconstant husbands, and treacherous friends." Here we have the secret of this traveller's sweeping censure. His hatred of republican institutions not only blinded him to all the privileges and merits of American life and character, but even to certain domestic traits and professional talents, recognized by every other foreign observer of the country. Yet, palpable as are his injustice and ignorance, contemporary critics at home failed to recognize them. One says, "his researches cannot fail to interest the politician, the statesman, the philosopher, and the antiquary;" while the *Quarterly Review* mildly rebukes him for having "spoiled a good book by engrafting incredible stories on authentic facts."

Rev. John Bristed, who succeeded Bishop Griswold in St. Michael's Church, at Bristol, R. I., published, in 1818, a work on "America and her Resources." He was a native of Dorsetshire, England, and, for two years, a pupil of Chitty. Strong in his prejudices of country, yet impressed with the advantages of the New World, his report of American means, methods, and prospects, though containing much useful, and, at the time, some fresh and desirable information, is crude, and tinctured with a personal and national bias, which renders it, superseded as most of its facts have been by the development of the country, of little present significance. It is, however, to the curious, as an illustration of character, a suggestive indication of the state of feeling of an English resident, and of the state of the country forty or fifty years since. The author was a scholar, with strong convictions. He died at Bristol a few years since, at an advanced age. He also published "A Pedestrian Tour in the Highlands," in 1804. His work on America was the result of several years' residence; and its scope, tone, and character are best hinted by the opinion of one of the leading Reviews of England, thus expressed soon after its publication: "We cannot avoid regarding Mr. Bristed with some degree of respect," says the *London Quarterly*. "In writing his book, his pride in his native country, which all his republicanism has been unable to overcome, has frequently had to contend with the flattering but unsubstantial prospect with which the prophetic folly that ever accompanies democracy has impressed his mind, to a degree almost equalling that of the vain people with whom he is domiciled." As an authentic landmark of economical progress, this work is useful as a reference, whatever may be thought of its social criticism.

An entire contrast to the record of Ashe appeared about the same time, in the "Travels through the Northern Parts of the United States,"* by Edward Augustus Kendall. No previous work on this country so fully explains the State polity and organization of New England, and the social facts connected therewith. "The intention of travel," says the intelligent and candid author, "is the discovery of truth." As unsparing in criticism as Ashe, he analyzes the municipal system and the social development with so much knowledge and fairness, that the political and economical student will find more data and detail in his work than, at that period, were elsewhere obtainable. It still serves as an authentic memorial of the region of country described, at that transition era, when time enough had elapsed, after the Revolutionary War, for life and labor to have assumed their normal

* "Travels through the Northern Parts of the United States, in the years 1807-'8," by Edward A. Kendall, 3 vols. 8vo., New York, 1809.

development, and before their scope had been enlarged and their activity intensified by the vast mechanical improvements of our own day. The local laws of Connecticut, for instance, are fully discussed; townships, elections, churches, prisons, schools, and the press—all the elements and principles which then and there manifested national and moulded private character. The famous "Blue Laws" form a curious chapter; and, in his account of the newspaper press, he notes the remarkable union of "license of thought with very favorable specimens of diction," and enlarges upon the prevalent "florid and tumid" language in America, its causes and cure; while his chapter on Hartford Poetry is an interesting illustration of our early local literature.

Scarcely any contemporary writer of American travels was more quoted and popular, sixty years ago, than Isaac Weld, whom the troubles of Ireland, in '95, induced to visit this country. That experience, we may readily imagine, caused him thoroughly to appreciate the importance of practical observations in a land destined to afford a prosperous home for such a multitude of his unfortunate countrymen. Accordingly we find, in his well-written work,* abundance of economical and statistical facts; and the interests and prospects of agriculture and commerce are elaborately considered. While this feature rendered Weld's Travels really useful at the time of their publication, and an authentic reference subsequently, his ardent love of nature lent an additional interest to his work; for he expatiates on the beauties of the landscape with the perception of an artist, and is one of the few early travellers who enriched his journal with authentic sketches of picturesque and famous localities. The French translation of Weld's Travels in America is thus illustrated; and the old-fashioned yet graphic view of an "Auberge et voiture publique dans les États Unis," vividly recalls the days anterior to locomotives, so suggestive of stage-coach adven-

* "Travels through the States of North America and the Provinces of Upper and Lower Canada, in 1795-'96-'97," by Isaac Weld, illustrated with fine engravings, 4to., 1799.

tures, deliberate travel, and the unmodified life and character of the rural districts. In describing the sanguinary attacks of New Jersey insects, he deals in the marvellous, giving Washington as authority that the mosquitos there bite through the thickest boots.

No writer on America has more singularly combined the political refugee and adventurer with the assiduous economist than William Cobbett. Born and bred a farmer, he fled, while a youth, from the peaceful vocation of his father, to become a soldier in Nova Scotia; but soon left the service, visited France, and, in 1796, settled in Philadelphia, where the fierce tone of his controversial writings involved him in costly libel suits. His interest in the political questions then rife in America is amply evidenced by the twelve volumes of the works of Peter Porcupine, published in London in 1801. Returning to England, he became the strenuous advocate of Pitt, and started the *Weekly Register*, which contained his lucubrations for thirty years; but, having once more rendered himself amenable to law by the combined freedom and force of his pen, he returned to the United States, and enjoyed the *prestige* of a political exile in the vicinity of New York; and when the repeal of the Six Acts permitted his return home, he conveyed to England the bones of Thomas Paine, whose memory he idolized. Cobbett is recognized under several quite distinct phases, according to the views of his critics—as a malignant radical by some, a philosophical liberal by others. His style is regarded as a model of perspicacity; and his love of agriculture, and faith in habits of inexpensive comfort and cheerful industry, made him, in the eyes of partial observers, quite the model of republican hardihood and independence; while the more refined and urbane of his day shrank from his vituperative language and bitter partisanship. He slandered the benign Dr. Rush, and Bentham declared "his malevolence and lying beyond everything;" while Kent remarked that his political writings afforded a valuable source of knowledge to those who would understand the parties and principles which agitated our country during his sojourn; and the London *Times* applauded the muscular vigor of his diction. But it is as a writer on the economical and social facts of American life, that Cobbett now claims our notice; and in this regard he differs from most authors in the same sphere, in the specific character of the information he imparts, and the deliberate conclusions at which he arrived. Some of our venerable countrymen remember his pleasant abode on Long Island, and the memorable discussions which sometimes took place there between the political exile, reformer, grammarian, and horticulturist, and his intelligent visitors from the city. The late Dr. Francis used to quote some of his emphatic sayings, and describe his frugal arrangements and agricultural trophies. In the preface to his "Year's Residence in America,"* Cobbett complains of English travellers as too extreme in their statements in regard to the country—one set describing it as a paradise, and the other as unfit to live in. He treats the subject in a practical way, and from patient experience. Enamored of a farmer's life, he boasts that he was "bred up at a ploughtail and among the hop gardens of Surrey," and that he was never eighteen months "without a garden." He expatiates on the superior condition of the agricultural class in America, where "a farmer is not a dependent wretch," and where presidents, governors, and legislators pride themselves on the vocation. He describes his own little domain, the American trees he has planted around his house, his experiments in raising corn, potatoes, and especially rutabaga. By "daily notes" he carefully reports the transitions of temperature and seasons, and gives definite accounts of modes of cultivation, the price of land, cost of raising kine and poultry; in a word, all the economical details which a practical man would prize. By the narrative of his own doings in the vicinity of New York, and of his observations during a journey to the West, the foreign reader must have obtained from Cobbett the most satisfactory knowledge of the mate-

---

* "A Year's Residence in the United States," 3 vols., 8vo., London, 1818.

rial resources of a large section of the country as it was forty years since. Through these agricultural items, however, the disappointment of the politician and the sympathies of the republican vividly gleam; for the truculent author constantly rejoices that no "spies, false witnesses, or blood-money men" beset the path of frugal toil and independent thought in this land of freedom. He justly laments the prevalence of intemperance, and compares the "Hampshire parsons" and their flocks—not at all to the advantage of either—with the "good, kind people here going to church to listen to some decent man of good moral character and of sober, quiet life." Despite the narrowness of the partisan and the egotism of the innovator, Cobbett, in some respects, is one of the more clear and candid reporters who sought to enlighten Europe about America. A critical authority in agriculture, while denying him scientific range, admits that he adorned the subject "by his homely knowledge of the art, and most agreeable delineation;" while some of the most essential social traits, remarkable political tendencies, and eminent public characters of the United States, have been most truly and impressively described by William Cobbett.

"I visited Parliament House," writes an American from London in 1833. "The question was the expediency of abrogating the right, under any circumstances, of impressing seamen for her Majesty's navy. Cobbett said but a few words, but they went directly to the question: 'One fact on this subject claims and deserves the attention of the House. The national debt consists of eight hundred millions of pounds; and seven hundred thousand of this debt was incurred in the war with America, in support of this right of impressing seamen.'"

However coarse the radicalism of Cobbett, there was a basis of sense and truth in his intrepid assertion of first principles—his recognition and advocacy of elementary political justice—that just thinkers respect, however uncongenial may be the manner and method of the man; no little of the offensive character thereof being attributable to a baffled and false position. An acute German writer * apostrophized him, not inaptly, thus: "Old Cobbett! dog of England! I do not love you, for every vulgar nature is fatal to me; but I pity you from my deepest soul, when I see that you cannot break loose from your chain, nor reach those thieves who, laughing, slip away their plunder before your eyes, and mock your fruitless leaps and unavailing howls."

While political reformers of the liberal school, drew arguments from American prosperity, popular bards gave expression to the common vexation, by taunting the republic with the taint of slavery, though a poisoned graft from the land of our origin—as Campbell, in his bitter epigram on the American flag—or with sarcasms upon democratic manners, as in Moore's ephemeral satire. And yet, when the prospect for men with more wit than money, and more learning than rank, in Great Britain, was all but hopeless, the Bard of Hope could discover no more auspicious home than the land he thus sneered at for a local and inherited stain. Alluding to a half-formed project of joining his brother in America, and earning his subsistence there by teaching, he observes, in a letter to Washington Irving: "God knows I love my country, and my heart would bleed to leave it; but if there be a consummation such as may be feared, I look to taking up my abode in the only other land of liberty; and you may behold me, perhaps, flogging your little Spartans in Kentucky into a true sense and feeling of the beauties of Homer."

Byron, an impassioned devotee of freedom, and disgusted by the social proscription his undisciplined and wilful career had entailed on him in his native land, turned a gaze of sympathy toward the West. It is said no tribute to his fame delighted him so much as the spontaneous admiration of Americans. He was highly gratified when one of our ships of war paid him the compliment of a salute in the harbor of Leghorn; and expressed unfeigned satisfaction when told of a well-thumbed copy of his poems at an inn near Niagara

---

* Heine.

Falls. Indeed, his restless mind often found comfort in the idea of making his home in the United States. Every schoolboy remembers his apostrophe to this country, in his Ode to Venice:

> "One great clime,
> Whose vigorous offspring by dividing ocean
> Are kept apart, and nursed in the devotion
> Of freedom, which their fathers fought for and
> Bequeathed—a heritage of heart and hand,
> And proud distinction from each other land—
> Yet rears her crest, unconquered and sublime,
> Above the far Atlantic. She has taught
> Her Esau brethren that the haughty flag,
> The floating wall of Albion's feebler crag,
> May strike to those whose red right hands have bought
> Rights cheaply earned with blood."

"One freeman more, America, to thee," Byron would have indeed added; and, had he followed the casual impulse and found new inspiration from nature on this continent, and outlived here the fever of passion and the recklessness of error, how easy to imagine his later manhood and his perverted name alike redeemed by faith and humanity into "victorious clearness."

A remarkable evidence of the prevalent fashion and feeling, on the other hand, is to be found in the writings of Tom Moore. His Life, so imprudently sent to the press by Lord John Russell, exhibits, in his own letters and diaries, as complete a fusion of the man of the world and the poet—if such a phenomenon is possible—as can be found in the whole range of literary biography. But Moore was a man of fancy and music rather than of deep or wide sympathies—a social favorite and graceful rhymer, who lived for the drawing room and the dinner, and was beguiled by aristocratic hospitalities from that great and true world of humanity wherein the true bard finds inspiration. Accordingly, it was to be expected that his hasty visit to America should be, as it was, made capital for satire and song, in the interest of British prejudice. There is so little originality or completeness in these desultory notes of his visit, with the exception of two finished and melodious lyrics—"The Lake of the Dismal Swamp" and "The Canadian Boat Song"—that only the prestige of his name makes them of present interest.

Moore arrived at Norfolk, Va., in the autumn of 1803, in H. B. M. frigate Phaeton, where he stayed ten days, and then went to Bermuda in the "Driver" sloop-of-war. Thence he proceeded in the "Boston" to New York; visited Washington and Philadelphia, Canada and Niagara Falls. At Bermuda he met Basil Hall, then a midshipman. At Washington he had an interview with Jefferson, "whom," he writes, "I found sitting with General Dearborn and one or two other officers, and in the same homely costume, comprising slippers and Connemara stockings." He enjoyed Philadelphia society, and addressed some verses to "Delaware's green banks" and "Fair Schuylkill." He describes Buffalo as a village of wigwams and huts; and part of his journey thence to Niagara he was obliged to perform on foot, through a half-cleared forest. On his arrival, he tells us he lay awake all night listening to the Falls; and adds, "The day following I consider a sort of era in my life; and the first glimpse I caught of that wonderful cataract gave me a feeling which nothing in this world will ever awaken again." His rhymes intended as "the song of the spirit of that region" are not, however, suggestive of these emotions. He spent part of his time with "the gallant Brock," who then commanded at Fort George, and, accompanied by him and the officers of the garrison, visited the Tuscarora Indians, and witnessed their dances, games, and rites with satisfaction. The Falls of the Mohawk also awoke his muse; and he was much delighted at the refusal of the captain of a steamboat on Lake Ontario to accept passage money from the "poet." Nearly all the period of Moore's sojourn was passed with British consuls or army and naval officers. From these and the Federalists of Philadelphia, he tells us, he "got his prejudices" in regard to America. The "vulgarity of rancor" in politics, and the "rude familiarity of the lower orders," were very offensive to him; and, although his opportunities for "cursory observation" were quite limited, he found America "at maturity in most of the vices and all the pride of civilization." Slavery, of course, is the chief object of his satire: of its origin he is silent. The crude state of border life, the prevalence of French sympathies, and the recklessness of partisan zeal, are among the special defects upon which he ironically descants, as usual ascribing them to the institutions of the country. He sneers at

> "The embryo capital, where fancy sees
> Squares in morasses, obelisks in trees;"

and scornfully declares that

> "Columbia's patriot train
> Cast off their monarch that their mob might reign;"

and assures his readers

> "I'd rather hold my beck
> In climes where liberty has scarce been named,
> Nor any right but that of ruling claimed,
> Than thus to live where bastard Freedom waves
> Her fustian flag in mockery over slaves."

He begins one of his tirades with

> "Arcady in this free and virtuous state,
> Which Frenchmen tell us was ordained by Fate;"

and his anti-Gallicism is as obvious as his hatred of the "equality and fraternity" principles, which he thinks so degrading. Yet it was here that he saw the picture of domestic peace and prosperity that prompted the lines, "I knew, by the smoke that so gracefully curled;" and the want of magnanimity in an Irish bard, in overlooking the blessings America has rained upon his countrymen, in flippant comments on temporary social incongruities, is the more apparent from his acknowledgment in the preface to his "Poems relating to America," subsequently written: "The good will I have experienced from more than one distinguished American, sufficiently assures me that any injustice I may have done to that land of freemen, if not long since wholly forgotten, is now remembered only to be forgiven."

Even a cursory examination of the British Travels in America already noticed, would suggest the facility and desirableness of a judicious compilation therefrom. It is easy to imagine a volume replete with information and attraction, gleaned by a discriminating hand from such copious but ill-digested materials. Omitting the mere statistics and the extravagant tales, the egotistical episodes and the coarse abuse, there remain passages of admirable description, racy anecdotes, and genial speculations enough to form a choice picture and treatise on nature, character, and life in the New World. It is surprising that such an experiment has not been tried by one of the many tasteful compilers who have sifted the grain from the chaff in so many other departments of popular literature. The attempt, on a small scale, was made, in 1810, by one of those clever female writers for the young, who, about that period, initiated the remarkable and successful department of juvenile literature, since so memorably illustrated by Maria Edgeworth, Mrs. Barbauld, Sir Walter Scott, Hans Andersen, and other endeared writers. "Excursions in North America, described in Letters from a Gentleman and his Young Companions in England," by Priscilla Wakefield, was a favorite little work among the children on both sides of the Atlantic, half a century ago. It is amusing to revert to these early sketches, which have given to many minds, now mature, their first and therefore their freshest impressions of this country. Mrs. Wakefield drew her materials from Jefferson, Weld, Rochefoucault, Bartram, Michaux, Carver, and Mackenzie, and, in general, uses them with tact and taste. The cities and scenery of the land, its customs and products, are well described. She notes some of the stereotyped so-called national vulgarities which have, in the more civilized parts of the country, sensibly diminished since the indignant protests of travellers reached their acme in Mrs. Trollope. "We have been," it is said in one of the letters, " once or twice to the theatre, but the company in the pit have such a disgusting custom of drinking wine or porter and smoking tobacco, between the acts, that I have no inclination to visit it again."

But the pleasantest parts of her book, especially considering for what class of readers it is intended, are those which delineate the natural features and productions. Here, for instance, we have a description of an indigenous tree, now exalted by the selfish and narrow passions of a small and sensitive community into an emblem of political hate and ungenerous faction. With this association there seems a latent satire in the details of the arborescent portrait. "The Palmetto Royal, or Adam's Needle, is a singular tree. They grow so thick together, that a bird can scarcely penetrate between them. The stiff leaves of this sword plant, standing straight out from the trunk, form a barrier that neither man nor beast can pass. It rises with an erect stem about ten or twelve feet high, crowned with a chaplet of dagger-like green leaves, with a stiff, sharp spur at the end. This thorny crown is tipped with a pyramid of white flowers, shaped like a tulip or lily; to these flowers succeeds a larger fruit, in form like a cucumber, but, when ripe, of a deep purple color."

"We scarcely pass ten or twelve miles," says another of these once familiar letters, "without seeing a tavern, as they call inns in this country. They are built of wood, and resemble one another, having a porch in front the length of the house, almost covered with handbills. They have no sign, but take their name from the person that keeps the house, who is often a man of consequence; for the profession of an innkeeper is far more respected in America than in England. Instead of supplying their guests as soon as they arrive, they make everybody conform to one hour for the different meals; so you must go without your dinner, or delay your journey till the innkeeper pleases to lay the cloth." This remark on the country taverns as they were before the "hotel" had become characterized by size, show, and costliness, strikes us as most natural, coming from one only acquainted with English inns; and the independent manners of the landlords are so obvious now, that a foreign writer declared they and the steamboat captains formed the only aristocracy he had encountered in America; while the custom of arbitrarily regulating the hours for meals, and the gregarious manner of feeding, led a Sicilian to complain that the guests of a public house in this country, were treated like friars in his own.

A sensible and pleasant but not very profound or methodical gentleman of Liverpool published "Remarks during a Journey through North America in 1819." This book, written by Adam Hodgson, Esq., was published in this country in 1823, and met with a kindly reception on account of the well-meaning aim and disposition of the writer, whose national prejudices were expressed in a more calm manner than by his more vulgar countrymen; while a tour of seven thousand miles had furnished him with a good amount of useful knowledge, not, however, well digested or arranged; and mingled therewith are certain personal tastes and views amusing and harmless, that lend a certain piquancy to the narrative. He examined the country with an eye to its facilities and prospects for the emigrant, and thus put on record important statistical facts, which are sometimes ludicrously blended with matters of no consequence. He so admired the chorus of frogs, heard in the stillness of the night at one place of his sojourn, that he opened his window to listen to their croaking, mistaking it, at first, for the notes of birds. He expressed the most *naïve* surprise at finding a copy of the "Dairyman's Daughter" at a shop in Mobile; and was so nervous in regard to the safety of his baggage, when travelling by stage coach, that he used a chain and padlock of his own, and held the cue thereof. He enjoyed Southern hospitality, which, however, was sadly marred, to his consciousness, by slaveholding. He dined on turkey every day for weeks, with apparently undiminished relish; and, with amusing pathos, laments that the "absence of the privileges of primogeniture, and the repeated subdivision of property, are gradually effecting a change in the structure of society in South Carolina, and will shortly efface its most interesting and characteristic features." "His book," wrote Jared Sparks, "is creditable to his heart and his principles. We should be glad if as much could be said for his discretion and judgment."

C. W. Janson, "late of the State of Rhode Island," resided in America from 1793 to 1806, and published in London, the year after the latter date, "The Stranger in America," * which the *Edinburgh Review* severely criticizes; while John Foster, in the *Eclectic*, awarded it much praise.

Henry Caswell, in 1849, published "America and the American Church, with some Account of the Mormons, in 1842;" and Robert Barclay issued "An Agricultural Tour in the United States;" a couple of volumes entitled "Travels through Parts of the United States and Canada in 1818-'19," and "A Sabbath among the Tuscaroras," are dedicated to Prof. Silliman, of Yale College. A small work appeared anonymously in London (1817), entitled "Travels in the Interior of America in 1809, '10, and '11," including a description of Upper Louisiana.

Isaac Holmes, of Liverpool, gave to the public, in 1823, "An Account of the United States of America, derived from Observations during a Residence of Four Years in that Republic;" of which the *Quarterly* observes that its author "is rather diffuse and inaccurate," yet gives "a modest and true statement of things as they are."

A rather verbose work of E. S. Abdy, previously known for a hygienic essay, was read extensively, at the time of its appearance, though its interest was quite temporary. It described, in detail, a "Residence and Tour in the United States in 1833-'34."

Sir J. Augustus Foster, Envoy to America in 1811-'12, wrote "Notes on the United States," which were not published, but privately circulated; although the *London Quar-*

* "The Stranger in America," by Charles William Janson, engravings, 4to., London, 1807.

terly declared its publication desirable "on both sides of the Atlantic;" and Godley's "Letters from Canada and the United States," published in London in 1814, contains valuable agricultural data, and is justly characterized by the critical journals of that day as sensible and impartial.*

There was, indeed, from the close of the war of 1812, for a series of years, an inundation of English books of travel, wherein the United States, their people and prospects, were discussed with a monotonous recapitulation of objections, a superficial knowledge, and a predetermined deprecation, which render the task of analyzing their contents and estimating their comparative merit in the highest degree wearisome. Redeemed, in some instances, by piquant anecdote,

* Among other works of British writers of early date worth consulting are Governor Bernard's Letters; Burton and Oldmixon on the British Empire in America; and of later commentators, as either amusing, intelligent, curious, or salient, sometimes flippant and sometimes sensible, may be mentioned Birkbeck's "Notes of a Journey in America in 1817;" Kingdom's "Abstract of Information relative to the United States" (London, 1820); "Tour in North America," by Henry Tudor, Barrister (1834); also the Travels of Bradbury, Shirreff, Byam, Casey, Cunningham, Chambers, Davison, Feroll, Finch, Head, Latrobe, Mackinnon, McNish, Majorbanks, Park, Sturge, Sutcliffe, Thomson, Thornton, Turnbull, Tasistro, Shraff, Warden, Waterton, Warburton, Weston, Keating, and Lamber; Dixon, Jameson, Wright, Dickinson, and Pursh; Vigne and Gleig's "Subaltern in America, a Military Journal of the War of 1812," which originally appeared in *Blackwood's Magazine*, vol. xxi.; J. M. Duncan's Travels (1818); Tremenhere's work on "The Constitution of the United States compared with that of Great Britain;" Prof. J. F. W. Johnson's "Notes on North America," chiefly agricultural and economical; Ousley's "Remarks on the Statistics and Political Institutions of the United States;" the statistical works of Seyber and Tucker; A. J. Mason's Lectures on the United States (London, 1841); and Flint's "Letters from America," chiefly devoted to the Western States (Edinburgh, 1822), of which it has been said that "James Flint was one of the most amiable, accomplished, and truthful foreign tourists who have visited America and left a record of their impressions: he died in his native country (Scotland), a few years after his book was published." Two English officers, Colonel Chesney and Lieut.-Colonel Freemantle, published brief accounts of what they saw and gathered from others, in regard to the war for the Union—too superficial and prejudiced to have any lasting value; and Mr. Dicey, the young correspondent of a liberal London journal, collected and published a narrative of his experience, candid, but of limited scope and insight.

interesting adventure, or some grace of style or originality of view, they are, for the most part, shallow, egotistical, and more or less repetitions of each other. So systematic and continuous, however, are the tone of abuse and the purpose of disparagement, that the subject claims separate consideration. Among those works that attracted special attention, from the antecedents of their authors or a characteristic manner of treating their subject, was the once familiar book of Captain Basil Hall, R. N., the Journal of Fanny Kemble, and the "Notes" of Dickens. Of the former, Everett justly remarked, in the *North American Review*, that "this work will furnish food to the appetite for detraction which reigns in Great Britain toward this country;" while even *Blackwood's Magazine*, congenial as was the spirit of the work to its Tory perversities, though characterizing Captain Hall's observations as "just and profound," declared they were "too much tinctured by his ardent fancy to form a safe guide on the many debated subjects of national institutions." A like protest against the authenticity of Fearon, a London surgeon, who published "A Narrative of a Journey of Five Thousand Miles through the Eastern and Western States of America,* was uttered by Sydney Smith, who wrote, as his critical opinion, that "Mr. Fearon is a much abler writer than either Palmer or Bradbury, but no lover of America, and a little given to exaggerate his views of vices and prejudices;" which estimate was confirmed by the *London Review*, which declared that the "tone of ill temper which this author usually manifests, in speaking of the American character, has gained for his work the approbation of persons who regard that country with peculiar jealousy."

So obvious and prevalent had now become this "peculiar jealousy," that when, in 1833, the flippant "Observations on the Professions, Manners, and Emigration in the United States and Canada," of the Rev. Isaac Fiddler, appeared, the

---

* "Narrative of a Journey of Five Thousand Miles through the Eastern and Western States, with Remarks on Mr. Birkbeck's Notes," by Henry B. Fearon, 8vo., London, 1818.

North American Review truly said of it : "This is another of those precious specimens of books with which John Bull is now regularly humbugged three or four times a year." It seemed to be deemed essential to every popular author of Great Britain, in whatever department, to write a book on America. In those instances where this task was achieved by men of science, valuable knowledge gave interest to special observation; as in the case of Lyell, Featherstonaugh, and Combe, three writers whose scientific knowledge and objects give dignity, interest, and permanent value to their works on America: but the novelists signally failed, from inaptitude for political disquisition, or a constant eye to the exactions of prejudice at home. Marryatt and Dickens added nothing to their reputations as writers by their superficial and sneering disquisitions on America. Yet, however philosophically superficial and exaggerated in fastidiousness, the great charm of Dickens as an author—his humanity, the most real and inspiring element of his nature—was as true, and therefore prophetic, in these "Notes," as in his delineations of human life. Of the long bane of our civic integrity and social peace and purity—of slavery, his words were authentic :

"All those owners, breeders, users, buyers, and sellers of slaves, who will, *until the bloody chapter has a bloody end*, own, breed, use, buy, and sell them at all hazards; who doggedly deny the horrors of the system, in the teeth of such a mass of evidence as never was brought to bear on any other subject, and to which the experience of every day contributes its immense amount; *who would, at this or any other moment, gladly involve America in a war, civil or foreign, provided that it had for its sole end and object the assertion of their right to perpetuate slavery*, and to whip, and work, and torture slaves, unquestioned by any human authority, and unassailed by any human power; who, when they speak of freedom, mean the freedom to oppress their kind, and to be savage, merciless, and cruel; and of whom every man, on his own ground, in republican America, is a more exacting, and a sterner, and a less responsible despot, than the Caliph Ilaroun Alraschid, in his angry robe of scarlet."

Of the female writers, there is more reflection and knowledge in the remarks of Mrs. Jameson and Miss Martineau; while nothing can exceed the indelicacy and want of insight, not to say absurdities, of the Hon. Amelia Murray—other books, however, by female writers, are, despite their unjustifiable personalities, grateful records of hospitalities and experiences, well enough for private letters.

The histrionic commentators, like Power and Fanny Kemble, and the naval annotators, like Hall and Mackinnon, are remarkable for a certain *abandon* and superficiality. Silk Buckingham * much enlarged the previous statistical data, and Francis Wyse collected some valuable expositions of America's "Realities and Resources." Abdy and Duncan, Finch and Graham, Lang and Latrobe, Waterton and Thomson, Palmer and Bradbury, Wright and Mellish, with scores of others, found readers and critics; and a *catalogue raisonné* of the series of books on America between Ashe and Anthony Trollope, would prove quite as ephemeral in character as voluminous. It is interesting to turn from the glowing impressions of American scenery, the ingenuous hatred of the "press gang," and unscrupulous personal revelations of Fanny Kemble's "Journal of Travel in America," written in the buoyant and brilliant youth of the gifted girl, to the details and descriptions of "Life on a Southern Plantation," recorded by the earnest and pitiful woman, and published at so critical a moment of our national struggle, to enlighten and chide her countrymen.

One of the most contemptible of the detractors was a vulgar English farmer, named Faux, whose "Memorable Days in America" was thought worthy of critical recognition by the once famous reviewer, Gifford. Among the

---

* "America, Historical, Statistic, and Descriptive," 3 vols.; "Eastern and Western States," 3 vols.; "Slave States," 2 vols.; "Canada, Nova Scotia, New Brunswick, and other British Provinces," 1 vol.; in all, 9 handsome vols. 8vo., by J. S. Buckingham, London, 1841–'3. One of the most interesting series of works descriptive of the New World which has ever emanated from the press. These volumes contain a fund of knowledge on every subject connected with America: its rise and progress; the education, manners, and merits of its inhabitants: its manufactures, trade, population, etc.

absurd calumnies of this ignorant scribbler, were such grave statements as that poisoned chickens were served to him at Portsmouth; that the Mississippi boatmen habitually rob the sheepfolds; that Boston people take their free negroes to Carolina, and sell them as slaves; and that, in America, "the want of an established religion has made the bulk of the people either infidels or fanatics."

Among the exceptions to that general rule of ignorance and crudity which marks the hasty records of American travel by English tourists, when a visit to America, while no longer adventurous, was yet comparatively rare, is the once famous book of Captain Thomas Hamilton. The author of a successful novel of modern life—as far as literary cultivation may be considered an element of success—this intelligent British officer claims the consideration which is due to a scholar and a gentleman, although he was not the highest exemplar of either title. He discussed "Men and Manners in America" neither as a philosopher nor as an artist. There is no great scope or originality in his speculations, no very profound insight; and the more refined tone of his work is somewhat marred by the same flippancy and affectation of superior taste, which give such a cockney pertness to so many of his countrymen's written observations when this country is the theme. Two merits, however, distinguished the work and yet make it worthy of attention—a better style, and superior powers of description. Captain Hamilton's prejudices warped his observation of our political and social life, and make his report thereof limited and unjust; but there is a vividness and finish about his accounts of natural beauty—such as the description of Niagara and the Mississippi—which, although since excelled by many writers, native and foreign, at the time (1833) was a refreshing contrast to previous attempts of a like nature. *Blackwood* recognized his political bias in commending the work "as valuable at the present crisis, when all the ancient institutions of our country are successively melting away under the powerful solvent of democratic institutions."

Parkinson was an English farmer, and therefore might be supposed capable of producing at least a valuable agricultural report; but impartial critics declared him both impudent and mendacious. Stuart's book * owed somewhat of its casual notoriety to the circumstance that he fled to America because he had killed Lord Auchinleck, Boswell's son, in a duel at Edinburgh; and beguiled months of his involuntary exile at Hoboken, N. Y., in writing his experience and impressions. The *Edinburgh Review* says of another of the countless writers on this prolific theme—Birkbeck: "Detesting his principles, we praise his entertaining volume." †

Harriet Martineau, through her Unitarian associations, became at once, on her arrival in the United States, intimate with the leading members of that highly intellectual denomination, and thus enjoyed the best social opportunities for acquiring a knowledge of the country and a favorable impression of its average culture. To this advantage she added liberal sympathies, an earnest spirit of inquiry, and a decided power of descriptive writing. Accordingly we find, in her work, a warm appreciation of what is humane and progressive in American institutions, right and wise in society, and beautiful or picturesque in nature. She often adopts a view and makes a general statement upon inadequate grounds. Her generalizations are not always authentic; but the spirit and execution of her work are a vast improvement upon the flippant detraction of less intelligent and aspiring writers. As in so many instances before and since, her gravest errors, both as to facts and reasoning, may be traced to inferences from partisan testimony, or the statements of uninformed acquaintance—a process which hasty travellers bent on book making are forced to have recourse to. Where she observed, she recorded effectively; when her informant was duly equipped for his catechism, she "set in a note book" what was worth preserving; but often, relying on hearsay evi-

---

* "Three Years in America," by James Stuart, 3 vols., Edinburgh, 1823.
† "Notes on a Journey from Virginia to the Territory of Illinois," by Morris Birkbeck, with a map, 8vo., Dublin, 1818.

dence and casual statements, inevitably mistakes occurred; but these do not invalidate her arguments or diminish her authority, when fairly provided with the opportunity to examine herself, or correctly informed by others. *Blackwood* condemned her book with an asperity that is *prima facie* evidence that it has considerable merit. "Nothing," says that trenchant and Tory oracle, in reference thereto, "nothing can rectify a reformer's vision, and no conviction of inadequacy prevent any of the class from lecturing all mankind."

Of this class of books, however, none made so strong a popular impression as the "Domestic Manners of the Americans," by Mrs. Trollope—a circumstance that the reader of our own day finds it difficult to explain, until he recalls and reflects upon the facts of the case; for the book is superior to the average of a like scope, in narrative interest. It is written in a lively, confident style, and, before the subjects treated had become so familiar and hackneyed, must have proved quite entertaining. The name of the writer, however, was, for a long period, and still is, to a certain extent, more identified with the unsparing social critics of the country than any other in the long catalogue of modern British travellers in America. Until recently, the sight of a human foot protruding over the gallery of a Western theatre was hailed with the instant and vociferous challenge, apparently undisputed as authoritative, of "Trollope!" whereupon the obnoxious member was withdrawn from sight; and the inference to a stranger's mind became inevitable, that this best-abused writer on America was a beneficent, practical reformer.

The truth is, that Mrs. Trollope's powers of observation are remarkable. What she sees, she describes with vivacity, and often with accurate skill. No one can read her Travels in Austria without acknowledging the vigor and brightness of her mind. Personal disappointment in a pecuniary enterprise vexed her judgment; and, like so many of her nation, she thoroughly disliked the political institutions of the United

States, was on the lookout for social anomalies and personal defects, and persistent, like her "unreasoning sex," in attributing all that was offensive or undesirable in her experience to the prejudice she cherished. Moreover, her experience itself was limited and local. She entered the country more than thirty years ago, at New Orleans, and passed most of the time, during her sojourn, amid the new and thriving but crude and confident Western communities, where neither manners nor culture, economy nor character had attained any well-organized or harmonious development. The self-love of these independent but sometimes rough pioneers of civilization, was wounded by the severe comments of a stranger who had shared their hospitality, when she expatiated on their reckless use of tobacco, their too free speech and angular attitudes; but, especially, when all their shortcomings were declared the natural result of republican institutions. Hence the outcry her book occasioned, and the factitious importance attached thereto. Not a single fault is found recorded by her, which our own writers, and every candid citizen, have not often admitted and complained of. The fast eating, boastful talk, transient female beauty, inadequate domestic service, abuse of calomel as a remedy, copious and careless expectoration, free and easy manners, superficial culture, and many other traits, more or less true now as then, here or there, are or have been normal subjects of animadversion. It was not because Mrs. Trollope did not write much truth about the country and the people, that, among classes of the latter, her name was a reproach; but because she reasoned so perversely, and did not take the pains to ascertain the whole truth, and to recognize the compensatory facts of American life. But this objection should have been reconciled by her candor. She frankly declares that her chief object is "to encourage her countrymen to hold fast by the Constitution that insures all the blessings which flow from established habits and solid principles;" and elsewhere remarks that the dogma "that all men are born free and equal has done, is doing, and will do much harm to this fair country." Her sympathies overflow toward an English actor, author, and teacher she encounters, and she feels a pang at André's grave; but she looks with the eye of criticism only on the rude masses who are turning the wilderness into cities, refusing to see any prosperity or progress in the scope and impulse of democratic principles. "Some of the native political economists," she writes, "assert that this rapid conversion of a bearbrake into a prosperous city is the result of free political institutions. Not being very deep in such matters, a more obvious cause suggested itself to me, in the unceasing goad which necessity applies to industry in this country, and in the absence of all resources for the idle." Without discussing the abstract merits of her theory, it is obvious that a preconceived antipathy to the institutions of a country unfits even a sensible and frank writer for social criticism thereon; and, in this instance, the writer seems to have known comparatively few of the more enlightened men, and to have enjoyed the intimacy of a still smaller number of the higher class of American women; so that, with the local and social data she chiefly relied on, her conclusions are only unjust inasmuch as they are too general. She describes well what strikes her as new and curious; but her first impressions, always so influential, were forlorn. The flat shores at the mouth of the Mississippi in winter, the muddy current, pelicans, snags, and bulrushes, were to her a desolate change from the bright blue ocean; but the flowers and fruits of Louisiana, the woods and the rivers, as they opened to her view, brought speedy consolation; which, indeed, was modified by disagreeable cookery, bad roads, illness, thunder storms, and unpleasant manners and customs—the depressing influence of which, however, did not prevent her expatiating with zest and skill upon the camp meetings, snakes, insects, elections, house moving, queer phrases, dress, bugs, lingo, parsons, politicians, figures, faces, and opinions which came within her observation.

With more perspicacity and less prejudice, she would have acknowledged the temporary character of many of the facts of the hour, emphasized by her pen as permanent. The superficial reading she notes, for instance, was but the eager thirst for knowledge that has since expanded into so wide a habit of culture that the statistics of the book trade in the United States have become one of the intellectual marvels of the age. Her investigation as to the talent, sources of discipline, and development, were extremely incurious and slight; hence, what she says of our statesmen and men of letters is too meagre for comment. The only American author she appears to have known well was Flint; and her warm appreciation of his writings and conversation, indicates what a better knowledge of our scholars and eminent professional men would have elicited from so shrewd an observer. The redeeming feature of her book is the love of nature it exhibits. American scenery often reconciles her to the bad food and worse manners; the waterfalls, rivers, and forests are themes of perpetual admiration. "So powerful," she writes of a passage down one of the majestic streams of the West, "was the effect of this sweet scenery, that we ceased to grumble at our dinners and suppers." Strange to say, she was delighted with the city of Washington, extols the Capitol, and recognizes the peculiar merits of Philadelphia. In fact, when she writes of what she sees, apart from prejudice, there are true woman's wit and sense in her descriptions; but she does not discriminate, or patiently inquire. Her book is one of impressions—some very just, and others casual. She was provoked at being often told, in reply to some remark, "That is because you know so little of America;" and yet the observation is one continually suggested by her too hasty conclusions. With all its defects, however, few of the class of books to which it belongs are better worth reading now than this once famous record of Mrs. Trollope. It has a certain freshness and boldness about it that explain its original popularity. Its tone, also, in no small degree explains its unpopularity; for the writer, quoting a remark of Basil Hall's, to the effect that the great difference between Americans and English is the want of loyalty, declares it, in her opinion, is the want of refinement. And it is upon this that she harps continually in her strictures, while the reader is offended by the identical deficiency in herself; and herein we find the secret of the popular protest the book elicited on this side of the water; for those who felt they needed to be lectured on manners, repudiated such a female writer as authoritative, and regarded her assumption of the office as more than gratuitous.

The interest excited by many of the now forgotten books at which we have glanced, can only be compared to that which attends a new novel by a popular author. Curiosity, pique, self-love, and indignation were alternately awakened. Hospitable people found themselves outraged, and communicative tuft hunters betrayed; provincial self-complacency was sadly disturbed, and the countless readers of the land, for weeks, talked only of the coarse comments of Mrs. Trollope, the descriptive powers of Captain Hamilton, the kindly views of the Hon. Augustus Murray, the conceit of Basil Hall, the good sense of Combe, the frankness of Fanny Butler, the impertinence of Fiddler, the elaborate egotism of Silk Buckingham, the scientific knowledge of Featherstonaugh and Lyell, the indelicate personalities of Fredrika Bremer, the masculine assurance of Miss Martineau, and the ungrateful caricatures of Dickens, as exhibited in their respective accounts of American life, institutions, resources, and manners.

One of the latest of this class of Travels in America, is an elaborate work entitled "Civilized America," by Thomas Colley Grattan. Although this writer commences his book by defining the Americans "a people easy of access, but difficult to understand," and declares that "no one who writes about the United States should be considered an oracle," he is behind none of his predecessors in the complacency and confidence with which he handles a confessedly difficult subject. He thinks that "it is in masses that the people of this country are to be seen to the greatest advantage;" not apparently recognizing the fact that this is the distinctive aim of republican institutions—the special compensation for the

absence of those monopolies and that exclusiveness whereby
the individual in Europe is gratified at the expense of the
multitude. He notes the "sacrifice of individual eminence,
and consequently of personal enjoyment"—a result of the
same spirit of humanity which cherishes manhood and womanhood as such, and, therefore, cheerfully loses the chance of
individual aggrandizement, in so far as it implies superiority
to and immunity from the universal and equal development
or opportunity therefor, whether of character, talent, material
welfare, or social position. Our educational system, public
men, some of the current political problems and parties, the
Irish in America, relations between England and the United
States, slavery, and other general subjects, are treated of
with little originality, but occasionally illustrated by facts
which to a British reader may be new and suggestive. The
old sarcasms about the bad architecture in our cities, and the
limited triumphs in art and literature yet achieved; the usual
sentimental protest against the slight local attachments, the
hurry, and the unrecreative habits and want of taste that
prevail; the hackneyed complaint of unscientific regimen,
with especial reference to the indigestible nature of dough-
nuts, salt fish and chowder; and the baneful variety of
alcoholic drinks, and their vulgar names, diversify the grave
discussion of questions of polity and character.

It is surprising that a native of Great Britain should find
punctuality at meals and the condition of women in America themes of animadversion; and that conceit and flippancy
should strike him as so common on this side of the water;
and narrowness of mind, as well as the want of independence, be regarded as characteristic. In these and several
other instances, the reader familiar with life and manners in
England, and alive to the indications of character in style
and modes of thought, cannot but suspect him of drawing
upon his experience at home and his own consciousness, quite
as much as from intelligent observation here. At all events,
it is obvious that he is piqued into indignation by some special experience of his own while British Consul in Boston;

for that "hub of the universe" is not the nucleus about which either his sympathies or his magnanimity revolve. Great ameliorations have occurred in "Civilized America" since Mr. Grattan left her shores. Nothing shows the progress of the country more emphatically than the obsolete significance of many of his remarks. They often do not apply to the United States of to-day; and both that country and the reading public generally have outgrown the need and the taste for this kind of petty fault-finding, which fails to comprehend the spirit of the people, the true scope of the institutions, the real law of life, labor, and love, whereof the communities gathered on this vast and prolific continent are the representatives. Not as a nursery of local manners, a sphere for casual social experiments, an arena for conventional development; but as the scene of a free expansion and assertion of the rights of humanity, a refuge for the victims of outgrown systems and over-populated countries, a home for man as such, a land where humanity modifies and moulds nationality, by virtue of the unimpeded range and frank recognition thereof, in the laws, the opportunities, the equal rights established and enjoyed, is America to be discussed and understood; for her civilization, when and where it is truly developed, is cosmopolitan, not sectional—human, not formal.

In 1850, the Earl of Carlisle delivered before the Mechanics' Institute of Leeds a lecture embodying his observations and comments during a tour in the United States; which was subsequently published and read with much interest by his lordship's numerous friends on this side of the Atlantic. A candid discussion of social defects and political dangers is mingled, in this work, with a just appreciation of the privileges and prosperity of the country. The American edition was widely circulated, and justly estimated as one of the most frank, kindly, and intelligent expositions of a familiar but suggestive theme, which had yet appeared. Though limited in scope, it is unpretending in tone and genial in feeling.

In 1862, thirty years after Mrs. Trollope gave to the world her opinion of the "Domestic Manners of the Americans," her son Anthony published his book on "North America."* His novels illustrative of Irish and ecclesiastical life, had made his name and abilities as a writer familiar on this side of the water. These works of fiction have for their chief merit an adherence to fact. The characters are not modelled on an ideal standard, the incidents are seldom extraordinary, and the style is the reverse of glowing. Careful observation, good sense, an apparently conscientious regard to the truth, make them a singular exception to the popular novels of the day. The author is no imaginative enthusiast or psychological artist, but he is an intelligent and accurate reporter of life as he sees it, of men and things as they are; and if the subject interests his reader, he will derive very clear and very just ideas of those forms and phases of British experience and economy with which these books so patiently deal. Mr. Trollope's account of his visit to the West Indies is recognized, by competent judges, as one of the most faithful representations of the actual condition of those islands, and especially of the normal traits and tendencies of the negro, which has appeared. Accordingly, he seems to have been remarkably fitted to record with candid intelligence what he saw and felt while visiting North America; and this he has done. The speciality of his book is, that it treats of the Rebellion, and is the first elaborate report thereof by a British eyewitness. Its defects are those of limited opportunities, an unfavorable period, and a superficial experience warped by certain national proclivities, which the feeling at work around him inevitably exasperated; and further modified by the circumstance that he is a Government *employé* and an English author. His spirit and intent, however, are so obviously manful and considerate, that his American readers are disarmed as soon as they are vexed, by whatever strikes them as unfair or indiscriminate. Yet, friendly as is the sentiment he challenges by his frankness,

* "North America," by Anthony Trollope, New York, 1862.

good sense, and good nature, one cannot avoid feeling somewhat impatient at the gratuitous tone of criticism, and the wearisome repetition and re-discussion of the most familiar subjects. If, as Mr. Trollope says, it has been "the ambition of his literary life to write a book about the United States," why did he not consult what has already been written, and give an adequate period and study to the subject? Scarcely a topic upon which he dilates as a grievance, has escaped like treatment from scores of his predecessors in this field, and been humorously exposed or cleverly discussed by our own authors; and yet he gravely returns to the charge, as if a newly discovered social anomaly claimed his perspicacious analysis. This unconsciousness of the hackneyed nature of the objections to American civilization, or want thereof, is the more amusing from a certain tone of didactic responsibility, common, indeed, to all English writers on America, as if that vast and populous country included no citizen or native capable of teaching her the proprieties of life and the principles of taste. We are constantly reminded of the reiterating insect who "says an undisputed thing in such a solemn way." Inasmuch as Mrs. Trollope, who came here thirty years ago to open a bazaar in a newly settled city of the West—which speculation failed—"with a woman's keen eye," saw, felt, and put "in a note book" the grievous solecisms in manners and deformities of social life which struck her in the fresh but crude American communities, her honest and industrious son now feels it incumbent upon him to complete the work, as "she did not regard it as part of hers to dilate on the nature and operation of those political arrangements which had produced the social absurdities which she saw; or to explain that, though such absurdities were the natural result of those arrangements in their newness, the defects would certainly pass away, while the political arrangements, if good, would remain." This, he thinks, is better work for a man than a woman, and therefore undertakes to do it—not apparently dreaming that it has been and is continually being done by those whose lifelong acquaintance with the problem, to say nothing of their personal interest in its solution, enables them fully to comprehend and clearly to analyze. This instinctive self-esteem is apparently the normal mood with which even the kindliest and the most sensible English travellers comment on America. They do not condescend to examine the writings of Americans on their own country, and ignore the fact that the lectures, essays, sermons, and humorous sketches of our own authors, have, for years, advocated reforms, exposed defects, and suggested ameliorations which these self-constituted foreign censors proclaim as original. Mr. Trollope seems extremely afraid of giving offence, continually deprecates the idea, and wishes it understood that it is very painful to him to find fault with anybody or anything in the United States, but he must censure as well as blame, and he means no unkindness. All this, however amiable, is really preposterous. It presupposes a degree of importance as belonging to his opinions, or rather a necessity for their expression, which seems to us quite irrational in a man of such common sense, and who has seen so much of the world. It is amusing, and, as a friend remarked, "comes from his blood, not his brain." It is the old leaven of self-love, self-importance, self-assertion of the Englishman as such. If he had passed years instead of months in America, and grown familiar with other circles besides the circle of *littérateurs* who so won his admiration in Boston, he would have found all he has written of the spoiled children, the hard women, the despotic landlords, disgusting railway cars, Western swindlers, bad architecture, official peculations, mud, dust, and desolation of Washington, misery of Cairo, and base, gold-seeking politicians of America, overheated rooms, incongruous *cuisine*, and undisciplined juveniles, thoroughly appreciated, perfectly understood, and habitually the subject of native protest and foreign report. On many of these points his views are quite unemphatic, compared to those of educated Americans; so that his discussion of civility *vs.* servility, of modern chivalry, of the reckless element of frontier life, of the unscrupulous " smartness" and the want of reverence in the American character, and the want of privacy and comfort in our gregarious hotels, seem to us quite as superfluous a task as to inveigh in England against fees, taxes, fog, game laws, low wages, pauperism, ecclesiastical abuses, aristocratic monopolies, or any other patent and familiar evil.

That "necessity of eulogium" which pressed upon Mr. Trollope, as it has upon so many of his countrymen in America, is regarded as the evidence of extreme national sensitiveness; but he himself unwittingly betrays somewhat of the same weakness—if it be such—by the deep impression made by an individual's remark to his wife, which remark, if made seriously to an Englishwoman, must have come from a person not overburdened with sense; and if from a man of intelligence, doubtless was intended as humorous. In either case, it would seem unworthy of notice; but Mr. Trollope refers to it again and again, as if characteristic: "I never yet met the down-trodden subject of a despot who did not hug his chains." Those English flags among the trophies at West Point, too, much as he delighted in the picturesque beauty of the place, sorely haunted his mind. The fact is, that this personal sensibility to national claims and associations is the instinct of humanity. Its expression here is more prevalent and its exactions more imperative, from the fact that, of all civilized countries, our own has been and is the chosen theme of criticism, for the reason that it is more experimental. In his somewhat disparaging estimate of Newport, R. I., Mr. Trollope strangely omits the chief attraction, and that is the peculiar climate, wherein it so much differs from the rest of the New England coast. He ignores this essential consideration, also, in his remarks upon the distinctive physiognomy of Americans. Yet such is its influence, combined with the active and exciting life of the country, that the "rosy cheeks," full habit, and pedestrian habitudes of Englishmen, often, after a few years' residence, give place to thin jaws and frames, and comparative indifference to exercise: the nervous temperament encroaches upon the sanguine; beef and beer, port and porter, are found too nutritive a diet; and a certain quickness of mind and movement, and sensibility to physical influences, transform John Bull even to his own consciousness. What Mr. Trollope says of the American press, whether just or not, comes with an ill grace from an Englishman, at a period wherein have been so absolutely demonstrated to the world the wilful perversity and predetermined falsehood of the leading press of Great Britain. As in the case of so many of his countrymen, the scenery of America proved to Mr. Trollope a compensation for her discomforts. Niagara, the White Mountains, the Alleghanies, and the Upper Mississippi, are described with more enthusiasm than anything else but Boston hospitality. Of course, for this feast of beauty, so amply illustrated by our writers, he suggests that only Murray can furnish the Guide Book.

It is curious that a man with such an eye for nature, and such an inquiring mind, should find the St. Lawrence so little attractive, fail to see President Lincoln, and feel no emotion at the scene of Wolfe's heroic death. Few visitors to "the States" have more intelligently appreciated the manliness of the frontier settlers, the sad patience there born of independent and lone struggling with nature, the immense cereal resources of the West, and the process of transportation thereof at Chicago and Buffalo. He follows his predecessors in attributing the chief glory of America to her provision for universal education, her mechanical contrivances, and the great average comfort and intelligence.

"The one thing," he remarks, "in which, as far as my judgment goes, the people of the United States have excelled us Englishmen, so as to justify them in taking to themselves praise which we cannot take to ourselves or refuse to them, is the matter of education; * * * and unrivalled population, wealth, and intelligence have been the results; and with these, looking at the whole masses of the people, I think I am justified in saying, unrivalled comfort and happiness. It is not that you, my reader, to whom, in this matter of education, fortune and your parents have probably been bountiful, would have been more happy in New York than in London. It is not that I, who, at any rate, can read and write, have cause to wish that I had been an American. But it is this: if you and I can count up in a day all those on whom our eyes may rest, and learn the circumstances of their lives, we shall be driven to conclude that nine tenths of that number would have had a better life as Americans than they can have in their spheres as Englishmen.

"If a man can forget his own miseries in his journeyings, and think of the people he comes to see rather than of himself, I think he will find himself driven to admit that education has made life for the million in the Northern States better than life for the million is with us.

"I do not know any contrast that would be more surprising to an Englishman, up to that moment ignorant of the matter, than that which he would find by visiting first of all a free school in London, and then a free school in New York. * * * The female pupil at a free school in London is, as a rule, either a ragged pauper or a charity girl, if not degraded, at least stigmatized by the badges and dress of the charity. We Englishmen know well the type of each, and have a fairly correct idea of the amount of education which is imparted to them. We see the result afterward, when the same girls become our servants, and the wives of our grooms and porters. The female pupil at a free school in New York is neither a pauper nor a charity girl. She is dressed with the utmost decency. She is perfectly cleanly. In speaking to her, you cannot in any degree guess whether her father has a dollar a day, or three thousand dollars a year. Nor will you be enabled to guess by the manner in which her associates treat her. As regards her own manner to you, it is always the same as though her father were in all respects your equal.

"That which most surprises an English visitor, on going through the mills at Lowell, is the personal appearance of the men and women who work at them. As there are twice as many women as there are men, it is to them that the attention is chiefly called. They are not only better dressed, cleaner and better mounted in every respect than the girls employed at manufactories in England, but they are so infinitely superior as to make a stranger immediately perceive that some very strong cause must have created the difference. * * * One would, of course, be disposed to say that the superior condition of the workers must have been occasioned by superior wages; and this, to a certain extent, has been the cause. But the higher payments is not the chief cause. Women's wages, including all that they receive at the Lowell factories, average about fourteen shillings a week; which is, I take it, fully a third more than women can earn in Manchester, or did earn before the loss of the American cotton began to tell upon them. But if wages at Manchester were raised to the Lowell standard, the Manchester woman would not be clothed, fed, cared for, and educated like the Lowell woman."

Charles Lamb aptly says, that the finer in kind things are, the more scope there is for individual taste; and therefore he was "always rather squeamish in his women and children." Mr. Trollope, judging of the latter by the *enfants terribles* encountered at inns and on steamboats in America, describes the nuisance of over-indulged and peremptory "Young America" with emphasis; and also draws the line, so remarkably obvious in this country, between female refinement and vulgarity. He is doubtless right in ascribing the Amazonian manners and expression of the latter class to that universal consideration for the sex so peculiar to our people. It certainly is abused, and offensively so by the selfish and arrogant. The conduct of Southern women, during the present war, to Northern officers, is the best proof of their consciousness of safety by virtue of this public sentiment of deference and protection. But has it ever occurred to Mr. Trollope that this sentiment, however abused by those lacking the chivalry to respond to it, is almost a social necessity in a land where people are thrown together so promiscuously, and where no ranks exist to regulate intercourse and define position? Crinoline and bad manners have, indeed, done much to encroach upon romance, and render modern gallantry thoroughly conventional; but the extravagant estimation in which the rights and privileges of woman are here held, is one of the most useful of our social safeguards and sanctions. Mr. Trollope pays the usual tribute of strangers to the beauty, intelligence, and grace of American women who are ladies by nature and not by courtesy; but he draws the reverse picture, not unfaithfully, in this mention of a species of the female sex sometimes encountered in a public conveyance:

"The woman, as she enters, drags after her a misshapen, dirty mass of battered wirework, which she calls her crinoline, and which adds as much to her grace and comfort as a log of wood does to a donkey, when tied to the animal's leg in a paddock. Of this she takes much heed, not managing it so that it may be conveyed up the carriage with some decency, but striking it about against men's legs, and heaving it with violence over people's knees. The touch of a real woman's dress is in itself delicate; but these blows from a harpy's fins are loathsome. If there be two of them, they talk loudly together, having a theory that modesty has been put out of court by women's rights.

"But, though not modest, the woman I describe is ferocious in her propriety. She ignores the whole world around her, as she sits with raised chin, and face flattened by affectation. She pretends to declare aloud that she is positively not aware that any man is even near her. * * * But every twist of her body, and every tone of her voice, is an unsuccessful falsehood. She looks square at you in the face, and you rise to give her your seat. You rise from a deference to your own old convictions, and from that courtesy which you have ever paid to a woman's dress, let it be worn with ever such hideous deformities. She takes the place from which you have moved without a word or a bow. She twists herself round, banging your shins with her wires; while her chin is still raised, and her face is still flattened, and she directs her friend's attention to another seated man, as though that place were also vacant, and necessarily at her disposal. Perhaps the man opposite has his own ideas about chivalry. I have seen such a thing, and have rejoiced to see it."

And of the spoiled children he thus discourses:

"And then the children—babies I should say, if I were speaking of English bairns of their age; but, seeing that they are Americans, I hardly dare to call them children. The actual age of these perfectly civilized and highly educated beings may be from three to four. One will often see five or six such seated at the long dinner table of the hotel, breakfasting and dining with their elders, and going through the ceremony with all the gravity and more than all the decorum of their grandfathers. When I was three years old, I had not yet, as I imagine, been promoted beyond a silver spoon of my own, wherewith to eat my bread and milk in the nursery; and I feel assured that I was under the immediate care of a nursemaid, as I gobbled up my minced mutton mixed with potatoes and gravy.

"But at hotel life in the States, the adult infant lisps to the waiter for everything at table, handles his fish with epicurean delicacy, is choice in his selection of pickles, very particular that his beefsteak at breakfast shall be hot, and is instant in his demand for fresh ice in his water. But perhaps his—or in this case her—retreat from the room when the meal is over, is the *chef d'œuvre* of the whole performance. The little precocious, full-blown beauty of four signifies that she has completed her meal—or is 'through' her dinner, as she would express it—by carefully extricating herself from the napkin which has been tucked around her. Then the waiter, ever attentive to her movements, draws back the chair on which she is seated, and the young lady glides to the floor. A little girl in old England would scramble down; but little girls in New England never scramble. Her father and mother, who are no more than her chief ministers, walk before her out of the saloon, and then—she swims after them."

The frequent change of occupation, and the hardihood with which misfortunes—especially pecuniary reverses—are met, impress him. "Everybody," he writes, "understands everything, and everybody intends, sooner or later, to do everything;" and, "whatever turns up, the *man* is still there, still unsophisticated, still unbroken." He thinks American coachmen the most adroit in the world; the houses more convenient than those of England of the same class; the green knolls and open glades of Kentucky more like what his countrymen love in a manorial estate, than any land or forest elsewhere in the country; and, of cities, gives the preference to Boston and Baltimore—the former on account of its culture, and the latter because of its "hunting-ground" vicinity, pleasant women, and "English look." It is amusing to find him gravely asserting, that "the mind of an Englishman has more imagination than that of an American," and that "squash is the pulp of the pumpkin." He thinks we suffer for "a national religion," and have found out that "the plan of governing by little men has certainly not answered;" and justly regards it as our special blessing to "have been able to begin at the beginning," and so, in many things, improve upon the Old World. Of Congress and Cambridge, Mr. Trollope gives details of parliamentary customs and educational habits, indicating wherein they differ from those of England. He repeats the old arguments for an international copyright. He discusses Canada in her present and prospective political relations with singular candor, and frankly admits the inferiority of her material development to that of the United States. "Everybody travels in America," he observes, "and nothing is thought of distance." In this fact he could easily have found the explanation of the discomforts of American travel, inasmuch as railroads that are built to lure emigrants to build towns in the wilderness, and cars that are intended to convey crowds of all classes, in the nature of the case do not admit of those refined arrangements which make foreign railways so agreeable, and the absence of which renders most American journeys a penance. Among the things which Mr. Trollope, however, finds superior, are canvas-back ducks, rural cemeteries, schools, asylums, city libraries, waterfalls, maize fields, authors, and women. But the special interest of his book is its discussion of the civil war. His own political views seem to us somewhat inconsistent. Repudiating the military despotism existing in France as a wrong to manhood and humanity, he yet thinks "those Chinese rascals should be forced into the harness of civilization." In allusion to our errors of government, he justly remarks, that "the material growth of the States has been so quick, that the political has not been able to keep up with it." In some respects he does justice to the war for the Union, asserting its necessity, and recognizing the disinterested patriotism of the North, and the wholly inadequate reasons put forth by the South for treachery and revolt. Yet he fails to grasp the whole subject—treating the exigency as political exclusively, and the Rebellion as analogous to that of Naples, Poland, and our own Revolution. This is, to say the least, a most inadequate and perverse view. Not only had the South no wrongs to redress for which the United States Government were responsible, but they violated State not less than National rights, in their seizure of property, persecution and murder of loyal citizens, and enforced votes and enlistments at the point of the bayonet. Citizens in their midst claimed and deserved Federal protection not less than those on this side of their lines. Moreover, the "landless resolutes" of the South proved, in warfare, barbarians in sacrilegious hate; so that, under any circumstances, it would have become a necessity for the North to fortify and defend her frontier. These circumstances make an essential difference between this Rebellion and other civil wars: they aggravate its turpitude, and vindicate the severest measures to repress it, irrespective of any question of political union. In like manner Mr. Trollope gives but a partial view of the feeling of America toward England. It was not sympathy in a mere political quarrel, between two equally justified parties, that she expected, and was grieved and incensed at not receiving. Such a feeling might be unmanly, as Mr. Trollope thinks, and also unreasonable; but when, for years, English statesmen, travellers, and journalists had taunted us with the slavery entailed upon the Southern States in colonial days, and by British authority; and when, at last, we had made the first grand step toward limiting, if not undermining the evil, and, by doing so, had incurred the hatred, treachery, and violence of the slaveholders, we had every reason to expect that a Christian nation, akin in blood and language, would throw the weight of her influence, social and political, into the scale of justice, instead of hastening to recognize the insurgents as standing before the world on an equal moral and civic footing with a Government and a people they had cheated, defied, and were seeking to destroy for no reason save the constitutional election of a President opposed to the extension of slavery. It was this that created the disappointment and inspired the bitterness which Mr. Trollope declares so unjust and unreasonable. He compares the struggle to a quarrel between a man and his wife, and with two parties throwing brickbats at each other across the street, to the great discomfort of neutral passengers. Mr. Gladstone recently compared it to a difficulty between two partners in business, the one wishing to retire from the firm, and the other attempting to force him to remain. Lord Brougham also spoke of a late treaty between England and the United States of America to suppress the slave trade, as "the treaty of the Northern Government." It requires no special candor and right feeling to perceive the *animus* of such expressions. They ignore the true state of the case; they betray a want of respect for historical accuracy, and an indifference, not to say contempt, for the Government and people of America, only to be explained by a brutal want of Christian sympathy, or mean desire to see a great and patriotic nation decimated and humbled. How sadly do such observations contrast with the just and kindly statements of De Gasparin, of John Bright, and of John Stuart Mill! All the solicitude which agitated England and America in regard to the capture of the rebel envoys, about which Mr. Trollope has so much to say, would have been avoided had Great Britain acted, thought, spoken, and felt in this matter with any magnanimity. To her the safe transit of those Secession commissioners was of no importance; to us it was, at the time, a serious misfortune. Their relinquishment, without war threats and war preparations, would have cost a friendly and noble nation no loss of dignity, no harm to private or public interests. The proceeding was assumed to be a premeditated insult, whereas it was purely an accident. An insult implies intention. In this case, the object of Captain Wilkes was manifestly to perform a duty to his own, not to injure or treat with disrespect another country. His act was illegal, but the exigency was peculiar. A generous man or woman personally incommoded by the representative of a just cause, and in the hour of misfortune, where there was no malice, no impertinence, but an important end to be achieved at the expense of a temporary discourtesy—not real, but apparent—would cheerfully waive conventional rights, and, from nobility of feeling, subdue or postpone resentment. In social life, examples of such forbearance and humane consideration often happen; and though it may be Utopian to apply the same ethical code to nations and individuals—in the view of a Christian or even a chivalric man, such an application of the high and holy instincts of our nature is far from irrational. In that sacred chart whereon rest the hopes and the faith, the precedents and the principles of Christianity—" the spirit we are of" is constantly referred to as the test of character and the evidence of feeling. Throughout our national sorrows, from the inception of this wicked Rebellion, through all its course, the spirit of the press and Parliament, the spirit of England, as far as it has found official expression, with a few memorable exceptions, have been unjust, disingenuous, and inimical; and when the history of this national crisis is written, the evidence of this will be as glaring as it is shameful.

Mr. Trollope has lost an opportunity to realize "the ambition of his literary life." His visit was too brief and unseasonable for him to do anything like justice to himself or his subject. He visited the West in winter—a comfortless period, when nature is denuded of the freshness and beauty which at more genial seasons cheer the natural "melancholy" he felt there. He saw the army of the Union in its transition state, and beheld the country and the people when under the shadow of war, and that war undertaken against a senseless and savage mutiny. He rapidly scanned places, with no time to ripen superficial acquaintance into intimacy; and he wrote his impressions of the passing scene in the midst of hurry, discomfort, and the turbulence and gloom of a painfully exciting and absorbing era. Moreover, his *forte* is not political disquisition. Still, the interests involved, the moral spectacle apparent, the historical and social elements at work, were such as to inspire a humanitarian and enlighten a philosopher; and if unambitious of either character, there remained a great duty and noble mission for an English author—to correct specifically, to deny emphatically, the current misrepresentations of British statesmen and journals, and to vindicate a kindred and maligned people. He has told many wholesome truths; he has borne witness to many essential facts about which the British public have hitherto, in spite of all evidence, professed utter incredulity. But he might have gone farther and done more, and so made his work signally useful now, and far more memorable hereafter.

The Scotch are far more discriminating and sympathetic than the English in their comments and comparisons in regard to America. The affinity between the North Britons and the New Englanders has often been noted. In habits of industry, native shrewdness, religious enthusiasm, frugal instincts, love of knowledge, and many other traits, a parallel may be easily traced. We have seen how genial was the appreciation of Mrs. Grant in her girlhood, of the independence, harmony, and social charms of colonial life in Albany. Alexander Wilson both loved and honored the home he found on our soil; and among the Travels in America of recent date, which, in their liberal spirit and their sagacity, form honorable exceptions to British misrepresentation, are two works written by Scotchmen, which our publishers, so ready to reproduce books that have the piquancy of abuse or the flash of extravagance, with singular want of judgment have ignored. The first of these is an unpretending little brochure, entitled "A Tour in the United States," by Archibald Prentice.* This writer has been a public-spirited citizen and an editor in Manchester, and was thus practically fitted intelligently to examine the economical features of the country. Of Covenanter stock, his sympathies were drawn to the Connecticut clergy; and the graves of kindred endeared the land which he visited in order to examine its physical resources with special reference to emigration, manufactures, trade, and labor. He is enthusiastic on entering, on a beautiful day, the harbor of New York, and, with all the zest of a practical economist, dwells upon the activity and scope of that commercial metropolis. "Here," he writes, "bright visions arise in the imagination of the utilitarian. He sees the farmer on the Hudson, the Mohawk, the Ohio, the Illinois, the Miami, and the lakes Michigan, Erie, and Ontario, cheerfully laboring in his own fields for the sustenance of the Manchester spinner and weaver; he sees the potter of Horsley, the cutler of Sheffield, the cloth manufacturer of Yorkshire, and the sewer and tambourer of Glasgow, in not hopeless or unre-

* London: Charles Gilpin, 1848.

warded toil, preparing additional comforts and enjoyments for the inhabitants of the American woods and prairies. He conjures up a great coöperative community, all working for mutual benefit; and sees, in the universal competition, the universal good." He finds the usual defects, as he extends his observations—the cheap railroads, the fragile women, the over-eagerness for foreign appreciation, the inadequate agricultural science, and, above all, the monstrous evil—political, economical, social, moral, and religious—of slavery. But while all these and other drawbacks are emphasized, the causes and conditions are frankly stated. This writer appreciates the favorable relations of labor to capital, and, although an anti-protectionist, recognizes cordially the advantages here realized by honest industry and intelligent enterprise in manufactures and trade. "Even the Irishman," he writes, "becomes commercial." "The Illinois coalfields," he notes, "are reached by drifts instead of shafts—horizontally, not perpendicularly." He lauds our comparatively inexpensive Government, the "moral machinery" of our manufacturing towns, the harmonious coexistence of so many religious sects. He considers the stern virtues bred by the hard soil and climate of New England a providential school, wherein the character of Western emigration was auspiciously predetermined. But Mr. Prentice has as keen an eye for the beauties of nature as for the resources of industry. He was constantly impressed, not only with the general but with the specific resemblance of American scenery to that of Great Britain; and compares an "opening" in the landscape between Baltimore and Washington to "the Esk below Langholm;" the view up the Shenandoah to the Clyde at Auld-Brig-End, near Lanark; the bluffs of the Ohio to the "irregular face which Alderley Edge presents Wilmstone;" and Lake Champlain to Windermere and Ulswater; while he finds the "footway to the Charter Oak, at Hartford, worn like the path to the martyr's grave in the Old Friar's Churchyard in Edinburgh. Although thus warmly alive to native associations, he is not less an ardent advocate for mutual forbearance and wise fellowship between Great Britain and America. "The citizens of the United States," he remarks, "do not dislike Englishmen individually. On the contrary, they are rather predisposed to like them, and to pay them most kind and respectful attention when they visit America. Their dislike is to John Bull—the traditional, big, bullying, borough-mongering and monopolizing John Bull; the John Bull as he was at the time of the American and the French Revolutions, before Catholic emancipation, before the repeal of the Orders in Council, before the Reform Bill." And, in conclusion, he thus benignly adjures the spirit of a candid mutual appreciation and harmony: "Would that men in both countries would drop all narrow jealousies, and, looking to the great mission of the Anglo-Saxon family, earnestly resolve that the sole struggle between those of its branches only geographically separated, should be which most jealously and most energetically should labor to Christianize and civilize the whole human race."

The other Scotch writer whose recent observations are worthy of that consideration which an honest purpose, elevated sympathies, and conscientious intelligence, should ever secure, is James Stirling,* a member of Parliament, whose "Letters from the Slave States," published seven years ago, but, strange to say, not reprinted here, seems to have anticipated many of the subsequent political events and social manifestations. This writer has evidently made a study of economical questions. He has that mental discipline which experience, legislative and professional, insures. Firm in his opinions, but liberal and humane in spirit, there is a combination of sagacity and generous feeling in his tone of mind which commands respect. These letters are candid and thoughtful; and, while some of the views advanced challenge argument, the general scope is just and wise. Mr. Stirling was chiefly struck with the rapidity of growth in the American settlements, and records many specific and authen-

* "Letters from the Slave States," by James Stirling. London: J. W. Parker, 1857.

tic facts illustrative of this peculiar feature in Western civilization, of which he calls railways "the soul." The conditions of success for new communities he regards as, first, an energetic population; second, fertile soil; third, favorable climate; and, fourth, easy means of communication; and he explains the prosperity and the failure of such experiments by these conditions. He is opposed to protection and to universal suffrage, and finds ample evidence to sustain these opinions in his observations in the United States. The subject, however, which mainly occupies his attention, is the actual influence and effects of slavery, the difficulties in the way of its abolition, and the probable consequence of its existence upon the destiny and development of the nation. His economical argument is strong. He indicates the comparative stagnation and degradation of the Slave States with detail, describes the *status* of the poor whites, notes the historical facts, and seems to anticipate the climax which three years later involved the country in civil war. "The South," he writes, "seems to me in that mood of mind which foreruns destruction;" and elsewhere observes that "the accident of cotton has been the ruin of the negro." He recognizes a "moral disunion" in the opposition of parties and social instincts in regard to slavery. "Like most foreigners," he observes, "I find it very difficult to appreciate the construction of American parties. There is a party called the Southern party, which is distinctly in favor of separation. It will carry along with it, notwithstanding its most insane policy, a great proportion of the low white population. Opposed to it is the conservative intelligence of the South." Mr. Stirling justly regards the "want of concentration" as the characteristic defect of American civilization; and regards the "aristocracy of the South" as almost identical with "the *parvenu* society of the mushroom cities" in Britain; and observes significantly that it is "on the importance of cotton to England that the philosophers of the South delight to dwell." Indeed, throughout his observations on the Slave States, there is a complete recognition of the facts and principles which the North has vainly striven for months past to impress upon English statesmen; and this testimony is the more valuable inasmuch as it is disinterested, and was recorded before any overt act of rebellion had complicated our foreign relations. Although this writer's experience in Alabama is more favorable to the social condition of that State than what fell under the observation of Mr. Olmsted, yet the latter's economical statistics of the Slave States are amply confirmed by Mr. Stirling. He is equally struck with the contrast between the two parts of the country in regard to providence and comfort. He agrees with other travellers in his estimate of popular defects, and is especially severe upon the evils of hotel life in the United States, and the superficial and showy workmanship which compares so unfavorably with substantial English manufactures. Many of these criticisms have only a local application, yet they are none the less true. Duelling, lynching, "hatred of authority," "passion for territory," inadequate police, and reckless travelling, are traits which are censured with emphasis. But the charm of these letters consists in the broad and benign temper of the writer, when from specific he turns to general inferences, and treats of the country as a whole, and of its relations to the Old World and to humanity. It is refreshing to find united in a foreign critic such a clear perception of the drawbacks to our national prosperity and incongruous elements in our national development, with an equally true insight and recognition of the individual and domestic rectitude, and the noble and high tendencies of life and character. A few random extracts will indicate these qualities of the man and merits of the writer:

"We have experienced, even from utter strangers, an officious kindness and sympathy that can only arise from hearts nurtured in the daily practice of domestic virtues."

"I have no fears but that the follies and crudities of the present effervescent state of American society will pass away, and leave behind a large residuum of solid worth."

"I cannot overlook that latent force of virtue and wisdom, which makes itself, as yet, too little felt in public affairs, but which assuredly is there, and will come forth, I am convinced, when the hour of trial comes to save the country."

"The American nation will wrestle victoriously with these social and political hydras."

Mr. Stirling gives a most true analysis of an American popular speaker in his estimate of Beecher. He discriminates well the local traits of the country, calling Florida the "Alsatia of the Union," because it is such a paradise for sportsmen and squatters; and explaining the superiority in race of the Kentuckians by their hunting habits and progenitors. "The little step," he writes, "from the South to the North, is a stride from barbarism to civilization—a step from the sixteenth to the nineteenth century."

Of the physiognomy of the people he says: "You read upon the nation's brow the extent of its enterprise and the intensity of its desires. The deepest-rooted cause of American disease is the overworking of the brain and the over-excitement of the nervous system."

Equally clear and earnest, humane and noble, is his view of the relation of this country to Great Britain: "Never were two nations," he writes, "so eminently fitted to aid and comfort each other in the vast work of civilization, than England and America." He reproaches Great Britain with her indifference, as manifest in sending second-class ambassadors to the United States; and invokes "the spiritual ruler, the press," to do its part, "by speaking more generously and wisely." If the prescience of this writer is remarkable in estimating aright the temper and tendencies of Southern treason while yet latent, and of Northern integrity and patriotism before events had elicited their active development, no less prophetic is his appeal to English magnanimity:

"Why, in God's name, should we not give them every assurance of respect and affection? Are they not our children, blood of our blood and bone of our bone? Are they not progressive, and fond of power, like ourselves? Are they not our best customers? Have they not the same old English, manly virtues? What is more befitting for us Englishmen, than to watch with intense study and deepest sympathy the momentous strivings of this noble people? It is the same fight we ourselves are fighting—the true and absolute supremacy of Right. Surely nothing can more beseem two great and kindred nations, than to aid and comfort one another in that career of self-ennoblement, which is the end of all national as well as individual existence."*

* "The stupendous greatness of England is factitious, and will only become natural when that empire shall have found its real centre: that centre is the United States."—"*The New Rome; or, The United States of the World*" (*New York*, 1843).

A remarkably bold and comprehensive theory of American progress, unity, and empire, by Theodore Pœsche and Charles Goepp—one an Americanized German, the other a Teutonic philosopher. In this little treatise the geography, politics, races, and social organization of the United States are analyzed, and shown to be "at work upon the fusion of all nations—not of this continent alone, but of all continents—into one people."

CHAPTER VII.

ENGLISH ABUSE OF AMERICA.

It has often been remarked, that there is a fashion in bookcraft, as in every other phase and element of human society; and the caprices thereof are often as inexplicable and fantastic as in manners, costume, and other less intellectual phenomena. The history of modern literature indicates extreme fluctuations of popular taste. Waller and Cowley introduced the *concetti* of the Italians into English verse, which, in Elizabeth's reign, was so preëminent for robust affluence; in Pope's day we had satire and sense predominant; Byron initiated the misanthropic and impassioned style; while Steele and Addison inaugurated social criticism, the lake poets a recurrence to the simplicity of nature, and the Scotch reviewers bold analysis and liberal reform. But the uniform tone of books and criticism in England for so many years, in relation to America, is one of those literary phenomena the cause of which must be sought elsewhere than among the whims and oddities of popular taste or the caprice of authors. A French writer, at one period, declared it was the direct result of official bribery, to stop emigration; but its motives were various, and its origin far from casual or temporary; and the attitude and *animus* of England during the war for the Union, give to these systematic attacks and continuous detraction a formidable significance. The American abroad may have grown indifferent to the derogatory facts or fictions gleaned for *Galignani's Messenger*, and served up with his daily breakfast; he may treat the prejudice and presumption of English censors with amusing nonchalance, when discussing them with an esteemed and kindly friend of that race; but the subject assumes a more grave aspect, when he finds his country's deadly struggle for nationality against a selfish and profane oligarchy, understood and vindicated by the press of Turin and St. Petersburg, and maligned or discouraged by that of London. Cockneyism may seem unworthy of analysis, far less of refutation; but, as Sydney Smith remarked by way of apology for hunting small game to the death in his zeal for reform, "in a country surrounded by dikes, a rat may inundate a province;" and it is the long-continued gnawing of the tooth of detraction that, at a momentous crisis, let in the cold flood at last upon the nation's heart, and quenched its traditional love.

We have seen how popular a subject of discussion were American manners, institutions, and character, by British writers; and it is amusing, in the retrospect, to consider with what avidity were read, and with what self-confidence were written, these monotonous protests against the imperfect civilization prevalent in the United States. That there was a certain foundation for such discussion, and a relation between the institutions of the country and the behavior of its people, cannot be denied; but both were exaggerated, and made to pander infinitely more to prejudice than to truth. The same investigation applied to other lands in the same spirit, would have furnished quite as salient material; and the antecedents as well as the *animus* of most of these self-appointed censors should have absolved their attacks from any power to irritate. The violations of refinement and propriety thus "set in a note book" were by no means universal. Many of them were temporary, and, taken at their best significance, to a philosophical mind bore no proportion to the more important traits and tendencies which invite the attention and enlist the sympathy of lovers of humanity. It is remarkable, also, that the most severe comments came from persons whose experience of the higher usages and refinements of social life was in the inverse ratio of their critical complaints. Lord Carlisle found, in the vast social possibilities of this country, an interest which rendered him indifferent to the discomfort and the anomalies to which his own habits and associations might have naturally made him sensitive; while the latter exclusively occupied Dickens, whose early experience had made him familiar with the least elegant and luxurious facilities of life. The arrant cockneyism and provincial impertinence of many of these superficial and sensation writers, on a subject whose true and grand relations they were incapable of grasping, and the mercenary or sycophantic motive of many of their tirades, were often exposed; while in cases where incidental popular errors were truly stated, the justice of the criticism was acknowledged, and, in some instances, practically acted upon. The reckless expectoration, angular attitudes, and intrusive curiosity which formed the staple reproach, have always been limited to a class or section, and are now comparatively rare; and these and similar superficial defects, when gravely treated as national, seem almost devoid of significance, when the grand human worth, promise, and beauty of our institutions and opportunities as a people, are considered and compared with the iron caste, the hopeless routine, the cowed and craven *status* of the masses in older and less homogeneous and unhampered communities.

We must look far back to realize the prevalent ignorance in regard to this country wherein prejudice found root and nurture. In colonial days, many bitter and perverse records found their way to the press; and Colonel Barre said to the elder Quincy, in England, before the Revolutionary war: "When I returned to this country, I was often speaking of America, and could not help speaking well of its climate, soil, and inhabitants; but—will you believe it?—more than two thirds of the people of this island thought the Americans were all negroes."

Goldsmith's muse, in 1765, warned the impoverished peasants, eager to seek a new home in the Western hemisphere, against perils in America so imaginary, that they would provoke only smiles but for the melodious emphasis whereby ignorance and error were thus consecrated.

And after our independence was acknowledged, Englishmen regarded it as a strictly political fact. We were independent of their Government, but not of themselves—the least of them assuming superiority, patronage, and critical functions, as a matter of course; so that Americans with any intelligence or manliness came inevitably to sympathize with Heine's estimate: "The English blockheads—God forgive them! I often regard them not at all as my fellow beings, but as miserable automata,—machines whose motive power is egotism." That insular and inevitable trait found expression, as regards America, through the Quarterly Reviews, Monthly Magazines, and a rapid succession of "Travels."

A pregnant cause of temporary alienation, fifty years ago, may be recognized in the last war with Great Britain. Our naval skill and prowess were a sore trial to the pride of Englishmen; although some of the popular authors of that day, like Southey, frankly acknowledged this claim to respect. "Britain had ruled the waves. So her poets sang; so nations felt—all but this *young* nation. Her trident had laid them all prostrate; and how fond she was of considering this emblem as identified with the sceptre of the world! Behold, then, the flag which had everywhere reigned in triumph supreme, sending forth terror from its folds—behold it again and again and again lowered to the Stars and Stripes which had risen in the new hemisphere! The spectacle was magnificent. The European expectation that we were to be crushed, was turned into a feeling of admiration unbounded. Our victories had a moral effect far transcending the number or size of their ships vanquished. For such a blow upon the mighty name of England, after many idle excuses, she had, at last, no balm so effectual as that it was inflicted and could only have been inflicted by a race sprung from herself." *

* "Occasional Productions: Political, Diplomatic, and Miscellaneous," by the late Richard Rush, Philadelphia, 1860.

Coincident with or ere long succeeding this naval prestige, our commercial marine advanced in character and prosperity. The cotton of the South became an essential commodity to Great Britain. In New England, manufactures were firmly established, with important mechanical improvements and facilities; while the Western States became more and more the granary of Europe. New territorial acquisitions, increase of mines, and a system of public instruction, which seemed to guarantee an improved generation of the middle and lower class—these, and other elements of growth, power, and plenty, tended to foster the spirit of rivalry and jealous criticism, and to lessen the complacent gaze wherewith England beheld her long chain of colonial possessions begird the globe. Thus a variety of circumstances united to aggravate the prejudice and encourage the animadversions of English travellers in America, and to make them acceptable to their countrymen. And it is a curious fact for the philosopher, an auspicious one for the humanitarian, that the undercurrent of personal and social goodwill, as regards individuals, of sympathy, respect, and, in many instances, warmer sentiments, flowed on uninterrupted; individual friendships of the choicest kind, hospitalities of the most frank and generous character, mutual interests and feelings in literature, religion, philanthropy, and science, consecrated the private intercourse and enriched the correspondence of select intelligences and noble hearts on opposite sides of the Atlantic. But the record of the hour, the utterances of the press, were as we have seen.

The importance attached to the swarm of English Travels abusive of America, upon calm reflection, appears like a monomania; and equally preposterous was the sensitiveness of our people to foreign criticism. Their exceptional fast eating, inquisitiveness, tobacco chewing, ugly public buildings, sprawling attitudes, and local lingo, were engrossed in so huge a bill of indictment, that their political freedom, social equality, educational privileges, unprecedented material prosperity, benign laws, and glorious country, seemed to shrink, for the moment, into insignificance before the monotonous scurrility and hopeless auguries of their censors. It was not considered that the motive and method of the most of these caustic strictures rendered them innocuous; that, to use the test of an able writer in reference to another class of narrow minds, they " endeavored to atone by misanthropic accuracy for imbecility in fundamental principles;" that few English men or women can write an authentic report of social and political facts in America, differences of habit and opinion therein being more fierce by approximation, thereby destroying the true perspective; add to which inability, the miserable cockney spirit, the dependent and subservient habit of mind, the underbred tone, want of respect for and sympathy with humanity as such, limited powers of observation, controlling prejudice, unaccustomed consideration, and native brutality, which proclaimed the incompetency and disingenuousness of the lowest class of these once formidable scribblers; and we realize why " folly loves the martyrdom of fame," and recognize an identical perversion of truth and good manners as well as human instincts as, in the ignorant arrogance which, in their own vaunted land of high civilization, incarcerated Montgomery, Hunt, and De Foe, exiled Shelley, blackguarded Keats, and envenoms and vulgarizes literary criticisms to-day in the *Saturday Review*—ignoring at home, as well as abroad, the comprehensive, the sympathetic, and the Christian estimate both of genius, communities, and character.

The prevalent feeling in relation to this injustice and unkindness of English writers on America, forty years ago, found graceful expression in a chapter of the Sketch Book, the first literary venture heartily recognized for its merits of style and sentiment, which a native author had given to the " mother country." Irving comments on the singular but incontrovertible fact, that, while the English admirably report their remote travels, no people convey such prejudiced views of countries nearer home. He attributes the vulgar abuse lavished on the United States by the swarm of visitors from Great Britain, first, to the misfortune that the worst class of English travellers have assumed this task; secondly, to the prejudice against democratic institutions; thirdly, to the lack of comforts in travelling here, whereby the humor is rendered splenetic; fourthly, to disappointed avarice and enterprise; and, finally, to jealousy, and a degree of consideration and hospitality to which men of the class of Birmingham and Manchester agents, being wholly unaccustomed, they were spoiled instead of being conciliated thereby. He descants, with a good sense equally applicable to the present hour, upon the short-sighted policy of incurring the resentment of a young and growing nation having a common language and innumerable mutual interests; and advances the claim which America possesses to every magnanimous people of Europe, as constituting the asylum of the oppressed and unfortunate. Since this amiable and just protest was written, the intellectual progress of the country has been as remarkable as the increase of its territory, population, resources, trade, and manufactures; while even the diplomatic conservatives across the sea, recognize in the United States a power vitally associated with that traditional "balance" whereon the peace and prosperity of the civilized world are thought to depend. But the improved and enlarged tone of foreign criticism has not quelled the original antipathy or prejudice, indifference or animosity of England—as the rabid and perverse comments of British journals, at this terrible crisis of our national life, too sadly demonstrate. The same wilful ignorance, the same disingenuous statements, the same cold sneers and defiant sarcasms find expression in the leading organs of English opinion to-day, as once made popular the shallow journals of the commercial travellers and arrogant cockneys; so that we and they may revert to Irving's gentle rebuke, now that he is in his grave, and feel, as of old, its strict justice and sad necessity. Hear him:

"Is this golden bond of kindred sympathies, so rare between nations, to be broken forever? Perhaps it is for the best: it may dispel an illusion which might have kept us in mental vassalage;

which might have interfered occasionally with our true interests, and prevented the growth of proper national pride. But it is hard to give up the kindred tie; and there are feelings dearer than interest, closer to the heart than pride, that will still make us cast back a look of regret, as we wander farther and farther from the paternal roof, and lament the waywardness of the parent that would repel the affections of the child."

And Allston echoed Irving's sense and sentiment with genial emphasis:

> "While the manners, while the arts,
> That mould a nation's soul,
> Still cling around our hearts,
> Between let ocean roll,
> Our joint communion breaking with the sun:
> Yet still from either beach,
> The voice of blood shall reach,
> More audible than speech,
>   'We are one.'"

The reader of the present day, who is inclined to doubt the justice of any reference to this contemptible class of writers, as representatives of English feeling toward America, has but to consult the best periodical literature, and note the style and imprint of the books themselves, to recognize in the fact of their eligible publication and reception, an absolute proof of the consideration they enjoyed; and this, be it remembered, in spite of the known character and objects of the authors, whose position and associations unfitted them for social critics and economical reporters such as an intelligent gentleman could endure, far less accord the slightest personal or literary credit. Ashe is openly described as a swindler; Faux as "low;" Parkinson was a common gardener; Fearon a stocking-weaver. Cobbett, who is the last person to be suspected of aristocratic prejudices, and was the most practical and perverse of democrats, observed, in reading the fastidious comments of one of these impudent travellers, upon an American meal, that it was "such a breakfast as the fellow had never before tasted;" and the remark explains the presumption and ignorance of many of this class of writers, who, never before having enjoyed the least social consideration or private luxury, became, like a beggar on horseback, intoxicated therewith.

Even a cursory glance at the catalogue of books thus produced will indicate how popular was the theme and how audacious the writers. We remember falling in with a clever but impoverished professor, several years ago, in Italy, who had resided in this country, but found himself in Europe without means. In obedience to an appeal which reached us, we sought his economical lodging, and found him pacing up and down a scantily furnished chamber, every now and then seizing a pen and rapidly noting the result of his cogitations. He had been offered, by a London publisher, a handsome gratuity to furnish, within a specified period, a lively anti-democratic book on life and manners in America. The contract, he assured us, provided that there should be enough practical details, especially in regard to the physical resources of the country, to give an air of solid information to the work. There were to be a vein of personal anecdote, a few original adventures, some exaggerated character painting, and a little enthusiasm about scenery: but all this was to be well spiced with ridicule; and the argument of the book was to demonstrate the inevitable depreciation of mind, manners, and enjoyment under the influence of democratic institutions. The poor author tasked his memory and his invention to follow this programme, without a particle of conviction in the emphatic declaration of his opinions, or any sympathy with the work other than what was derived from its lucrative reward. The incident illustrates upon what a conventional basis the rage for piquant Travels in America rested.

Contemporary periodical literature echoed constantly the narrow comments and vapid faultfinding of this class of English travellers, most of whose sneers may be found repeated with zest in the pages of the *Quarterly* and *Blackwood*. Somewhat of the personal prejudice of these articles is doubtless to be ascribed to political influences. Then, as now, the encroachment of democratic opinions excited the alarm of the conservatives. The reform party had made extraordinary advances, and the extension of the right of suffrage became the bugbear of the aristocracy. To represent the country where that right had such unlimited sway, as demoralized thereby, became the policy of all but the so-called radical writers; and the Reviews, fifty years ago, exhibited the worst side of American life, manners, and government, for the same reason that the *London Times* and *Blackwood's Magazine** to-day persist, in the face of truth and history, in ascribing the Southern Rebellion to republican institutions, instead of their greatest bane and most anomalous obstacle on this continent—slavery. Thus the organs of literature and opinion encouraged the cockney critics in their flippant strictures upon this country, and did much to prolong and disseminate them where the English language is spoken. But the journals of the United States were not less trenchant on the other side. In the *North American Review*, especially, several of the most presuming and ignorant of the books in question were shown up with keen and wise irony, and an array of argumentative facts that demolished their pretensions effectually. It should be remembered, in regard to this period, when expediency, fashion, and prejudice combined to make our country the favorite target of opprobrious criticism in Great Britain, that America began to excite fears for that "balance of power" which was the gauge of political security among the statesmen of that day. Moreover, the literary society then and there had not been propitiated by success on this side of the water, nor its respect excited by the intellectual achievements which have since totally reversed the prophecies and the judgments of English reviewers; nor had the United States then become, as now, the nation of readers whose favor it was the interest as well as the pride of popular authors abroad to win

* "It would perhaps be too much to say that the tendencies of our Constitution toward democracy have been checked solely by a view of the tattered and insolent guise in which republicanism appears in America."—*Blackwood's Mag.*, 1862.

and cherish. In reverting to some of the articles which proved most offensive and to the tone of all that more or less sanctioned the spirit of vituperative travellers in America, it should also be considered that private feeling, in certain instances, lent vigor to the critical blows. Some of the writers had been annoyed by the intrusion or disgusted with the indelicacy of pertinacious and underbred tourists from this side of the Atlantic. Many were the current anecdotes illustrative of Yankee impudence which the friends of Southey, Maria Edgeworth, and Sir Walter Scott used to relate—anecdotes that, unfortunately, have found their parallels since in the experience of Carlyle, Tennyson, and other admired living writers. And, although these and their predecessors have found reason to bless the "nation of bores," as in many instances their most appreciative and remunerative audience, personal pique did and still does sharpen the tone and scope of British authorship when America is referred to, as in the case of Sydney Smith,* whose investments were unfortunate, or Leigh Hunt, whose copyrights were invaded, or Dickens and other British lions, who found adulation and success less a cause for gratitude than for ridicule; while every popular British novelist has a character, an anecdote, or an illustration drawn from traditional caricatures of American manners and speech. A comprehensive mind and a generous heart turns, however, from such ephemeral misrepresentation and casual reproach as the bookwrights and reviewers in question delighted in, not so much vexed as wearied thereby; but it is a more grave reflection upon English probity and good sense, that so many of her standard writers, or those who aspire to be such, are disinclined to ascertain the facts of history and social life in America.

* Notwithstanding the deserved rebuke he administered to our State delinquency in his American letters, Sydney Smith vindicates his claim to the title of Philo-Yankeeist. No British writer has better appreciated the institutions and destiny of the United States. He recognized cordially the latent force of Webster, the noble eloquence of Channing, and the refined scholarship of Everett. "I will disinherit you," he playfully writes to his daughter, "if you do not admire everything written by Franklin."

Such wilful errors as those of Lord Mahon and Alison, to say nothing of the vast display of ignorance evoked by the recent discussion in British journals of the Rebellion in America, are utterly unworthy of men of professed candor and scholarship in this age. The specific objections to American civilization, political and social, emphasized with such zeal and unanimity, by certain English writers, are often just and true; but the statement thereof is none the less disingenuous because the compensatory facts are withheld, and incidental, particular, and social faults treated as normal and national. This kind of sophistry runs through the Travels, Journals, and conversation of that illiberal class of British critics who, then as now, from policy, prejudice, or personal conceit or disappointment, habitually regard every question, character, and production of American origin with dislike and suspicion.

This inveterate tendency to look at things exclusively from the point of view suggested by national prejudices, is apparent in the most casual notice of American localities. A writer in *Blackwood's Magazine*,* describing his visit to the "Cave of the Regicides," at New Haven, is disgusted by the difference of aspect and customs there exhibited from those familiar to him at the old seats of learning in England; and, instead of ascribing them to the simple habits and limited resources of the place, with a curious and dogmatic perversity, finds their origin in political and historical opinions, about which the students and professors of Yale care little and know less; as a few quotations from the article will indicate:

"I suspect the person who leaned over the bulwarks of the steamer and gave me the facts, was a dissenting minister going up to be at his college at this important anniversary. There was a tone in his voice which sufficiently indicated his sympathies. The regicides were evidently the calendared saints of his religion." * * *
* * * "The streets were alive with bearded and mustached youth; but they wore hats, and flaunted not a rag of surplice or

---

* *Blackwood's Mag.*, vol. lxi., p. 333.

gown. They are devoutly eschewed as savoring too much of popery; nor master, doctor, or scholar appears with the time-honored decency which, to my antiquated notion, is quite inseparable from the true regimen of a university."

"It was really farcical to see the good old president confer degrees with an attempt at ceremony, which seemed to have no rubric but extemporary convenience and the despatch of business." * * *

"In this college one sees the best that Puritanism could produce; and I thought what Oxford and Cambridge might have become, under the invading reforms of the usurpation, had the Protectorate been less impotent to reproduce itself."

The memorable papers which first established the reputation of Dickens, curiously indicate the prevalence of this deprecatory and venal spirit in English writers on America, at a later period. The elder Weller, in suggesting to Samivel his notable plan for the escape of Pickwick from the Fleet prison, by concealing himself in a "pianner forty," significantly adds: "Have a passage ready taken for 'Merriker. Let the gov'ner stop there till Mrs. Bardell's dead, and then let him come back and write a book about the 'Merrikens as 'll pay all his expenses, and more, if he blows 'em up enough."

The preëminence of the British colonies in America early proved the Anglo-Saxon destiny of this continent. The long wars with the aborigines, and the memorable struggle between the French and English, resulting in the confirmed possession and sway of the latter rule and colonies, and, finally, the American Revolution and its immediate and later consequences, furnish to a philosophic and benevolent mind so remarkable an historical series of events, combining to results of such infinite significance, not to this country and nation alone, but to the world and humanity, that it is surprising English speculation and criticism so long continued narrow, egotistic, and unsympathizing. Noble exceptions, indeed, are to be remembered. Chatham, the most heroic, Burke, the most philosophic of British statesmen, early and memorably recognized the claims, the character, and the destiny of our country; and many of the intellectual nobility of Great Britain, in the flush of youthful aspirations, baffled by political or social exclusiveness, turned their hopes and their tributes toward the Western continent. But among the numerous English visitors who undertook to describe, to illustrate, and to criticize nature, government, and society in the United States for the benefit of their countrymen, few have proved adequate or just; and still less is the number who rose to the philosophy of the subject.

Many of the French writers seize upon practical truths of universal interest, or evolve the sentiment of the theme with zest: either process gives a vital charm to descriptions and speculations, and places the reader in a genuine human relation with the writer. The same distinction between the English and French method of treating our condition, history, and character, is observable in the current literature of both countries, as well as in the works of their respective travellers. How rarely in an English writer do we encounter episodical remarks so generous in tone as this page from Michelet's little treatise, "La Mer":

"L'Amérique, est le désir. Elle est jeune, et elle brûle d'être en rapport avec le globe. Sur son superbe continent, et au milieu de tant d'États, elle se croit pourtant solitaire. Si loin de sa mère l'Europe, elle regarde vers ce centre de la civilization, comme la terre vers le soleil, et tout ce qui la rapproche du grand luminaire la fait palpiter, qu'on en juge par l'ivresse, par les fêtes si touchantes auxquelles donna lieu là-bas le télégraphe sous-marin qui mariat les deux rivages, promettait le dialogue et la réplique par minutes, de sorte que les deux mondes n'auraient plus qu'une pensée!"

The historical character of France and England explains the discrepancy so evident in their recorded estimate of and sentiments in regard to America. The former nation envied the Spaniards the renown of their peerless discovery, and blamed their king for not having entertained the project of Columbus. As a people, they love power more than gain, and are ever more swayed by ideas than interest; whereas, in the earliest chronicles of English polity, we find a spirit of calculation. On that side of the Channel, we are told, they "seldom voted a subsidy without bargaining for a right;" and in a sketch of the wars between the two countries, one of their own writers observes: "Our character at that time (1547) was more economical than heroic; and we seldom set our foot in France, unless on the careful calculation of how much the enemy would give us for going away again."

This sharp appreciation of material results has had much to do with the civic prosperity of England, for thereby the popular mind has grown alert and efficient in securing those privileges in which consists the superiority of the English Constitution, and the absence of which enabled Philip Augustus, Richelieu, and Louis XIV. to establish in France such absolute despotism. On the other hand, so exclusive and pertinacious a tendency to self-interest is and has proved, in the case of England, a serious obstacle to those generous national sentiments which endear and elevate a people and a Government in the estimation of humanity; and it is only necessary to recall the caricatures of the French, the Dutch, the German, and Italian character, which pervade English literature, to realize the force of insular prejudice and self-concentration thus confirmed by national habits and polity.

"Some years ago," says a popular English writer, "it would have been an unexampled stretch of liberality to have confessed that France had any good qualities at all. Our country was an island—we despised the rest of the world; our county was an island—we despised the other shires; our parish was an island, with peculiar habits, modes, and institutions; our households were islands; and, to complete the whole, each stubborn, broad-shouldered, strong-backed Englishman was an island by himself, surrounded by a misty and tumultuous sea of prejudices."*

A curious illustration is afforded by the entire series of English Travels in America, of this national egotism so characteristic of England, which regards foreign countries and people exclusively through the narrow medium of self-

* Rev. James White.

love. The tone of these records of a sojourn or an exploration in America is graduated, almost invariably, as to the sympathy or the depreciation, by the relation of the two countries to each other at different times. For a long period after the early colonization, so remote and unprofitable was the New World, that indifference marks the allusions to, and superficiality or contempt the accounts of, those thinly settled and unprosperous communities. As they grew in population and resources, and glimpses were obtained of a possible future alike promising to the devotees of gain, of ambition, and of political reform and religious independence, English writers dwell with complacency upon the natural beauties and fertility of the land, upon the prospect here opened for enterprise; and as a colonial tributary to their power and wealth, America, or that part of it colonized by the British, is described with pride and pleasure; even its social traits occasionally lauded, and the details of observation and experience given with elaborate relish. Especially do we find political malcontents at home, and social aspirants or benign and intelligent visitors, dwelling upon the novel features and free scope of the country with satisfaction. Immediately subsequent to the Revolution, a different spirit is manifest. When the choicest jewel of her crown had been wrested from the grasp of Great Britain, numerous flaws therein became at once evident to the critical eyes of English travellers; and, though occasionally a refreshing contrast is afforded by the candid and cordial estimate of a liberal writer, the disingenuous and deprecatory temper prevails. It is impossible not to perceive that the rapid growth and unique prosperity of a country governed by popular institutions, without an established church, a royal family, an order of nobility, and all the expensive arrangements incident to monarchical sway, however free and constitutional, has been and is a cause of uneasiness and hatred to a nation of kindred language and character. "Freedom," wrote Heine, "has sprung in England from privileges—from historical events. All England is congealed in mediæval, never-to-be-rejuvenated institutions, behind which her aristocracy is intrenched, awaiting the death struggle." Hence the example of America has been to a large political party, to a proud social organization, inauspicious; to the popular, the liberal, the democratic masses, encouraging. Hence the base jubilee at our recent internal dissensions, whose root—slavery*—was planted by the English themselves. Hence their constant assertion that "the republic is a failure."

One of the chief grounds of complaint stated, when the Declaration of Independence was first written, against the British Government, was that it had, contrary to the wishes of the colonies, planted African slavery on our soil. Hence the extreme baseness of ignoring this primal and positive cause of our domestic troubles on the part of writers and rulers in England, and striving to make republican institutions responsible exclusively therefor—a course referable to shameful jealousy, and to the want of cotton and the desire for free trade. In all British history there is no more remarkable illustration of what De Tocqueville, whose English proclivities and philosophic candor no intelligent reader can question, remarked, in one of his letters:

"In the eyes of an Englishman, a cause is just if it be the interest of England that it should succeed. A man or a Government that is useful to England, has every kind of merit; and one that does England harm, every possible fault. *The criterion of what is honorable, or just, is to be found in the degree of favor or of opposition to English interests.* There is much of this everywhere; but there is so much of it in England that a foreigner is astonished."

The mineral wealth and adaptation of mechanical processes to manufacture, which laid the foundation of England's commercial prosperity, are no longer a monopoly. Identical resources have been elsewhere developed and employed, and her productions and enterprise have become, in the same proportion, less essential to the industry of the

---

* It was the monopoly of the infamous traffic in negroes, which, during the ministry of Sir Robert Walpole, so greatly increased the mercantile prosperity of London, and founded that of Bristol and Liverpool.

world. Her power, therefore, in more than one direction, is on the wane. But to a liberal and philosophic mind, the grand natural provision for the subsistence of her impoverished laborers, and the permanent amelioration of their *status*, on this continent, should be regarded as a vast blessing, not a selfish vexation; as a cause of religious gratitude, and not of jealous detraction. Will it not prove a suggestive anomaly to the rational historian of the wonderful age in which we live, when science, letters, adventure, economy, education, and travel are making human beings every day less local and egotistic, and more cosmopolitan and humane, in their relations and sentiments—that in such an age, when, for the privilege of holding black people in servitude unchallenged, a class of American citizens rose in arms against national authority, the nobles of England, and a portion of her traders and manufacturers, became the allies of the insurgents; while the royal family, the starving thousands of Lancashire—who are the real sufferers from the war—and the bravest and wisest representatives of the people in Parliament, gave to the United States, and to the cause of justice and of freedom, their sympathy, advocacy, and respect? The real fear of America in Great Britain is of our moral influence, which, of course and inevitably, is democratic; and if her detractors in England are pensioned, the working class there spontaneously, through faith and hope, attach themselves to her cause.

The superior candor of the French writers on America is obvious to the most superficial reader. The urbanity and the philosophical tendency of the national mind account for this more genial and intelligent treatment; but the striking difference of temper and of scope between the French and English Travels in America, is accounted for mainly by the comparative freedom from political and social prejudice on the part of the former, and the frequent correspondence of their sentiments with those of the inhabitants of the New World. From the descriptions of primeval nature by the early Jesuit missionaries to the gallant gossip and speculative enthusiasm of the French officers who coöperated in our Revolutionary struggle, a peculiar sympathy with the prospects and affinity with the conditions of nature and of life, on this continent, inspire the Gallic writers. Nor did this partiality or sense of justice diminish with the growth of the country. From the swarm of dilettante critics and arrogant or shallow authors of books on the United States, during the last fifty years, the only philosophical work wherein the principles of democratic institutions are fairly discussed, and their peculiar operation in America justly defined, is the standard treatise of Alexis de Tocqueville; while the first able and eloquent plea for our nationality, the first clear and honest recognition of the causes and significance of our present civil war from abroad, came from a French publicist. What a contrast between the considerate argument and noble vindication of De Gasparin, and the perverse dogmatism, disingenuous tone, and malicious exaggeration of a large part of the English periodical press! "We are not just toward the United States," says the former. "Their civilization, so different from ours, wounds us in various ways, and we turn from them in the ill humor excited by their real defects, without taking note enough of their eminent qualities. This country, which possesses neither church nor state, nor any governmental protection; this country, born yesterday—born under a Puritan influence; this country, without past history, without monuments, separated from the middle ages by the double interval of centuries and beliefs; this rude country of farmers and pioneers, has nothing fitted to please us. It has the exuberant life and the eccentricities of youth; that is, it affords to our mature experience inexhaustible subjects of blame and raillery."

This frank statement explains while it does not excuse the long tirades of English writers against the crudities of our national life: not because these were not often truly reported, but because the other side of the story was omitted. Our sensitive pride of country took offence, and thus gave new provocation to the "blame and raillery" of which De

Gasparin speaks. No American familiar with Europe can wonder that refined visitors from the Old World to the New should find the gregarious habits, the unventilated and promiscuously crowded railway cars, the fragile high-pressure steamboats of the Western rivers, the *cuisine*, the flashiness, the conceit, the hardihood, the radicalism, the costume, the architecture, the social standards, the money worship, and the countless incongruities, especially on the outskirts of the older settlements, distasteful, and often revolting; but it requires no remarkable powers of reflection to understand, and no extraordinary candor to admit, that many of these repugnant and discordant facts are incidental to great and benign innovations and improvements upon the hopeless social routine and organization of Europe; that they coexist with vast human privileges; that they are compensated for by new and grand opportunities for the mass of humanity, however much they may trench upon the comfort and sense of decency of those accustomed to exclusive privileges and luxury. It is precisely because, as a general rule, the French writers recognize, while so many of the English ignore such palliations and compensations, in judging of and reporting life in America, that the former, as a whole, are so much more worthy of respect and gratitude. Any shallow vagabond can compare disadvantageously the huge and hot caravansaries of Western travel with the first-class carriages of an English railway; the bad whiskey and tough steaks of a tavern in America with the quiet country inn and the matchless sirloin and ale of old England. The social contrasts are easily made; the defects of manners patent; but when it is considered that what is applied by way of privilege or superiority to a class in Europe, is open—in a less perfect way, indeed, but still open—to all; that the *average* comfort and culture here are unequalled in history; and, above all, that the prospect and the principle of civil and social life are established on an equal and prosperous basis—the superficial defects, to the eye of wisdom and the heart of benevolence, sink into comparative insignificance. "America," writes De Tocqueville, "is the place of all others where the Christian religion has preserved the most power over souls."

Other reasons for the difference of English and French interpretation of American questions are well stated by a recent writer in the *Revue des Deux Mondes:*

"Frenchmen and Englishmen cannot be impressed alike by what is passing in the United States. At the bottom of the quarrel there is, it is true, the abolition of slavery, to which the English are devoted by a glorious beginning; but, on the other hand, what relates to the United States, awakens in England memories, interests, antipathies, which can have no parallel in the politics or feelings of France. In the first place, the Star-spangled Banner (*le drapeau semé d'étoiles*) is the only flag that France has never met in the coalition of her enemies. To the English, the United States are always the rebellious colony of the past; to us, they are a nation whose independence we contributed to establish by common victories carried in the teeth of British obstinacy. For British politics, in spite of the accidental importance of cotton, it would be a satisfaction to see the American Union enfeebled by a division. For French politics, the breaking up of the American republic, which would destroy the balance of maritime power, would be a serious misfortune. The English cherish the disdain of an aristocratic race for the republican Yankee; democratic France (!) has been enabled to take lessons from American democracy, and has more than once made itself envied by the latter. The two young volunteers who have just enrolled themselves in the army of the North have thus remained faithful, in their choice of the cause which they would serve, to the traditions of their country."

How uncandid English writers are, even when quoting respectable authorities, is evinced in the remark of a late quarterly reviewer, in alluding to De Tocqueville's hopeful views of democracy in America in contrast with the Southern Rebellion: "If he had lived a little longer, what an example of the fallacy of man's profoundest thoughts and acutest inference would he himself have mournfully acknowledged, in the unnatural and incredible convulsion of the United States of America;" whereas, so far from being unnatural and incredible, the whole argument of De Tocqueville is prophetic thereof. He knew the incubus of slavery—the anomaly of local despotism in the heart of a republic—must be thrown off, as a loathsome disease in the body politic: how and when, he did not pretend to say; but still proclaimed his faith in the strength of the Constitution—the vital power of political justice embodied in a democratic Government, and a vast, industrious, educated, and religious nation—to triumph over this accidental poison, which had been allowed to taint the blood but not blast the heart of the republic. Moreover, this same scientifically humane writer beheld, in the triumph of the democratic principle, the progress of the race and the will of God; but he inferred not therefrom any roseate dreams of human perfection or individual felicity. On the contrary, as the responsibility of governing, and the privileges of citizenship expanded and became confirmed, he saw new claims upon the serious elements of life and character; the need of greater sacrifices on the part of the individual; a necessity for effort and discipline calculated to solemnize rather than elate. It is one of the most obvious of compensatory facts, that, as we are more free to think and to work, we are less able to enjoy, as that word is commonly understood. Where occupation is essential to respectability, and public spirit a recognized duty, pleasure has but infrequent carnival, and duty perpetual vigil. With all his elasticity of temperament, the self-dependence and the exciting scope of the life of an American tax the powers of body and mind as much as they inspire.

Geographical ignorance, and errors in natural history, inexcusable now that so many authentic accounts of the country are accessible to all, continue to be manifest even in the higher departments of English literature. Goldsmith's melancholy exaggeration of the unhealthy shores of Georgia, in his apostrophe to the peasantry, finds a parallel in the tropical flowers Campbell ascribes to the valley of Wyoming; while the last Cambridge prize poem places Labrador in the United States, and confuses the locality of American rivers with more than poetic license. Philosophical keep pace with geographical errors. Despite the evidence of common sense and patent facts, the English press insisted that Mississippi repudiation of State debts was a direct and legitimate result of republican institutions. It now ascribes the slaveholders' rebellion to the same cause; and a religious review of high standing recently attributed the high-flown and exaggerated style of Parke Custis, in his "Recollections of Washington," to the undisciplined American method of expression.

Ignorance of the social life incident to republican institutions betrays itself continually in an indirect manner. In a work recently published in London, called the "Book Hunter," the writer observes of a work on American private libraries: "The statement that there is in Dr. Francis's library a complete set of the 'Reccuil des Causes Célébres,' &c., would throw any of our book knight-errants in convulsions of laughter;" and elsewhere, speaking of thus publishing the catalogue of private libraries, he says: "That the privacy of our ordinary wealthy and middle classes should be invaded in a similar shape, is an idea that would not get abroad without creating sensations of the most lively horror. They manage these things differently across the Atlantic; and so here we have over fifty gentlemen's private collections ransacked and anatomized. If they like it, we have no reason to complain, but rather have occasion to rejoice in the valuable and interesting result." How little this writer seems to understand that the facts which excite his wonder and disgust are legitimate results of democratic society, wherein we are accustomed to forego private for public good, and to liberally exchange intellectual privileges! Monopolies are forced to yield to the pressure of humane exigencies. It is made known that a benevolent physician has a copy of the "Causes Célébres," not because the work is rare, but that some poor scholar may know where he can refer to it; for in America we are bred to the recognition of mutual aid in culture as in economy, and, like Sir Thomas Brown, "study for those who will not study for themselves." It may be said of many English critics, as was said of a recent traveller in America, that, "living as he had so long in an atmosphere of country houses and parsonages, he is constantly exclaiming against the absence of those complicated rules of social intercourse which have so long engaged his attention."

"When will the English learn how to write correctly about this country?" asks a recent writer. "A very friendly press, the *Daily News*, reviewing Hawthorne's book, says, very compassionately, that our 'national life has been too short' for the formation 'of a homogeneous character' among our people. We should like to know what homogeneity there is among the British people, though a thousand years old, composed of Welshmen who cannot speak English, of Irishmen always in revolt and forever at enmity with their rulers, of Scotchmen who are distinct in dialect, manners, and customs, and even now are not too fond of the Sassenachs? How much of this is there in the English counties of Yorkshire, Kent, Cornwall? The truth is, there is far more homogeneity in the United States, notwithstanding its short national life, than there ever has been in Great Britain, from the time of the heptarchy down."

Much ridicule has been wasted upon our national sensitiveness to criticism; and the hardihood and self-love of English writers and talkers often repel, as weak and irrational, the expectation of sympathy which finds utterance in every unfortunate crisis on this side of the water. Yet even John Bull winced at Hawthorne's choicely worded and thoughtfully insinuated hits at his tendency to obesity and stagnation. Without defending that natural and honorable instinct that cherishes the tie of a common language and literature, historical, social, and domestic associations with a distant people, in the present age and among enlightened nations, it is certainly justifiable to demand scientific observation in all those deliberate estimates of a country or a race, a government or a cause, wherein mutual and permanent interests are concerned. One chief cause of protest and complaint against British commentators on America, is their ignorance of facts whereof but slight investigation would requisitely inform them, and their wilful repudiation of the inferences thence resulting. It is a significant truth, that throughout the vast discussion by newspapers, reviews, magazines, pamphlets, club and dinner talk, lectures and parliamentary speeches, which the Southern Rebellion and its consequences in the United States, have induced in Great Britain, scarcely any evidence appears of cognizance and appreciation as regards the simple geographical facts of the case; without a knowledge of which it is impossible to perceive the scope or judge the merits of this question. Long ago Humboldt and other naturalists recognized in the fact that this continent is placed between two oceans, the provision and pledge of a grand destiny; long ago economists found, in the remarkable number, size, and relative situation of its lakes and rivers, the means established by nature to bring together and render mutually dependent and helpful the most widely separated regions; long ago philanthropists hailed in the variety of climate and the liberal political institutions, a vast asylum and arena predestined to shelter and succor the independent but proscribed, and the impoverished and hopeless victims of over-populated and down-trodden Europe. Yet, when these institutions and this prosperous nationality were threatened by a minority in the interest of African slavery, and the civil war inevitably consequent thereon, challenged the sympathy of the world, in order to give a plausible excuse for their advocacy of our disunion, the writers and speakers of England, with very rare exceptions, assumed that a geographical line isolated the two communities, by kinds of labor, forms of society, political and personal interests so in conflict, that a peaceable separation was not only practicable, but wise, humane, and requisite. Had these malign and specious advocates merely ignored the fact that our power and prosperity have been the offspring of our union, it might have been tolerated in silence; but when they refused to acknowledge that this immense country * known as the United States of North Amer-

---

* Its greatest length is from Cape Cod to the Pacific, near lat. 42°, 2,600 miles; in breadth from Maine to Florida, 1,600 m.; there are 3,303 m. of frontier toward British America, and 1,456 of that toward Mexico; on the ocean the boundary line, including indentations, is 12,609 m.; the total area of the States and Territories in 1853 was 2,963,606 square miles.

ica is intersected by a mountain range inhabited by a people absolutely one in attachment to their Government and devotion to free labor, and that the slave interest borders upon, intersects, and isolates rather than divides this homogeneous and patriotic race, so that, to break up the political unity of the country is to expose these citizens to the despotic cruelty of rebels—to abandon the highest duty of a state and the noblest principle of human government, we cannot but feel that ignorance degrades or sophistry impugns the honest humanity of these ostensible interpreters of public opinion in Britain. To illustrate the practical bearing of geographical facts in this instance, note the language of an intelligent native [*] of one of the border States, a kinsman of one of the unprincipled politicians who fomented, when in office under the Government he betrayed, this wicked rebellion:

"Whoever will look at a map of the United States, will observe that Louisiana lies on both sides of the Mississippi River, and that the States of Arkansas and Mississippi lie on the right and left banks of this great stream—eight hundred miles of whose lower course are thus controlled by these three States, unitedly inhabited by hardly as many white people as inhabit the city of New York. Observe, then, the country drained by this river, and its affluents, commencing with Missouri on its west bank, and Kentucky on its east bank. There are nine or ten powerful States, large portions of three or four others, several large Territories—in all a country as large as all Europe, as fine as any under the sun, already holding many more people than all the revolted States, and destined to be one of the most populous and powerful regions of the earth. Does any one suppose that these powerful States, this great and energetic population, will ever make a peace that shall put the lower course of this single and mighty national outlet to the sea in the hands of a foreign Government far weaker than themselves? If there is any such person, he knows little of the past history of mankind; and will, perhaps, excuse us for reminding him that the people of Kentucky, before they were constituted a State, gave formal notice to the Federal Government, when General Washington was President, that if the United States did not acquire Louisiana, they would themselves conquer it. The mouths of the Mississippi belong, by the gift of God, to the inhabitants of its great valley. Nothing but irresistible force can disinherit them.

[*] Dr. Breckinridge, of Kentucky.

"Try another territorial aspect of the case. There is a bed of mountains abutting on the left bank of the Ohio, which covers all Western Virginia and all Eastern Kentucky to the width, from east to west, in those two States, of three or four hundred miles. These mountains, stretching southwestwardly, pass entirely through Tennessee, cover the back parts of North Carolina and Georgia, heavily invade the northern part of Alabama, and make a figure even in the back parts of South Carolina and the eastern parts of Mississippi; having a course of perhaps seven or eight hundred miles, and running far south of the northern limit of profitable cotton culture. It is a region of eighty thousand square miles, trenching upon eight or nine Slave States, though destitute of slaves itself—trenching upon at least five Cotton States, though raising no cotton itself. The western part of Maryland and two thirds of Pennsylvania are embraced in the northeastern continuation of this remarkable region. Can anything that passes under the name of statesmanship be more preposterous, than the notion of permanent peace on this continent, founded on the abnegation of a common and paramount Government, and the idea of the supercilious domination of the cotton interest and the slave trade, over such a mountain empire, so located, and so peopled?"

When, in the calm and kindliness of meditation, we remember the solemn assemblies of wise and intrepid English men and women who, two centuries and more ago, left their native shore with tears and prayers, only "comforted to live" by the thought that they took with them a great principle and a cherished faith to transplant and bequeath in another hemisphere; when we recall the proud and fond associations with which their descendants sought and yet seek the ancestral homes and graves of these brave and holy exiles; and how tenderly the traditions, the literature, the laws, and the liberties of the Old World have been cherished by the enlightened and earnest natives of the New; how the kings of thought and the heralds of freedom regarded the Anglo-Saxon settlements in America, when persecution and strife made England to many a perilous sojourn; how eagerly John Milton questioned Roger Williams; how ardently Berkeley appealed to Walpole; what Vane and Penn, Calvert, Winthrop, Puritan, Churchman, Quaker, Catholic, Huguenot, thought, felt, wrote, and did to colonize what to all of them was a land of promise; and how, during the long lapse of time, the civilization that originated when the world had reached a period of glorious development, has ever responded to and often quickened that of older date but identical character, like the "child of Earth's old age" as she is—it seems incredible that disdain and indifference, especially in a crisis of national life, should mark and mar nearly all public expression in England regarding a country thus morally assimilated and historically identified with her. Not strange, indeed, that traders and shallow egotists should ignore or sneer at a nation of kindred language and memories; but strange that legislators and writers, who profess to instruct, should prove their want of interest by gross ignorance, historical and geographical. How perversely blind have they shown themselves to the facts that the experiment of State sovereignty has been fully tried during the perilous interval between the acknowledgment of our independence and the adoption of the Constitution, whereby industry was paralyzed, fiscal and social confidence lost, and advantage taken of the weakness of the isolated fragments of a nation by foreign powers; that federal union, from all this chaos and imbecility, created and confirmed a nation whose growth, freedom, and self-reliant resources are unparalleled; that so essential, by the laws of nature, is one section to the prosperity of the other, that the chief motive and absolute condition whereby the new Southwestern States indissolubly linked their destiny and allegiance to the old thirteen, were that the free navigation of the Mississippi should be permanently guaranteed—that noble stream, like a main artery, vitally connecting the heart with the extremities of the body politic; that what the practical effect is of a faction, however large, undertaking illegitimate opposition to a Government based upon popular will, was memorably illustrated by Shay's Rebellion in Massachusetts in 1785-'86; by the career of Citizen Genet in '93—his wild and anomalous partisan success, and his ignominious practical failure; by the Virginia Resolutions of '85 and '86, by the base and futile conspiracy of Burr, and the prompt overthrow of Calhoun's sophistical theories. Equally blind to the present as the past, the fraud and coercion whereby the present Rebellion was initiated, the inhuman cause for which it was undertaken, the despotic violence resorted to for its maintenance, the latent barbarism made patent by its career, were all, from base policy or selfish malice, studiously kept out of view by these ostensible interpreters of public opinion. It is, indeed, one of those singular exhibitions of the blindness induced by self-love, that vituperation should mark the press of England in discussing American institutions, when often, in the identical sheet, glares the evidence of her own inadequacy in providing for the masses. It is a striking coincidence, that, when an American banker* in London desired to indicate his interest in and gratitude to the country where he had acquired a colossal fortune, the best method his sagacious observation could discover, was to provide homes for the working classes, whose physical degeneracy is thus noted in a recent issue of the most widely circulated and implicitly trusted organ of British opinion:

"We have only to take a walk through any of our populous quarters — Shoreditch, Bethnal Green, the Borough, Lambeth, all the river side, Clerkenwell, Gray's Inn Lane, and those numerous smaller districts of which the working classes, for one reason or another,

---

* "When Mr. Peabody, the celebrated American banker, who is about to quit this country, first heard of the national memorial of the late Prince Consort, he authorized Sir Emerson Tennent to state that, should that memorial be a charitable institution, he would give £100,000 toward it; and his disappointment was great on learning that the money would not be expended in that way. However Mr. Peabody, still resolved on carrying out his charitable scheme—as a token, he says, of gratitude to the English nation, for the many kind acts he has received from them, and also in memory of his long and prosperous career in this country—has decided on erecting a number of houses for the working class, who, through the innumerable improvements in the metropolis, have been rendered almost homeless. For this purpose he gives £100,000, and also undertakes to pay the first year's interest of the money— £5,000. Sir Emerson Tennent is appointed one of three trustees; Lord Stanley, M. P., it is hoped, will be the second; the third has not yet been nominated."—*London Paper.*

have obtained inalienable possession; take them at the hours when they show—going to their work or returning from it, or making their purchases, or cooling themselves in the open air: look at them, and please remember, that when you have deducted half a million people rather better off, there remain two millions of the sort you see before you."

It would prove, indeed, a more ungracious than difficult task to enumerate social anomalies and characteristic defects, quite adequate to counterbalance, in English civilization, those so constantly proclaimed as American. Deans and poachers, snobs and weavers, sempstresses and governesses, convicts, pretended lunatics, might figure as unchristian monopolists or pitiable victims; and poor laws, costly and useless governmental arrangements, the ravages of gin and beer, the pressure of taxation, the inhumanity of rank and fashion, the cold egotism of the social code, the material routine of life, the absurd conventionalities, the servility of one class and the arrogance of another, the law of primogeniture, ecclesiastical abuses, the hopeless degradation of labor, and numerous kindred facts and figures in the economical and social statistics of the British realm, not only offer ample range for relentless and plausible defamation, akin to that which has been so bitterly indulged by English writers on America; but the indictment would be confirmed by the testimony of popular and current English literature—Crabbe, Hood, Dickens, Mrs. Gaskell, Reade, and Thackeray having elaborated from patent social wrongs their most vivid pictures of human suffering and degradation.

Nor, were the test applied to specific traits, would the comparison be less disadvantageous. The vulgarity and brutality of an Englishman, when he is vulgar and brutal, are unparalleled. The stolidity of their lower class is more revolting than the inquisitiveness of ours. The history of England's criminal code, of her literary criticism, of her artists and authors, of her colonial rule, of her aristocratic privileges, of her army, naval, and merchant service, has furnished some of the darkest pictures of cruelty, neglect, selfishness, and abuse of power to be found in the annals of the world.

The favorite subject of *Punch*—the trials of an "unprotected female"—betrays a national trait in brutal contrast with the habits and sentiments of the kindred people whose "domestic manners" have so long been the subject of their sneers. "Not a day passes," remarks an English lady of intelligence and character, but without rank or wealth, in writing to an American friend, "but I regret that paradise of my sex—your country. There my womanhood alone was my safeguard and distinction."

Centuries ago, the very "land question" which led to the recent controversy whereby the *Times* was unmasked, offered the same ominous problem to humane and liberal Englishmen, and was, to not a few, the motive of emigration to America.

"This land growes weary of her inhabitants," writes Winthrop, "soe as man, whoe is the most pretious of all creatures, is here more vile and base than the earth we treade upon. All townes complaine of the burthen of theire poore, and we use the authoritie of the Law to hinder the increase of or people by urginge the statute against colleges and inmates. The fountaines of Learning and Religion are soe corrupt as (besides the insupportable charge of theire education) most children are perverted. Why, then, should we stand striving here for places of habitation, many men spending as much labour and coste to recover or keepe sometimes an acre or twoe as would procure them many and as good or better in another Countrie." *

Compare this ancient statement with one in a journal of this year:

"In the main, landed property is still in the same condition in England to-day as it was immediately after the Norman conquest. The foreign invaders at that time divided the land among a small number of nobles and brigand captains with the point of the sword;

---

* "Reasons for the Intended Plantation in New England," by John Winthrop, 1629. Life of John Winthrop, by Robert C. Winthrop.

and in the Doomsday Book it was then laid down that their right to the possession of these lands was as high as heaven and as deep as hell, and that the hand of him should wither who would dare to touch it. In course of time a number of free proprietors crept in between the landholding aristocracy; but subsequent parliamentary acts, known as the 'Enclosure Acts,' restricted once more the number of free proprietors by forcible expropriation. With the exception of a few localities, England possesses no peasantry in the sense of France and of Southern and Western Germany. There is only the aristocratic proprietor, the steward, or the farming tenant and the laborer. The condition of the laborer is worse than anywhere in Central or Western Europe. The political power British feudalism wields is immense. A statistical table shows that, with regard to the representation of the people in the so-called House of Commons, there are about thirty popular constituencies; one hundred constituencies slightly influenced by personal or family control, and most of them by money; *two hundred and forty constituencies almost wholly under such family and aristocratic influence;* and thirty constituencies which may be regarded as mere family property."

With such social and political evils—a portentous report whereof, in their actual results upon labor and life, may be found in the work of Mr. Kay,* lately published—emigration to America has been and is a resource to Great Britain which should have engendered gratitude instead of growls. An acute French writer attributes to it no small degree of England's prosperity:

"Let others denounce, if they will, as culpable want of foresight, the energetic multiplication of the English people, and felicitate France on being preserved from this misfortune by the demi-sterility of marriages; but, for my part, faithful to the ancient morality and patriotism which regarded a numerous posterity as a blessing from God, I point out this exhaustion of vital sap as a symptom of malady and decline. I see the people who emigrate redouble efforts to fill up voids, redouble virtues, savings, and labor to prepare departures and new establishments. Among a people who do not emigrate, I see wealth disbursed in the superfluities of vain luxury; young men idle, without horizons, and without lofty ambition, consuming them-

* "The Social Condition and Education of the People in England," by Joseph Kay, Esq., M. A., of Trinity College, Cambridge, Barrister-at-Law, and late Travelling Bachelor of the University of Cambridge, 12mo., New York, 1863.

selves in frivolous pleasures and petty calculations; and families alarmed at a fecundity which would impose on them modest and laborious habits. Like stagnant waters, stagnant populations become corrupt. Moved by this spectacle, I should dread for the sedentary race an early degradation, if this inequality revealed a decree of Providence, instead of being a fault of man." *

If from the graver interests we turn to the superficial traits of the English people, it requires little acumen to discover materials for ridicule quite as patent and provocative of satire as the "domestic manners of the Americans" yield. Leach and Doyle have long since stereotyped for the public, certain traits of physiognomy, costume, and manners, somewhat monotonous, certainly, but quite as absurd and vulgar as any so-called American, characteristic and popularly recognized as such. The pronunciation, snobbishness, egotism, bad taste, stolidity, and arrogance of different classes are thus caricatured. Deference to wealth and rank, perverse adherence to obsolete and unjust as well as irrational systems, habits, and opinions, in England, are the staple themes of satirical novelists, eloquent liberals, and comic draughtsmen; while the "English abroad" furnish a permanent subject of ridicule to their more vivacious neighbors, and figure habitually in French farces and after-dinner anecdotes. But this mode of discussing national character is not less unworthy a philosopher than a Christian; it is essentially one-sided, prejudiced, and inhuman. Yet it is worth while to suggest the recognized vulnerable points of English life, manners, and institutions, that it may be seen how easily their reproach and ridicule of Americans can be retaliated.

But we do not cite such national defects and misfortunes in the spirit of retaliation, but simply to indicate how unjust and uncharitable it is to regard a country or a people exclusively in the light of reproach and animadversion, and how universal is that law of compensation whereby good and evil in every land are balanced in the scale of Divine wisdom. It

* "Histoire de l'Emigration au XIXe Siècle, par M. Jules Duval," Paris, 1863.

is indeed a remarkable evidence of inconsistent and perverse feeling, that a course which no man of sense and common humanity would think of applying to an individual, is confidently adopted in the discussion of national character and destiny. That allowance which the mature in years instinctively make for the errors of youth—the compassion which tempers judgment in regard to the indigence, the ignorance, or the blind passions of the outcast or the criminal, is ignored when the faults or the calamities of a whole people are described. Yet such a fearful exposition of "London Labor and London Poor," which Mayhew has made familiar, should excite only emotions of shame and pity in the Christian heart. But the hardihood that so long coldly admitted or wantonly sneered at the wrongs of Ireland and Italy, gives a bitter edge or a narrow comprehension to the class of English writers on America we have, perhaps too patiently, discussed.

The simple truth is, that there is scarcely a vulnerable point in our system, social, political, or religious, but has its counterpart in the mother country. For every solecism in manners or inhuman inconsistency in practice, growing out of democratic radicalism on this side of the water, a corresponding defect or incongruity is obvious in the ecclesiastical or aristocratic monopolies and abuses on the other. For our well-fed African slaves, they have half-starved white operatives; for the tyranny of demagogues here, there is the bloated rule of duke and bishop there; for the degraded squatter life in regions of whiskey drinking and ague in America, there is the not less sad fate of the miner and the poacher in the heart of civilized England; and there is reason to believe that, if a philosophical collector of the data of suicides, railway catastrophes, and financial swindlers, were to be equally assiduous in the United States and Great Britain, the figures, in the ratio of space, time, and population, would be nearly parallel. Even the philological blunders and absurdities over which cockney travellers here have been so merry, may be equalled in many a district of England; and if the classic names applied to new towns on this continent savor of tasteless pedantry, a similar lack of a sense of the appropriate stares us in the face in the names of villas in the suburbs of London; while the same repetition and consequent confusion of names of places occur in English shires as in our States.

Language has been one of the most prolific sources of ridicule and animadversion; especially those peculiarities of tone and speech supposed to belong exclusively to the Eastern States, and popularly designated as Yankeeisms. Yet it has been made obvious at last, that, instead of being indigenous, these oddities of speech, with very few exceptions, were brought from England, and are still current in the localities of their origin. In the preface to his "Dictionary of Americanisms," Mr. Bartlett tells us that, after having collected, he imposed upon himself the task of tracing to their source these exceptional words, phrases, and accents. "On comparing these familiar words," he writes, "with the provincial and colloquial language of the northern counties of England, a most striking resemblance appeared, not only in the words commonly regarded as peculiar to New England, but in the dialectical pronunciation of certain words, and in the general tone and accent. In fact, it may be said without exaggeration, that nine tenths of the colloquial peculiarities of New England are derived directly from Great Britain; and they are now provincial in those parts from which the early colonists emigrated, or are to be found in the writings of well-accredited authors of the period when that emigration took place."

Neither has the long-standing reproach of a lack of literary cultivation and achievement present significance. Sydney Smith's famous query in the *Edinburgh Review*, "Who reads an American book?" is as irrelevant and impertinent to-day as the other famous dictum of Jeffrey in regard to Wordsworth's poetry—"This will never do." In history, poetry, science, criticism, biography, political and ethical discussions, the records of travels, of taste, and of romance, universally recognized and standard exemplars, of American origin, now illustrate the genius and culture of the nation.

In thus referring the liberal and philosophical inquirer, who desires to comprehend the character, destinies, and history of the United States, and thence infer the relation of and duty to them on the part of Europe, to the several departments of literature which bear the impress of the national mind, another form of prejudice and phase of injustice habitual with British writers inevitably suggest themselves. Fifty years ago, American literature was declared by them beneath contempt; but as soon as leisure and encouragement stimulated the educated and the gifted natives of the soil to enter upon the career of authorship; when the literary products of the country attained a degree of merit that could not be ignored, these same critics objected that American literature was unoriginal—only a new instalment of English; that Irving reproduced the manner of the writers of Queen Anne's day; that Cooper's novels were imitated from those of Scott; that Brockden Brown plagiarized from Godwin, Hoffman from Moore, Holmes from Sterne, Sprague from Pope; and, in short, that, because Americans made use of good English, standard forms of verse, and familiar construction in narrative, they had no claim to a national literature. It seems a waste of time and words to confute such puerile reasoning. If the number of English authors who have written popular books in any and all of the British colonies, should have their literary merits questioned on the ground that these works, although composed and published in the vernacular, were not actually conceived and written in London, the absurd objection would be deemed too ridiculous to merit notice. Not only the language, but the culture; not only the political traditions, but the standards of taste, the religious and social education, the literary associations, the whole mental resource and discipline of an educated American, are analogous to or identical with those of England; but, as a people, the statistics of the book trade and the facts of individual culture prove that the master minds of

British literature more directly and universally train and nurture the American than the English mind. Partly from that distance that lends enchantment, and partly from the vast number of readers produced by our system of popular education, Shakspeare and Milton, Bacon and Wordsworth, Byron and Scott have been and are more generally known, appreciated, and loved, and have entered more deeply into the average intellectual life, on this than on the other side of the Atlantic; and the best thinkers, the most refined poets of Great Britain in our own day, find here a larger and more enthusiastic audience than they do at home. Accordingly, until the laws of mind are reversed, there is no reason to expect any different manifestation of literature, as far as form, style, and conventional rules are concerned, here than there. The subjects, the scenery, the characters, the opinions of our historians, poets, novelists, and essayists, are as diverse from those of British writers as the respective countries. Cooper's local coloring, his chief personages, the scope and flavor of his romances, are as unlike those of Scott as are the North American Indians from Highlanders, and Lake Ontario from Loch Leven. The details of Bryant's forest pictures are full of special traits of which there is not a trace in Thomson or Burns. The author of "Caleb Williams" acknowledged his obligations to the author of "Weiland" and "Arthur Mervyn." There are pages of the "Sketch Book" and "Bracebridge Hall" which Addison might have written, for their subjects are English life and scenes; but when the same graceful pen expatiates, with rich humor, among the legends of the Hudson or Dutch dynasties in New York, describes the prairies or colonial times in Virginia, except in the words used, there is not the slightest resemblance in subject, tone, impression, or feeling to the "Spectator." Why should Motley write otherwise than Hallam, Prescott than Macaulay, Emerson than Carlyle, Channing than Arnold, Hawthorne than Kingsley, as regards the technical use of a language common to them all, and a culture identical in its normal elements? All the individuality to be looked for is in the treatment of their several subjects, in the style incident to their respective temperaments and characters, and in the literary genius with which they are severally endowed. Yet, if it were desirable to vindicate the American quality as a distinction of these and other approved authors, it would be an easy task to indicate a freedom and freshness, an independence and humanity, so characteristic as to prove singularly attractive to foreign readers, and to be recognized by high continental criticism as national.

The mercenary spirit so continually ascribed to our civilization by English writers, long before was the habitual reproach cast on their own by continental critics. Thrift is a Saxon trait, and the "nation of shopkeepers" cannot appropriately thus make the love of or deference to money our exclusive or special weakness; whereas the extreme and appalling diversity of condition in England, the juxtaposition of the duke and the drudge, the pampered bishop and the starving curate, the magnificent park and the malarious hovel, the luxurious peer and the squalid operative, bring into such melancholy relief the sharp and bitter inequalities of human lives and human creatures, that not all the latent and obvious resources, energy, self-reliance, and power which so beguiled the wonder and love of Emerson in the aspect of England and Englishmen in their prosperous phase, can reconcile that social atmosphere to the large, warm, sensitive heart of an unselfish, sympathetic, Christian man. Clubs and races, cathedrals and royal drawing rooms, the freshness of rural and the luxury of metropolitan life, Parliament and the *Times*—all the elements, routine, substantial bases and superficial aspects of England and the English, however adequate to the insular egotism, and however barricaded by prejudice, pride, and indifference, do not harmonize, to the clear, humane gaze of soulful eyes, with what underlies and overshadows this stereotyped programme and partial significance. We hear the "cry of the human" that rang so drearily in the ear of the noblest woman and poet of the age:

> "I am listening here in Rome ;
>   Over Alps a voice is sweeping :
> 'England's cruel! Save us some
>   Of these victims in her keeping.'"

> . . . . . . "Let others shout,
>   Other poets praise my land here ;
> I am sadly setting out,
>   Praying, 'God forgive her grandeur!'"

Nor less authoritative is the same earnest and truth-inspired voice, in its protest against the inhumanity that ignores or wilfully repudiates the claims of other nations :

"I confess that I dream of the day when an English statesman shall arise with a heart too large for England, having courage, in the face of his countrymen, to assert of some suggestive policy, 'This is good for your trade ; this is necessary for your domination : but it will vex a people hard by ; it will hurt a people farther off ; it will profit nothing to the general humanity ; therefore away with it ! It is not for you or me.' When a British minister dares so to speak, and when a British public applauds him speaking, then shall the nation be so glorious, that her praise, instead of exploding from within, from loud civic mouths, shall come to her from without, as all worthy praise must, from the alliances she has fostered, and from the populations she has saved." *

Voltaire compared the English to beer—"the bottom dregs, the top froth, and the middle excellent." The first and last class, for a considerable period, alone reported us ; low abuse and superficial sneers being their legitimate expression, and an inability to understand a people, sympathize with an unaccustomed life, or rise above selfish considerations, their normal defects ; whereof the last three years have given memorable proof.

'Instead of the vague title of *Annus Mirabilis* which Dryden bestowed upon a memorable year in English history, these might more appropriately be called, as far as our country is concerned, the *Test Years*. Not only have they proved the patriotism, the resources, and the character of the people

---

* Elizabeth Browning.

and their institutions, but they have applied specific tests, the result of which has been essentially to modify the convictions and sentiments of individuals. Any thinking man who will review his opinions, cannot fail to be astonished at the changes in his estimate of certain persons and things, which have taken place since the war for the Union began. Thousands, for instance, who entertained a certain reverence for the leading British journal, simply as such, without any familiarity therewith, having become acquainted with the *Times* in consequence of its gratuitous discussion of our national affairs, and perceiving its disingenuous, perverse, inimical spirit toward their country in the hour of calamity; and, of their own personal knowledge, proving its wanton falsehoods, have been enlightened so fully, that henceforth the mechanical resources and intellectual appliances of that famous newspaper weigh as nothing against the infamy that attends a discovered quack.*

In countless hearts and minds on this continent, pleasant and fond illusions in regard to English character, government, and sentiment are forever dispelled, first by the injustice of the official, and then by the uncandid and inimical tone of the literary organs of the British people. There lies before us, as we write, a private letter from an American scholar and gentleman, who, on the score of lineage as well as culture and character, claims respect for his deliberate views. What he says in the frank confidence of private correspondence, indicates, without exaggeration, the change which has come over the noblest in the land: 'Let John Bull beware. War or no war, he has made an enduring enemy of us. I am startled to hear myself say this, but England is henceforth to me only historical—the home of *our* Shak-

---

* Cobden thus characterizes the *Times* with reference to its treatment of a home question and native statesmen: "Here we have, in a compendious form, an exhibition of those qualities of mind which characterize the editorial management of the *Times*—of that arrogant self-complacency, that logical incoherence, and that moral bewilderment which a too long career of impunity and irresponsibility could alone engender."

speare, and Milton, and Wordsworth; for all her best writers are ours by necessity and privilege of language: but farewell the especial sympathy I have felt in her political, social, and total well-being. With her present exhibition and promulgation of jealousy and selfishness and heartlessness and ungentlemanly meanness, she has cut me loose from the sweet and cordial and reverent ties that have kept her so long to me a second fatherland.'"

CHAPTER VIII.

NORTHERN EUROPEAN WRITERS.

KALM; MISS BREMER; GUROWSKI, AND OTHERS; GERMAN WRITERS:
HUMBOLDT; SAXE WEIMAR; VON RAUMER; PRINCE MAXIMILIAN
VON WEID; LIEBER; SCHULTZ; OTHER GERMAN WRITERS:
GRUND; RUPPIUS; SEATSFIELD; KOHL; TALVI; SCHAFF.

IN the North of Europe, since the beginning of the present century, French literature has been the chief medium of current information in regard to the rest of the world. Within the last twenty years the English language has become a fashionable accomplishment; and, with the wonderful development of German literature, books of science and travel, in that language, have furnished the other northern races with no small part of their ideas about America. In Russia, Sweden, and Denmark, many of our best authors have been translated; and the *Journal de St. Petersbourg, L'Abeille du Nord, Vedemosti* (*Bedemoctu*), during the civil war, have, by the accuracy of their facts and the justness of their reasoning, evidenced a remarkably clear understanding of the struggle, its origin, aim, and consequences. A pleasant book of "Impressions" during a tour in the United States, by Lakieren, a Russian, was published in that language in 1859; and a Swedish writer—Siljestroem*—gave

* "The Educational Institutions of the United States, their Character and Organization," translated from the Swedish by Frederica Rowan, London,

to his countrymen an able description and exposition of the American system of popular education, which is justly esteemed for its fulness and accuracy; while the great work of Rafn on "Northern Antiquities" identifies the profound researches of a Danish scholar with the dawn of American history.

It is refreshing alike to the senses and the soul, to turn from the painfully exciting story of those early adventurers on this continent, whose object was conquest and personal aggrandizement, whose careers, though signalized often by heroism and sagacity, were fraught with bloodshed, not only in conflicts with the savages, but in quarrels among their own followers and rivals, to the peaceful journeys and voyages—attended, indeed, with exposure and privation—of those who sought the woods and waters of the New World chiefly to discover their marvels and enjoy and record them. We find in all the desirable reports of explorers, whether men of war, diplomacy, or religion, more or less of that observation, and sometimes of that love of nature, so instinctively active when a new scene of grandeur or beauty is revealed to human perception. But these casual indications of either a scientific or sympathetic interest in the physical resources of the country are but the episodes in expeditions, whose leaders were too hardy or unenlightened to follow these attractions, for their own sake, with zeal and exclusiveness. Other and less innocent objects absorbed their minds; and it is chiefly among the missionaries that we find any glowing recognition of the charms of the untracked wilderness, the mysterious streams, and the brilliant skies, which they strove to consecrate to humanity by erecting, amid and beneath them, the Cross, which should hallow the flag that proclaimed their acquisition to a distant but ambitious monarch. To the naturalist, America has ever abounded in peculiar interest; and

1853. Other Swedish works on America are C. D. Arfevedson's "Travels," (1838); Gustaf Unonecis' "Recollections of a Residence of Seventeen Years in the United States" (1862–'3). Munck Rieder, a Norwegian, wrote a work on his return from the United States in 1849—chiefly statistical.

all with an inkling of that taste have found their loneliest wanderings cheered thereby. Nor has it been the scientific love of nature alone to which she has here ever appealed. To the adventurous and poetical, to the brave lover of independence and freedom, like Boone, and the enthusiast, like Chateaubriand, the forest and the waterfall have possessed a memorable charm. From Bartram to Wilson, and from Audubon to Agassiz, the world of animal and vegetable life in America has yielded a long array of naturalists the richest materials for exploration.

One of the earliest scientific visitors to our shores was Peter Kalm, who was sent from Sweden, with the approbation of Linnæus, in 1745. His salary was inadequate, and he so trenched upon his private resources, in order to carry out the objects of his journey, as to be compelled, after his return home, to practise rigid economy. Kalm was born in Osterbotten, in 1715, and educated at Upsal. On his return from America, he was appointed professor of natural history at Abo, where he died in 1779. A charming memorial of his visit to our country is the botanical name given to the wild laurel of our woods, first made known by him to Europe, and, in honor thereof, called the Kalmia. His work, "En resa til Norra Amerika," appeared in Stockholm in 1753-'61, in three volumes, and was translated into Dutch, German, and English—the latter by John R. Foster, under the title of "Travels in North America" (2 vols., London, 1772).* He passed the winter of 1749 among the Swedes settled at Racoon, New Jersey. He explored the coast of New York, visited the Blue Mountains, the Mohawk, Iroquois, Oneida, Tuscarora, and Onondaga Indian tribes, Lake Ontario, and the Falls of Niagara. His description of the latter was long popular. In his diary, while at Philadelphia, he notes the variety of religious sects and their peculiarities, the exports, and the hygiene. Some of the facts recorded by him of the

* "Travels in North America, containing its Natural History, and Civil, Ecclesiastical, and Commercial State," &c., by Peter Kalm, 3 vols. 8vo., best edition, map, plates Warrington, 1770.

City of Brotherly Love a century ago, enable us to realize how rapid has been the advance from suburban wildness to the highest metropolitan luxury. When Kalm sojourned there, elks, beavers, and stags were hunted where now is "the sweet security of streets." So abundant were the peaches, that they served as the food of swine. The noisy midsummer chorus of frogs, locusts, and grasshoppers vibrated through what is now the heart of a great city. Maize was to the Swedish botanist the most wonderful staple of the soil. He discovered a species of Rhus indigenous to the region. The murmur of the spinning wheel was a familiar sound; and sassafras was deemed a specific cure for dropsy.

Kalm's picture of Albany in 1749 is an interesting parallel and contrast to Mrs. Grant's more elaborate description, and to the pleasant social glimpses of its modern life given by the late William Kent in a lecture before the young men there of this generation. The Swedish traveller tells us that all the people spoke Dutch, that the servants were all negroes, and that all the houses had gable ends to the street, with such projecting gutters that wayfarers were seriously incommoded in wet weather. He describes the cattle as roaming the dirty streets at will; the interior of the dwellings as of an exemplary neatness, and the fireplaces and porches thereof of an amplitude commensurate with the wide and genial hospitality and liberal social instincts of the people, whose prevalent virtues he regarded as frugality in diet and integrity of purpose and character. In their houses the women were extremely neat. "They rise early," says Kalm, "go to sleep late, and are almost over nice and cleanly in regard to the floor, which is frequently scoured several times a week." Tea had been but recently introduced among them, but was extensively used; coffee seldom. They never put sugar and milk in their tea, but took a small piece of the former in their mouths while sipping the beverage. They usually breakfasted at seven, dined at twelve or one, and supped at six; and most of them used sweet milk or buttermilk at every meal. They also used cheese at breakfast and dinner, grated instead of sliced; and the usual drink of the majority of the people was small beer and pure water. The wealthier families, although not indulging in the variety then seen upon tables in New York, used much fish, flesh, and fowl, preserves and pastry, nuts and fruits, and various wines, at their meals, especially when entertaining their friends or strangers. Their hospitality toward deserving strangers was free and generous, without formality and rules of etiquette, and they never allowed their visitors to interfere with the necessary duties of the household, the counting room, or the farm.

In describing his visit to Niagara Falls, in a letter dated Albany, September 2, 1750, Kalm furnishes us with an interesting contrast between the experience of a traveller to this long-frequented shrine of nature, a century ago, when such expeditions were few and far between, and the magnificent scene with its frontier fort was isolated in the wilderness, and the same visit now, when caravans rush thither many times a day, with celerity, to find all the comforts, society, and amenities of high civilization:

"I came, on the 12th of August, to Niagara Fort. The French there seemed much perplexed at my first coming, imagining I was an English officer, who, under pretext of seeing the Falls, came with some other view; but as soon as I showed them my passport, they changed their behavior, and treated me with the greatest civility. In the months of September and October, such immense quantities of dead waterfowl are found, every morning, below the fall, on the shore (swept there), that the garrison of the fort for a long time live chiefly upon them, and obtain such plenty of feathers in autumn as make several beds."

The Swedish colony on the banks of the Delaware early associated that brave nationality with the settlement of America.* Longfellow's translation of Tegner's "Children

---

* 1. "Description of New Sweden in America, and the Settlements in Pennsylvania by Companies," Stockholm, 1792, a small quarto, with primitive engravings.

2. "Description of the Province of New Sweden, now called by the English Pennsylvania," translated and edited by Peter S. Duponceau. Phila., 1824.

3. "The Swedes on the Delaware," by Rev. Jehu Curtis Clay, Phila.

of the Lord's Supper," with the prefatory sketch of life in Sweden, gave us a pleasant glimpse of its primitive and rural traits; and the vocalism and beneficence of Jenny Lind endeared the very name of that far-off land to American hearts. But the novels of Fredrika Bremer first made known in this country the domestic life of Sweden, which, delineated with such *naiveté* and detail in "The Neighbors," charmed our households, and prepared them to give a cordial welcome to the author. The first impression she made, however, was not highly attractive. A journal of the day well describes it, and the natural reaction therefrom :

"The slowness with which she spoke, and the pertinacity with which she insisted on understanding the most trifling remark made to her, a little dashed the enthusiasm of those who newly made her acquaintance. Further intercourse, however, brought out a quaint and quiet self-possession, a shrewd vein of playfulness, a quick observation, and a truly charming simplicity, which rewon all the admiration she had lost, and added, we fancy, even to the ideal of expectation."

There are few situations in modern life more suggestive of the ludicrous, than that of a woman "of a certain age," professedly visiting a country for the purpose of critically examining and reporting it and its people. Every American of lively imagination who has been thrown into society with one of these female philosophers on such a voyage of discovery, must have caught ideas for a comedy of real life from the phenomena thus created. "Asking everybody everything," the self-appointed inspector is propitiated by one, quizzed by another, feared by this class and contemned by that, all the time with an unconscious air, looking, listening, noting down, and, from the most evanescent and unreliable data, "giving an opinion" or drawing a portrait, not of a wellknown place or familiar person, but of an unknown country and a strange nation! To see Miss Martineau vigilantly thridding crowds and paying out the flexible tube of her cartrumpet, like a telegraph wire, into the social sea; or Dickens astride a chair in a hotel, receiving gratuitous and exaggerated reports of the state of the nation, from a group of lion-struck republicans, are tableaux that will recur to many, as illustrations of this comedy of travel in America.

It was our lot to see Miss Bremer at a manorial domicile on the Hudson, in all the glory of her "mission." It was in the autumn, and no one could pass along the river without being struck with admiration at the splendid colors that kindled the woods: it was the common theme of remark. She, however, resented this assumed superiority of the American autumn, saying, "The Lord also has done something for Sweden. Our foliage is brilliant in the fall." In the same spirit she refused to believe a lady fresh from Kentucky, who, in describing to her the Mammoth Cave, mentioned the familiar fact that the fish therein have only the rudiment of an optic nerve. At dinner, her inquiries about the material and preparation of the viands would have led to the supposition that she meditated a manual of cookery; and, on returning to the drawing room, she whipped out a sketch book, and coolly drew a likeness of Irving, the most illustrious of the guests. The fabrics of the ladies' dresses, the modes of dancing, the style of meals, the trees, furniture, books, schools, and private history of all persons of note, and even of those unknown to fame, were investigated with perfect good humor and *nonchalance;* but the process and idea of the thing, when considered, are a singular commentary upon modern life and social dignity; and when the long-expected book appeared, the kind people who had entertained Miss Bremer, were dismayed to find their sayings and doings recorded, and their very looks and characters analyzed for the public edification. This breach of good faith and good taste, however, did not prevent her Swedish readers from learning, through her very frank and *naïve* but often superficial report, many details of domestic economy, and some novelties of American life; while here the effect was once more to "give us pause" in our hospitable instincts, and to feel the necessity of a new sumptuary law, whereby to eat one's salt should be a pledge against the freedom of pen-craft.

Adam Gurowski's book on America is noteworthy as the observations of a Pole. It appeared in 1857, and has few elements of popularity, being alike devoid of statistics and gossip—the staple elements of favorite records of travel on this side of the water; but it is honorably distinguished from these by a vein of grave speculation and historical reasoning, of which the author's subsequent hasty, irate, and irrational comments on the war for the Union, give no indication. Being a publicist and a well-read political philosopher, as well as a political refugee, the Count's experience as a Polish revolutionist, an *employé* of Russia, and a long resident in America, fits him eminently to discuss the tendencies and traits of this country by the light of the past. He compares our civilization with that of Europe. The tone of his work is liberal and rational. He is a sincere and earnest admirer of our institutions, a trenchant social critic. The pulpit, press, and "manifest destiny" of the nation are keenly analyzed, and slavery is discussed from an historical stand-point, and thoroughly condemned by practical argument. As a treatise on government and society, the book contains an unusual amount of thought, and grasps salient questions with a comprehensive scope. It is, indeed, defective in style, and contains palpable errors of statement and inference; but these are more than atoned for by its philosophical spirit.

A highly educated Swiss, K. Meier, in a pleasant work entitled "To the Sacramento," has described his journey from the Northern States to California *via* Panama, in the German language, with the interest which ever attaches to the tour of an intelligent votary of the natural sciences; and an officer of the same nation, Colonel Lecomte, has published, in the French language, a report of our military operations during the first months of the war for the Union, which has been translated into English.*

* "The War in the United States: a Report to the Swiss Military Department; preceded by a Discourse to the Federal Military Society, assembled

An accomplished member of the Belgian Representative Chamber wrote an able little treatise on "La Question Américaine,"* in which he arrays facts and arguments in a lucid and forcible manner, and discusses, with rare fulness and perspicacity, the causes and consequences of the civil war. His views of the mutual interests of his own and our country are worth citing:

"It will not seem out of place to show here, briefly, that, as regards Belgium, the cotton question is not the only one which interests her in the affairs of America. We have close constitutional analogies with the United States. If their institutions should fall, ours would suffer by reaction. We have copied the American Constitution, not only as to municipal and provincial decentralization, as to that of industrial, financial, charitable associations, &c., as to the great liberties of worship, of instruction, and of the press (of which the English charter offered us equally the model); but we have followed America particularly as regards the absence of a state religion, of which Catholic Maryland gave the first example. We have imitated her in the institution of an elective Senate, in that of a House of Representatives identified with the democratic interest. The national Congress voted the Belgian Constitution with their eyes fixed on the American Union. Were we to consult only the interest of Belgium, we ought to desire that the United States should continue to remain what they have been, and to give us the example of union, of the spirit of liberty, and of decentralization—qualities which characterize the Anglo-Saxon race, with which the Belgians have bonds of relationship and close affinities." (P. 63.)

No Europeans, in our own day, have had more reason to regard North America with hopeful interest than the Germans. To their indigent agricultural population this country has proved a prosperous home; and the zeal with which our Teutonic fellow citizens, of all classes, volunteered for the war on whose issues hang the liberties of this continent, is the best evidence of their appreciation of the privileges of

at Berne, August 18th, 1862," by Ferdinand Lecomte, translated from the French by a Staff Officer, New York, 1863.

* "La Question Américaine dans ses Rapports avec les Mœurs, l' Esclavage, l' Industrie et la Politique." Par Le Chanoine de Haerne, Membre de la Chambre des Représentants, Bruxelles, 1862, 8vo., pp. 72.

American citizenship. No foreigners seem to organize their national life among us with such facility. The guilds and pastimes of the fatherland are as familiar in our cities as on the Rhine. German scholars and thinkers are attached to our colleges, contribute to our literature, and enrich our society; while large sections of the Western States are cultivated by German peasants. Moreover, the literature of Germany has essentially modified the culture of the present generation of American scholars; and thus, in the sphere of intellectual and of utilitarian life, a mutual understanding and sympathy, and a community of political interests, have tended to bring the two nationalities into nearer relations.

Many statistical works on the United States have been published in Germany as guides to emigrants; and many sensible treatises explaining and describing our institutions, manners, resources, and characteristics, like those of Von Raumer, Lieber, and other residents and visitors. A certain philosophical impartiality of tone makes the German record a kind of middle ground between the urbane and enthusiastic French and the prejudiced and sneering English writers. Some of the most just views and candid delineations have emanated from German writers. Their political sympathies, extensive information, and patient tone of mind, alike fit them for the task of investigating and reporting physical and social facts. The record may lack sprightliness, and be tinged with a curious vein of speculation, but is nevertheless likely to convey solid and valuable knowledge, and suggest comprehensive inferences. Gerstaecker, who travelled on foot over a large part of the Southwest, and Trochling, have given to many of their countrymen the first vivid impressions of America. Writing in the novelistic form, they reached the sympathies of many who would neglect a merely statistical work. Private letters, and the current journals and translations of Cooper and Irving, are, however, the popular sources of specific information and romantic impressions in Germany in regard to the United States. Although Baron Humboldt's American researches were chiefly confined to the

Southern continent, he was keenly alive to the human interest and civic problems of the United States. "We would simply draw attention," he writes in "Cosmos," "to the fact that, since this period" (that of the discovery and colonization of America), "a new and more vigorous activity of the mind and feelings, animated by bold aspirations and hopes which can scarcely be frustrated, has gradually penetrated through all grades of civil society; that the scanty population of one half of the globe, especially in the portions opposite to Europe, has favored the settlement of colonies, which have been converted, by their extent and position, into independent States, enjoying unlimited power in the choice of their mode of free government; and, finally, that religious reform—the precursor of great political revolutions—could not fail to pass through the different phases of its development, in a portion of the earth which had become the asylum of all forms of faith, and of the most different views regarding Divine things. The daring enterprise of the Genoese seaman is the first link in the immeasurable chain of these momentous events. Accident, and not fraud and dissension, deprived the continent of America of the name of Columbus. The New World, continuously brought nearer to Europe during the last half century by means of commercial intercourse and the improvement of navigation, has exercised an important influence on the political institutions, the ideas and feelings of those nations who occupy the eastern shores of the Atlantic, the boundaries of which appear to be constantly brought nearer and nearer to one another."

There is a curious illustration of the first impressions of the highly educated Germans in America, in a phrase of Baron Furstenwärther, and its explanation by Mr. Schmidt: "With all the facility," writes the former, "particularly of the material life, there is no idea, not a distant suspicion, of a high and fine existence." "By material," observes the latter, "we mean men who take more pleasure in a cattle show or a breed of swine, than a Venus de Medici or a Laocoon." Very patient and informing, but quite tame and didactic, are the "Travels in North America" by His Highness, Bernhard, Duke of Saxe-Weimar-Eisenach, republished in Philadelphia in 1828. The kindliness and intelligence of the Duke are apparent on every page of these two volumes; but there is little new in the subjects or mode of treatment. It is a work which excites respect for the man more than admiration for the writer. His benevolent interest and his detailed account of what he sees and hears, are the most remarkable traits. He gives a favorable report of the hospitality of Americans; describes his visit to the elder Adams, and a Virginia rail fence, a granite machine in New England, and a Hudson River steamboat or horse ferry, the Creek Indians, and Owen's community, with the same fulness and apparent interest. He criticizes West's painting of "Christ Healing the Sick" judiciously, bestows the epithet "dear" upon Philadelphia, was astonished "to hear Virginians praise hereditary nobility and primogeniture," and greatly enjoyed a visit to the Moravian settlement at Bethlehem, the Natural Bridge, and a dinner at Monticello. It is remarkable that the travellers of rank show so much more human and so much less conventional interest in American life, manners, and resources than those who belong to a class we should imagine especially alive to the opportunities and privileges of a new and free country. Yet the Cavalier Castiglione, the Marquis of Chastellux, the Duke of Saxe-Weimar, and Lord Morpeth are more just and generous in their observation and sympathies, as travellers in America, than a Hall, a Trollope, or a Dickens.

Friedrich Von Raumer, more of an historian than an observer, a professor in the University of Berlin, and author of several political and historical treatises, after travelling in England and publishing his observations on that country, which were translated by Mrs. Austin (5 vols., London, 1836), visited this country, and, in 1843, wrote a book thereon, entitled "America and the American people," subsequently translated and published in New York.* It contains

* "America and the American People," by Frederick Von Raumer,

much valuable information, and is written with the love of knowledge and patient exposition thereof characteristic of a German professor, but evidently drawn much more from books than from life.

The German edition of the "Travels"* in America of the Prince Maximilian von Wied, is superbly illustrated, and much used as an authentic reference by his countrymen, for whom the work was expressly written: it is wholly descriptive, and therefore contains little that is new to a well-informed native. The work was translated into English, and with its superb illustrations republished in London. One of the best known here of the German writers on this country is Dr. Francis Lieber. He was born at Berlin in 1800, and received a doctor's degree at the University of Jena. Like so many ardent and cultivated young Europeans, he espoused the cause of Greece during her Revolution; became a political exile, received a letter of encouragement from Richter, wrote poems in prison, and, in 1827, came to America. He edited the *Cyclopædia Americana*, and was professor in Columbia College, South Carolina, several years, and now holds a like situation in Columbia College, New York. Dr. Lieber is an eminent publicist. His views on political economy are original and profound. His expositions of international law, and his occasional political essays, are alike remarkable for extensive knowledge and acute reasoning. His "Letters to a Gentleman in Germany," or "The Stranger in America," † exhibit his ability in his special line of studies, applied to our institutions and resources. They give remarkably full statements of judicial and penitentiary systems, and of social traits. Dr. Lieber's ample opportunities of observation, his

---

translated from the German by W. W. Turner, 8vo., pp. 512, New York, 1846.

* "Journey through North America," by Prince Max v. New-wied-Wied, a most valuable work, rich in characteristic sketches of nature and life, as well as in scientific results.

† "The Stranger in America; comprising Sketches of the Manners of Society, &c.," by Francis Lieber, 2 vols. 8vo., London, 1835.

familiarity with society and life both North and South, and the philosophical tendency of his mind, make him a remarkably apt expositor of the most important questions relating to our country. His work was translated into English by a son of the celebrated jurist Hugo.

Christian Schultz made an inland tour through the United States, in 1807–'8, of six thousand miles, his description whereof was published in New York in 1810.* Though not intended for the public, his letters are intelligent, and, for the most part, accurate. Those referring to the Western Territories must have afforded seasonable and desirable information at that period; and his account of the Middle States is in some respects highly satisfactory. A good illustration of the absence of locomotive facilities at that time on one of the most frequented lines of travel in our day, occurs in the notes of his journey from Albany to Oswego. The latter place, he tells us, was then "wholly dependent upon the salt trade." He went there by canal and through Wood Creek and the Onondaga River; in fact, by the route described in Cooper's "Pathfinder," substituting a barge for a canoe. As to the town itself, thus slowly approached by water, and long the goal of fur trader, missionary, and military expeditions, this author thought its "appearance very contemptible from the irregular and confused manner in which the inhabitants build their houses;" but his impression of the place changed when he surveyed the lake from the shore, and recognized so many local advantages and so vast and beautiful a prospect.

A volume, written also from personal experience, of the same date, by Ludwig Gale, entitled "My Emigration to the United States," is another of the early specimens of German Travels therein, since forgotten in the more complete and careful reports of later writers. Nor should the essay of a political philosopher and naturalist, E. A. W. Zimmerman, be neglected. It is entitled "France and the Free States of

* "Travels on an Inland Voyage through the States of New York, Pennsylvania, Virginia, Ohio, Kentucky, and Tennessee, &c.," by Christian Schultz, with numerous maps and plates, 2 vols. 8vo., New York, 1810.

North America," and appeared in 1795. Its author, a native of Hanover, and educated at Leyden and Gottingen, died in 1815, and, " during the whole period of the French ascendency in Europe, was distinguished for his bold denunciation of the usurpations and oppressions of that Government."

In 1839, a view of " Social and Public Life in the United States," by Nicholas H. Julius, appeared at Leipsic. It is written in a very intelligent and humane spirit, and with practical judgment. Paul William Duke of Wurtemberg's " Journey in North America in the Years 1825–'26," is finely descriptive, with vivid sketches of social life. It contains a detailed account of some of the German settlements. William Grisson characterizes ably the juridical, religious, and military relations of America, and comments on life there from careful observation. F. W. von Wrede drew some authentic " Pictures of Life in the United States and Texas." In Count Gorsz's " Journey Round the World," the first volume is devoted to America; and, the author having remained there longest, it is the best of the series. M. Busch's " Wanderings in the United States " is written with candor, and presents the extremes of light and shade, with no small humor; while Francis Loher has some excellent national portraits in his " Lands and People in the Old and New World," and describes at length the " Germans in America," with whom he long resided. Frederick Kapp published, at Gottingen, in 1854, a treatise on the slavery question, in its historical development, full of facts and just reasoning, although recent events have negatived its prophetic inductions. Louis von Baumbach's " New Letters from the United States" (Cassel, 1856), is a useful guide to the candid study of American life and institutions; and Julius Frobel's " From America" (Leipsic, 1857) treats with *esprit* and geniality social and political questions.

In a work entitled " The Americans in their Moral, Social, and Political Relations," a German writer, Francis J. Grund (subsequently a naturalized citizen and active politician), exposed some of the superficial and false reasoning of English travellers in America. Published in Boston * and London in 1837, and claiming to be the result of fourteen years' residence in the country, it discussed, with much acuteness and candor, several unhackneyed topics of this prolific theme: among them, the aversion to amusements, the reception of foreigners, the relation of American literature to the English periodical press, and the influence of the Western settlements on the political prospects of America; while the more familiar topics of education, universal suffrage, slavery, and industrial enterprises, are treated with much discrimination. The political sympathies of the author give an emphasis to his arguments; but he is by no means blind to the national deficiencies; and in a subsequent work, evidently more especially devoted thereto—which, although ostensibly edited only, was written by him, and entitled "Aristocracy in America"—he exhibits them with sarcastic vigor. His first book, however, was timely, true, and remarkably well written. He professes to have arrived at strict impartiality, and was chiefly inspired by an "honest desire to correct prejudices, American and English, and not to furnish them with fresh aliment." He declares that the "Americans have been greatly misrepresented;" and this not so much by ascribing to them spurious qualities, as by omitting to mention those which entitle them to honor and respect, and representing the foibles of certain classes as weaknesses belonging to the nation. In the opinion of this writer, "a remarkable trait of English travellers in the United States consists in their proneness to find the same faults with Americans which the people of the continent of Europe are apt to find with themselves." He recognizes an "air of busy inquietude" as characteristic of the people, and "business" as the "soul" of American life; yet he considers the tendency of their democracy "not to debase the wealthy in mind or fortune, but to raise the inferior classes to a moral elevation where they no longer need be

---

* "The Americans in their Moral, Social, and Political Relations," by Francis J. Grund, 2 vols. in 1, 12mo., Boston, 1837.

degraded and despised." As to the "unhallowed custom of talking about trade and business, I must confess," he says, "not to have remarked it half as often as Hamilton. I rather think an honorable exception was made in his favor, in order to acquaint him the better with American affairs, on which they knew he was about to write a book." To this natural explanation of a circumstance which the English traveller magnifies into a national defect, the more kindly continental observer adds another which accounts for many false inferences: "From the writings of Basil Hall and Hamilton, it is evident that neither of the gentlemen became acquainted with any but the fashionable coteries of the large cities, and that the manners of the people, and especially of the respectable middle class, escaped altogether their immediate attention." He observes that "the most remarkable characteristic of Americans is the uncommon degree of intelligence that pervades all classes;" and thinks that "their proneness to argue lends a zest to conversation." To popular education he attributes the mental activity and enlightenment so striking to a European as general traits. "The German system," he remarks, "favors the development of the mind to the exclusion of all practical purposes. The American aims always at some application, and creates dexterity and readiness for action." In the Western communities, he finds an attractive "*naïveté* of manners and grotesqueness of humor." No one, he says, can travel in the United States without making a business of it. "He must not expect to stop except at the place fixed upon by the proprietors of the road or the steamboat." The position of a man of leisure in this country, unless he is interested in literary or scientific pursuits, he deems forlorn, because it is companionless. "There is no people on earth," he observes, "with whom business constitutes pleasure and industry amusement, to an equal degree as with the inhabitants of the United States." Hamilton attributes the "total absence of the higher elegancies of life" in this country to the "abolition of primogeniture;" while this German commentator cheerfully accepts the condition that he "must resign his individual tastes to the wishes of the majority" in view of the compensatory benefits. "Every new State," he writes, "is a fresh guarantee for the continuance of the American Constitution, and directs the attention of the people to new sources of happiness and wealth. It increases the interest of all in the General Government, and makes individual success dependent on national prosperity." With such broad sympathies and liberal views, he protests against the narrowness and the injustice of British writers, who have so pertinaciously misrepresented the country, its institutions and prospects, declaring that "the progress of America reflects but the glory of England. All the power she acquires extends the moral empire of England. Every page of American history is a valuable supplement to that of England. It is the duty of true patriots of both countries to support and uphold each other to the utmost extent compatible with national justice; and it is a humiliating task either for private individuals or public men to make the foibles of either the subject of ridicule to the other."

In his novels, Otto Ruppius, who resided for a considerable period in the United States, undertook, in this form, to make his countrymen familiar with the various aspects of life in America. They are interesting and suggestive, and in many respects authentic, though not always free from those partial or overdrawn pictures which are inseparable from this form of writing.

Another German author, for some years a resident in the United States, has made life and nature there the subject of several interesting and effective novels—after having, on his return home in 1826, published the general result of his observation and experience on this side of the water. He came back the following year, and his first American romance appeared in Philadelphia soon after, under the title of "Tokeah; or, The White Rose." Charles Seatsfield thus became known as an author. In 1829 and '30 he was one of the editors of the *Courier des Etats Unis*, and, soon after, went to Paris as correspondent of the *New York Courier and*

Enquirer. In 1832 he visited Switzerland, and there published a translation of "Tokeah." So popular was this work abroad, that he resolved to compose a series of romances illustrative of American life. His keen observation, strong sympathies, and imaginative zest enabled him to mould into vivid pictures the scenes and characters with which he had become familiar in America, where the six novels devoted to that subject soon became known through partial translations which appeared in *Blackwood's Magazine.* The intensity and freshness of these delineations excited much interest. They seemed to open a new and genuine vein of romance in American life, or, rather, to make the infinite possibilities thereof charmingly apparent. This was an experiment singularly adapted to a German, who, with every advantage of European education, in the freshness of life had emigrated to this country, and there worked and travelled, observed and reflected, and then, looking back from the ancient quietude of his ancestral land, could delineate, under the inspiration of contrast, all the wild and wonderful, the characteristic and original phases and facts of his existence in Texas, Pennsylvania, or New York. "Life in the New World" was soon translated and published in the latter city. It was followed by "The Cabin Book; or, Sketches of Life in Texas," and others of the series which abroad have given to thousands the most vivid impressions of the adventure, the scenery, and the characters of our frontier, and of many of the peculiar traits of our more confirmed civilization. Seatsfield resides alternately in Switzerland and the United States.

Few modern travellers have won a more desirable reputation for intelligent assiduity and an honest spirit than John G. Kohl, who, born at Brême in 1808, was educated at Gottingen, Heidelberg, and Munich, and, after filling the office of private tutor in two noble families, established himself at Dresden, and thence made numerous excursions through various parts of Europe and America; describing, with care and often with a singular thoroughness, the countries thus visited. Few records of travel convey so much interesting information.

The attainments and the temper of Kohl alike fit him for his chosen department of literature; for, to much historical and scientific information, an enlightened and ardent curiosity, and a habit of patient investigation, he unites a liberal, urbane disposition, and a rare facility of adaptation. He deals chiefly with facts that come under his own observation, and views them in the light of history. Imagination is quite secondary to rational inquiry in the scope of his studies from life; but he is not destitute of sensibility to nature, nor wanting in that philosophic interest in man, whereby the records of travel become so suggestive and valuable. Still, to most of his readers the charm of his books is mainly their candid and complete report of local features, social circumstances, and economical traits; so that one is often surprised to find a hackneyed subject arrayed in fresh interest, through the new facts noted or the special vein of inquiry pursued by this genial and intelligent *cicerone*. Kohl has written thus of Russia, Poland, Hungary, Styria, Bavaria, England, Scotland, Ireland, Denmark, Switzerland, Holland, Istria, Dalmatia, and other countries, explored by him with obvious zeal and vigilant observation. The tone of his mind may be inferred, not only from the extent of his books of travels and their fulness and authenticity, but also from the casual subjects which have occupied his indefatigable pen; such as the "Influence of Climate on the Character and Destiny of the People;" and "Esquisses de la Vie, de la Nature et des Peuples." The inquiries and impressions of so experienced a traveller and comprehensive a student cannot be destitute of interest and value. During his sojourn among us, Kohl cultivated the acquaintance of men of letters. He was eager in searching for the earliest maps and charts of the country and the coast. He domesticated himself where there was most to be learned, and won the esteem of all who knew him, by his *naive*, candid, and intelligent companionship. Thus far his published writings on America consist of an account of his visit to Canada, an expedition to Lake Superior, an elaborate sketch of the History of Discovery on this Continent, and various local delineations, which have appeared in the London periodicals. He differs from other writers by his geographical knowledge and the comparisons founded on extensive observations in other parts of the world. Although not blind to the incongruities and inequalities of our civilization, he is keenly alive to the progressive tendencies and actual privileges here realized. His eye for nature is scientific, his interpretation of national character acute, his judgments often historical in their basis; and it is in the spirit of a kindly man of the world, and a scholar and thinker, that he looks on the spectacle of American life. With a true German patience and zest, he seeks the men and the things, the facts of the past and the traits of the present that interest him, and have, in his estimation, true significance as illustrative of national character or local traits. How he thus regarded some of our literary and political celebrities and social aspects and traits, appears from his account of Boston. It is curious to compare his impressions of the metropolis of New England, viewed in such a spirit and for such an end, at this period, with the primitive picture of the Abbé Robin and the imbittered reminiscences of Consul Grattan:

"Of all the cities of the American Union, Boston is the one that has most fully retained the character of an English locality. This is visible upon the first glance at its physiognomy and the style of building. The city is spread out over several islands and peninsulas, in the innermost nook of Massachusetts Bay. The heart of Boston is concentrated on a single small peninsula, at which all the advantages of position, such as depth of water, accessibility from the sea and other port conveniences, are so combined, that this spot necessarily became the centre of life, the Exchange, landing place, and market.

"The ground in this central spot rises toward the middle, and formerly terminated in a triple-peaked elevation (the Three Mountains), which induced the earliest immigrants to settle here. At the present time these three points have disappeared, to a great extent, through the spread of building; but for all that, the elevation is perceptible for some distance, and the centre of Boston seems to tower over the rest of the city like an acropolis. From this centre numerous streets run to the circumference of the island, while others have

14

been drawn parallel with it, just as Moscow is built round the Kremlin. All this is in itself somewhat European, and hence there are in Boston streets running up and down hill; at some spots even a drag is used for the wheels of carts. The streets, too, are crooked and angular—a perfect blessing in America, where they generally run with a despairing straightness, like our German everlasting poplar alleys. At some corners of Boston—which is not like other American cities, divided chess-board-wise into blocks—you actually find surprises: there are real groups of houses. The city has a character of its own, and in some parts offers a study for the architect—things usually unknown in America.

"The limitation of the city to a confined spot, and the irregularity of the building style, may partly be the cause that the city reminds us of Europe. But that the city assumed so thorough an English type, may be explained by the circumstance that Boston received an entirely English population. In 1640, or ten years after its formation, it had five thousand English denizens, at a period when New York was still a small Dutch country town, under the name of New Amsterdam. Possibly, too, the circumstance that it was the nearest seaport to England, may have contributed to keep up old English traditions here. The country round Boston bears a remarkable likeness to an English landscape, and hence, no doubt, the State obtained the name of New England; but as in various parts of New England you may fancy yourself in Kent, so, when strolling about the streets of Boston, you may imagine yourself in the middle of London. In both cities the houses are built with equal simplicity, and do not assume that pomp of marble pilasters and decoration noticeable at New York and elsewhere. The doors and windows, the color and shape, are precisely such as you find in London. In Boston, too, there is a number of small green squares; and, amid the turmoil of business, many a quiet *cul de sac*, cut off from the rest of the street system.

"Externals of this nature generally find their counterpart in the manners and spirit of the inhabitants, and hence I believe that Boston is still more English and European than any other city of the Union. This is visible in many things; for instance, in the fact that the police system and public surveillance are more after the European style than anywhere else in America. Even though it may not be 'quite so bad' as in London, it strikes visitors from the West and South, and hence they are apt to abuse Massachusetts as a police-ridden State. Even in the fact that the flag of the Revolution was first raised in Boston—and hence the city is generally called 'The Cradle of American Freedom'—we may find a further proof that the population was penetrated with the true Anglo-Saxon temperament.

"This is specially perceptible in the scientific and social life of Boston, which suits Europeans better than the behavior in other American towns. Boston, in proportion to the number of its population, has more public and private libraries and scientific societies than any other metropolis of the Union; and, at the same time, a great number of well-organized establishments for the sick, the poor, the blind, and the insane, which are regarded as models in the United States. Boston has, consequently, a fair claim to the title of the 'American Athens.' There are upward of one hundred printing offices, from which a vast number of periodicals issue. The best and oldest of these is the *North American Review*, supplied with articles by such men as Prescott, Everett, Channing, Bancroft, &c. Among the Boston periodicals there has existed for some time past one devoted to heraldry, the only one of the sort in the Union, which, perhaps, as a sign of the aristocratic temper of the Bostonians, evidences a deeply rooted Anglicanism.

"The Historical Society of Boston is the oldest of that nature in the country. Since the commencement of the present century, it has published a number of interesting memoirs; and the history of no portion of the Union has been so zealously and thoroughly investigated as that of New England. The 'Lowell Institute,' established and endowed by a rich townsman, is an institution which works more efficaciously for the extension of knowledge and education than any other of the same character in America. It offers such handsome rewards for industry and talent, that even the greatest scientific authorities of England—for instance, Lyell—have at times found it worth while to visit Boston, and lecture in the hall of the Lowell Institution. In one of its suburbs—Cambridge—Boston possesses Harvard College, the best and oldest university in America; and it has also in the heart of the city a medical school. The city library, in its present reformed condition, surpasses in size and utility most of such establishments to be found in Germany.

"At Boston, too, private persons possess collections most interesting for science and art, which prove the existence of a higher feeling among the inhabitants of the city. During my short stay there I discovered and visited a considerable number. For instance, I met with a linen draper, who first showed me his stores near the waterside, then took me in his carriage to his suburbanum, where I found, in a wing expressly built for its reception, a library containing all the first editions of the rarest works about the discovery and settlement of America, which are now worth their weight in gold.

This worthy Boston tradesman was a very zealous member of the Historical Society, and has already published several memoirs upon his speciality (the earliest history of the American settlements). I was also taken to the villa of another tradesman, who made it the business of his life to make the most perfect collection of editions of the Bible. His collection is the only one of the sort in America, and, at the time I saw it, consisted of no less than twelve hundred Bibles, in every sort of edition and shape, published in all the languages and countries of the world, among them being the greatest typographical rarities. I was also enabled to inspect a splendid collection of copperplate engravings, equally belonging to a tradesman: it consisted of many thousand plates, belonging to all schools, countries, and epochs. The owner has recently presented it to Cambridge University, where it is now being arranged by a German *connoisseur*.

"One evening I was invited to the house of a Boston tradesman, where I found, to my surprise, another variety of artistic collections. It was a partly historical, partly ethnographical museum, which the owner has arranged in a suite of most elegant rooms, and which he allowed us to inspect after tea. His speciality lay in weapons and coats of mail, and the walls were covered with magnificent specimens bought up in all parts of Europe, regardless of cost. He possesses all the weapons employed before the invention of gunpowder; while in an adjoining room were all the blood-letting tools of Japan. In another was a similar collection from China, and several other countries. Never in my life have I seen so many different forms of knives, hatchets, battle axes, and lances collected together as at this house.

"At the same time, the company assembled on that evening was of great interest. Among others, we were honored by the presence of Fanny Kemble, who, as is well known, belongs to the United States since her marriage with an American. The fact that this most intellectual of *artistes* has selected Boston as her abode, will also bear good testimony to the character of the city. During my stay in Boston she was giving readings from Shakspeare, and I heard her in the 'Merchant of Venice.' The readings took place in a magnificent hall capable of containing two thousand persons, and it was quite full. I have frequently heard Tieck, Devrient, and many others of our best dramatic readers; but I am bound to say that Fanny Kemble is the best of all I ever heard. She is graceful in her movements, and possesses a well-formed chest, and an energetic, almost masculine organ. On the evening I heard her she was hoarse, in consequence of a cold, and, by her own statement, weak and languid; but, for all that, managed so admirably that nothing of the sort was perceptible. She developed all the male and female parts in the play—especially the Jew's—so characteristically and clearly, that I could not help fancying I had the whole thing before me, brilliantly designed on Gobelin tapestry. She accompanied her reading with lively gesticulations, but did not lay more stress on them than is usual in an ordinary reading. The Boston public were silent and delighted; and it is on account of this public that I insert my remarks about Fanny Kemble. I was charmed with the praise which this excellent English lady bestowed on our German actors during a conversation I had with her. She told me that she preferred to see Shakspeare acted on a German stage, especially by Devrient. And this, she added, was the opinion of her father, Charles Kemble. The circumstance that his wife was a native of Vienna may have contributed, however, to make Charles Kemble better acquainted with the character of the German stage.

"Of course it was not in my power to inspect all the collections of Boston, and I need scarcely add that I found magnificent libraries in the houses of a Prescott, a Ticknor, an Everett, &c. In Boston, a good deal of the good old English maxim has been kept up, that every one buys a book he requires. A great quantity of rare and handsome books wander from all parts of Europe annually to these libraries. In the same way as the Emperor Nicholas had his military agents in every state, the Americans have their literary agents, who eagerly buy up our books. In London I was acquainted with a gentleman permanently residing there, who was a formidable rival to the British Museum, and found his chief customers among the Boston amateurs, though he had others in New York and elsewhere.

"When they desire to satisfy any special craving, the Americans are not a whit behind the English in not shunning expense or outlay. Thus I was introduced, at Philadelphia, to a book collector, whose speciality was Shakspeare. He had specimens of every valuable edition of the poet's works. Only one of the oldest and rarest editions, of which but three copies exist, was missing from his shelves; and when he heard that one of these would shortly be put up for sale in London, he sent a special agent over with secret instructions and *carte blanche*. He succeeded, though I am afraid to say at what an outlay of dollars, and the expensive book was shipped across the water. When it arrived at Philadelphia, the overjoyed owner invited all the friends of Shakspeare in the city, and gave them a brilliant party, at which the jewel—an old, rusty folio—was displayed under a brilliant light upon a gold-embroidered velvet cushion. Interminable toasts and speeches were given, and finally the volume was incorporated in the library, where it occupied but a very small space.

"In other American cities I saw various remarkable collections of rarities—as, for instance, Mr. Lenox's, at New York, who has a mania for bringing together all the books, documents, and pamphlets referring to the history of America. Mr. Peter Force, of Washington, has a similar one; but I will not stop to describe it, but return to Boston, which is to some extent the metropolis of such collections.

"Alexander von Humboldt's library has been made known to the world in a copperplate, but I must confess that I could draw a much more attractive picture of some of the studies of the Boston savans. In their arrangement, in the picturesque setting out of the books and curiosities, in the writing tables, and chairs, as ingenious as they are comfortable, in the wealth of pictures and busts found in these rooms, generally lighted from above, you find a combination of the English desire for comfort and the American yearning after external splendor. The Americans are the only people in the world who possess not merely merchant princes, but also author princes.

"I visited several of these distinguished men in their spacious and elegant studies. One morning I was taken to the house of the celebrated Edward Everett, one of the great men of Boston, who, first as preacher, then as professor of Greek, and lastly as author and speaker, has attained so prominent a position in the Union, and is still an active and busied man in spite of sixty odd years having passed over his head. Any remarkable book a man may have written, or any sort of notoriety that brings him before the public, can be employed in America as political capital, and lead to position and influence in the state. The preacher and professor, Everett, who for a season edited the *North American Review*, and very cleverly praised and defended in its pages the manners and Constitution of his country, soon after became, in consequence of his writings, member of Congress, a leader of the old Whig party, Governor of Massachusetts, and lastly a diplomatist and American ambassador to England. Like many American politicians who have held the latter office, he was frequently proposed as candidate for the Presidency, but did not reach the chair, because the old Whigs had lost much of their former influence. On the final dissolution of his party, Everett devoted himself to the sciences and *belles lettres*. At the time when I formed his acquaintance, he was engaged in delivering a public lecture in all the cities of the Union on the character of Washington. The great man's qualities naturally had a brilliant light thrown on them, and, in comparison with our renowned monarchs, such as Frederick the Great, Joseph II., and Napoleon I., the latter came off second best. Everett had learned his lecture by heart, and delivered it with great emphasis and considerable success, though I confess that when I heard it I could not conscientiously bestow such praise on it as did the patriotic Americans. In order that the lecture might not lose the charm of novelty, all the American papers were requested to give no short-hand report of it: hence it remained unknown in each city until the lecturer had publicly delivered it. Everett saved up his earnings for a patriotic object—namely, the purchase of Washington's estate of Mount Vernon, for which purpose a ladies' committee had been formed. In 1857, Everett had collected more than forty thousand dollars toward this object. There is hardly another country besides America in which such a sum could be collected by reading a lecture of a few pages, however effective it might be. Moreover, the whole affair is characteristic of the land and that is why I have related it.

"Boston has ever been not only the birthplace, but the gathering ground of celebrated men. In politics it frequently rivalled Virginia, while in the production of poets and literary men it stands far above all other cities of the Union. Starting from Benjamin Franklin, who was born on one of the small islands in Boston harbor, down to Everett and his contemporaries, there has never been a deficiency of great and remarkable men in the city. Hancock, who drew up with Jefferson the Constitution of the United States, lived in Boston; and the most distinguished of the few Presidents the North has produced—the two Adamses—belonged to Boston, where they began and closed their career. Daniel Webster, the greatest American orator of recent times, received his education in Boston, and spent all that portion of his life there when he was not engaged at Washington. There are, in fact, entire families in Boston—as, for instance, the Winthrops, Bigelows, &c.—which have been rich in talented persons ever since the foundation of the city.

"When I visited Boston in 1857, the circle of celebrated, influential, and respected men was not small, and I had opportunity to form the acquaintance of several of them. Unfortunately, I knocked to no purpose at the door of the liberal and gifted Theodore Parker, whose house is ever open to Germans. The noble, equally liberal, and high-hearted Channing, whose pious, philanthropic, and philosophic writings I had admired from my earliest youth, and who had labored here as the apostle of the Unitarians, I only found represented by a son, who does honor to his great father's memory. The Websters and Adamses had also been dead for some years, though I formed the acquaintance of several of their personal friends, who told me numerous anecdotes about them.

"I am sorry to say, too, I missed seeing George Ticknor, the great historian of Spanish literature, a true child of Boston, where he was born and educated, and where he spends his time in study when he is not travelling in Europe, which was unfortunately the case at the period of my visit. I saw nothing of him but his splendid Spanish library, which he exclusively collected for the purpose of his classical work, which has been translated into almost every language.

"As a compensation, Prescott, who was summoned away some time ago, to the regret of all his friends, was at home to receive me, and he was one of the most amiable men I ever met. I saw him both at his own house and in society, and greedily took advantage of every opportunity that offered for approaching him. As he was descended from an old New England family, and was educated, and lived, and worked almost entirely in Boston—he had only visited Europe once, and had travelled but little in the United States—I could consider him as a true child of Boston, and as an example of the best style of education that city is enabled to offer. He was a man of extremely dignified and agreeable manners, and a thorough gentleman in his behavior. I met but few Americans so distinguished by elegance and politeness; and when I first met him, and before knowing his name, I took him for a diplomatist. He had not the slightest trace of the dust of books and learning, and, although he had been hard at work all day, when he emerged into daylight he was a perfect man of the world. I found in him a great resemblance, both in manner and features, with that amiable Frenchman Mignet. He was at that time long past his sixtieth birthday, and yet his delicate, nobly-chiselled face possessed such a youthful charm that he could fascinate young ladies. In society his much-regretted weakness of sight was hardly perceptible; and at dinner he made such good use of his limited vision, that he could help himself without attracting the slightest attention. He frequently remarked that this weakness of sight, which others lamented so greatly, was the chief cause of his devoting himself to historical studies. Still it impeded his studies greatly; for he was obliged to send persons, at a terrible expense, to copy the documents he required in the archives of Spain. He could only employ these documents and other references—partially, at any rate—through readers. He was obliged to prepare much in his mind and then dictate it, without the help of his hand and fingers, which, as every author knows, offer such aid to the head, and, as it were, assist in thinking. At times he could only write by the help of a machine that guided his hand. I say purposely 'at times,' for every now and then the sight of his own eyes became so excellent and strong, that he could undertake personally the mechanical part of his labor. Still, literature is indebted to Prescott's semi-blindness for his elaborate historical works on Peru, Mexico, Isabella, and Philip II.; for, had he kept the sight of both eyes, he would have continued the career he had already begun as barrister, and in all probability have ended as a politician and a statesman.

"Another somewhat younger literary talent Boston was proud of at that period, was Motley, the historian, who in many respects may be placed side by side with Prescott. Like him, he also belongs to a wealthy and respected Boston family; and like him, too, he has devoted himself to history, through pure love. His union with the Muse is no *marriage de convenance*, but he entered into it through a hearty affection. The subject that Motley selected, ' The History of the Netherlands in the Sixteenth and Seventeenth Centuries,' had a special interest for his countrymen. At that period Holland was remarkably influential all over the New World, and, *inter alia*, laid the foundations of New York State. This State and its still somewhat Dutch inhabitants consequently regard the Netherlands to some extent as the mother country, and their history as a portion of their own. They feel as much interested in it as the French do in the history of the Franks in Germany. Moreover, they like to compare an event like the insurrection of the Netherlands against Spain with their own revolt against England. Motley, therefore, selected a very popular theme. After learning something of the world as *attaché* to the American embassy at Petersburg, he travelled in Germany, and stayed for several years at Dresden, the Hague, and other European cities, in order to employ the libraries for his purpose. Nine years ago, he read to a small circle of friends in Dresden, myself among the number, extracts from his historical work—for instance, his description of the execution of Counts Egmont and Horn—and then returned to America, where he published it. This work was a great success; and when I met Motley again at Boston, he had just been crowned with laurel. He was a handsome man, in the prime of life, with dark curly hair. Unluckily, he did not like his country sufficiently well to remain in it, and returned quickly to Europe, during my visit to Boston. Perhaps he had lived too long upon our continent, and had not the patience to go through the process of re-Americanizing, to which an American who has long been absent is bound to subject himself. He proceeded to London, where he resided several years, continuing his studies, and always a welcome guest in fashionable society, until the recent troubles forced him to return home.

"We might fairly speak of a thorough historical school of Boston, for nearly all the recent remarkable historians of America have issued from this school. Among these I may specially mention George Bancroft, who has selected the history of his native land as his special study. His career has a great likeness to that of Everett: like him, he went to Gottingen when a young man, and acquired his tendency for historic research from Heeren, Eichhorn, and Schlosser. Like Everett, he began his career as a professor at Cambridge University, and like him, also, his talent and the growing popularity of his books led him up to important offices and posts under Government. He was for a time secretary to the navy at Washington, then American ambassador in England, and at last, as he was not successful in politics, like Everett, he retired from public life into the calmer atmosphere of his study, where he has remained for several years, dividing his time between literary work and pleasant society. During the winter he now resides at New York, and during the summer at a charming villa near that pretty little watering place, Newport, on Narraganset Bay, whence he pays a visit now and then, though, to his old Boston. I had the good fortune to visit this active and energetic historian at both his winter and summer abode. At New York, he passes the whole winter shut up in his splendid library, like a bee in his honey cell. In the midst of the turmoil of business, his lamp may be seen glimmering at an early hour; and he lights it himself, as he does his fire, in order not to spoil the temper of his lazy American helps for the day.

"I am forced to remark that the result of my observations is, that this zeal and this 'help yourself' are no rarity among American men of letters. Thus I always remember with pleasure old Senator Benton, whose 'History of the American Congress,' although an excellently written work, and a thorough mine in which to study the politics, parties, and prominent men of America, is, unfortunately, but little known on this side the water. This brave old Roman Benton, of Missouri, a man otherwise greatly attacked for his vanity and eccentricities, I remember seeing, one morning at six, lighting his fire, boiling his coffee, and then devoting the morning hours to his History.

"This Benton was, at that period, above seventy years of age, and long a grandfather. He wrote his 'History' with so firm and current a hand, that the copy went almost uncorrected from his table to the printing office, and within a few months entire volumes could be worked off. And yet he could only devote his morning and late evening hours to the task; for, so long as the sun was up, he thought it his duty to take part in the debates of Congress and quarrel in the committee rooms. At times, he broke his labors entirely off, because he considered it necessary to take a trip to Missouri, and agitate for some political purpose or other. One evening, it happened that his entire library, with all the manuscripts it contained, fell a prey to the flames. He had temporarily taken up his quarters in a small wooden house in the vicinity of the Capitol, which caught fire.

"These fires are an almost regular and constantly menacing calamity to American authors, their libraries, and manuscripts. During my short stay in the United States, I heard of a whole series of cases in which valuable literary undertakings were completely interrupted by fire. Senator Benton, on the occasion to which I refer, lost his entire library, a large portion of manuscript ready for the press, and a heap of materials, extracts, and references, which he had collected for a new volume of his 'History.' As I was on rather intimate terms with him and his family, and, as an author myself, felt a special compassion for him, I visited him a few days after to offer him my sympathy. As it happened, President Pierce came up at the same moment, and for the same object. We found the aged man, to our surprise and admiration, not in the slightest degree affected or excited. He had removed from the ruins to the house of his son-in-law, the celebrated traveller Fremont, had had a new table put together, and was busy rewriting his manuscript. With Anglo-Saxon coolness and a pleasant face, which reminded me of the stoic referred to by Montaigne, who did not allow himself to be disturbed in his speech when a dog tore a piece out of the calf of his leg, he told us the story of the burning of his books. Mr. Benton allowed that a quarto volume of his work, with all the materials belonging to it, was entirely destroyed; but he said, with a smile, while tossing a little grandchild on his knee, 'It is no use crying over spilled milk.' He had begun his work afresh on the next day, and retained in his head most of what he had written down. He hoped that he should be able to collect once more the necessary materials—partly, at any rate—and he expected that the printing would not be delayed for many days.

"This man, in his present position—and there could not be a more lamentable one for an author—appeared to me like an old Roman. And, in truth, old Senator Benton had something thoroughly Roman in his features, just as you might expect to find on an ancient coin. And all this was the more remarkable to me, because I discovered such an internal value in a man who in the external world afforded such scope for jibes. In Congress I saw him twice play the part of a quarrelsome and impotent old man. At times—especially when he marched into the field to support the claims of his son-in-law Fremont, or any other distinguished members of his family of whom he was proud, and whom he thought he must take under his wing, like a patriarch of old—he grew so excited, that the President several times tried in vain to stop him. Once I saw him leave Congress cursing and gesticulating, and loudly declaring that he would never again appear in that assembly. When, too, he rode up and down the main street of Washington, with his grandson on a little pony by his side, and keeping as close as possible to the pavement, that he might be bowed to by the ladies and gentlemen, they certainly saluted, but afterward ridiculed the 'great man.' Hence it caused me special pleasure, I repeat, to recognize in so peculiar a man an inner worth, and find the opportunity to say something in his praise. After all, there were heroes among the wearers of full-bottomed wigs and pigtails.

"Since then, the inexorable subduer of all heroes has removed old Senator Benton forever from his terrestrial activity. He was enabled stoically to withstand the fire; but death, which caught him up four years ago, did not allow him to complete his work. Still, the fragments of it that lie before us contain extraordinarily useful matter for the history of the Union from the beginning of this century, and I therefore recommend them strongly to public writers at the present moment, when everybody wishes to know everything about America. But I will now return to Boston.

"In the hot summer, when Longfellow, Agassiz, and other distinguished men of Boston fly to the rock of Nahant, Bancroft, as I said, seeks shelter on the airy beach of Newport; and I remember, with great pleasure, the interesting trip I took thither for the purpose of spending a couple of days with the historian. The pleasant little town of Newport, which a hundred years back was a promising rival of New York, is now only known as the most fashionable watering place in the Union. Most of the upper ten, as well as the politicians and diplomatists of Washington, congregate here in July and August. Splendid steamers, some coming from New York through Long Island Sound, others from Boston through the archipelago of Narraganset Bay, bring up hundreds of people daily. On one of these green islands in the bay, Newport is built, surrounded by a number of villas and gardens, which stretch out along the beach. And one of these hospitable villas belongs to the celebrated historian, who in that character, and as ex-minister and statesman, is reverently regarded as one of the 'lions' of Newport.

"When I entered his house, at a late hour, I found him surrounded by the ladies of his family, to whom he was reading a newly finished chapter of his 'History' from the manuscript. He invited me to listen, and told me that it was his constant practice to read his works in this fashion in the domestic circle, and take the opinion of his hearers, but, above all, of his amiable and highly educated wife. This, he said to me, was the best way of discovering any lack of clearness or roughness of style, and after this trial he made his final corrections.

"Newport is also known, to those versed in American antiquities, as the spot where an old octagonal building still stands, which the Danish savans believe to have been erected long prior to Columbus, and which they consider was built by the old Norman seafarers and heroes who visited America about the year 1000. This monument was very interesting to me to visit in the company of the historian of the United States, even though the townspeople regard it as the foundation of an old windmill, that belonged to a former inhabitant of Newport. Bancroft was of opinion that the good people of Newport were more likely to hit the truth than the scientific men of Copenhagen. I, too, after an inspection, *in situ*, consider the opinion of the latter so little founded, that it is hardly worth contradicting. As is well known, to the south of New England, in the middle of a swamp on Taunton River, there is a huge rock covered with all sorts of grooves and marks, which the Danish savans regard as a Runic inscription, also emanating from the Normans. The Danes have even gone so far as to decipher the word 'Thorfiun,' as the name of one of the Norman heroes, while others believe that they are marks and memoranda made by an Indian hand; while others, again, are of opinion that the grooves and scratches are produced by natural causes.

"Bancroft described to me the difficulties he experienced in reaching this rock—at one moment wading through the water, at another forcing his way through scrub. He was, however, unable to convince himself of the truth of any one of the above three hypotheses; and hence, in his 'History of the United States,' he could only say that the much-discussed Taunton River inscription did not afford a certainty of the presence of the Normans in these parts. But I must hasten back to Boston, where I have many an excellent friend awaiting me.

"First of all rises before my mental eye the image of that noble senator, Charles Sumner, one of the most honored men of Boston, whom I visited not only here in his birthplace, where he spends his leisure hours with his mother and relatives, but also at Washington, where he was delivering his bold and fiery speeches against slavery. While at the capital, I heard him deliver that magnificent speech which, although it lasted for several hours, was listened to in speechless silence by the whole Senate, even by the Southern members who were boiling over with fury, and entailed on this noble man the brutal attack from one of the chivalry of the South, which laid him on a bed of sickness for weeks, where he hovered between life and death.

"How painful and sad it was to see this tall and stately man felled like a pine tree, and writhing in agony on his couch! His noble face, in which his lofty intellect and towering mind spoke out, was swollen and lacerated, as if he had been under the claws of a bear. English, Germans, French, Spaniards, and Italians were the first to hurry to him on the day of the outrage, to display their sympathy and respect, and lay a crown of honor on his bleeding temples. With this great man, after his return from Europe, and several kindred spirits, I used to spend pleasant evenings *en petit comité* in Boston, and felt delighted at the opportunity of discussing with them the great questions of the day. Not so pleasant, though equally remarkable, were my feelings when I returned home at night from such an intellectual and sympathizing circle, and was compelled to listen to the expectorations of a Colonel B——, of Carolina, who lodged in the same hotel. He made it a point to lie in ambush for me every night, to smoke a cigar, drink a glass of grog, and take the opportunity of explaining to me his views about the North. Although he had travelled in France and Germany, associated with the nobility, and belonged to the Southern aristocracy, the Colonel was so full of prejudices against the North, that he walked about among the New Englanders of Boston like a snarling sheep dog among a flock of lambs. He 'pished' and 'pshawed,' even abused loudly and bitterly all he saw, both the men—the accursed Yankees, their narrow-hearted views, their stiff regulations, their unpolished manners—as well as things, such as the Northern sky, the scenery, the towns, villages, and country houses. All that Boston or a Bostonian had or possessed seemed to him infected with abolitionism. He would even look on, with a sarcastic smile, when, during our conversation, I stroked a pretty little spaniel belonging to a Boston lady. He could not endure this Boston animal, and if ever it came within his reach he was sure to give it a harmless kick. Nothing was right with him, of course—least of all the Boston newspapers, in which he pointed out to me articles every evening, which, according to his opinion, were horrible, perfidious, atheistical, full of gall and poison, although I could not discover anything of the sort in them when he read them aloud to me with many gesticulations. To the people who surrounded us he generally behaved politely, because, as I said, he was a Southern gentleman, and did not let it be seen how his heart heaved and boiled. But if any one took up the cudgels with him, merely expressed an opinion that had the remotest connection with the slavery question, or smelled of abolitionism, he would break out into the most enthusiastic diatribes in defence of the peculiar institution. His glances would become passionate, and his tone insulting. He appeared evidently bent on war, and I was often surprised that the Yankees put up with so much from him, and let him escape with a whole skin. In the South, had a Northerner gone to one tenth of the same excess, it would have been enough to hand him over to the tender mercies of Judge Lynch.

"If I asked him why he had come to this North, which he so heartily despised, he would reply that, unhappily, his physicians had found it necessary to send him into this exile for the sake of his health; and he had long had an intention of visiting, on the Northern lakes, the poor Indians who were so shamefully maltreated by the Yankees. The sufferings of these unhappy tribes, who perished beneath the heel of the oppressor, and pined away in their shameful fetters, had long touched his heart. He could never think of them without emotion, and he now intended to go as far as the cataracts of St. Anthony to give the Sioux a feast, and offer them some relief from their shameful martyrdom. I remembered that I had once before noticed the same compassion for the Indians in a Southern slaveowner, and consequently that it is, in all probability, traditional among these people, to answer the reproaches cast on them for slaveholding, by accusing their hostile brethren of ill-treating the Indians. Although I in no way shared my Southern friend's views of slavery and abolition, but was generally in the opposition, as a foreigner I did not seem to him so utterly repulsive as these God-forgotten Yankees. At first, at any rate, he believed that he should not be washing a blackamoor white with me. If I only would visit the South, he expressed his opinion I should be speedily converted, and grow enthusiastic for his side. Hence he condescended to argue with and instruct me, while he gnashed his teeth at his Northern countrymen when they dared to address him on the vexed question. Toward the end, however, I began to perceive that he was giving me up as incorrigible, and extended his enmity to me as well. We at length parted, not exactly as sympathetic souls; and when I now think of my Southerner stalking about Boston like a tornado in a human shape, I do not understand how it was that I did not then see civil war *ante fores* in that country.

"It may be imagined what a relief, joy, and comfort it was for me, after the stormy evenings I spent with the Southerner, to be invited the following day to a dinner table, where I found all the men with whom I sympathized, and whom I respected, assembled. The old Flemish painters, in their fruit and flower pieces, and in what is called 'still life,' have striven to represent the roast meats, wine-flasks, crystal glasses, grapes, and oranges which decorated the tables of their rich contemporaries. But how can I depict such a dinner at Boston, where a Longfellow took the chair, an Agassiz acted as *croupier*, a Prescott was my left, a Motley my right hand neighbor, and where my *vis-à-vis* was a tall, thin, dry-looking man, who, I was told, was Ralph Waldo Emerson? Between the epergnes and flower vases I could see also the characteristic features of noble and distinguished men; the gray head of a Winthrop, or the animated face of such a benefactor to humanity as Dr. Howe, whom the blind and the deaf and dumb combine to bless. When I reflect how rare such highly gifted men are in the world, and how much more rare it is to be enabled to see a dozen of them sitting together cheerfully and socially over their wine, I find that we cannot sufficiently value such moments which accidents produce, and which, perhaps, never again occur in the traveller's life. When we read such books as those of Mrs. Trollope, Captain Basil Hall, or Dickens, we might suppose that there is nothing in America that can be called 'good society.' But when a man finds himself in such company as fell to my lot in Boston, he begins to think differently, and is at length disposed to allow that in America a good tone peculiar to the country, and possessing highly characteristic qualities, exists. I concede that it is rare, and I believe that the American, in order to appropriate this tone, must have passed the ocean several times between America and Europe; in this, imitating his twice-across-the-line Madeira (which, by the by, is magnificent in some Boston houses). The American, as a rule, becomes really full flavored in and through Europe. What I would assert, though, is, that the American has a peculiar material to take the polish which Europe can impart, and that, when he has rubbed off his American horns—for it is quite certain that the American is as much of a greenhorn in Europe as the European seems to be in the United States—a species of polish is visible, which possesses its peculiar merit, and nothing like it is to be found in Europe. There is no trace of mannerism or affectation; none of that insipid politeness, prudery, and superfinedom into which Europeans are so apt to fall. In the well-educated American we meet with a great simplicity of manner, and a most refreshing masculine dignity. Both in Boston and New York I visited private clubs, and met gentlemen belonging to the bar, the church, the mercantile classes, &c., who possessed all these qualities in an eminent degree. In these small retired clubs —they may have been select, and I am unable to decide how many of the sort may exist—humor and merriment were so well controlled, wit and jesting were so pleasantly commingled with what was serious and instructive, that I never knew pleasanter places for men."

In our inadequate because inevitably brief summary of German writers on America, should not be forgotten the learned widow of the lamented Professor Edward Robinson, who, among other notable writings published under the name of "Talvi," gave to her countrymen (Leipsic, 1847) "The Colonization of New England"—an able historical digest of the early history of that region and people, subsequently translated by a son of William Hazlitt, and published in London (1851) in two handsome duodecimo volumes. In this work the details of each original State organization are given, and much incidental light thrown on the character of the people and the tendencies and traits of local society at this primitive era. Relying upon the Diary of Bradford, first Governor of Plymouth, the New England Memorial, Governor Dudley's Report, Johnson's, and "America Painted to the Life, a True History" (London, 1658), the Relations of Higginson, Wood, Lechford, Joscelyn, the Reports of Munson, Underhill, Gardiner, &c., with the writings of "founders" such as Clark, Gorges, Roger Williams, &c., and for later facts referring to Hubbard, Mather, Church, Miles, Neale, and others, Mrs. Robinson eliminated from these and other authentic sources the essential facts, and moulded them into a most significant and lucid narrative—the more so from being the work of a mind trained in the older civilization of Europe. "I look upon the early days of New England," she naïvely remarks, "with love certainly—but as a German." Comparatively impartial as she is, even in this primitive record we find indications of the prejudice which subsequent events fostered into a habit, and almost a mania, in "the mother country." "In the Revolutionary period," she writes, "S. A. Peters, a degenerate son of Connecticut, published a 'General History' of that State (London, 1781)—a mesh of lies, and deformed with enormous slander. Nothing could be more characteristic of the feeling at that time prevalent in England toward America, than the fact that this contemptible and slanderous work survived, the following year, in a second edition."

We cannot, perhaps, more appropriately close this cursory notice of German writers on America, than by referring to two lectures by Dr. Philip Schaff, whose fame as a Church historian, and labors as a theological professor at Mercersburg, Pennsylvania, give special interest and authority to his views. When Dr. Schaff revisited his native country, in 1854, he gave, at Berlin, two discourses, part of a series by eminent scholars. Carl Ritter, and other illustrious friends, advised their publication; and this is the origin of his unpretending but comprehensive "Sketch of the Political, Social, and Religious Character of the United States of North America." It was translated from the German, and published in New York in 1855. The latter branch of the subject naturally occupies the largest space; and it is in relation to German emigration and the Evangelical Church that he chiefly discusses the condition and prospects of his adopted country. In view of the fact that, the very year of his visit to his fatherland, the emigration of his countrymen to the port of New York alone, amounted to more than one hundred and seventy-nine thousand, he descants upon the privileges, needs, dangers, and destinies involved in this vast experiment, with the knowledge of a good observer and the conscience of a Christian scholar. He laments the evil attending so large a proportion of ignorant and irreligious *emigrés*, and the low condition of the German press in America; but, on the other hand, anticipates the happiest results from the coalition of the American and Teutonic mind. "With the one," he observes, "everything runs into theory, and, indeed, so radically, that they are oftentimes in danger of losing all they aim at; with the other, everything runs into practice, and it is quite possible that many of the best and worst German ideas will yet attain, in practical America, a much greater importance than in the land of their birth, and first become flesh and blood on the other side of the ocean, like certain plants, which need transplanting to a foreign soil in order to bear fruit and flowers." He describes with candor the prominent traits of our country and people. The latter, he says, "are restlessness and agitation personified: even when seated, they push themselves to and fro in their rocking chairs, and live in a state of perpetual excitement in their business, their politics, and their religion. They are excellently characterized by the expressions 'help yourself' and 'go ahead,' which are never out of their mouths." "The grandest destiny is evidently reserved for such a people. We can and must, it is true, find fault with many things in them and their institutions—slavery, the lust of conquest, the worship of mammon, the rage for speculation, political and religious fanaticism and party spirit, boundless temerity, boasting, and quackery; but we must not overlook the healthy vital energies that continually react against these diseases—the moral, yea, Puritanical earnestness of the American character, its patriotism and noble love of liberty in connection with deep-rooted reverence for the law of God and authority, its clear, practical understanding, its inclination for improvement in every sphere, its fresh enthusiasm for great plans and schemes of moral reform, and its willingness to make sacrifices for the promotion of God's kingdom and every good work. They wrestle with the most colossal projects. The deepest meaning and aim of their political institutions are to actualize the idea of universal sovereignty, the education of every individual. They wish to make culture, which in Europe is everywhere aristocratic and confined to a comparatively small portion of society, the common property of the people, and train up, if possible, every youth as a gentleman, and every girl as a lady; and in the six States of New England, at least, they have attained this object in a higher degree than any country in the Old World, England and Scotland, not excepted. There are respectable men, professedly of the highest culture, especially in despotic Austria, who have a real antipathy to America, speak of it with the greatest contempt or indignation, and see in it nothing but a grand bedlam, a rendezvous of European scamps and vagabonds. Such notions it is unnecessary to refute. Materialism, the race for earthly gain, and pleasure, find unquestionably rare encouragement in the inexhaustible physical resources of the country; but it has a strong and wholesome counterpoise in the zeal for liberal education, the enthusiastic spirit of philanthropy, the munificent liberality of the people, and, above all, in Christianity. Radicalism finds in republican America free play for its wild, wanton revellings, and its reckless efforts to uproot all that is established. But there is unquestionably in the Anglo-Saxon race a strong conservatism and deeply-rooted reverence for the Divine law and order; and, even in the midst of the storms of political agitation, it listens ever and anon to the voice of reason and sober reflection. Despotism and abuse of the power of government make revolution; while moderate constitutional liberalism forms the safest barrier against it: radicalism, therefore, can never have such a meaning and do so much harm in England and America, as in countries where it is wantonly provoked to revolutionary reaction."

Dr. Schaff sketches the size, growth, polity, social life, and religious tendencies and traits of America, in a few authentic statements, and expresses the highest hope and faith in the true progress and prosperity of the nation. "To those," he remarks, "who see in America only the land of unbridled radicalism and of the wildest fanaticism for freedom, I take the liberty to put the modest question: In what European state would the Government have the courage to enact such a prohibition of the traffic in all intoxicating drinks, and the people to submit to it, as the Maine liquor law? I am sure that in Bavaria the prohibition of beer would produce a bloody revolution."

Education in America, and the state of literature and science, are ably discussed and delineated. The press there is fairly estimated; and the Church, as an organization and a social element, analyzed with remarkable correctness as to facts and liberality as to feeling. The influence of German literature in America is duly estimated, and the character and tendencies of foreign immigration and native traits justly considered. Without being in the least blind to our national faults, Dr. Schaff has a comprehensive insight as to our national destiny, and a Christian scholar's appreciation of our national duties. "The general tendency in America," he observes, "is to the widest possible diffusion of education; but depth and thoroughness by no means go hand in hand with extension. A peculiar phenomenon is the great number of female teachers. Among these are particularly distinguished the 'Yankee girls,' who know how to make their way successfully everywhere as teachers—as in Europe the governesses from French Switzerland. Domestic life in the United States may be described as, on an average, well regulated and happy. The number of illegitimate births is perhaps proportionally less than in any other country. The American family is not characterized by so much deep good nature, and warm, overflowing heartiness, as the German; but the element of mutual respect predominates."

No foreign writer has more clearly perceived or emphatically stated the moral and economical relation of America to Europe than Professor Schaff. His long residence in this country, and his educational and religious labors therein, gave him ample opportunity to know the facts as regards emigration, popular literature, social life, and enterprise; while his European birth and associations made him equally familiar with the wants of the laboring, the theories of the thinking, and the exigencies of the political classes. "America," he writes, "begins with the results of Europe's two thousand years' course of civilization, and has vigor, enterprise, and ambition enough to put out this enormous capital at the most profitable interest for the general good of mankind. America is the grave of all European nationalities; but it is a Phœnix grave, from which they shall rise to new life. Either humanity has no earthly future, and everything is tending to destruction, or this future lies, I say not exclusively, but mainly in America, according to the victorious march of history, with the sun, from east to west." *

* "America, Political, Social, and Religious," by Dr. Philip Schaff, New York, C. Scribner, 1855.

CHAPTER IX.

ITALIAN TRAVELLERS.

NATIONAL RELATIONS: VERRAZZANO; CASTIGLIONE; ADRIANI; GRASSI; BELTRAMI; D'ALLESSANDRO; CAPOBIANCO; SALVATORE ABBATE E MIGLIORI; PISANI.

FROM the antiquated French of the missionary Travels, and the inelegant English of the uneducated and flippant writers in our vernacular, it is a vivid and pleasant change to read the same prolific theme discussed in the "soft bastard Latin" that Byron loved. Although no Italian author has discoursed of our country in a manner to add a standard work on the subject to his native literature, America is associated with the historical memorials of that nation, inasmuch as Columbus discovered the continent to which Vespucci gave a name, and Carlo Botta wrote the earliest European history * of our Revolution; while the great tragic poet of Italy dedicated his "Bruto Primo," in terms of eloquent appreciation, to Washington; and the leading journal of Turin to-day has a regular and assiduous correspondent in New York, who thus made clear to his countrymen the cause, *animus*, and history of the war for the Union, and whose able articles on the educational system and political condition

* Botta's "History of the War of the Independence of the United States of America," translated by Otis, 2 vols. 8vo. in 1.

of the United States, which have appeared in the *Rivista Contemporenea*—the ablest literary periodical in Italy—are a promising foretaste of the complete and well-considered work on our country that he is preparing for his own : a task for which long residence and faithful study, as well as liberal sympathies and culture, eminently fit him.* At the banquet given in New York to the officers of the Italian frigate Re Galantuomo, on the occasion of her visit to bring the equipment for the Re d'Italia, a magnificent ship of war built in this country for the navy of Italy, the same writer, in response to a sentiment in honor of the king, aptly observed : " Con qual animo non pronuzieremo il nome de Vittorio Emmanuele, in questo solenne occasione, quando per la prima volta nella storia d'Italia i rappresentati della marina nazionale, toccano a questi lidi e mettono piede su questo continente che da quasi quattro secoli un marinaio italiano scopriva e dava alla civiltà del mondo ! " †

Within a recent period, the despotism of Austria, and the reactionary and cruel vigilance of the local rulers in the peninsula, which succeeded the fall of Napoleon and the conspiracies and *emeutes* thence resulting among the Italian people, brought many interesting exiles of that nation to our shores. The establishment of the Italian opera created a new interest in the language of Italy—which, with her literature, were auspiciously initiated in New York by Lorenzo Daponte forty years ago ; and the popular fictions of Manzoni, Rufini, Mariotti, d'Azeglio, and Guerazzi, have made the story of their country's wrongs and aspirations familiar to our people; while such political victims as Maroncelli, Garibaldi, and Foresti challenged the respect and won the love of those among whom they found a secure and congenial asylum ; and thus,

---

* Professor Vincenzo Botta.

† " With what emotions shall we not pronounce the name of Victor Emmanuel, on this occasion, when, for the first time in the history of Italy, the representatives of her national navy touch the shores and tread the continent which, nearly four centuries ago, an Italian mariner discovered and gave to the civilized world ! "

although the least numerous class of *emigrés*,* the Italian visitors became among the most prominent from their merits and misfortunes. To the vagabond image venders and organ grinders, musicians and confectioners, were thus added eminent scholars and patriots, and endeared members of society. Nowhere in the civilized world was the national development of Italy more fondly watched than here. The lecture room, the popular assembly, and the press in the United States, responded to and celebrated the reforms in Sardinia, the union of that state with Lombardy, Tuscany, and Naples, the liberal polity of Victor Emmanuel, and the heroic statesmanship of Cavour. Garibaldi has received substantial tokens of American sympathy; and current literature, love of art, and facilities of travel, have made the land of Columbus and the Republic of the West intimately and mutually known and loved. The café, the studio, the lyric drama, letters, art, and society in our cities attest this;† and should steam communication be established, as proposed, between Genoa and

---

* Between 1820 and 1860, about 13,000 Italian emigrants reached this country. At present, in New York, the Italian population is estimated at 2,000—most of them peasants and peddlers, who earn a precarious subsistence as organ players, venders of plaster casts, &c. Colonies of them live in limited quarters in the most squalid part of the city—monkeys, organs, images, and families grotesquely huddled in the same apartment. An evening school for these *emigrés* has been in successful operation for some years, and with good results.

† Scanty as is the record of Italian travel in the United States, the emigration of that people being chiefly directed to South American cities, where, as at Montevideo, they have large communities, the Spanish is still more meagre, and contrasts in this respect with the prominence of that race in the chronicle of maritime enterprise and exploration centuries since. Among the few books of Spanish travel of recent origin, are the following: 1. "Viage a los Estados-Unidos del Norte de America," por Don Lorenzo de Zavala, Paris, 1834, 1 vol. 8vo., pp. 374. The author was, at one time, Minister from Mexico to France. His book is a slight affair.—2. "Cinco Meses en los Estados-Unidos de la America del Norte desde el 20 de Abril el 23 Setiembre, 1835, Diario de Viage de D. Ramon de la Sagra, Director del Jardin Botanico de la Habana, eč.," Paris, 1836, 1 vol. 8vo., pp. 437. Le Sagra has published an important book about Cuba, been concerned in Spanish politics, and is well considered as a man of science; but his book, says an able critic, is not much better than Zavala's.

New York, the emigration will improve. When the war for the Union commenced, many Italian citizens volunteered, and some have acquired honor in the field; while not a few can find in the following anecdote, which recently appeared in a popular daily journal, a parallel to their own recent experience:

"Ten or twelve years ago an Italian emigrated from Northern Italy, and, after various wanderings, pitched his tent at Jackson, Mississippi. He prospered in business, increased and multiplied. He also managed to build two comfortable little houses, and altogether was getting on quite well in the world. At the time the war broke out he was North on business; and finding, from his well-known Union sentiments, that it would be dangerous to return, he took what money he had with him, and, accompanied by his wife, sailed for Europe, while his sons entered the Union army.

"In the beautiful Val d'Ossola, not far from the town of Domo d'Ossola, on the great thoroughfare where the Simplon road, issuing from the Alps, and but just escaped from the rocky frowns of the gorge of Gondo, passes amid fringes of olive groves to the great white 'Arch of Peace' and the brilliant city of Milan, is located one of those unpretending inns or locandas which abound in Italy— a low, rambling house, half hid in trellised vines, and prefaced as to doorway by several rude stone tables, at which transient guests may sit and sip the country wine.

"A few months ago, two American pedestrians stopped at this place and ordered wine, and, while sipping it, were accosted in tolerable English by the landlord, who wanted to know their views about the war, and particularly when the State of Mississippi would be regained for the Union. The question, coming from such a source, led to a conversation, during which it was revealed that the worthy innkeeper was none other than the Italian emigrant and the houseowner in the town of Jackson.

"At that time there was no early prospect of the taking of the capital of Mississippi; but, now that General Sherman is in that very vicinity, if not in the city itself, there will probably be good news for the innkeeper of the Simplon road. And this is but one instance out of many, in which each of even the minor phases of the war strikes directly at some personal interest or some chord of affection in individuals in the most remote corners of the continent of Europe."

A curious waif that gives us tokens of early exploration, is what remains of the journal of the old Italian navigator

15

Verrazzano—a relic still preserved among the treasures of the public library at Florence. In a summer sail down the bay of New York, or an excursion in and around the harbor of Newport, R. I., we easily recognize the local features thus noted by Verrazzano; but to which scene they apply, seems to have been doubtful to nearly all the commentators upon this ancient mariner; although to us the former place seems obviously intended. "The mouth of the haven," he writes, "lieth open to the south, half a league broad, and being entered within it, it stretcheth twelve leagues, and waxeth broader and broader, and maketh a gulf about twenty leagues in compass, wherein are five small islands very fruitful and pleasant, and full of hie and broad trees, among the which islands any great navie may ride itself." So New York Bay struck the eyes of Verrazzano in 1524, and so he described it in a letter to the king of France, wherein he also speaks of the "great store of slate for houses," the abundant wild grapevines, the mullets in the waters, and the "okes, cipresses, and chestnuts" of the islands.

There is something that excites the imagination into a more objective view of familiar things, when they are described and commented on in a foreign tongue; and certain peculiarities of American life and scenery thus derive a fresh aspect from the vivacious pictures and observation of French writers. We seem to catch glimpses of our country from their point of view, and to realize the salient diversities of race and customs, as we never do when discussed in our vernacular. A similar though equally characteristic effect is produced by reading even hackneyed accounts of men and things in America when couched in Italian. Accordingly, though we find little original information in the "Viaggio negli Stati Uniti dell' America Settentrionale, fatto negli anni 1785, '6, e '7, da Luigi Castiglione," to one who has visited Italy there is a charm in the record of a "Patrizio Milanese." His book was printed in Milan, 1790. He paid especial attention to those vegetable products of the New World which are valuable as commodities and useful in domestic economy.

He observed with the eye of a naturalist. Climate, sects, food, edifices, and local history occupied his mind; and when we remember the almost incredible ignorance prevalent even among educated Italians, within a few years, in regard to the United States, we cannot but think that Castiglione's copious and generally accurate narrative must have been valuable and interesting to such of his countrymen as desired information, seventy years ago, about America. To a reader here and now, however, the work has but a limited significance, the writer's experience being so identical with that of many better-known authors. It is curious, however, in this, as in other instances, to note the national tendency in the line of observation adopted. Castiglione says more about architecture than manners, meagre as that branch of the fine arts was in our land at the time of his visit. He is much struck with Long Wharf on arriving at Boston: " Il Gran Molo per cui si discenda a terra, è uno da piu magnifici degli Stati Uniti; e si dice avere un mezzo miglia di lunghezza." He specifies "l' isola di Noddle" in describing the harbor. The shingles which then covered most of the roofs proved a novelty to him; and a salt-fish dinner, with shellbarks and cider, he found so indigestible, that it made quite an impression both upon his stomach and brain. Alive to the charm of great memories, as lending dignity to cities, he recalls with delight the fact that Franklin, Hancock, Adams, and other patriots, were born in Boston; the republican equality of which community is to him a memorable fact, as is the sight of the statue of Pitt in New York, and the simultaneous advertisement of a negro and a horse to be sold at auction there. As the Signore frequently travelled on horseback, he was exposed to the caprices of our temperature, and vividly realized the extremes of the climate. He alludes to his visit at Mount Vernon in the same terms with which all intelligent foreigners dwell upon the privilege of a personal acquaintance with the spotless patriot, whose recent career was then the moral marvel of the age. There is so much in this contemporary testimony that agrees with and anticipates the verdict of history, that we never can read the spontaneous expression thereof, from so many and such various sources, without a fresh emotion of love and honor, inspired not less by the blessing such a character and career have proved to humanity, than by our own national preëminence. Never was there such identity of sentiment in so many different languges, in regard to the same human being. "Ivi," writes Castiglione of his visit to Mount Vernon, " passai quattro giorni favorito del Generale Washington colla maggiore ospitalità. Il Generale ha cerca cinquante setti anni, ó grande di statura, di robusta complessione, di aspetto maestoso e piacevole, e benche incallito nel servizio militare, sembra ancora di étá non avanzata. Voglia il Cielo, che, vivendo molti anni, serva, per lungo tempo, d'esempio nella virtù e nella industria a suoi concittadini, come servi d'esempio all' Europa, nelle vittorie che consacrarono il sou nome ad un' eterna fame."

In 1790, Count Adriani, of Milan, brought an ode from Alfieri to Washington, and afterward wrote an abusive book about America, of which the General wrote to Humphrey, it is "an insult to the inhabitants of a country where he received more attention and civility than he seemed to merit."

Whoever visited the Roman Catholic convent at Georgetown, twenty years ago, chatted with the priests, and perhaps tasted the old Malaga with which they used to beguile their guests, must, especially if fresh from Washington society, have experienced a curious kind of old-world sensation, inspired by the contrast between this glimpse of the monastic life of Europe and the vivacious, hopeful, experimental tone of American society. It is easy, with these impressions, to imagine what kind of a report of our country, its prospects, manners, and tendencies, an isolated priest of such an establishment would be likely to prepare. Its main character would, of course, be deprecatory of the religious freedom of the land; its social comments would naturally be founded on convent gossip and hear-say evidence; and it would be natural to expect traces of that waggery with which our quick-witted people, when provoked by the perversity or amused by the credulity of their foreign visitors, are apt to quiz these seekers "of knowledge under difficulties;" as when a complacently curious lady scribe was made to believe the water carts used to lay the summer dust in our Northern cities, sprinkled the streets thrice daily with vinegar, to obviate infection; or when the cockney accepted the statement that a rose bug was a flea, everything, from hotels to mountains and insects, being on a large scale in America.

Accordingly, the reader of a now rare pamphlet, written by a former inmate of the Georgetown convent, will not be disappointed in any of these anticipations. Originally published in Rome, it was reprinted at Milan in 1819, and is entitled "Notizie Varie sullo stato presente della Republica degli Stati Uniti dell' America Settentrionale da Padre Giovanni Grassi della compagnia de Gesu." This Jesuit writer is of the urbane class. Take away the priestly *animus*, and there is nothing consciously uncandid in his account, narrow and superficial as it is. The marvellous growth of the country in population and resources is fairly indicated, and some agricultural information given. He declares "the mass of the people are better provided with food" than elsewhere in the world, but are not as well off as regards drink, wine being very dear and beer quite rare. The seventh part of the population, he says, are negroes, and are kindly treated. He is severe on "the passion for elegant preaching," on the extravagance in dress, on the prevalence of duels and dancing, on the superficial education, and the practice of gambling. The two last defects come with an ill grace from an Italian, the bane of whose nation they have been for ages. Padre Grassi must have been hoaxed by some report of the Connecticut Blue Laws, for he speaks of the superstitious observance of the Sabbath as constituting religion in the view of American Protestants, who "saddle a horse the day before Sunday to go to church on, and have no beer made on Saturday, lest it should work the next day." He gravely declares that cider is substituted for wine at the communion service, from motives of economy. He is not at all complimentary to the people of the Eastern States, of whom he probably heard a Southern report. "Among the inhabitants of the United States," he writes, "those of New England are regarded as thorough knaves, and are called Yankis." He mentions, as ordinary infractions of good breeding, that people in America "pare the nails and comb the head in company" (in Italy the latter is a street occupation), and "sit with their feet braced on a wall or a chair." He inveighs against the "display of piety," and indulges in some rather coarse jokes and some very free caricatures, that suggest rather the licentious than the disciplined side of monastic life; yet, withal, there is something kindly in the spirit as there is absurd in the prejudices of Father Grassi, whose summing up, however, is rather discouraging: "The unrestrained freedom which obtains, the drunkenness which abounds, the rabble of adventurers, the great number of negro slaves, the almost infinite variety of sects, and the little real religion that is met with, the incredible number of novels that are read, and the insatiable eagerness for gain, are, indeed, circumstances that would hardly give reason to expect much in point of manners. At first view, however, one is not aware of the depravity of this country, because it is hidden, for a time, under the veil of an engaging exterior."

J. C. Beltrami, previously a judge of a royal court in the kingdom of Italy, in his "Pilgrimage in Europe and America," published in London in 1828, gives his impressions of the West with much vividness. He had much to say of the aborigines, and expatiates upon the natural history and scenery of the region he visited with intelligence and enthusiasm. Of the latter he writes, "one wants the pencil of Claude and the pen of Delille to describe it."

Twenty years ago, there resided in Boston a Sicilian refugee, still affectionately remembered. He celebrated in graceful verse the solemn beauty of Mount Auburn,* and was

* "Monte Auburno: Poemetto da Pietro d'Alessandro."

esteemed by many of our scholars and citizens for his genial disposition and refined mind. His first impressions of New England manners were essentially modified when time and opportunity had secured him friends; but his early letters are interesting because so natural; and they express, not inadequately, the feelings of a sensitive and honest Italian, while yet a stranger in the "land of liberty." They indirectly, also, bring the sentiment of the two countries, before the days of Italian unity, into suggestive contrast. Not intended for publication, they are all the more candid on that account. I obtained permission to translate them, and they are now quoted as a faithful local sketch of personal experience of an educated Sicilian patriot in the American Athens:

"BOSTON, 183-.

"'I was reading Yorick and Didimo* on the 26th of December, the very day preceding your departure; and I wept for you, for Didimo, and myself, earnestly wishing, at the moment, that our countrymen would yield at least the tribute of a tear to the memory of Foscolo, recalling his sublime mind and the history of those lofty but hopeless feelings which drove him a wanderer, out of Italy, to find repose only in the grave.'

"I often ponder upon these few words written by you on the blank leaf of my Didimo. I can never read them unmoved, for they awaken a sad emotion in my heart, as if they were the last accents I am destined to hear from your lips. Never have I so vividly felt the absence of your voice, your presence, and your counsel, as now that, driven by my hapless fortune to a distant land, I have no one either to compassionate or cheer me, nor any with whom to share my joy or sorrows. Believe me, Eugenio, the love of country and friends was never so ardent in my bosom as now that I am deprived of them; and time, instead of healing, seems rather to irritate the wound which preys so deeply upon my heart. I often wrote you while on the Atlantic, describing the various incidents of our voyage, the dangers we encountered, and the fearful and sweet sensations I alternately experienced, as the sea lashed itself into a tempest, or reposed beneath the mild effulgence of a tranquil night. But, upon reviewing those letters, I find they breathe too melancholy a strain, and are quite too redolent of my wayward humor, even for a dear

* The name assumed by Foscolo as translator of Sterne's "Sentimental Journey."

friend's perusal; and, besides reaching you too late, they could only serve to grieve both yourself and my poor mother. But at length I have arrived at a place whence I can give you some definite account of my welfare.

"On the night of the 15th of March, notwithstanding the contrary wind which had beat us about here and there for several successive days, we cast anchor in Boston harbor. That night was long and wearisome to me. Obliged to remain on board until dawn, I passed it like many others during the passage, unable to sleep. The weariness and anxiety consequent upon a long sea voyage, were at length over. Indeed, the moment I caught the first glimpse of land, they were forgotten. Yet I could scarcely persuade myself that I had reached America. The remembrance of the last few months of excitement and grief, passed in that dear and distant country which, perhaps, I am never destined again to behold, came over me anew, and, contrasting with my present situation, awoke in my mind the most painful sense of uncertainty. I felt doubtful of everything, even of my own existence. I experienced, at that moment, an utter want of courage. The flattering hopes which had brightened the gloomiest hours of my voyage, all at once abandoned me. My imagination no longer pictured scenes of promise. I looked within and around, and beheld only the naked reality of things. I realized only the sad certainty, that a new life was before me. I revolved the various necessities of my situation: the importance of immediately forming new acquaintances—the uncertainty how I should be received by the few to whom I had brought introductions—my own natural aversion to strangers—and a thousand other anxious thoughts, which made me long for day as the signal of relief from their vexation. At length the morning dawned; but it was obscured by a damp fog and heavy fall of snow. All around wore a gloomy and cheerless aspect. In a few moments, the captain came to greet me as usual, but with more than wonted urbanity. He informed me I was now at liberty, and, whenever I pleased, the boat should convey me to the nearest wharf. I did not wait for him to repeat the summons, but, throwing off my sea dress, assumed another; and, descending the ship's side, soon touched the shore so long and ardently desired. It is true, I then felt intensely what it is to be alone. Yet not less sincere was my gratitude to that invisible and benignant Being, who had guided and preserved me through so many dangers. I landed with tearful eyes; and, although no friend, with beating heart, was there to welcome me, I stooped reverently to kiss the land sacred to liberty, and felt then for the first time that I, too, was a *man*.

"*17th April.*

"I have now passed several days in strolling through the streets of this city, amusing myself with the sight of so many objects of novelty and interest. I find the place rather pretty than otherwise; much more so, indeed, than I had imagined. The buildings, however, are in a style so peculiar, as to suggest the idea that the principles of architecture are here entirely unknown, or purposely disregarded. And then, the people all seem in such a hurry!—ladies and gentlemen, boys and girls, white and black, horses, hacks, wagons, and omnibuses hastening so furiously along the streets, that, unless you are on your guard, there is no little danger of awkward rencontres. How delightful to my sea-worn sight, this spectacle of animated life! How gladly would I, too, have assumed a part in the busy scenes in which the multitude about me were engaged! With what delight should I have rejoiced with them, in anticipating the comforts and the greetings of *a home!* But, situated as I was during these first days succeeding my arrival, the scenes around me served but to make me realize anew my loneliness; and, but for the gratification afforded my curiosity, I would have willingly remained immured in the little chamber of my hotel. I am, however, anxiously seeking employment; but, as yet, my efforts have been unsuccessful. My letters of introduction I do not think will be of much service to me, except the one proposing a credit in my favor, from our mutual friend, which has been duly honored by his correspondents. These gentlemen, like many others here, have expressed great pleasure in seeing me. They have introduced me to such individuals as I have chanced to meet in their company, either at the counting house, or in the streets. They have also made innumerable proffers of assistance. In short, they have received me kindly, and yet with a curious species of kindness, certainly not Italian; and, as yet, I know not if I can properly characterize it as American. Polite or not, however, they certainly seem to aim first to satisfy their curiosity; for, after having beset one with a thousand questions—many more, indeed, than it is agreeable to answer—they make no scruple of waiving all ceremony, and leaving you very abruptly, without even a hasty *addio.* This has occurred to me very often, though I cannot say invariably. The figure which I have presented more than once, on such occasions, I am sure must have been ridiculous. Taken by surprise at the abrupt termination of the interview, I have stood immovable and half mortified, following with my eyes the receding form of my friend, walking so coolly off, intent upon his own affairs.

"Another kind of courtesy, which some, perhaps, might ascribe to frankness, but which certainly wears the appearance of perfect indifference, is their habit of inviting one to their houses and tables, in terms so very vague and general, that I assure you, during the month I have been here, it has been frequently impossible for me to make up my mind to accept many of the civilities offered me. I question, however, whether there will be frequent occasion for scruples of this kind, as I apprehend there is little danger of such courtesies being repeated: yet the good people seem in earnest, and to tender their hospitalities with all their hearts. I am inclined to think they do. But, to tell the truth, I feel no small degree of delicacy in accepting such courtesies, because the experience I daily acquire of their customs and manner of thinking, forces upon my mind the conviction, that the reputation they have for egotism, especially as regards foreigners, is not without foundation.

"Boston people may be ranked among that large class who content themselves with respecting all who respect them, and refrain scrupulously from doing the slightest injury to all who are equally harmless. They are, however, exceedingly wary of foreigners, and not, perhaps, without much reason; since many who have sojourned among them have shown themselves both ignorant and unprincipled, and, besides leaving a bad impression of their individual characters, have also induced the most unfavorable opinions of the countries whence they came. In Italy, the very name of stranger is a passport to civility and kindness. Here, while you require no sealed and signed document from any of their European majesties to insure free communication and travel, you can scarcely ask the slightest civility, or approach one of your kind, without exciting a certain degree of suspicion; and your disadvantage is still enhanced, if, in addition to the name of foreigner—which, like original sin, is deemed a common taint—you also bring the still less pardonable sin of poverty. The necessity of earning a livelihood, however honestly, is certainly the worst recommendation with which to enter a foreign country; nor is it less so in the New World, since here, as well as elsewhere, a well-filled purse, and the disposition liberally to dispense its contents, will insure the heartiest welcome. The Americans, too, being universally intent upon gain, are naturally indisposed to encourage new competitors, and their time is too completely absorbed in business to allow of their devoting many moments to the interests of foreigners. Their lives are entirely spent in striving after new accumulations; and the whole glory of their existence is reduced to the miserable vanity of having it said, after their death, that they have left a considerable estate; and this short-lived renown is awarded according to the greater or less heritage bequeathed. This is not only the course of the father, but of the children; for they, being by law entitled to an equal portion of their father's property, are obliged to follow in his footsteps, in order to obtain their shares of this same glory: that the question, 'How much has he left?' may be answered as much to their credit as it was to that of their sire. Thus the young and the old, those barely possessing a competence and those rolling in wealth, with equal zeal bend all their energies to the common end. Intent upon gain and traffic, they are too absorbed to think of any but themselves. They calculate, with watch in hand, the minutes and seconds as they pass, and seem naturally averse to any conversation of which trade and speculation are not the subject. Hence results, as a natural consequence, the prevailing mediocrity of ideas and feelings, derived from the uniform system of education and manner of thinking, as well as the great similarity of interests. Hence, too, the equal tenor of life, and the absence of great vices, as well as of great virtues; hence the social calmness and universal prosperity, and hence the apparent insensibility to the appeal of misfortune, resulting from the want of exercise of feelings of ready sympathy and compassion incident to such a social condition.

"You may infer, from what I have said, the condition of the stranger in the midst of such a community—of him of whom it may be said with truth, that he interests no one. For my part, I cannot be too grateful for the generosity of my relatives: without it, God knows what, by this time, would have become of your wretched friend. Still, I am anxious about the future—the more so since I have discovered that political misfortunes, which have driven into exile so many of our countrymen, furnish no claim to the sympathies of these republicans. Many of those with whom I am already acquainted are so foolishly proud of their political privileges, that, instead of pitying, you would fancy they intended to ridicule the less favored condition of other lands. I beg you, however, to consider what I have said on this subject as hastily inferred, and not dogmatically affirmed. I may be quite mistaken; and, indeed, to pretend to give a correct idea of a country entirely new to me, after only a month's residence, especially where the aspect of things differs so essentially from what I have been accustomed to, would, I am well aware, appear very absurd. Yet there is a very just proverb which says, that from the dawn we may augur the day; and if it be true, I regret to say that the dawn before me seems most unpromising. Would that a bright and cheerful sun would arise to dispel the mists of doubt, and throw gladness upon the heart of your devoted friend!

"*28th April.*

"Often, during my voyage, I promised myself great delight, upon my arrival, in visiting the plains of Cambridge, and the heights of Dorchester and Bunker Hill, renowned as the early scenes of the American war. As I read Botta's 'History,' my imagination often transported me to those spots which he so vividly pictured. I longed to find myself upon the hallowed ground, to render my tribute of grateful admiration to the memory of those noble men who there perished fighting for the liberty of their country. The inclement season, however, has not yet allowed me to realize my anticipations. We are at the end of April, and yet the spring seems scarcely to have commenced.

"The aspect of the environs of Boston is most desolate. The earth is still buried under the snow; the streets are covered with ice, here and there broken by the constant travelling, which renders them almost impassable. In addition, there prevails here, at this season, a most disagreeable wind. It blows from the east, and is so exceedingly chilly and penetrating, that it not only destroys one's comfort, but undermines the health. It seems to freeze my very soul, and effectually drives away all disposition for romance. I have been, therefore, constrained to remain in town, and rest satisfied with a distant view of the environs, until the coming of a more genial season.

"Although the city is scarcely less gloomy than the country, it is still some amusement for the stranger to note the pedestrians. On both sides of the principal street you may behold men of all sorts and sizes, muffled up to their eyes in cloaks, high-collared surtouts, or quilted wrappers, fur caps and gloves, woollen capes, heavy boots and heavier overshoes; and, although thus burdened with garments—weightier far than the leaden cloaks of Dante's hypocrites—they contrive to shuffle along at the usual rapid rate, for they are *business men.* Now and then the light figure of a dandy flits by, arrayed in raiment quite too light for the weather, and looking as blue as winter and misery can make him. And then the women—*ladies,* I mean, God bless them! women, there are none here—all in their gala dresses, all satin and muslin, light feathered bonnets, silk stockings and dancing shoes, with a bit of fur round their necks, or the skirt of their pelisses, to *whisper* of *comfort.* Thus attired, they glide over the ice with a calm indifference worthy of heroines, stopping occasionally to purchase blonde lace or cough candy, and then moving on in the very face of the April breeze I have described to you.

"To speak seriously, I had thought to find in this country, if not the original, at least the remains of ancient simplicity. I flattered myself that I should see, among the descendants of those Puritan colonists, who were 'wise and modest in all their wishes,' a complete absence of pretension. But it is not so. The habits which prevail, and especially those relating to dress, are most extravagant. In the houses, in the streets, at every hour of the day, you see displayed—I say not with how much taste—the same dresses which our female nobility, who are as extravagant as any countesses in the United Kingdom, are accustomed to wear only at *soirées*, weddings, or the opera. It is much the same with our sex. I will not now pretend to account for these extravagant habits, although I fancy I have divined the reason. Yet I must believe that, in this republic, female dress is the great item of domestic expense. The *materiel*, being imported from abroad, is very dear. Indeed, the price of everything is exorbitant. As the saying is with us, those who have not a house pay for every sigh; and here they cost not less than half a dollar or seventy-five cents each. And this adds another to the disadvantages of the stranger, especially if, like myself, he has indulged the idea that, in this young country, dress was not thought to make the man in the same degree as elsewhere, and finds that, with all their vaunted progress, the Americans have not gone an iota beyond their predecessors in establishing a just standard of estimating mankind; and are quite as prone to base their judgments upon appearance rather than character. Nor can you practically oppose such customs either with your philosophy or indifference, since the individual who avails himself of the privileges of social life is bound, as far as he can without self-debasement, to conform to popular prejudices; and, indeed, it seems to me that here appearances are peculiarly imposing. Wherever you turn, you behold the names of every description of dealer, from the poor huckster to the rich merchant, blazoned upon signs in gilt letters, as if to impress the stranger with the idea that he had entered the most prosperous country of the earth.

"But I will speak to you of the more noteworthy objects around me, which, however, are not numerous. Notwithstanding the unpleasant season, I have visited Cambridge, with the situation of which I have been much pleased. The village is about three miles and a half from Boston; and, in its centre, you find the most ancient and best-endowed seat of learning existing in the United States. It is called Harvard University, and the establishment consists of several buildings, containing lodging and recitation rooms, built of brick, with one exception, all in a simple style, which struck me as happily accordant with the character of the institution. The law and theological schools constitute a part of the University. But what particularly pleased me was the library, which, from what I hear, is the best in the country, and, in truth, is excellent. Among other works, there is quite a collection of Italian books; and many of the editions are beautiful, and very neatly bound. You cannot imagine how much I enjoyed the sight of so many of our beloved authors. Amid the legacies of these illustrious dead, I, for the moment, forgot all my private griefs and anxiety. I seemed no longer to be among strangers, for in every one of those books I recognized an honored and dear friend of my youth: so long unseen, and so unexpectedly encountered, they seemed to transport me to a new world. In truth, this was the first moment that I felt really encouraged. Who knows, I asked myself, but these ancient allies of mine will introduce me to their friends of the New World?—and then Yorick's unfortunate adventure with the police of Paris occurred to me.

"Of the University, the method of instruction pursued, and the progress it has made, I will tell you when I am better informed. It grieves me, at present, that I cannot go every day to Cambridge. The season being so bad, it is necessary to ride thither. Then, there is my dinner. So that, by a broad calculation (you see how I have already begun to calculate), the pleasure of six hours' reading would daily make me minus a dollar. 'But,' you ask, 'cannot you dine upon your return in the evening?' Yes, if they would let me! But here, even at the hotels, it is not the custom to order your dinner when you please. They treat us quite like friars; and it is necessary, if you would not lose your dinner, to be at the table punctually at the stroke of two; otherwise—but, Holy Virgin! it is the dinner bell. Wait only a moment, for I must make haste to be in time for the roast beef. In three minutes (all that is required here) I will return, and continue my letter.

"I went, the other day, with one of our countrymen, to visit the Athenæum, which is the only literary establishment in the city. It is supported by the *savans* and aristocracy of Boston. It has a library composed chiefly of donations of books, among which are many of the principal works published in Europe and America, several literary and scientific journals, and numerous gazettes. There are also rooms containing casts and a few marble statues, a small collection of medallions, and two apartments for the study of architecture and drawing, but destitute both of masters and pupils, and one large hall, on the lower floor, used as a reading room. The shareholders and their friends are only admitted to the Athenæum. These are, for the most part, gentlemen of leisure or *idle people*, according to the complimentary title bestowed on them by their fellow citizens; and they go, as their taste may be, to occupy their time in the reading room, which is open from early morning till nine at night. In this room, there is a rule inscribed expressly prohibiting conversation; and you see, to far more advantage than in our libraries, so many living statues in every variety of attitude, often not the most graceful, all with a book in hand, or intent upon a newspaper. The librarian, a very good sort of man, has shown himself, like many others, very glad to see me. He told me that, as a stranger, the Athenæum would be open to me for the period of one month; but that after that time, if I remained, and wished to continue my visits, it would be necessary for me to become a subscriber, like the other frequenters of the institution. I thanked him for his politeness, and have shown how sincerely I valued it, by going almost every day to the Athenæum; and as to the end of the month, I do not trouble my head about it, because, by that time, I hope the weather will allow me to walk frequently to Cambridge. What and how great are the advantages which result from this institution, I leave you to estimate. The Athenæum, however, now in its infancy, seems destined to advance greatly; and if, one day, it should become a public establishment, it cannot but be of lasting benefit to Boston. And truly, in a city like this, which I hear called the Athens of America, there should be, if nothing else, a rich library freely open to the people. Thus you see that, both in and out of town, I have not failed to find the means of becoming learned and illustrious. All these literary advantages, however, are reduced to nothing to a poor devil who is in the situation of being obliged to derive profit from the little he knows, rather than from what still remains to him to be acquired. And this necessity has urged me to seek an occupation at every sacrifice; and, having gone the rounds with the diploma of a young *letterato*, the office which, for the moment, I can most certainly obtain, is that of a teacher of our language. And I have, indeed, one scholar, a lean doctor of medicine, to whom, as he has the merit of being connected with a relative who is intimate with one of the family of ———, who pays me my remittances, I give my lessons gratis. This has been, thus far, my greatest resource. But this gentle minister of death gives me promise of an introduction among his patients—of whom, as yet, I have not caught even a glimpse. However, I am obliged to trot every day, at the expense of my poor legs, to the doctor's door, which is no little distance from mine. I go very punctually, but often only to find him asleep in his chair, and dozing while I read the lesson—which, moreover, I am obliged to explain through the medium of a French grammar. This avaricious Sangrado piques himself not a little upon his egregious lisping of the French; and to this day I have been unable to induce him to buy another grammar. But, somehow or other, I hope soon to send him on a journey to Elysium, to carry my compliments to his master Hippocrates.

"*May 7th.*

"I am angry with you. Five packets have arrived since I landed; and every day I hurry anxiously to the post office, only to hear the same chilling negative to my ardent inquiry for letters. I have even conceived quite an antipathy to the stiff, laconic postman, who sometimes deigns no other reply than a cold shake of the head. Yet you promised to write me at the end of the first month after my embarkation. How can I forgive such neglect? And what reasonable excuse can you offer? Perhaps you allege the uncertainty of my fate. Yet, had I gone to my last sleep in the bosom of old Neptune, think you a friendly letter would not have been a pleasant offering to my manes? Nay, Eugenio, you know not the comfort a few lines from you would bring to the heart of a poor friend. I am homesick. My feelings seem dead to all that surrounds me. I seem condemned to the constant disappointment of every cherished hope; and, were I able to express all I feel, I could unfold a most pitiable story of mental suffering. Do you realize, Eugenio, how far I am from home, and all that is dear to me?—that I am living in a weary solitude which I sometimes fear will drive me mad? With affections most tenderly alive, and a nature that would fain attach itself to all around, I find not here a single congenial being or idea upon which my heart can repose. A stranger to everything, I am by all regarded as a stranger, and read that forbidding name in the expression of all whom I approach. Did I carry the remorse of a criminal in my bosom, I could not meet the gaze of my fellow beings with less confidence. The few whom I have known thus far, are, for the most part, merchants or commonplace people, too much occupied in their own affairs to relish interruption during their leisure hours. But when I fall in with them, they instantly tender the old salutation, 'Glad to see you,' coupled with an invitation to their counting houses, where they are too busy to talk, and content themselves with proffering a chair and the newspaper. These manners result from a mode of life very different from that which prevails in Europe: still they are painfully striking to the novice, especially if he be one of those who know not how to support the toil and vexation of existence, unsoothed by those cheering palliatives with which we are wont to sweeten the bitter cup of life. You well know that I was never over fond of general society, nor took much delight in the heartless glitter of fashionable life. But what I voluntarily avoided at home, is not a little desirable here, as a relief from the loneliness of my position. Yet the only house at which I can spend an evening with any pleasure, is that of our countryman B——, who, with the true feeling of Italian hospitality, at once made me at home under his roof. I meet him, too, occasionally in my walks, and we converse of our country, our literature, and, most frequently, of our misfortunes. God knows how grateful I am for his sympathy, without which it seems as if I should have died of weariness and grief. Yet our conversations sometimes serve to renew most keenly the memory of my sorrows—which I fain would bury in the bottom of my heart—and send me back to my little chamber to find more sadness than before, in the companionship of my own thoughts. That which renders me most anxious, is the harassing doubt which seems to attend my steps. I feel already that I am a burden to my relatives. Every day, which passes without advancing me in an occupation from which I can derive support, seems lost. Although I have not neglected, nor shall neglect, seeking for every honest mode of relieving them from this care, yet I feel a species of remorse, as if I were abusing their generosity; and the bread I eat tastes bitter, when I reflect that the expense of my bare subsistence, even with all the economy I can practise, in these times, and under existing circumstances, would half support the family of my afflicted mother. Thus my days pass, sustained only by hope and the promises of my new friends. Now and then, as at this moment, I write to those dear to me by way of solacing my bleeding heart; but even this occupation is painful to me, since I can only write of my afflictions.

"Ah, Eugenio, how aggravating is now the remembrance of all your kind advice! It is true, in an important sense, that man is the creator of his own destinies. With how much care and ingenuity do we raise the funeral pile, which is to consume our hopes and burn our very hearts! It is true, indeed, that if I had reconciled myself to existing circumstances, and allowed to subside the first force of those feelings which even you, with all your natural wisdom, could not but confess were generous and noble; and especially had I opened my eyes, and calmly looked those illusions in the face, in which so many of our young men, and I among the rest, so inconsiderately confided, it is true I should not have experienced the bitterness of the present. But how could I contemplate the miseries of our country, and not glow with indignation at beholding all the rare gifts which Heaven and nature had so benignantly bestowed, rendered unavailing—made but the occasion of tears to us all—every fountain of good dried up, or poisoned by the envy and iniquity of man? How could I admit the idea that I ought to sacrifice my thoughts and dearest sentiments, merely for the sake of pursuing, at home, one of our genteel professions, which, after all, could not preserve me from the general degradation, nor, perhaps, from infamy? And should I have done so? And why? From the cowardly fear, perhaps, of being exiled from the land of my fathers, when, in the buoyancy of youth, I could turn to another country—far distant, it is true, but free; to a country in which I could obtain a subsistence without sacrificing *one* of my opinions; where, even now, notwithstanding I may be made deeply to realize the axiom that mankind are the same everywhere, I do not see all around me the aspect of misery and unhappiness, nor daily instances of the petty vengeance and cold-hearted injustice of our tyrants; where the cheerful prospect of peace and universal prosperity almost reconciles one to the inevitable evils incident to human society; where, at least, thought and speech are not crimes, and you can cherish the hope of a better future without seeing beside you the prison or the gallows; where the mind can expand unfettered by any servile chain—yes, the *mind*, which I now feel as free within me as when it was first bestowed by God.

"And yet I complain! It is true; and I well know what you will reply to these letters, which I write only for the pleasure of being with you, even while we are separated. But if you have the heart to charge all the blame to me, I would beg you, Eugenio, to remember that every tear teaches a truth to mortals, and that I, too, am one of those numerous creatures, made up of weaknesses and illusions, who drag themselves blindly, and without knowing where or why, in the path of inexorable fate. Now that I feel that there never existed so great a necessity for bringing about an alliance between my reason and my heart, I cannot discover the method by which to accomplish it, and the task never seemed more impracticable. Reason, which levels everything with her balance to a just equilibrium, and reduces, by calculation, all things to a frigid system, you have adopted as your goddess; and truly she is a most potent divinity, and often have I invoked her aid, and supplicatingly adored her power. Yet this heart of mine is such a petty and obstinate tyrant, that it will never yield the palm even when fairly conquered; and, in its waywardness, takes a wicked pleasure in pointing out the naked coldness of your divinity, and setting her before me in a most uninviting light. Hence it is that I am devoured with the desire of home; nor will all the charms of glory, or the smiles of fortune, lure me from the dearer hope of reunion with the land and the loved of my heart. Yet who knows where I shall leave my bones? Who knows if these eyes shall close eternally to the light amid the tears of my kindred, or whether friendship and love will linger sorrowfully near to receive my last sigh?

"*Addio.* I commend to you my mother. This phrase would be meaningless to any but you. I have used it to express all I feel for that tenderest of beings—for her whom I continually behold in imagination, weeping and desolate. If the voice of pity and friendship are powerful in your heart, I pray you, Eugenio, leave her not unconsoled. Thou must be as another child to her, and ever remember that she is the mother of thy friend.

"*May 15th.*

"This morning I rose full of anxiety. The moment I awoke, my first thought was of you, of my family, and of the delay of your letters; and the sound of the breakfast bell first aroused me from my painful reverie. I descended, swallowed a single cup of coffee, and, quick as thought, hastened to the office. I did not expect to find letters, but having given my name, and perceiving that the postman did not return the customary nod of refusal, my heart began to palpitate strongly. I did not deceive myself. I have my mother's letter to which you have made so large an addition, and I have been till this moment shut up in my room, reading it over and over again, and bathing every line with my tears. God reward you for all your care and your love for me! I trust that, ere this, you have received my first letters, and thus been relieved of all anxiety on my account. I thank you for all the news you give me, and especially for what you tell me respecting our young companions, who, I rejoice to know, are now quite free from the ill-founded suspicions of Government. The condition of Italy, however, seems to grow more sad every day; and you write me that many are rejoicing at the rumor of imminent war, and in the hope that our old liberators will again reappear among us. For my part, however, I cannot but tremble with you, since now there is less certainty than ever that aught will remain to us but injuries and derision. The present and past misfortunes of our country should have taught us that, if there is anything to hope, it is from ourselves alone; and it is certain, that if the new subjects of the new citizen-king descend again from the mountains, there is reason to believe that the disgraces of bygone times will be renewed in Italy, and it will be our lot to transmit another record of shame and cowardly execrations.

"From your literary news, I learn that the Anthology of Florence has been abolished, and, as usual, by command of Austria. I had made no little search for the last number. Be it so. The suppression of that work is only one other insult to our condition, but not a serious loss to the nation, since the writers, who perhaps set out with the idea of undeceiving the Italians, are themselves the very ones who propagate their unfortunate illusions; and in that journal, which was doubtless the best we had, they also said too much, and without profit. In these times, there exist no Alfieris or Foscolos; and the new school, which promised so much by its historical romances, has thus far accomplished little enough, if we except one or two sermons on passive obedience. Botta remains, but he is alone; and the soul of Tacitus, which should be devoted to so exalted a work, is wanting to him. Moreover, his thoughts, although grand and sacred, are rather understood readily by those who think, than felt deeply by the mass, with that profound sense of desperation, from which alone a real change and constancy of opinion are to be hoped for among the Italians.

"To tell you the truth, I believe we are so susceptible of illusions, that the intellectual energy of no writer whatever can avail anything in eradicating from the hearts of our countrymen the weaknesses which are as old as our servitude, and which are strongly maintained by the consciousness of general debasement and actual incapacity, as well as by the small degree of virtue and the total absence of ambition on the part of our princes. I desired to allude to these circumstances, in reply to that part of your letter wherein you recommend me not to forget Italy and our studies. But, as yet, you seem unaware, that in this land I have conceived a love of country not only more powerful than ever, but instinct with a desperate earnestness which consumes my heart. Wherever I turn, the aspect of all the civil and social benefits enjoyed by this fortunate people, fills me, at the same time, with wonder, admiration, and immense grief. Not that I envy the Americans their good fortune, which, on the contrary, I ardently rejoice in, and desire, as much as any one of themselves, may be forever continued to the land. But I think of Italy, and know not how to persuade myself why her condition should be so different and so sad. I do not allude to the general policy of the country, but I speak of what I see every day while walking the streets—a quiet population, incessantly intent upon industry and commerce, without being retarded by civil restrictions or tyrannical extortions, by the subterfuges of official harpies, or by the machinery of so many hungry and shameless financiers, nor yet continually irritated by the insufferable and cowardly insolence of the ministers of the law, who, either in the military garb, or as civil officers, or in the form of police, are the vilest instruments of European tyranny—the pests of the state, consuming its substance and resources, and corrupting the manners and morals of the people. Here, I have not yet seen in the streets a single soldier, nor one patrol of police, nor, in fact, any guard of the public safety; and, having occasion to go to the Custom House, I was quite astonished to see the simplicity of the forms, the expedition with which affairs were conducted, and the small number of officers employed. Indeed, this people seem like a large and united family, if not bound together by affection and reciprocal love, at least allied by a common and certain interest, and the experience that the good of all is the good of the individual. Every one who has the will to labor will easily find occasion for its free practice and most adequate recompense. Not being incited by opportunity and the keen necessities of life, crimes are rare, violences almost unheard of, and poverty and extreme want unknown. In the streets and markets, and in every place of public resort, you behold an activity, a movement, an energy of life, and a continual progress of affairs; and in the movements and countenances of the people, you can discern a certain air of security, confidence, and dignity, which asks only for free scope. I know not how it is, but often I pause thoughtfully in the midst of the thoroughfare, to contemplate the scene around me. I sometimes find myself standing by some habitation, and my fancy begins to picture it as the sanctuary of every domestic and social virtue—as the cradle of justice and piety—as the favorite sojourn of love, peace, and every human excellence. And my heart is cheered, and bleeds at the same time, as I then revert to Italy, and imagine what might be her prosperity, and how she might gloriously revive, and become again mistress of every virtue and every noble custom, among the nations of the world.

"Judge, then, if I have forgotten, or if it will be possible for me to forget Italy, as long as I remain in this country. For the rest, as I have before said, I am only made the more constantly to remember my native land. I am told, and begin to realize, that here, as well as there, Utopian views of politics, morals, religion, and philosophy, have long prevailed, and promise to grow more luxuriously than ever, and become, perhaps, fatal to the prosperity and liberty of this land. It is, however, no small consolation for the moment, to reflect, that the doctrines of this nation do not depend upon the *letterati*, or rather, that the country does not look to that class for its salvation; which, as such, has no voice in the capital. There are here no mere questions of language; no *romanticists* or *classicists* who cannot understand each other; no imperial nor royal academicians of grammar; no furious pedants who are continually disputing how we should write, nor any that pretend to dictate how we should think. Eloquence is here the true patrimony, and, in fact, the most formidable weapon for good or for evil, in the hands of the people, who estimate it more or less by the standard of their wants or individual

partialities. I will tell you, however, from time to time, in future letters, as I become better informed on these subjects. Yet expect not, I pray you, from me, either statistics, disquisitions, or a traveller's journal, since you know I came hither in quite another capacity. There goes, with this, another letter to our young friend B——, who writes me that he desires to come and seek his fortune in the United States. You will see my reply; and, to dissuade him still more from the project, let him see what I have written you. *Addio.* Live ever in the love of your friends, of letters, of your country, and of yours,
"———."

An errant countryman of ours, with the ready wit of an educated New Englander, when sojourning in London, after a long visit to the Continent, being disappointed in his remittances, conceived the idea of replenishing his purse by a spirited article for one of the popular magazines, wherein he imagined the sayings and doings of a Yankee ruler suddenly placed at the head of affairs in the kingdom of Naples. The picture was salient and unique, and amused the public. We were irresistibly reminded thereof by a little brochure wherein the process here described is exactly reversed, and, instead of a Yankee *letterato* in Naples, we have a Neapolitan priest in America. So grotesquely ignorant and absurdly superstitious and conservative is the spirit of this brief and hasty record,* that we cannot but regret the *naive* writer had not extended his tour and his chronicle; for, in that case, we should have had the most amusing specimen extant of modern Travels in America. The author was a chaplain in the navy of his Majesty of Naples. He describes the voyage of the frigate Urania during a nearly two years' cruise from Castellamare to Gibraltar, thence *via* Teneriffe to Pernambuco, Rio Janeiro, and St. Helena, to New York and Boston, and back to Naples by way of England and France. In his dedication of the "Breve Racconto" to the very reverend chaplain of Ferdinand II, he declares he finds "non pochi

---

* "Breve Racconto delle cose Chiesastiche piu Importanti occorse nel viaggio fatto sulla Real Fregata Urania, dal 15 Agosto, 1844, al 4 Marzo, 1846, per Raffaele Capobianco, Cavaliere del Real Ordine del Merito di Franceses I. e Capellano della Real Marina," Napoli, 1846.

consolazioni" in having gathered "some fruits in the vineyard of the Lord" during his perilous voyage; but he adds, "the rivers are but little grateful for the return of the water they yielded in vapor;" and so this dedication and description are but a poor return to "our fountain of wisdom and virtue." The style, spirit, ideas in this little journal are quite mediæval. The simplicity and ignorance and bigotry of the roving ecclesiastic are the more striking from their contrast with the times and places of which he writes. Imagine a priest or friar suddenly transported from the Toledo to Broadway, and it is easy to solve what would otherwise be enigmatical in this childish narrative. He mentions, with pious reflections, the death of a mariner at sea from "nostalgia;" lauds, at the South American ports, the Roman Catholic religion, remarking its aptitude to "generalmente insinuarsi nel cuore del popolo docile." At Rio Janeiro he celebrates the feast of the Virgin; and to the devout manner in which the ship's company commended themselves to her, he attributes their subsequent miraculous escape from shipwreck. Thus, he writes, "God showed himself content with our homage to the Virgin." They keep Palm Sunday on board, with palms brought from St. Helena. He describes summarily the aspect of the cities they visit, gives the altitude of the peak of Teneriffe, notes the zones and tropics, the rites, and rate of their progress. "La navigazione felice," he observes, "arrise alle pie devozioni." On entering New York harbor, the chaplain says we passed "il grande forte Hamilton, e finalmente la Fregata," after six thousand miles of navigation, "dropt her anchor opposite the Battery garden, built in the sea, and joined to the *continent* by a wooden bridge about two hundred feet long." He remarks upon the public buildings, observing that the Exchange was "rebuilt in 1838, and is destined for a hospital;" that the Croton water "serves for conflagrations, which are very frequent," and that "il commercio é attivissimo." He descants upon "la immensita de vapori," declaring that the ferry boats carry "not only loaded carts, ten or fifteen at a time, but also bath-houses, with every convenience." His most elaborate descriptions, however, are reserved for the Catholic churches —St. Patrick's, St. Peter's, St. Giuseppe, and the Church of the Transfiguration, where he celebrated mass. He admires the "Campanile" of "il Tempio colossale degli Episcopali" (Trinity Church), and is charmed with the "Seminario Cattolico," through which he was conducted by "quel gentile e virtuoso vescovo Monsignore Hus"—doubtless the late Bishop Hughes. The Italian priests, the juvenile choristers, and the church music excite his enthusiasm. Crowds of Catholics, he tells us, came on board the frigate to hear the sailors sing "Salva Regina." Romanism, he declares, has "profound root" in the United States, and "daily grows," though the Episcopalians still strive "to infuse into the human heart the poison that, in 1603, came from Elizabeth's successor." He calls the Protestant sects "tristi pianté," and gives a list thereof, adding, "and to finish the noisome catalogue, to confusion add confusion, with the Quakers and Hebrew synagogues." "Il nemico infernale," he says, tried to insinuate his "veleno dell' errore" into the ship. Protestant emissaries from the Bible Society came on board to distribute the Scriptures "senza spirito santo!" His indignation at this proceeding is boundless. "Era mai possibile," he exclaims, "che i ciechi illuminassero gli illuminati e che intiepidessoro nel el cuore de Napolitani quella Religione che il Principe stesso degli Apostoli venne a predicare nella loro citta!"*

Leaving New York, the pious chaplain was "swept from the shores of the Hudson to Cape Cod," and, on the 3d of June, entered "the wonderful and picturesque bay" of Boston, to the sound of greeting cannon, and surrounded "by gondolas, whence arose cordial hurrahs" ("ben venga"). Boston, says the erudite chaplain, "was founded by English colonists from Boston in England. Bunker Hill monument was commenced in 1827 by the celebrated engineer, O'Don-

---

* "As if it were possible for the blind to enlighten the enlightened, and weaken in the hearts of Neapolitans that religion which the Prince of the Apostles himself came to preach in their own city."

nell Webster, under the presidency of the celebrated Lafayette!" He describes the public edifices, and, among them, the "Casa di Città," "which rises from a height near the public garden, and presents a majestic appearance, *with columns of white marble.*" Among the memorable names of streets, he observes, is "that of Franklin, who drew the lightning from heaven." Of the churches, he only remembers the Cathedral, the care and prosperity of which he ascribes "to that excellent prelate, Fitzpatrick." Again he congratulates himself upon the progress of his Church— thanks to the labors " della propagazione delle fede "—and declares that "the net of St. Peter does not fail to fish up many new souls from the turbid sea of error." Although made up of all nations, "the Americans," says the Neapolitan *padre*, " follow the habits and customs of the English." From Boston the frigate went to Holland and to England, from Plymouth to Brest, thence to Carthagena and Toulon, the island of Zante and Navarino, all of which places are briefly noted; and from the latter they proceed to Naples, which harbor and city the delighted chaplain hails as the cradle of Tasso and the tomb of Virgil; saluting, in the facile rhetoric of his native tongue, Mergellina, " where rest the ashes of Sannazaro," Herculaneum, Pompeii, and the light " del nostro sole, un perpetuo e vivissimo verde, l'ombrifero pino, il pomposo cipresso, l'odorato arancio, una sopredente moltitudine di eleganti casine sparse per tutta quanto la costa, stanze di un popolo vivacissimo ed amorevole!" At length, two steamers sent by " la benignità de Rò " approach the Urania, and the loyal and loving Padre Capobianco invokes Heaven's blessing on his head and reign, and, " in the midst of the joy and affection of kindred and friends," kisses his native earth.

Every American who has travelled in Europe has some extraordinary anecdote to relate of the ignorance there existing in regard to the geography, history, and condition of his country; but, perhaps, the questions asked him are nowhere so absurd as in Sicily. Her isolated position before the advent of Garibaldi, and the prevalent want of education, explain the phenomenon. Two things chiefly the Sicilians know about America—that she imports fruit, sulphur, and rags from the island, and affords a safe asylum for political refugees. At the seaports, especially in Syracuse, our naval officers are remembered as the most liberal of gentlemen. A deputation, not many years since, when the American squadron in the Mediterranean wintered there, waited on the commodore, and offered to coöperate with him in annexing Sicily to the United States. A spacious hotel was built at Syracuse, under the expectation that the fine harbor of that ancient city would become the permanent rendezvous of our fleet; but the jealousy of Bomba interposed, and Mahon continued to be the depot of our national ships, until Spezzia was substituted. Within a short period it was impossible to find in Sicily a book that could enlighten a native, in the Italian language, as to the actual resources and institutions of America. In 1853, however, one of the Palermo editors published a volume giving an account of his experience in the United States, with statistics and political facts, interspersed with no small amount of complacent gossip. The novelty of the subject then and there seemed to atone for the superficial and egotistic tone. Very amusing it was to an American sojourner in the beautiful Sicilian capital, to glance at the "Viaggio nella America Settentrionale di Salvatore Abbate e Migliori." We have seen what kind of gossip the French and English indulge in while recording their experience in America; let us compare with it a Sicilian's. He avows his object in visiting the New World—to ascertain for himself how far the unfavorable representations of a well-known class of British travellers are correct. He gravely assures his countrymen that, although foreigners are kindly received there, the Government does not pay for the transit of *emigrés*. The great characteristic which naturally impressed a subject of Ferdinand of Naples, was the non-interference of Government with private persons and affairs, except when the former have rendered themselves directly amenable to the law, by some invasion of the rights of others—an inestimable privilege in the view of one who has lived under espionage, *sbirri*, and the inquisition. All things are gauged by the law of contrast in this world; and it is curious, with the bitter and often just complaints of Englishmen of the discomforts of travel in America fresh in mind, to note the delight with which a Sicilian, accustomed to the rude *lettiga*, hard mule, precarious fare, and risk of encountering bandits, expatiates upon the safety, the society, and abundant rations accorded the traveller in the Western world. "Ecco," exclaims Salvatore, after describing a delightful *tête-à-tête* with a fair companion in the cars, and a hearty supper on board the steamer *en route* from Boston to New York, "Ecco il felice modo di viaggiare negli Stati Uniti sia per terra che per acqua; divertimenti sociali e senza prejudizii, e celerità di viaggio libero dai furtori e dagli assassini."

The *festa* bells of some saint are forever ringing in Sicily; and, although our traveller found holidays few and far between in this busy land, he describes, with much zest, the first of May, New Year's, and St. Valentine's Day in New York. His journal, while there, is quite an epitome of what is so familiar to us as to be scarcely realized, until thus "set in a note book," as the strange experience of a Southern European. To him, intelligence offices for domestics, mock auctions, the Empire Club, anniversaries of national societies, the frequency of conflagrations, matrimonial advertisements, the extent of insurance, the variety and modes of worship of Protestant sects, the number and freedom of public journals, the unimpeded association of the sexes, and the size and splendor of the fashionable stores and hotels, are features and facts of metropolitan life so novel as to claim elaborate description. Amusement is an essential element of life to an Italian, fostered by his sensibility to pleasant excitement, and his long political vassalage. Accordingly, Salvatore devotes no inconsiderable portion of his book to the public entertainments available in our cities. Few Americans imagine how much an enthusiastic foreigner can find to gratify his taste and divert his mind in New York. The careers of the celebrated English actors, Italian opera singers, and German pianists, the concerts of Ole Bull and De Meyer, the military balls, travelling circuses, public dinners, private *soirées*, and theatres, afford Salvatore a theme upon which he dilates as only one of his sensitive and mercurial race can; and the American reader is astonished to discover what abundant provision for the pleasure seeker may be found in our utilitarian land.

More grave interests, however, are not forgotten. A succinct but authentic account is given of some of the aboriginal tribes; our constitutional system is clearly stated; the details of government in the Eastern and Middle States are defined; the means and methods of education; the cereals, trees, rivers, charitable institutions, agricultural and mechanical industry of the country, are intelligently explained and illustrated; and thus a considerable amount of important information afforded, altogether new to the mass of his countrymen. This is evidently collected from books of reference; and its tone and material form an absolute contrast to the light-hearted and childish egotism of the writer's own diary, wherein the vanity of a versifier and sentimentalism of a beau continually remind us of the amiable gallants and dilettante *littérateurs* we have met among Salvatore's countrymen. His generalizations are usually correct, but tinctured with his national temperament. He describes the Americans as "a little cold, thoughtful, sustained, grave, positive in speech and argument, brave, active, intelligent, and true in friendship." The Northerners, he says, "are born with the instinct of work, and in physiognomy are like Europeans." Though there are "not many rich, most are comfortable; and, though few are learned, the great majority are intelligent. Labor is a social requisition; moderate fortunes and large families abound; and the test question in regard to a stranger is, 'What can he do?'" He sums up the peculiar advantages of the country as consisting of "a good climate, a fertile soil, salubrious air and water, abundance of provisions, adequate pay for labor, good laws, affable women, encouragements to matrimony, freedom, and public education"—each and all of which he seems to appreciate from the contrast they afford to the civil wrongs and social limitations of his own beautiful land, not then emancipated from the most degrading of modern despotisms. He notes the temperature with care, and has occasion to realize its extreme alternations. To a Sicilian, a snowstorm and sleighing must prove a winter carnival; and Salvatore gives a chapter to what he calls " La città nel giubello della neve." He finds the American women charming, and marvels at the extent and variety of their educational discipline, giving the programme of studies in a fashionable female seminary as one of the wonders of the land; and also a catalogue of popular and gifted female writers, as an unprecedented social fact in his experience. Salvatore was a great reader of newspapers while in this country, and was in the habit of transcribing, from those "charts of busy life," characteristic incidents and articles wherewith to illustrate his record of life in America. He was puffed by editorial friends, and mentions such compliments, as well as the publication of some of his own verses, with no little complacency; as, for instance, " Quest' oggi, contra ogni mia aspettazione, si è pubblicato nel giornale—*Evening Post*, un elogio dando a conoscere agli Americani lo scopo del mio viaggio," &c.; and elsewhere, " il mio addio all' America è stato messo in musica."

One of the latest publications of Italian origin, although written in the French language and by a French citizen, is that of a Corsican officer, one of Prince Napoleon's suite, on his brief visit to the United States, in the summer of 1861.*

Eighteen hundred leagues traversed in two months, "more with eyes than ears or mind," would seem to afford a most inadequate basis for discussion where grave facts of national polity and character are its subjects; but when the author of such a record begins by confessing himself mistaken as a

* " Lettres sur les États-Unis d'Amerique," par le Lieutenant-Colonel Ferri Pisani, Aide-de-camp de S. A. I. le Prince Napoleon, Paris, 1862.

prophet, and disclaims all pretensions to other accuracy and interest than can be found in a "point de vue general," and "portraits saisis au vol," and "resumés de conversations fugitives," we accept his report and speculations with zest, if not with entire satisfaction, and accompany his rapid expedition, animated descriptions, and thoughtful though hasty commentary, with the more pleasure inasmuch as the temper and tone of both indicate an experienced traveller, a shrewd observer, and a cultivated thinker. The time of this visit and date of its record give thereto an interest apart from any intrinsic claim. America had just been converted from a world of peaceful industry to a scene of civil war. The Gallic visitors compared the crisis to that which had once hurled France into anarchy and military despotism; and beheld here a mighty army improvised in the Free States, with no apparent check to their industrial prosperity; and governmental powers assumed to meet the exigency without provoking any popular distrust in the rectitude of the authorities or the safety of their rights; arrests, proscription, and enlistments were sanctioned by public confidence; in a word, the patriotism of an *instructed people* was the safeguard of the republic.

It is remarkable that a writer whose mind was so preoccupied with the exciting military scenes and imminent political problems of the day, should have become so thoroughly and justly impressed with the religious phenomena of the Eastern States, tracing their development from the Pilgrims to Edwards, and thence to Whitfield and Channing; and the conflicts of faith thus foreshadowed. "Les États-Unis," he writes, "présentent en ce moment des spectacles bien émouvants. Les armées s'entrechoquent sur tous les points de leur immense territoire. Une race qui semblait devoir realiser l'ideal pacifique de l'humanité moderne se transforme tout à coup en un peuple belliqueux et se déchire de ses propres mains. D'autre part l'esclavage se dresse, au milieu des horreurs de la guerre, come une question de vie ou de mort, devant laquelle reculent et le philosophe, et l'homme d'état et l'économiste. Eh bien! faut-il vous l'avouer, mon colonel, tous ces faits extraordinaires, dont nous sommes témoins, et qui rempliront un jour l'histoire de ce siècle, ont à mes yeux une portée moins redoutable que celui que nous venons de trouver à Boston, un de ces faits qui bouleversent la condition de l'homme, sans s'inscrire, comme les grands événements politiques, en traits de feu et du sang, dans sa mémoire. Je veux parler de l'établissement du Déisme dans le nouveau monde sous la forme d'une religion, d'une Eglise, du Déisme, non plus enseigné par une philosophie spéculative, mais pratiqué comme un culte, comme un principe moral et social, par l'élite de la société Americaine, et faisant, au dépens du Protestantisme, les progrès les plus effrayants." Thereupon we have a treatise on "Protestantism," from Edwards and Whitfield to Channing; the Puritans, the voluntary church system, rationalism, &c., " face à face avec le Catholicisme;" and he concludes with the prophecy that " ce sera entre ces deux champions que se livrera le combat suprême qui décidera des destinées futures de l'humanité."

Colonel Pisani's letters are a striking illustration of the facilities of modern travel. He describes the complete and elegant appointments of the swift and safe steam yacht in which Prince Napoleon, his wife, and suite, after visiting various points of the Old World, crossed the ocean, and, in a very few weeks, saw half a continent. They entered the harbor of New York, after days of cautious navigation owing to the dense fog, which, fortunately, and almost dramatically, lifted just as they sailed up the beautiful bay, revealing, under the limpid effulgence of a summer day, a spectacle which enchanted the Colonel, familiar as he was with the harbors of Naples and Constantinople.

The reader can scarcely help finding a parallel in this sudden and delightful change in the natural landscape, with that which exists between the preface and the text of this work, in regard to the national cause. Arriving at the moment when the defeat of the Federal army at Bull Run had spread dismay among the conservative traders, and warmed to imprudent exultation the traitors of the North, all the travellers heard from the official representatives of their country who greeted their arrival, was discouraging—almost hopeless for the republic. His Highness thought otherwise, and viewed the national cause with unshaken confidence; but Colonel Pisani, in giving his letters to the public, a year afterward, found himself obliged to retract premature forebodings, and admit a reaction and reversal, not only of the fortunes of war, but of the vital prospects of the nation. Midsummer is the worst period of the year for a foreigner to arrive in New York—a fact this writer scarcely appreciated, as he regards the deserted aspect of the palatial residences as their normal condition, and speaks of the then appearance of the population as if it were characteristic. Surprised by the courteous urbanity of those with whom he came in contact in shops, streets, and public conveyances, he contrasts this superiority of manners with his anticipations of ruffianism, and with the utter neglect of municipal method and decency. The American steamboats and railways are fully discussed and described. Broadway seems to Pisani a bazaar a league and a half in length. He misses the taste in dress familiar to a Parisian's eye, thinks the horses and harnesses fine, but the horsemen and equipages inferior. Despite "les industries de luxe," men of leisure, varied culture, and special tastes seemed quite rare, and the average physiognomy unattractive. The architecture and aspect of the hotels strike him as sombre compared with those of Paris; and he declares every *gamin* of that metropolis would ridicule our popular and patriotic *fêtes* as childish attempts thereat, which he attributes to the basis of Anglo-Saxon reserve in the national character, wherein "l'expression de la pensée est rarement dans un rapport exact avec la pensée elle-même." Decentralization, and all its phenomena, naturally impress his mind, accustomed to routine and method; and the manner of recruiting and organizing—in fact, the whole military *régime* of the country—offers salient points of comment and criticism to one who has long witnessed the results of professional life in this sphere. Visiting Philadelphia, Washington, and the great lakes, adapting themselves to the customs and the people, examining all things with good-natured intelligence, this record contains many acute remarks and suggestive generalizations. We have numerous portraits of individuals, sketches of scenery, reflections on the past, and speculations as regards the future. The absence of a *concierge* at the White House, the *naïveté* of the new President, the character and principles of statesmen and of parties, are subjects of candid discussion. The mines of Lake Superior, the community of Rappists, McCormick's manufactory of "engins agricoles," the local trophies and the economical resources of the country, find judicious mention. While the Colonel is indignant at the "curiosité brutale" encountered in the West, he pays a grateful tribute to the hospitality of the people. At Pittsburg, the site of Fort Duquesne, he reverts with pride and pathos, to the French domination on this continent, recalls its military successes, and laments its final overthrow. At Mount Vernon he thinks of Lafayette's last visit, and sadly contrasts that period of republican enthusiasm and prosperity with the sanguinary conflict of the passing hour. Indeed, the value and interest of these letters consist in the vivid glimpses they afford of the darkest hour in our history as a free people, and the indirect but authentic testimony thus afforded to the recuperative and conservative power of our institutions and national character. Colonel Pisani accompanied Prince Napoleon in his visits to the camps of both armies, and heard their respective officers express their sentiments freely. Rare in the history of war is such an instance of dual observation apparently candid; seldom has the same pen recorded, within a few hours, impressions of two hostile forces, their aspect, condition, aims, *animus*, and leaders. Rapid as was the journey and hasty the inspection, we have many true and vivid pictures and portraits; and it is interesting to note how gradually but surely the latent resources of the country, the absolute instincts of the popular will, and the improved because sustained force of the Government, are revealed to the mind of this pleasant *raconteur*, who brings home to the American reader the moral crisis, so memorable in the retrospect, which succeeded our premature battle for national honor and life—whose vital current, thus baffled, shrank back to the heart of the republic, only to return with fresh and permanent strength to every vein in the body politic, and vitalize the popular brain and heart with concentrated patriotic scope, insight, and action. Absorbing, however, as was the question of the hour even to a casual sojourner, the physical, social, and economical traits of the country were only more sympathetically examined by the intelligent party of the Prince because of the war cloud that overhung them; and we are transported from inland sea and lonely prairie to the capital of New England, where, says the Colonel, " for the first time I believed myself in Europe," and to quite other society than the governmental circles at Washington or the financial cliques of New York. At Cambridge and Boston, with Agassiz, Felton, Everett, and others, he found congenial minds. The speech of the latter at a parting banquet given the Prince, is noted as a model of tact and rhetoric; while " Vive la France," the refrain of Holmes' song, with happy augury cheered their departure.

CHAPTER X.

AMERICAN TRAVELLERS AND WRITERS.

JOHN AND WILLIAM BARTRAM; MADAME KNIGHT; LEDYARD; CARVER; JEFFERSON; IMLAY; DWIGHT; COXE; INGERSOLL; WALSH; PAULDING; FLINT; CLINTON; HALL; TUDOR; WIRT; COOPER; HOFFMAN; OLMSTED; BRYANT; GOVERNMENT EXPLORATIONS; WASHINGTON; MRS. KIRKLAND; IRVING; AMERICAN ILLUSTRATIVE LITERATURE; BIOGRAPHY; HISTORY; MANUALS; ORATORY; ROMANCE; POETRY; LOCAL PICTURES; EVERETT, HAWTHORNE, CHANNING, ETC.

THERE is one class of travellers in America that have peculiar claims upon native sympathy and consideration; for neither foreign adventure nor royal patronage, nor even private emolument, prompted their journeyings. Natives of the soil, and inspired either by scientific or patriotic enthusiasm—not seldom by both—they strove to make one part of our vast country known to the other; to reveal the natural beauties and resources thereof to their neighbors, and to Europeans; and to promote national development by careful exploration and faithful reports. All the intelligent pioneers of our border civilization more or less enacted the part of beneficent travellers. Public spirit, in colonial and later times, found scope in expeditions which opened paths through the wilderness, tested soil, climate, and natural productions, and estimated the facilities hitherto locked up in primeval solitudes. Washington's early surveys, Boone's first sojourn in the woods of Kentucky, Clinton's visit to Western New York to trace the course of the Erie Canal, are examples of this incidental kind of home travel, so useful to the early statesmen and the political economists. At subsequent periods, the natural features of the Great West were revealed to us by Flint and Hall; New England local and social traits were agreeably reported by Tudor and Dwight; Lewis and Clarke gave the first authentic glimpses of the Rocky Mountains and the adjacent plains, afterward so bravely traversed by Fremont and others; and Schoolcraft gathered up the traditions and the characteristics of those regions still occupied by the aborigines; and while Audubon tracked the feathered creation along the whole Atlantic coast, Percival examined every rood of the soil of Connecticut.

Among the most interesting of the early native travellers in America, are the two Bartrams. Their instinctive fondness for nature, a simplicity and veneration born of the best original Quaker influence, and habits of rural work and meditation, throw a peculiar charm around the memoirs of these kindly and assiduous naturalists, and make the account they have left of their wanderings fresh and genial, notwithstanding the vast progress since made in the natural sciences. John Bartram's name is held in grateful honor by botanists, as "the first Anglo-American who conceived the idea of establishing a botanic garden, native and exotic." He was lured to this enterprise, and its kindred studies, by the habit of collecting American plants and seeds for his friend, Peter Collinson, of London. Encouraged by him, Bartram began to investigate and experiment in this pleasant field of inquiry. He was enabled to confirm Logan's theory in regard to maize, and to illustrate the sexes of plants. From such a humble and isolated beginning, botany expanded in this country into its present elaborate expositions. The first systematic enumeration of American plants was commenced in Holland, by Gronovius, from descriptions furnished by John Clayton, of Virginia. As early as 1732, Mark Catesby, of Virginia, had published a volume on the "Natural History of Carolina, Florida, and the Bahamas." Colden, of New York, corresponded with European botanists, from his sylvan retreat near Newburg. We have already noticed the visit to America of a pupil of Linnæus—Peter Kalm. The labors of Logan, Dr. Mitchell, Dr. Adam Kuhn of Philadelphia, the first professor of botany there, the establishment of Hosack's garden in New York, Dr. Schoeff's, Humphrey Marshall, Dr. Cullen of Berlin, the two Michauxs, Clinton, and the Abbé Correa, promoted the investigation and elucidation of this science in America, until it became associated with the more recent accomplished expositors. But with the earliest impulse and record thereof, the name of John Bartram is delightfully associated; and it is as a naturalist that he made those excursions, the narrative of which retains the charm of ingenuous zeal, integrity, and kindliness. John Bartram was born in Delaware, then Chester County, Penn., in 1699. His great-grandfather had lived and died in Derbyshire, England; his grandfather followed William Penn to the New World, and settled in the State which bears the famous Quaker's name; his father married, "at Darby meeting, Elizabeth Hunt," and had three sons, of whom John, the eldest, inherited from an uncle the farm. His early education was meagre, as far as formal teaching is concerned. He studied the grammar of the ancient languages, and had a taste for the medical art, in which he acquired skill enough to make him a most welcome and efficient physician to the poor. It is probable that, as a simpler, seeking herbs of alleviating virtues, he was won to that love of nature, especially fruits, flowers, and plants, which became almost a ruling passion. But, according to the exigencies of the time and country, Bartram was an agriculturist by vocation, and assiduous therein; yet this did not prevent his indulging his scientific love of nature and his philosophic instinct: he observed and he reflected while occupied about his farm. The laws of vegetation, the loveliness of flowers, the mysteries of growth, were to him a perpetual miracle. To the thrift and simplicity of life common among the original farmers of America, he united an ardent love of knowledge and an admiration of the processes and the products of nature—partly a sentiment and partly a scientific impulse. Purchasing a tract on the banks of the Schuylkill, three miles from Philadelphia, he built, with his own hands, a commodious dwelling, cultivated five acres as a garden, and made continual journeys in search of plants. The place became so attractive, that visitors flocked thither. By degrees he gained acquaintances abroad, established correspondence and a system of exchanges with botanists, and so laid the foundation of botanical enterprise and taste in America. This hale, benign, and wise man, rarely combining in his nature the zeal and observant habitude of the naturalist with the serene self-possession of the Friend, travelled over a large part of the country, explored Ontario, the domain of the Iroquois, the shores and sources of the Hudson, Delaware, Schuylkill, Susquehanna, Alleghany, and San Juan. At the age of seventy he visited Carolina and Florida.

Peter Collinson wrote of him to Colden as a "wonderful natural genius, considering his education, and that he was never out of America, but is a husbandman." "His observations," he adds, "and accounts of all natural productions, are much esteemed here for their accuracy. It is really astonishing what a knowledge the man has attained merely by the force of industry and his own genius."

The journal* of his tour was sent to England, and was published "at the instance of several gentlemen." The preface shows how comparatively rare were authentic books of Travel from natives of America, and how individual were Bartram's zeal and enterprise in this respect. "The inhabitants of all the colonies," says the writer, "have eminently

---

* "Observations on the Climate, Soil, Rivers, Productions, &c., made by John Bartram in his Travels from Pensilvania to Onondaga, Oswego, and the Lake Ontario in Canada; to which is annexed a Curious Account of the Cataracts of Niagara, by Mr. Peter Kalm, a Swedish Gentleman who travelled there," London, 1751.

deserved the character of industrious in agriculture and commerce. I could wish they had as well deserved that of *adventurous inland discoverers ;* in this they have been much outdone by another nation, whose poverty of country and unsettled temper have prompted them to such views of extending their possessions, as our agriculture and commerce make necessary for us to imitate."

The region traversed by Bartram a little more than a century ago, and described in this little volume, printed in the old-fashioned type, and bearing the old imprimatur of Fleet street, is one across and around which many of us have flown in the rail car, conscious of little but alternate meadows, woodland, streams, and towns, all denoting a thrifty and populous district, with here and there a less cultivated tract. Over this domain Bertram moved slowly, with his senses quickened to take in whatsoever of wonder or beauty nature exhibited. He experienced much of the exposure, privation, and precarious resources which befall the traveller to-day on our Western frontier; and it is difficult to imagine that the calm and patient naturalist, as he notes the aspects of nature and the incidents of a long pilgrimage, is only passing over the identical ground which the busy and self-absorbed votaries of traffic and pleasure now daily pass, with scarcely a consciousness of what is around and beside them of natural beauty or productiveness. It is worth while to retrace the steps of Bartram, were it only to realize anew the eternal truth of our poet's declaration, that

> "To him who in the love of nature holds
> Communion with her visible forms, she speaks
> A varied language."

It was on the 3d of July, 1743, that John Bartram set out, with a companion, from his home on the Schuylkill. His narrative of that summer journey from the vicinity of Philadelphia to Lake Ontario, reads like the journal of some intelligent wayfarer in the far West; for the plants and the animals, the face of the country, the traveller's expedients, the Indian camps, and the isolated plantations, bring before us a thinly scattered people and wild region, whereof the present features are associated with all the objects and influences of civilization. Flocks of wild turkeys and leagues of wild grass are early noted; the variety and character of the trees afford a constant and congenial theme; swamps, ridges, hollows alternate; chestnuts, oaks, pines, and poplars are silent but not unwelcome comrades; snakes, as usual, furnish curious episodes: Bartram observed of one, that he "contracted the muscles of his scales when provoked, and that, after the mortal stroke, his splendor diminished." He remarks, at one place, "the impression of shells upon loose stones;" he is annoyed by gnats; and, in an Indian lodge, "hung up his blanket like a hammock, that he may lie out of fleas." He lingers in an old aboriginal orchard well stocked with fruit trees; swims creeks, coasts rivers, lives on duck, deer, and "boiled squashes cold;" smokes a pipe—"a customary civility," he says, "when parties meet." Here he finds "excellent flat whetstones," there "an old beaver dam;" now "roots of ginseng," and again "sulphurous mud;" one hour he is drenched with rain, and another enraptured by the sight of a magnolia; here refreshed by the perfume of a honeysuckle, and there troubled by a yellow wasp. No feature or phase of nature seems to escape him. He notes the earth beneath, the vegetation around, and the sky above; fossils, insects, Indian ceremonies, flowers; the expanse of the "dismal wilderness," the eels roasted for supper, and the moss and fungus as well as locusts and caterpillars. He travelled on foot to the Onondaga, and paddled down in a bark canoe to the Oneida, "down which the Albany traders come to Oswego." He stops at a little town thereabout "of four or five cabins," where the people live "by catching fish and assisting the Albany people to haul their bateaux." In this region of railways and steamboats, such were then the locomotive facilities. Nor less significant of its frontier wilderness is Bartram's description of the spot which has long flourished as the grain depot and forwarding mart of Western New York, where immense warehouses line the river, and fleets of barges, steamers, and schooners cluster along the lake shore. Oswego is identified with his picture mainly by the topography. "On the point formed by the entrance of the river stands the fort, or Trading Castle. It is a strong stone house, encompassed by a stone wall twenty feet high and one hundred and twenty paces round, built of large square stones very curious for their softness. I cut my name in it with my knife. The town consists of about seventy log houses, of which half are in a row near the river; the other half opposite to them, on the other side of a fair, where two streets are divided by a row of posts in the midst, where each Indian has his house to lay his goods, and where any of the traders may traffic with him. This is surely an excellent regulation for preventing the traders from imposing on the Indians. The chief officer in command at the castle keeps a good look-out to see when the Indians come down the lake with their poultry and furs, and sends a canoe to meet them, which conducts them to the castle, to prevent any person enticing them to put ashore privately, treating them with spirituous liquors, and then taking that opportunity of cheating them. Oswego is an infant settlement made by the province of New York, with the noble view of gaining to the crown of Great Britain the command of the five lakes; and the dependence of the Indians in their neighborhood to its subjects, for the benefit of the trade upon them, and of the rivers that empty themselves into them. At present the whole navigation is carried on by Indian bark canoes; but a good Englishman cannot be without hopes of seeing these great lakes one day accustomed to English navigation. It is true, the famous Fall of Niagara is an insurmountable barrier to all passage by water from the Lake Ontario into the Lake Erie. The honor of first discovering these extensive fresh-water seas is certainly due to the French. The traders from New York come hither up the Mohawk River, but generally go by land from Albany to Schenectady; about twenty miles from the Mohawk the carriage is but three miles to the river, that falls into the Oneida Lake, which discharges itself into the Onondaga River. It is evident, from the face of the earth, that the water of Lake Ontario has considerably diminished."

It is interesting to contrast the vague and timid conjectures of Bartram with the subsequent facts in the development of that intercourse between the lakes, the far interior, and the seacoast, whence dates so much of the commercial and agricultural prosperity not only of the State of New York, but of the metropolis, and the vast regions of the West. Bartram observed, at Oswego, "a kitchen garden and a graveyard to the southwest of the castle," which reminds him that "the neighborhood of this lake is esteemed unhealthful." This opinion, however, refers only to a large swampy district, and not to the elevated site of the present town. Draining and population have long since redeemed even the low lands from this insalubrity; and now, in consequence of the constant winds from that immense body of pure water, Oswego enjoys a better degree of health than any place in Western New York. Its summer climate is preferable to that of any inland city of the State. Bartram notes many traits of Indian life there—the girls playing with beans, and the squaws addicted to rum, and "drying huckleberries." As usual, he expatiates on the trees, and especially admires specimens of the arbor vitæ and white lychinus. The last entry in this quaintly pleasing journal is characteristic of the writer's domestic and religious faith, and of the adventurous nature of a tour which then occupied seven or eight weeks, and is now practicable in a few hours. Under date of August 19th, he writes: " Before sunset I had the pleasure of seeing my own home and family, and found them in good health; and with a sincere mind I returned thanks to the Almighty Power that had preserved us all."

At an advanced age Bartram embarked at Philadelphia for Charleston, S. C., and went thence, by land, through a portion of Carolina and Georgia, to St. Augustine, in Florida. While there, he received the appointment of botanist and naturalist to the king of England, with directions to trace the San Juan River to its source. Leaving St. Augustine, he embarked in a boat at Picolata, ascended and descended that beautiful river nearly four hundred miles, making careful observations not only as to distances, width, depth, currents, shores, &c., but recording all the physical facts, vegetable and animal. The full and accurate report thereof he sent to the Board of Trade and Plantations, in England. The labor of love this exploration proved to him, may be imagined from the enthusiastic terms in which Florida, its coast, its flowers, and its climate, are described by subsequent naturalists, especially Audubon and Agassiz. The latter thinks the combination of tropical and western products and aspects there unrivalled in the world. It is, indeed, a paradise for the naturalist, from its wonderful coral reefs to its obese turtles, and from its orange groves, reminding the traveller of Sicily, to its palms, breathing of the East. When old John Bartram, in his lonely boat, glided amid its fertile solitudes, it was a virgin soil, not only to the step of civilization, but the eye of science; and later and far more erudite students of nature have recognized the honest zeal and intelligent observation wherewith the venerable and assiduous botanist of the Schuylkill recorded the wonders and the beauty of the scene. But it was amid his farm and flowers that Bartram appeared to memorable advantage. His manners, habits, and appearance, his character and conversation, seem to have embodied, in a remarkable manner, the idea of a rural citizen of America as cherished by the republican enthusiasts of Europe. The comfort, simplicity, self-respect, native resources, and benign faith and feeling incident to a free country life, religious education, and a new land, were signally manifest in the home of the Quaker botanist. A Russian gentleman, who visited him in 1769, describes these impressions in a letter. He was attracted to Bartram's house from knowing him as a correspondent of French and Swiss botanists, and even of Queen Ulrica, of Sweden. Approaching his home, the neatness of the buildings, the disposition of fields, fences, and trees, the perfect order and the prosperous industry apparent, won the stranger's heart at a glance. Nor was he less charmed with the greeting he received from "a woman at the door, in a simple but neat dress," in answer to his inquiry for the master. "If thee will step in and take a chair, I will send for him." He preferred walking over the farm. Following the Schuylkill, as it wound among the meadows, he reached a place where ten men were at work, and asked for Mr. Bartram; whereupon one of the group, "an elderly man, with wide trousers and a large leather apron on, said, "My name is Bartram; dost thee want me?" "Sir," replied the visitor, "I came on purpose to converse, if you can be spared from your labor." "Very easily," he replied; and, returning to the house, the host changed his clothes, reappeared, conducted his guest to the garden, and they passed many hours in a conversation so delectable, that the foreign visitor grows enthusiastic in his delight at this unique combination of labor and knowledge, simplicity of life and study of nature. One remark of Bartram's recalls a similar one of Sir Walter Scott's, as to the best results of literary fame; and it is a striking coincidence in the experience of two of nature's noblemen, so widely separated in their pursuits and endowments: "The greatest advantage," observed the rural philosopher to his Russian visitor, "which I receive from what thee callest my botanical fame, is the pleasure which it often procures me in receiving the visits of friends and foreigners." Summoned to dinner by a bell, they entered a large hall where was spread a long table, occupied, at the lower end, by negroes and hired men, and, at the other, by the family and their guest. The venerable father and his wife "declined their heads in prayer"—which "grace before meat," says the visitor, was "divested of the tedious cant of some, and ostentatious style of others." Nor was he less charmed with the plain but substantial fare, the cordial manners, the amenities of the household, and the dignity of its head. Madeira was produced; an Æolian harp vibrated melodiously to the summer breeze; and they talked botany and agriculture to their heart's content. The knowledge of Bartram surprised his auditor. He found a coat of arms amid all this primitive life, and learned that it was possible to unite the simplicity of American with the associations of European domiciles. To him, the scene and the character whence emanated its best charm, were a refreshing novelty; and he endeavors to solve the mystery by frankly questioning his urbane host, whose story was clear enough. " 'What a shame,' said my mind, or something that inspired my mind," observed the latter, in explaining the first impulse to his career, " 'that thou shouldst have employed so many years in tilling the earth, and destroying so many flowers and plants, without being acquainted with their structure and their uses.' By steady application," he added, " for several years, I have acquired a pretty general knowledge of every plant and tree to be found on this continent." But it was the social phenomena of Bartram's house that impressed " the stranger within his gates," not less than the " pursuit of knowledge under difficulties;" the skilful method of the farming operation; the deference, without servility, of the workmen; the gentle bearing of the negroes, and the serene order and dignity, yet cheerfulness of the household, struck the *habitué* of courts as a new phase of civilization. He became enamored of the Friends, attributing much of what he admired in Bartram and his surroundings to their influence. He sojourned among them in the vicinity, attended their meetings, and, after two months thus passed, declared " they were the golden days of my riper years." Few and far between are such instances of primitive character and association now exhibited to the stranger's view in our over-busy and extravagant land. It is pleasant to look back upon those days, and that venerable, industrious, benign philosopher; to remember his pleasant letters to and from Franklin, Bard, Logan, Catesby, and Colden at home, and Gronovius, Sir Hans Sloane, Collinson, and Fothergill abroad; the medal he received from " a society of gentlemen in Edinburgh;" the seeds he sent Michaux and Jefferson; the books sent him by Linnæus. It is pleasant to retrace that peaceful and wise career to its painless and cheerful close—the career of one whose great ambition was the hope, as he said, "of discovering and introducing into my native country some original productions of nature which might be useful to society;" and who could honestly declare, "My chief happiness consisted in tracing and admiring the infinite power, majesty, and perfection of the great Almighty Creator." Philosopher as he was, he never coveted old age; dreaded to become a burden; hoped "there would be little delay when death comes;" and deemed the great rule of life "to do justice, love mercy, and walk humbly before God." Cheerful and active to the age of seventy-eight, he died content, September 22, 1777. His name stands next to Franklin's in the record of the American Philosophical Society. The war of the Revolution shortened his days; as the approach of the royal army, after the battle of Brandywine, agitated him with fear that his "darling garden," the "nursling of half a century," might be laid waste.

Bartram was a genuine Christian philosopher. His healthful longevity was mainly owing to his temperance and out-of-door life, the tranquil pleasures he cultivated, and the even temper he maintained. Hospitable, industrious, and active, both in body and mind, he never found any time he could not profitably employ. Upright in form, animation and sensibility marked his features. He was "incapable of dissimulation," and deemed "improving conversation and bodily exercise" the best pastimes. Meditative, a reader of Scripture, he was born a Quaker, but his creed was engraved by his own hand over the window of his study—a simple but fervent recognition of God.

It is as delightful as it is rare to behold the best tastes and influence of a man reproduced and prolonged in his descendants; and this exceptional trait of American life we find in the career and character of John Bartram's son William, who was born at the Botanic Garden, Kingsessing, Pennsylvania, in 1739, and died in 1823. One of his early tutors was Charles Thomson, so prominent in the Continental Congress. He began life as a merchant, but was formed, by nature, for the naturalist and traveller he became. A letter from John Bartram to his brother, dated in 1761, alludes to this son as if his success in business was doubtful: "I and most of my son Billy's relations are concerned that he never writes how his trade affairs succeed. We are afraid he doth not make out as well as he expected." Having accompanied his father in the expedition to East Florida, he settled on the banks of the St. John River, after assisting in the exploration of that region. In 1774 he returned to his home in Pennsylvania; and soon after, at the instance of Dr. Fothergill, of London, made a second scientific tour through Florida. His observations on the Creek and Cherokee Indians there made were written out in 1789, and have been recently reprinted from the original manuscript, by the American Ethnological Society. He aided Wilson in his ornithological investigations, and Barton in his "Elements of Botany," of which science he was elected professor by the university of his native State. Dunlap the painter, and Brockden Brown the novelist, refer to him with interest; and the former has left a personal description of him, as he appeared when visited by the writer, whereby we recognize the identical simplicity of life, brightness of mind, industry, kindliness, and love of nature which distinguished his father. "His countenance," says Dunlap, "was expressive of benignity and happiness. With a rake in his hand, he was breaking the clods of earth in a tulip bed. His hat was old, and flapped over his face. His coarse shirt was seen near his neck, as he wore no cravat. His waistcoat and breeches were both of leather, and his shoes were tied with leather strings. We approached and accosted him. He ceased his work, and entered into conversation with the ease and politeness of nature's nobleman." A similar impression was made upon another visitor in 1819, who informs us that the white hair of William Bartram, as he stood in his garden and talked of Rittenhouse and Franklin, of botany and of nature, gave him a venerable look, which was in keeping with his old-fashioned dress, his genial manners, and his candid and wise talk. He was elected professor of botany in the University of Pennsylvania in 1782, and "made known and illustrated many of the most curious and beautiful plants of North America," as well as published the most complete list of its birds, before Wilson. "The latest book I know," wrote Coleridge, "written in the spirit of the old travellers, is Bartram's account of his tour in the Floridas." It was published in Philadelphia in 1791, and in London the following year.* The style is more finished than his father could command, more fluent and glowing, but equally informed with that genuineness of feeling and directness of purpose which give the most crude writing an indefinable but actual moral charm. The American edition was "embellished with copperplates," the accuracy and beauty of which, however inferior to more recent illustrations of natural history among us, form a remarkable contrast to the coarse paper and inelegant type. These incongruities, however, add to the quaint charm of the work, by reminding us of the time when it appeared, and of the limited means and encouragement then available to the naturalist, compared to the sumptuous expositions which the splendid volumes of Audubon and Agassiz have since made familiar. In the details as well as in the philosophy of his subject, Bartram is eloquent. He describes the "hollow leaves that hold water," and how "seeds are carried and softened in birds' stomachs." He has a sympathy for the "cub bereaved of its bear mother;" patiently watches an enormous yellow spider capture a humblebee, and describes the process minutely. The moonlight on the palms; the notes of the mockingbird in the luxuriant but lonely woods; the flitting oriole and the

---

* "Travels through North and South Carolina, Georgia, East and West Florida, the Cherokee Country, the extensive Territories of the Muscogulges, or Creek Confederacy, and the Country of the Choctaws; containing an Account of the Soil and Natural Productions of those Regions, together with Observations on the Manners of the Indians," embellished with copperplates (turtle, leaf, &c.), by William Bartram, Philadelphia, 1791, London, 1792.

cooing doves; the mullet in the crystal brine, and the moan of the surf at night; the laurel's glossy leaves, the canes of the brake, the sand of the beach, goldfish, sharks, lagoons, parroquets, the cypress, ash, and hickory, Indian mounds, buffalo licks, trading houses, alligators, mosquitos, squirrels, bullfrogs, trout, mineral waters, turtles, birds of passage, pelicans, and aquatic plants, are the themes of his narrative; and become, in his fresh and sympathetic description, vivid and interesting even to readers who have no special knowledge of, and only a vague curiosity about nature. The affluence and variety in the region described, are at once apparent. Now and then, something like an adventure, or a pleasant talk with one of his hospitable or philosophical hosts, varies the botanical nomenclature; or a fervid outbreak of feeling, devotional or enjoyable, gives a human zest to the pictures of wild fertility. Curiously do touches of pedantry alternate with those of simplicity; the matter-of-fact tone of Robinson Crusoe, and the grave didactics of Rasselas; a scientific statement after the manner of Humboldt, and an anecdote or interview in the style of Boswell. It is this very absence of sustained and prevalence of desultory narrative, that make the whole so real and pleasant. The Florida of that day had its trading posts, surveyors, hunters, Indian emigrants, and isolated plantations, such as still mark our border settlements; but nowhere on the continent did nature offer a more "infinite variety;" and the mere catalogue of her products, especially when written with zest and knowledge, formed an interesting work, such as intelligent readers at home and abroad relished with the same avidity with which we greet the record of travel given to the world by a Layard or a Kane, only that the restricted intercourse and limited education of that day circumscribed the readers as they did the authors.

In 1825 was published, from the original manuscript, "The Private Journal kept by Madame Knight; or, A Journey from Boston to New York in the year 1704." This lady was regarded as a superior person in character and culture.

She indulged in rhyme, and had a vein of romance, as is evident from her descriptions of nature, especially of the effect of moonlight, and the aspect of the forest at night. This curious specimen of a private diary gives us a vivid and authentic description of the state of the country, and the risks and obstacles of travel in a region now as populous, secure, and easy of access and transit as any part of the world. A fortnight was then occupied in a journey which is now performed several times a day in seven or eight hours. It seems that the fair Bostonian, even at that remote period, tinctured with the literary proclivities that signalize the ladies of her native city to this day, had certain business requiring attention at New Haven and New York, and, after much hesitation, formed the heroic resolution of visiting those places in person. The journey was made on horseback. She took a guide from one baiting place to another, and was indebted to the "minister of the town," to the "post," and relatives along the route, for hospitality and escort. She often passed the night in miserable inns—if such they can be called—and was the constant victim of hard beds, indigestible or unsavory food, danger from fording streams, isolated and rough tracks, and all the alarms and embarrassments of an "unprotected female" crossing a partially settled country. Narraganset was a pathless wild. At New Haven she notes the number and mischievousness of the Indians, and that the young men wore ribbons, as a badge of dexterity in shooting. She satirizes the phraseology of the people there, such as "Dreadful pretty!" "Law, you!" and "I vow!" and criticizes the social manners as faulty in two respects—too great familiarity with the slaves, and a dangerous facility of divorce; yet, she remarks, though often ridiculous, the people "have a large portion of mother wit, and sometimes larger than those brought up in cities." Pumpkin and Indian bread, pork and cabbage, are the staple articles of food, varied, at "Northwalk," by fried venison. Of Fairfield she says: "They have abundance of sheep, whose very dung brings them great gain, with part of which they pay their parson's sallery; and they grudge that, preferring their dung before their minister." She is charmed with the "vendues" at New York, where they "give drinks;" and mentions that the "fireplaces have no jambs;" and "the bricks in some of the houses are of divers colors, and laid in checkers, and, being glazed, look very agreeable." "Their diversions," she says of the inhabitants, "is riding in sleys about three or four miles out of town, where they have houses of entertainment at a place called the Bowery."

Nor, among the early explorers of New England, can we fail to remember the intrepid John Ledyard, Captain Cook's companion and historiographer, and one of the bravest pioneers of African travel. Born in 1751, he ran away from the frontier college of Hanover, and fraternized with the aboriginal Six Nations in Canada. Returning to his native region, he cut down a tree, and made a canoe three feet wide and fifty long, wherein, with bear skins and provisions, he floated down the Connecticut River, stopping at night, and reading, at intervals, Ovid and the Greek Testament. Interrupted in his lonely voyage by Bellows' Falls, he effected a portage through the aid of farmers and oxen, and, continuing his course, reached Hartford. This exploration of a river then winding through the wilderness, was inspired by the identical love of adventure and thirst for discovery which afterward lured him to the North of Europe, around the world with Cook, and into the deserts of Africa.

Captain John Carver traversed an extent of country of at least seven thousand miles, in two years and a half, at a period when such a pilgrimage required no little courage and patience. He was induced to undertake this long tour partly from a love of adventure, and, in no small degree, from public spirit and the desire to gain and impart useful information. Carver was to be seen at the *reunions* of Sir Joseph Banks, where his acquaintance with the natural productions of this continent made him a welcome guest; and his straitened circumstances won the sympathy of that benign *savant*, who promoted the sale of his "Travels," which were published in London,* and passed through three editions. This work contains many facts of interest to economists and scientific men not then generally known. The narrative refers to the years 1766, '67, and '68. Carver also published a "Treatise on the Culture of Tobacco." The region of country described by this writer was then attracting great inquiry on account of the prevalent theories regarding a Northwest Passage. Carver went from Boston to Green Bay *via* Albany, and explored the Indian country as far as the Falls of St. Anthony; following, in a great degree, the course of Father Hennepin in 1680. He has much to say of the aborigines, their ceremonies, character and vocabulary, of the phenomena of the great lakes, and of the birds, fishes, trees, and reptiles; although, as a reporter of natural history, some of his snake stories excited distrust. Carver's enterprise, intelligence, and misfortunes, however, commend him to favorable remembrance. He was born at Stillwater, Connecticut, and was a captain in the French war. Dr. Lettsom wrote an interesting memoir of him, which was appended to the posthumous edition of his writings; and it is a memorable fact, that the penury in which this brave seeker after knowledge died, as described by his biographer, in connection with his unrecognized claims as an *employé* of the English Government, induced the establishment of that noble charity, the Literary Fund.

One of the French legation in the United States, in 1781, requested Jefferson to afford him specific information in regard to the physical resources and character of the country. This course is habitual with the representatives of European Governments, and has proved of great advantage in a commercial point of view; while political economists and historical writers have found in the archives of diplomacy invaluable materials thus secured. M. Marbois could not have applied to a better man for certain local facts interesting and

---

* "Travels through the Interior Parts of North America, in 1766–'68," by John Carver, Captain of a Company of Provincial Troops in the late French War, 8vo., third edition, portrait, maps, and plates, London, 1781.

useful in themselves, and as yet but partially recorded, than Thomas Jefferson, who was a good observer of nature, as far as details are concerned, and accurate in matters where taste and opinion were not essential. His love of such inquiries had led him to record whatever statistical knowledge or curious phenomena came under his observation. As a planter, he had ample opportunity to observe the laws of nature, the methods of culture, and the means of progress open to a circumspect agriculturist. He had read much in natural history, and was fond of scientific conversation; so that, with the books then at command, and the truths then recognized in these spheres, he was in advance of most of his countrymen. The inquiries of Marbois induced him to elaborate and arrange the data he had collected, and two hundred copies of the work were privately printed, under the title of "Notes on Virginia,"* a bad translation of which was soon after published in Paris. The reader of Jefferson's collected writings, whose taste has been formed by the later models of his vernacular authors, will not be much impressed with his literary talents or culture. In eloquence and argumentative power he was far inferior to Hamilton. His memoir of himself has little of the frank simplicity and *naïve* attraction that have made Franklin's Life a household book; while the fame of the Declaration of Independence wholly eclipses any renown derived from the wisdom and occasional vivacity of his correspondence, or the curious knowledge displayed in his "Notes" on his native State. The eminence of the writer in political history and official distinction, the extraordinary circumstances amid which he lived and acted, the part he took in a great social and civic experiment, his representative character in the world of opinion, the coincidence of his death with the anniversary of the most illustrious deed of his life, and with the demise of his predecessor in the Presidential office and political opponent, all throw a peculiar interest and impart a personal significance to what his pen recorded; so

* "Notes on the State of Virginia," 8vo., map, London, 1787.

that, although there is comparatively little of original scientific value in his "Notes on Virginia," they are a pleasing memorial of his assiduous observation, and are characteristic of his turn of mind and habits of thought. It has been justly said of the work, that "politics, commerce, and manufactures are here treated of in a satisfactory and instructive manner, but with rather too much the air of philosophy." The description of the Natural Bridge, and of the scenery of Harper's Ferry and the Shenandoah Valley, as well as of other remarkable natural facts, drew many strangers to Virginia; and the "Notes" are often quoted by travellers, agriculturists, and philosophers.

Captain Imlay, of the American army, is considered the best of the early authorities in regard to the topography of the Western country. The original London edition of his "Topographical Description of the Western Territory of North America,"* is the result of observations made between 1792 and 1797. The third edition is much enhanced in value as a reference, by including the works of Filson, Hutchins, and other kindred material. In 1793, this author embodied another and most interesting phase of his experience in that then but partially known region, in a novel called "The Emigrants," which contains genuine pictures of life.

The "Travels in New England and New York"† of Timothy Dwight are probably as little read by the present generation as his poetry; and yet both, fifty or sixty years ago, exerted a salutary influence, and are still indicative of the benign intellectual activity of a studious, religious, and patriotic man, whose name is honorably associated with early American literature, as well as with the educational progress

---

* "Topographical Description of the Western Territory of North America," by Gilbert Imlay, second edition, with large additions, 8vo., with correct maps of the Western Territories, 1793. Comprises a valuable mass of materials for the early history of the Western country, embodying the entire works of Filson, Hutchins, and various other tracts and original narratives.

† "Travels in New England and New York," by Timothy Dwight, illustrated with maps and plates, 4 thick vols., 8vo., 1823.

and theological history of New England. A descendant of Jonathan Edwards, a chaplain in the army of the Revolution, a member of the Connecticut Legislature, farmer, clergyman, scholar, patriot, and bard, whether giving religious sanction to his brave countrymen in their struggle for freedom, toiling for the support of his family, teaching, rhyming, talking, or filling, with assiduous fidelity, the office of President of Yale College, Dwight was one of the most useful, consistent, and respected men of letters of his day in America. Idolized by his pupils, admired by his fellow citizens, and the favorite companion of Trumbull, Barlow, and the elder Buckminster, his simple style of life harmonized nobly with his urbane self-respect, intellectual tastes, and public spirit. His revision of the Psalms of Watts was a service practically recognized by all sects. The conscientiousness which formed the basis of his character, not less than the exigencies of his life, promoted habits of versatile and indomitable industry. In youth, his ardent nature found vent in verse, much of which, especially some heroic couplets, have the ring and emphasis of a muse enamored of nature and fired with patriotism. His vacations, while President of Yale, were devoted to travel, not in the casual manner so usual at the period, but with a view to explore carefully and record faithfully. It is true that, compared to the scientific tourists of our day, Dwight was but imperfectly equipped for a complete and minute investigation of nature; but, keenly observant, intelligent, and honest, loving knowledge for its own sake, and eager to diffuse as well as to acquire practical information, we find in this voluntary choice of recreation, at that period, a signal evidence of his superior mind.

Many comparatively unknown regions of New England and New York Dwight traversed on horseback, communicating the results of his journeys in letters, which were not given to the public until several years after his death. We know of no better reference for accounts of the prominent men and the economical and social traits of the Eastern

States, at the period, than may be gleaned from Dwight's Travels. They preserve some original features and facts which a locomotive age has since swept away. They furnish an interesting picture of life in New England and New York, when the towns therein were scattered and lonely, the agricultural resources but partially developed, and the primitive tastes and customs yet dominant. Although seldom read, this early record of travel over scenes so familiar and unsuggestive to us, will be precious to the future delineator of manners, and even to the speculative economist and philosopher. A future Macaulay would find in them many elements for a picturesque or statistical description; for in such details, when authentic and wisely chosen, exist the materials of history. Among the earliest modern accounts, at all elaborate, of the White Mountains, Lake George, Niagara, and the Catskills, are those gleaned by Timothy Dwight, in his lonely wanderings at a time when, to travel at all, was to isolate oneself, and be inspired with an individual aim, and the "solitary horseman" was a significant fact, instead of a resource of fiction. It was Dwight's habit to take copious notes and accumulate local facts, which he afterward wrote out and illustrated at his leisure. His "Travels" were first published in 1821. Their range would now be thought quite limited; but, in view of the meagre facilities for moving about then enjoyed, and the comparative absence of enterprise in the way of journeys of observation, these intelligent comments and descriptions must have been very useful and entertaining, as they are now valuable and agreeable. Robert Southey, whose literary taste was singularly catholic, and who had labored enough in the field of authorship to duly estimate everything that contributes to the use or beauty of the vocation, wrote of Dwight's "Travels," in the *Quarterly Review:*

"The work before us, though the humblest in its pretences, is the most important of his writings, and will derive additional value from time, whatever may become of his poems and sermons. A wish to gratify those who, a hundred years hence, might feel curiosity concerning his native country, made him resolve to preserve a faithful description of its existing state. He made notes, therefore, in the summer vacation tours, and collected facts on the spot. The remarks upon natural history are those of an observant and sagacious man, who makes no pretensions to science; they are more interesting, therefore, than those of a merely scientific traveller."

Here we have another striking illustration of the conservative worth of facts in literature over the fruits of speculation or of fancy, unless the latter are redeemed by rare originality. Only the most gifted poets and philosophers continue to be read and admired; while the humblest gleaner among the facts of life and nature, if honest and assiduous, is remembered and referred to with gratitude and respect.

As Commissioner of the Revenue, Tench Coxe, of Philadelphia, investigated and wrote upon several economical interests of the country, and, in 1794, published his "View of the United States of America," in a series of papers written in 1787–'94.* There is much statistical information in regard to trade and manufactures during the period indicated. The progress of the country at that time is authentically described, and the resources of Pennsylvania exhibited. Two chapters of the work are curious—one on the "distilleries of the United States," and the other giving "information relative to maple sugar, and its possible value in some parts of the United States." The facts communicated must have been useful to emigrants at that period; and, in summing up the condition and prospects of the country, a remarkable increase of foreign commerce, shipbuilding, and manufactures, in the ten years succeeding the War of Independence, is shown. The author congratulates his fellow citizens that "the importation of slaves has ceased;" that "no evils have resulted from an entire separation of church and state, and of ecclesiastical from the civil power;" that Europeans "have rather accommodated themselves to the American modes of life, than pursued or introduced those of Europe;" that no monarchy over

---

* "View of the United States of America," in a series of papers written between 1787 and 1794, by Tench Coxe, 8vo., Philadelphia and London, 1795.

"an equally numerous people has been so well able to maintain internal tranquillity;" and that the "terrifying reports of danger from Indians" are unfounded. The work is a valuable statistical landmark of national development.

In the year 1810, a book on America* by a native author excited much attention, partly from the special facts it recounted, and partly because of a humorous vein, wherein European criticisms and travellers' complaints were met and refuted. The volume was timely, in some respects quite able, and often piquant. The literary artifice adopted served also to win the curious. It was pretended that Inciquin, a Jesuit, during a residence in the United States, had written numerous letters descriptive of the country, and in reply to current aspersions by prejudiced visitors—a portion of this correspondence having been discovered on a bookseller's stall, at Antwerp, and the "packet of letters" being published on this side of the water as the work of some unknown foreigner. A distinct account of political parties, about which great misapprehensions then prevailed in Great Britain, is given; numerous falsehoods then prevalent regarding the social condition and habits of the people are exposed; and the hypercritical and fastidious objections propagated by shallow writers are cleverly ridiculed; while a more kindly and just estimate of American manners and culture is affirmed. The idea of the book was excellent; but its execution is not commensurate therewith, being comparatively destitute of that literary tact and graceful vivacity essential to the complete success of such an experiment. It, however, served a good though temporary purpose, more adequately fulfilled by Walsh's "Appeal." In his account of American literature, the author, at that date, had but a meagre catalogue to illustrate his position, Marshall's "Life of Washington" and Barlow's "Columbiad" being most prominent. Perhaps the political information was the most important element of the work; and the intimate acquaintance with our

---

* "Inciquin the Jesuit's Letters, during a late Residence in the United States of America," New York, 1810, 8vo.

system of government, and the appreciation of the social condition of the republic manifest throughout, suggest that, with the attraction of a more pleasing style, "Inciquin's Letters" might have claimed and won a more permanent interest. It soon became known that they were written by Charles J. Ingersoll, of Philadelphia, a political *littérateur* and well-known citizen, who has since figured in public life, and died within a few years. The *London Quarterly*, with characteristic unfairness, assailed the work, which malicious criticism was promptly answered by Paulding.

The calumnies of the English bookwrights and reviewers were ably confuted also by Irving, Dwight, and Everett; but the most efficient and elaborate reply, at this time, emanated from Robert Walsh, whose industry in the collection of facts, practice as a writer, and familiarity with history and literature, made him an able champion. He had long entertained the idea of a carefully prepared work—historical, economical, and critical—on the United States, and had arranged part of the materials therefor. A peculiarly bitter and unjust article, ostensibly a review of "Inciquin's Letters," induced Mr. Walsh to abandon, for the time, his intended work, in favor of a less elaborate but most seasonable one. He did not attach undue importance to these attacks, but, like all educated and experienced men, perceived that the wilful misrepresentations and vulgar prejudice with which they abounded, insured their ephemeral reputation, and proved them the work of venal hands; yet, in common with the best of his countrymen, he recognized, in the popularity of such shallow and often absurd tirades, in the demand as a literary ware of such aspersions upon the name, fame, and character of the republic, a degree of ignorance and prejudice in England, which it became a duty to leave without excuse, by a clear and authentic statement of facts. Accordingly, his "Appeal from the Judgments of Great Britain" *

---

* "An Appeal from the Judgments of Great Britain respecting the United States, &c., with Strictures on the Calumnies of British Writers," by Robert Walsh, 8vo., Philadelphia, 1819.

appeared in 1819. Its political bias made it somewhat unacceptable to a portion of his countrymen; and, with the more full exposition of our intellectual resources which the growth of American literature has subsequently induced, it is obvious that he might have made the argument in this regard more copious. But, as a whole, it was admirably done. Much of the testimony adduced is English; and the chapters on the British maladministration of the colonies, on the hostility of the British Reviews, and on slavery, are of present significance and permanent interest. It was a timely vindication of our country, and so absolutely fixed the lie of malice upon many of the flippant writers in question, and the bigotry of prejudice upon their acquiescent readers, that an obvious improvement was soon apparent, especially in the Reviews—more care as to correctness in data, and less arrogance in tone. The work is a landmark to which we can now refer with advantage, to estimate the degree and kind of progress attained by the United States at the period; and it serves no less effectually as a memorial of the literary, political, and social injustice of England.

In addition to Irving, Ingersoll, Walsh, Everett, and Cooper, many of our citizens have "come to the rescue" abroad, in less memorable but not less seasonable and efficient ways. Through the journals of Europe, many a mistake has been corrected, many a prejudice dispelled, and many a right vindicated by public-spirited and intelligent citizens of the republic. In *Blackwood's Magazine*, 1823-'6, for instance, are several articles on American writers and subjects, wherein, with much critical nonchalance and broad assertion, there are many facts and statements fitted to enlighten and interest in regard to this country. They were written by John Neal, of Portland, whose dramatic but extravagant and rapidly concocted novels and poems, by their spirit and native flavor, had won their author fame, and gained him literary employment abroad; where he became a disciple of Bentham, and aspired, despite strong personal likes and dislikes, to be an impartial *raconteur* and reporter of his country, in a British periodical of wide circulation and influence.

No Southern State has been so fully described by early and later writers, as Virginia. As the home of Washington and Jefferson, it attracted visitors when the journey thither from the East was far from easy or convenient. The partially aristocratic origin of the first settlers gave a distinctive and superior social tone to the region. Hunting, political speculation, convivial courtesies, and the Episcopal Church, were local features whereby the life of the Virginia planter assimilated with that of English manorial habits and prestige. Moreover, a certain hue of romance invests the early history of the State, associated as it is with the gallantry and culture of Sir Walter Raleigh and the self-devotion of Pocahontas. The very name of "Old Dominion" endeared Virginia to many more than her own children; and that other title of "Mother of Presidents" indicates her prominence in our republican annals. Novelists have delighted to lay their scenes within her borders—to describe the shores of the Rappahannock, the ancient precincts of Jamestown, the beautiful valley of the Shenandoah, and the picturesque attractions of the Blue Ridge; as well as to elaborate the traits of character and the phases of social life fondly and proudly ascribed to the country. Lovers of humor find an unique comic side to the nature of the Virginia negro—one of whose popular melodies plaintively evinces the peculiar attachment which bound the domestic slave to the soil and family; while the countless anecdotes of John Randolph, and other eccentric country gentlemen, indicate that the independent and provincial life of the planter there was remarkably productive of original and quaint characteristics. Naturalists expatiated on the wonders of the Natural Bridge; valetudinarians flocked to the Sulphur Springs; and lovers of humanity made pilgrimages to Mount Vernon. 'There Washington, a young surveyor, became familiar with toil, exposure, and responsibility, and passed the crowning years of his spotless career; there he was born, died, and is buried; there Patrick Henry roamed and mused, until the hour struck for him to rouse, with invincible eloquence, the instinct of free citizenship; there Marshall drilled his yeomen for battle, and disciplined his judicial mind by study; there Jefferson wrote his "Political Philosophy" and "Notes of a Naturalist;" there Burr was tried, Clay was born, Wirt pleaded, Nat Turner instigated the Southampton massacre, Lord Fairfax hunted, and John Brown was hung, Randolph bitterly jested, and Pocahontas won a holy fame; and there treason reared its hydra head, and profaned the consecrated soil with vulgar insults and savage cruelty; there was the last battle scene of the Revolution, and the first of the Civil War; there is Mount Vernon, Monticello, and Yorktown; and there, also, are Manassas, Bull Run, and Fredericksburg; there is the old graveyard of Jamestown, and the modern Golgotha of Fair Oaks; there is the noblest tribute art has reared to Washington, and the most loathsome prisons wherein despotism wreaked vengeance on patriotism; and on that soil countless martyrs have offered up their lives to conserve the national existence.

What Wirt, Kennedy, Irving, the author of "Cousin Veronica," and others, have written of rural and social life in Virginia, from the genial sports of "Swallow Barn" to the hunting frolics at Greenway Court—what Virginia was in the days of Henry and Marshall, she essentially appeared to Chastellux and to Paulding. It is nearly fifty years since the latter's "Letters from the South"* were written; and, glancing over them to-day, what confirmation do recent events yield to many of his observations! This is one of the unconscious advantages derived from faithful personal insight and records. However familiar the scene and obsolete the book, as such, therein may be found the material for political inference or authentic speculation. "It seems the destiny of this country," writes Paulding from Virginia, in 1816, "that power should travel to the West;" and again, "the blacks diminish in number as you travel toward the

* "Letters from the South," by a Northern Man.

mountains;" and elsewhere, "I know not whether you have observed it, but all the considerable States south of New York have their little distrusts and separate local interests, or rather local feelings, operating most vehemently. The east and west section of the State are continually at sixes and sevens. The mountains called the Blue Ridge not only form the natural, but the political division of Virginia." Recent events have confirmed emphatically the truth of this observation; and what Paulding says of the people, agrees with previous and subsequent testimony—"gallant, high-spirited, lofty, lazy sort of beings, much more likely to spend money than to earn it." We have noted the evidence of earlier travellers as to the decadence of slavery in Virginia, before the invention of the cotton-gin made the institution profitable; and our own countryman, writing nearly fifty years ago, quotes the remark of a farmer's daughter: "I want father to buy a black woman; but he says they are more trouble than they are worth." Even at that period, the primitive methods of travel continued through the Southern country much as they are described by the French officers who made visits to the South immediately after or during the Revolutionary war. "Travellers' Rests," says Paulding, "are common in this part of the world, where they receive pay for a sort of family fare provided for strangers. The house, in frequent instances, is built of square pine logs lapping at the four corners, and the interstices filled up with little blocks of wood plastered over and cemented." The ridges of mountain ribbed with pine trees, the veins of copper and iron revealed by the oxydated soil, the nutritious "hoecake," the marvellous caves and Natural Bridge, the comical negroes, the salubrious mineral springs, the occasional hunts such as cheered the hospitable manor of Fairfax, the conclaves of village politicians, the horse racing, cock fighting, the hard drinking, the famous "reel" of the dancers and turkey shooting of the riflemen, were then as characteristic of the Old Dominion as when the judicial mind of her Marshall, the eloquence of her Henry, the eccentricities of her Randolph, or the matchless patriotism of her Washington made her actual social life illustrious. The field of Yorktown, the memorable "Raleigh tavern," and the ubiquitous "first family," had not ceased to be favorite landmarks and jokes, any more than tobacco the staple or slavery the problem of this fertile but half-developed region and incongruous community.

Paulding gave vent to his indignant patriotism, when the second war with England broke out, in "The Diverting History of John Bull and Brother Jonathan,"* in the manner of Arbuthnot. In this work, the two countries are made to figure as individuals, and the difficulties between the two nations are exhibited as a family quarrel. England's course is the subject of a severe but not acrimonious satire. It was republished abroad and illustrated at home, and the idea still further developed in a subsequent story entitled "Uncle Sam and his Boys."

A visit to Ohio from New England was formidable as late as 1796, when Morris Cleveland, whose name is now borne by the city where then spread a wilderness, accompanied the survey as agent of those citizens of Connecticut to whom she gave an enormous land grant in Ohio, to indemnify them for the loss of their property destroyed by the British during the Revolution. The party ascended the Mohawk in bateaux, which they carried over the "portage" of Little Falls to Fort Stanwix, now Rome, where there was another portage to Wood Creek, which empties into Oneida Lake; thence they passed through its outlet and the Oswego River into Lake Ontario, following the south shore thereof to the mouth of the Niagara River; crossing seven miles of portage to Buffalo, and thence to the region of which Cleveland now forms the prosperous centre. The descendants of these landowners—some of whom yet may be found in the towns that suffered from the enemy's incursions eighty years ago, such as New London, Groton, and Fairfield—if they possess

---

* "John Bull in America; or, New Munchausen," second edition, 18mo., pp. 228. The original and genuine edition, New York, 1825.

any record of the hardships thus endured and the time consumed, might find a wonderful evidence of progress and growth, in the facility with which they can now reach the same spot by a few hours of railway travel along the picturesque track of the Erie road.

We must revert to such memorials to appreciate what "going West" implied forty or fifty years ago, and to understand the interest which the narratives of travellers there then excited. Before this experience became familiar, there were two writers who enjoyed much popularity in the North and East, and were extensively read abroad, as pioneer delineators of life and nature in the Western States, when that region fairly began its marvellous growth: these were Timothy Flint and James Hall.

There are writers whose works lack the high finish and the exhaustive scope which insures them permanent currency; and yet who were actuated by so genial a spirit and endowed with so many excellent qualities, that the impression they leave is sweet and enduring, like the brief but pleasing companionship of a kindly and intelligent acquaintance met in travelling, and parted with as soon as known. Those who, in youth, read of the West as pictured by Timothy Flint, though for years they may not have referred to his books, will readily accord him such a gracious remembrance. He wrote before American literature had enrolled the classic names it now boasts, and when it was so little cultivated as scarcely to be recognized as a profession. And yet a candid and sympathetic reader cannot but feel that, however defective the products of Flint's pen may be justly deemed when critically estimated, they not only fulfilled a most useful and humane purpose at the time they were given to the public, but abound in the best evidences of a capacity for authorship; which, under circumstances more favorable to discipline, deliberate construction, and gradual development, would have secured him a high and permanent niche in the temple of fame. Flint had all the requisite elements for literary success—uncommon powers of observation, a generous tone of mind, habits of industry, a command of language, imagination, scientific tastes, and a vein of originality combined with a kindliness of heart that would honor and elevate any vocation. On the other hand, it was not until the mature age of forty-five that he fairly embarked in authorship. That business was far from profitable, and, to make it remunerative, he was obliged to write fast, and publish without revision. His health was always precarious. He had few of those associations whereby an author is encouraged in the refinements and individuality of his work by the example and critical sympathy of his peers. It is not, therefore, surprising that his success varied in the different spheres of literary experiment; that the marks of haste, sometimes a desultory and at others a crude style, mar the nicety and grace of his productions; and that many of these are more remarkable for the material than the art they exhibit. Yet such was the manly force, such the kindly spirit and fresh tone of this estimable man and attractive writer, that he not only gave to the public a large amount of new and useful information, and charmed lovers of nature with a picturesque and faithful picture of her aspects in the West, then rarely traversed by the people of the older States, but it is conceded that his writings were singularly effective in producing a better mutual understanding between the two extremes of the country. For several years Timothy Flint was almost the only representative of the American authorship west of the Alleghanies. Travellers speak of an interview with him as an exceptional and charming social incident. When that long range of mountains was tediously crossed in stages; when a visit to the West was more formidable than a passage across the Atlantic now; and when material well-being was the inevitable and absorbing occupation of the newly settled towns along the great rivers, it may easily be imagined how benign an influence an urbane and liberal writer and scholar would exert at home, and how welcome his report of personal experience would prove to older communities. Accordingly, Timothy Flint was extensively read and widely beloved. A native of Massachusetts, and by profession a clergyman, he entered on a missionary life in the Valley of the Mississippi in 1815; sojourning in Ohio, Indiana, Kentucky, Missouri, Arkansas, and Louisiana, now as a teacher and now as a preacher; at home in the wilderness, a favorite in society, winning children and hunters by his wisdom and eloquence, and endearing himself to the educated residents of St. Louis, New Orleans, or Cincinnati, by his liberal and cultivated influence. It is, perhaps, impossible to imagine how different these cities and settlements were before facility of communication had enlarged and multiplied their social resources; but we have many striking evidences of the characteristics of each in Flint's writings. He wrote several novels, which are now little considered, and, compared with the present standard in that popular department of letters, would be found indifferent; yet, wherever the author has drawn from observation, he leaves a vital trace. In "Francis Berrian," which is a kind of memoir of a New Englander who became a Mexican patriot, and in " Shoshonoe Valley," there are fine local pictures and touches of character obviously caught from his ten years' experience of missionary life. Flint wrote also lectures, tales, and sketches. He edited magazines both in the North and West, and contributed to a London journal. But the writings which are chiefly stamped with the flavor of his life and the results of his observations—those which, at the time, were regarded as original and authentic, and now may be said to contain among the best, because the most true, delineations of the West— are his " Condensed Geography and History of the Mississippi Valley,"* and his " Recollections of Ten Years" (1826) residence therein. These works were cordially welcomed at home and abroad. They proved valuable and interesting to *savant*, naturalist, emigrant, and general readers; and, while more complete works on the subject have since

---

* " History and Geography of the Mississippi Valley, with the Physical Geography of the whole American Continent," by Timothy Flint, 2 vols. in 1, 8vo., Cincinnati, 1832.

appeared, the period which gave birth to them, and the character and capacity of their author, still endear and render them useful. The *London Quarterly* was singularly frank and free in its commendation of Flint, whom it pronounced " sincere, humane, and liberal" on the internal evidence of these writings; declaring, also, that the author indulged " hardly a prejudice that is not amiable."

In 1840, on his way to his native town—Reading, in Massachusetts—Flint and his son were at Natchez, when the memorable tornado occurred which nearly destroyed the place, and were several hours buried under the ruins. The father's health continued to decline, and, although he reached his early home and survived a few weeks, the summons that called his wife reached her too late.

The peculiar value of Timothy Flint's account of the remarkable region of whose history and aspect he wrote, consists in the fact that it is not the result of a cursory survey or rapid tour, but of years of residence, intimate contact with nature and man, and patient observation. The record thus prepared is one which will often be consulted by subsequent writers. The circumstances, political and social, have greatly changed since our author's advent, nearly half a century ago; but the features of nature are identical, and it is pleasant to compare them with his delineation before modified by the adorning and enriching tide of civilization. There is one portion of these writings that has a permanent charm, and that is the purely descriptive. Flint knew how to depict landscapes in words; and no one has more graphically revealed to distant readers the shores of the Ohio, or made so real in our language the physical aspects of the Great Valley.

Of native travellers, the unpretending and brief record called "The Letters of Hibernicus"* possesses a singular charm, from being associated with the recreative work of an eminent statesman, and with one of the most auspicious eco-

* "Letters on the Natural History and Internal Resources of the State of New York," by Hibernicus, New York, 1822, 18mo.

nomical achievements which ever founded and fostered the prosperity of a State and city. When De Witt Clinton explored the route of the Erie Canal, he communicated his wayside observations in a series of familiar epistles, wherein the zest of a naturalist, the ardor of a patriot, and the humor of a genial observer are instinctively blended.

"This account of his exploration of Western New York,* which originally appeared in one of the journals of the day, offers a wonderful contrast to our familiar experience. Then, to use his own language, 'the stage driver was a leading beau, and the keeper of a turnpike gate a man of consequence.' Our three hours' trip from New York to Albany was a voyage occupying ten times that period. At Albany stores were laid in, and each member of the commission provided himself with a blanket, as caravans, in our time, are equipped at St. Louis for an expedition to the Rocky Mountains. Here they breakfast at a tollkeeper's, there they dine on cold ham at an isolated farmhouse; now they mount a baggage wagon, and now take to a boat too small to admit of sleeping accommodations, which leads them constantly to regret their 'unfortunate neglect to provide marquees and camp stools;' and more than six weeks are occupied in a journey which now does not consume as many days. Yet the charm of patient observation, the enjoyment of nature, and the gleanings of knowledge, caused what, in our locomotive era, would seem a tedious pilgrimage, to be fraught with a pleasure and advantage of which our flying tourists over modern railways never dream. We perceive, by the comparison, that what has been gained in speed is often lost in rational entertainment. The traveller who leaves New York in the morning, to sleep at night under the roar of Niagara, has gathered nothing in the magical transit but dust, fatigue, and the risk of destruction; while, in that deliberate progress of the canal enthusiast, not a phase of the landscape, not an historical association, not a fruit, mineral, or flower was lost to his view. He recognizes the be-

* From the author's "Biographical and Critical Essays."

nign provision of nature for sugar, so far from the tropics, by the sap of the maple; and for salt, at such a distance from the ocean, by the lakes that hold it in solution near Syracuse. At Geddesburg he recalls the valor of the Iroquois, and the pious zeal of the Jesuits; at Seneca Lake he watches a bald eagle chasing an osprey, who lets his captive drop to be grasped in the talons of the king of birds; the fields near Aurora cheer him with the harvests of the 'finest wheat country in the world.' At one place he is regaled with salmon, at another with fruit, peculiar in flavor to each locality; at one moment he pauses to shoot a bittern, and at another to examine an old fortification. The capers and poppies in a garden, the mandrakes and thistles in a brake, the bluejays and woodpeckers of the grove, the bullet marks in the rafters of Fort Niagara, tokens of the siege under Sir William Johnson, the boneset of the swamp, a certain remedy for the local fever, a Yankee exploring the country for lands, the croaking of the bullfrog and the gleam of the firefly, Indian men spearing for fish, and girls making wampum—these and innumerable other scenes and objects lure him into the romantic vistas of tradition, or the beautiful domain of natural science; and everywhere he is inspired by the patriotic survey to announce the as yet unrecorded promise of the soil, and to exult in the limitless destiny of its people. If there is a striking diversity between the population and facilities of travel in this region as known to us and as described by him, there is in other points a not less remarkable identity. Rochester is now famed as the source of one of the most prolific superstitions of the age; and forty years ago there resided at Crooked Lane, Jemima Wilkinson, whose followers believed her the Saviour incarnate. Clinton describes her equipage—'a plain coach with leather curtains, the back inscribed with her initials and a star.' The orchards, poultry, cornfields, gristmills noted by him, still characterize the region, and are indefinitely multiplied. The ornithologist, however, would miss whole species of birds, and the richly-veined woods must be sought in less civilized districts. The prosperous future which the varied products of this district foretold, has been more than realized; with each successive improvement in the means of communication, villages have swelled to cities; barges and freight cars with lumber and flour have crowded the streams and rails leading to the metropolis; and, in the midst of its rural beauty, and gemmed with peerless lakes, the whole region has, according to his prescient conviction, annually increased in commerce, population, and refinement.

A more noble domain, indeed, wherein to exercise such administrative genius, can scarcely be imagined than the State of New York. In its diversities of surface, water, scenery, and climate, it may be regarded, more than any other member of the confederacy, as typical of the Union. The artist, the topographer, the man of science, and the agriculturist, can find within its limits all that is most characteristic of the entire country. In historical incident, variety of immigrant races, and rapid development, it is equally a representative State. There spreads the luxuriant Mohawk Valley, whose verdant slopes, even when covered with frost, the experienced eye of Washington selected for purchase as the best of agricultural tracts. There were the famed hunting grounds of the Six Nations, the colonial outposts of the fur trade, the vicinity of Frontenac's sway, and the Canada wars, the scenes of André's capture, and Burgoyne's surrender. There the very names of forts embalm the fame of heroes. There lived the largest manorial proprietors, and not a few of the most eminent Revolutionary statesmen. There Fulton's great invention was realized; there flows the most beautiful of our rivers, towers the grandest mountain range, and expand the most picturesque lakes; there thunders the sublimest cataract on earth, and gush the most salubrious spas; while on the seaboard is the emporium of the Western world.

A poet has apostrophized North America, with no less truth than beauty, as 'the land of many waters;' and a glance at the map of New York will indicate their felicitous distribution within her limits. This element is the natural and primitive means of intercommunication. For centuries it had borne the aborigines in their frail canoes, and afterward the trader, the soldier, the missionary, and the emigrant, in their bateaux; and, when arrived at a terminus, they carried these light transports over leagues of portage, again to launch them on lake and river. Fourteen years of Clinton's life were assiduously devoted to his favorite project of uniting these bodies of water. He was the advocate, the memorialist, the topographer, and financier of the vast enterprise, and accomplished it, by his wisdom and intrepidity, without the slightest pecuniary advantage, and in the face of innumerable obstacles. Its consummation was one of the greatest festivals sacred to a triumph of the arts of peace ever celebrated on this continent. The impulse it gave to commercial and agricultural prosperity continues to this hour. It was the foundation of all that makes the city and State of New York preëminent; and when, a few years since, a thousand American citizens sailed up the Mississippi to commemorate its alliance with the Atlantic, the ease and rapidity of the transit, and the spectacle of virgin civilization thus created, were but a new act in the grand drama of national development, whose opening scene occurred twenty-seven years before, when the waters of Lake Erie blended with those of the Hudson.

The immense bodies of inland water, and the remarkable fact that the Hudson River, unlike other Atlantic streams south of it, flows unimpeded, early impressed Clinton with the natural means of intercourse destined to connect the seaboard of New York with the vast agricultural districts of the interior. He saw her peerless river enter the Highlands only to meet, a hundred and sixty miles beyond, another stream, which flowed within a comparatively short distance from the great chain of lakes. The very existence of these inland seas, and the obvious possibility of uniting them with the ocean, suggested to his comprehensive mind a new idea of the destiny of the whole country. Within a few years an ingenious geographer has pointed out, with singular acumen, the relation of his science to history, and has demonstrated, by a theory not less philosophical than poetic, that the disposition of land and water in various parts of the globe predetermines the human development of each region. The copious civilization of Europe is thus traceable to the numerous facilities of approach that distinguish it from Africa, which still remains but partially explored. The lakes in America prophesied to the far-reaching vision of Clinton her future progress. He perceived, more clearly than any of his contemporaries, that her development depended upon facilities of intercourse and communication. He beheld, with intuitive wisdom, the extraordinary provision for this end, in the succession of lake and river, extending, like a broad silver tissue, from the ocean far through the land, thus bringing the products of foreign climes within reach of the lone emigrant in the heart of the continent, and the staples of those midland valleys to freight the ships of her seaports. He felt that the State of all others to practically demonstrate this great fact, was that with whose interests he was intrusted. It was not as a theorist, but as a utilitarian, in the best sense, that he advocated the union by canal of the waters of Lake Erie with those of the Hudson. The patriotic scheme was fraught with issues of which even he never dreamed. It was applying, on a limited scale, in the sight of a people whose enterprise is boundless in every direction clearly proved to be available, a principle which may be truly declared the vital element of our civic growth. It was giving tangible evidence of the creative power incident to locomotion. It was yielding the absolute evidence then required to convince the less far-sighted multitude that access was the grand secret of increased value; that exchange of products was the touchstone of wealth; and that the iron, wood, grain, fruit, and other abundant resources of the interior could acquire their real value only through facilities of transportation. Simple as these truths appear now, they were widely ignored then; and not a few opponents of Clinton predicted that, even if he did succeed in having flour conveyed from what was then called the 'Far West' to the metropolis, at a small expense of time and money, the grass would grow in the streets of New York. The political economists of his day were thus converted into enemies of a system which, from that hour, has continued to guide to prosperous issues every latent source of wealth throughout the country. The battle with ignorance and prejudice, which Clinton and his friends waged, resulted in more than a local triumph and individual renown. It established a great precedent, offered a prolific example, and gave permanent impulse and direction to the public spirit of the community. The canal is now, in a great measure, superseded by the railway; the traveller sometimes finds them side by side, and, as he glances from the sluggish stream and creeping barge to the whirling cars, and thence to the telegraph wire, he witnesses only the more perfect development of that great scheme by which Clinton, according to the limited means and against the inveterate prejudices of his day, sought to bring the distant near, and to render homogeneous and mutually helpful the activity of a single State, and, by that successful experiment, indicated the process whereby the whole confederacy should be rendered one in interest, in enterprise, and in sentiment.

Before the canal policy was realized, we are told by its great advocate that 'the expense of conveying a barrel of flour by land to Albany, from the country above Cayuga Lake, was more than twice as much as the cost of transportation from New York to Liverpool;' and the correctness of his financial anticipations was verified by the first year's experiment, even before the completion of the enterprise, when, in his message to the legislature, he announced that 'the income of the canal fund, when added to the tolls, exceeded the interest on the cost of the canal by nearly four hundred thousand dollars.' Few, however, of the restless excursionists that now crowd our cars and steamboats, would respond to his praise of this means of transportation when used for travel. His notion of a journey, we have seen, differed essentially from that now in vogue, which seems to aim chiefly at the annihilation of space. To a philosophic mind, notwithstanding, his views will not appear irrational, when he declares that fifty miles a day, 'without a jolt,' is his ideal of a tour—the time to be divided between observing, and, when there is no interest in the scenery, reading and conversation. 'I believe,' he adds, 'that cheaper or more commodious travelling cannot be found.'"

James Hall wrote a series of graphic letters in the *Portfolio*—one of the earliest literary magazines, published in Philadelphia—which were subsequently collected in a volume, and were among the first descriptive sketches of merit that made the West familiar and attractive to the mass of readers. Born in Philadelphia in 1793, the author entered the army, and was engaged in the battle of Lundy's Lane, at the siege of Fort Erie, and on other occasions during the war of 1812. Six years later he resigned his commission, and, in 1820, removed to Illinois, where he studied and practised law, became a member of the legislature and judge of the circuit court. In 1833 he again changed his residence to Cincinnati, where he was long occupied as cashier of a bank, and in the pursuits of literature. From his intimate acquaintance with the Western country, his experience as a soldier and a legislator, habits of intelligent observation, and an animated and agreeable style, he was enabled to write attractively of a region comparatively new to the literary public, and for many years his books were a popular source of information and entertainment for those eager to know the characteristics and enjoy the adventurous or historical romances of the Western States first settled. He successively published letters from and legends of the West, tales of the border, and statistics of and notes on that new and growing region.*

---

* "Legends of the West," 12mo., Philadelphia, 1833.
"Sketches of History, Life, and Manners in the West," 2 vols. 12mo., Philadelphia, 1835.
"Notes on the Western States," 12mo., Philadelphia, 1838.
"The Wilderness and the War Path," 12mo., New York, 1846.
"The West, its Soil, Surface, and Productions," Cincinnati, 1848.

With the progress of the country, and the leisure and its consequent literary taste which peace and prosperity induce, more deliberate works began to appear from native authors, which, without being literally Travels, contain their best fruits, and possess a more mature attraction. The same causes led to critical observation and pleas for reform. Two books especially won not only attention, but fame: they were the productions of men of classical education, genial tastes, and public spirit, but diverse in subject as their authors were in vocation—one an eloquent lawyer, and the other an enterprising merchant. "Letters from the Eastern States," by William Tudor, appeared in 1819. Their originality and acuteness were at once acknowledged; and, although the discussion of some questions now seems too elaborate, they are an excellent memorial of the times and the region they describe. Tudor was an efficient friend of the first purely literary periodical established in New England, one of the founders of the first public library, and the originator of the Bunker Hill Monument. William Wirt, in Virginia, at an early date exhibited the same love of elegant letters, initiated a work similar in scope and aim to Addison's *Spectator*, and was not only an eloquent speaker and favorite companion, but a scholar of classic taste and literary aspirations. In the winter of 1803 he published, in the *Argus*—a daily journal of Richmond, Va.,—"Letters of a British Spy," which were collected and issued in a book form.* Like Irving in the case of "Knickerbocker," he resorted to the ruse of a pretended discovery of papers left in an inn chamber. The success of these "Letters" surprised

---

* "The British Spy; or, Letters to a Member of the British Parliament," written during a tour through the United States, by a Young Englishman of Rank, 18mo., pp. 103, Newburyport, 1804.—" The above is the original edition of the now celebrated letters of the British Spy, written by the American Plato, William Wirt. For the amount of what he has written, no American author has won so permanent and widespread a reputation. His story of the blind preacher is one of the most beautiful and affecting in the language. This book has gone through fifteen editions, and is destined to go through as many more."—*Gowan's Catalogue.*

the author, as it would the reader of the present day unacquainted with the circumstances. Superior in style to any belles-lettres work of the kind, of native origin, that had yet appeared, and analyzing the merits of several popular orators of the time, the book had a charm and interest for its first readers greatly owing to the rarity of an intellectual feast of domestic production. Besides his remarks on the eloquence of the forum and bar, Wirt discussed certain physical traits and phenomena with zest and some scientific insight, and gave incidental but graphic sketches of local society and manners. His reflections on the character of Pocahontas, and his portrait of the "Blind Preacher," are familiar as favorite specimens of descriptive writing. Although now little read, the "Letters of a British Spy" are a pleasing landmark in the brief record of American literature, and give us a not inadequate idea of the life and region delineated. In 1812, an edition was published in London, with an apologetic preface indicative of the feeling then prevalent across the water in regard to all mental products imported from the United States, aggravated, perhaps, by the *nom de plume* Wirt had adopted. The publisher declares his "conviction of its merit" induces him to offer the work to the public, though "it is feared the present demand on the English reader may be considered more as a call on British courtesy and benevolence than one of right and equity."

When our national novelist returned to America, after a residence of many years in Europe, he undertook to give his countrymen the benefit of his experience and reflections in the shape of direct censure and counsel. "The Monnikins"—a political satire—"The American Democrat," "Homeward Bound," "Home as Found," "A Letter to his Countrymen," and other productions in the shape of essays, fiction, and satire, gave expression to convictions and arguments born of sincere and patriotic motives and earnest thought. In his general views, Cooper had right and reason on his side. What he wrote of political abuses and social anomalies, every candid and cultivated American has known and felt to be true, especially after a visit to Europe. But the manner of conveying his sentiments was injudicious. Description, not satire, was his *forte ;* action, and not didactics, had given *éclat* to his pen ; hence his admirers believed he had mistaken his vocation in becoming a social and political critic ; while many were revolted by what they conceived to be a sweeping and unauthorized condemnation. Moreover, in offending the editorial fraternity, by a caricature of their worst qualities, he drew around himself a swarm of virulent protests, and thus was misjudged : the consequence was a series of libel suits and a wearisome controversy. Now that the exaggerated mood and the gross misapprehensions therein involved, have passed away, we can appreciate the abstract justice of Cooper's position, the manly spirit and the intelligent patriotism of his unfortunate experiments as a reformer, and revert to this class of his writings with profit, especially since the crisis he anticipated has been reached, and the logic of events is enforcing with solemn emphasis the lessons he ungraciously perhaps, but honestly and bravely, strove to impress upon his wayward countrymen. If ever an American had a right to assume the office of censor, it was Cooper. He had, soon after his arrival in Europe, taken up his pen in behalf of his country, and thenceforth advocated her rights, defended her fame, and brought to reckoning her ignorant maligners. His " Notions of the Americans" did much to correct false impressions abroad ; and its author was involved in a long controversy, and became an American champion and oracle, whose services have never yet been fully appreciated, enhanced as they were by his European popularity as an original American novelist. Well wrote Halleck :

> " Cooper, whose name is with his country's woven,
> First in her files, her pioneer of mind,
> A wanderer now in other climes, has proven
> His love for the young land he left behind."

It requires a love of nature, an adventurous spirit, and an intelligent patriotism, such as, in these days of complex associations and fragmentary interests, are rarely found in the same individual, to observe and to write with effect upon the scenes and the character of this republic—especially those parts thereof that are removed from the great centres of trade and society. Political economists there are who will patiently nomenclate the physical resources; sportsmen who can discourse with relish of the bivouac and the hunt, and their environment and incidents; poetical minds alert and earnest in celebrating particular local charms: but the American of education who delights in exploring the country and invoking its brief past in a historical point of view, while dwelling *con amore* upon its natural features, so as to produce an animated narrative—who delights in the life and takes pride in the aspect, even when least cultivated, of his native land, is the exception, not the rule, among our authors. The reasons are obvious: for the scholar there is too little of that mysterious background to the picture which enriches it with vast human interest; to the imaginative there is too much monotony in the landscape and the experience; to the sympathetic, too little variety and grace of character in the people; and the man who can be eloquent in describing Italy, and vivacious in his traveller's journal in France, and speculative in discussing English manners, will prove comparatively tame and vague when a traveller at home—always excepting certain shrines of pilgrimage long consecrated to enthusiasm. He may have profound emotions at Niagara, confess the inspiration of a favorite seacoast, and expatiate upon the White Mountains with rapture; but find a tour in any one section of the land more or less tedious and barren of interest, or, at best, yielding but vague materials for pen or talk. Exceptions to this average class, many and memorable, our survey of Travels in America amply indicates; but the fact remains, that the feeling that invests Scott's novels, Wilson's sketches, the French memoirs, the German poets, the intense partiality, insight, and sentiment born of local attachment and national pride, has seldom impregnated our literature, especially that of travel; for the novels of

Cooper, the poems of Bryant, and other standard productions in more elaborate and permanent spheres, do not invalidate the general truth. Among the native writers who, from the qualities already mentioned, have known how to make the narrative of an American tour pleasant and profitable, is Charles Fenno Hoffman, whose " Winter in the West" is quite a model of its kind. It consists of a series of letters addressed to a New York journal, describing a journey on horseback in 1835.* There was the right admixture of poetical and patriotic instinct, of knowledge of books and of the world, and of the love both of nature and adventure, to make him an agreeable and instructive delineator of an experience which, to many equally intelligent travellers, would have been devoid of consecutive interest. In his novels, tales, and verses, there is a positive American flavor, which shows how readily he saw the characteristic and felt the beautiful in his own country. To him the Hudson was an object of love, and the history of his native State a strong personal interest. Unspoiled by European travel, and fond of sport, of the freshness and freedom of the woods, and the independence incident to our institutions, he, although infirm, bore discomforts with cheerfulness, easily won companionship, and delighted in exercise and observation. Accordingly, he notes the weather, describes the face of the country, recalls the Indian legends, speculates on the characters and modes of life, and discusses the historical antecedents, as he slowly roams over Eastern Pennsylvania, Michigan, Kentucky, Virginia, and Illinois, with a lively tone and yet not without grave sympathy. Scenery is described with a robust and graphic rather than with a dainty and rhetorical pen, obviously guided by an excellent eye for local distinctions and charms; men and manners are treated with an acute, generalized, and manly criticism; the animals, the river craft, the flowers, the game, the origin and growth of towns, the aspect and resources of the country, are each and all congenial themes. He so enjoys the observation thereof, as to put

* "A Winter in the West," by a New Yorker, 2 vols., New York, 1835.

his reader in relation with himself, as he did the diverse characters he encountered in tavern, log house, military outpost, and drawing room. He is neither revolted by coarseness nor discouraged by inconveniences. He takes us sociably along a route now familiar to thousands who traverse it on railways with scarce a thought of the latent interest more tranquil observation and patient inquiry would elicit. At Detroit we are entertained by an historical episode, and at Prairie du Chien with a veritable picture of military life, character, and routine in America. A conversation here, an anecdote there, a page of speculation now, and again one of description, something like an adventure to-day, and of curious observation to-morrow, beguile us with so cheerful and intelligent a guide, that, at the end of the journey, we are surprised it yielded so many topics of reflection and scenes of picturesque or human interest.

The statistics whereby the practical inquirer, and the agencies and examples whereby the social philosopher, may decide whether Cotton is king, may be found in the books of Southern Travel in America written by Frederick Law Olmsted. The actual economical results of slave labor upon the value of property, the comfort and the dignity of life and manners, mind, domestic economy, education, religion, social welfare, tone and tendency, may there be found, copious, specific, and authentic. What nature is in the Cotton States, and life also, are therein emphasized discreetly. How the solemn pine woods balmily shade the traveller; how gracefully dangle the tylandria festoons in hoary grace; how cheerily gleam the holly berries, and glow the negroes' fires; how sturdily are gnarled the cypress knees; how magnificent are the liveoaks, and luxuriant the magnolias, and desolate the swamps, and comfortless the dwellings, and reckless the travel, and shiftless the ways, and rare the vaunted hospitality, and obsolete the "fine old country gentleman;" and how proud and poor, precarious and unprogressive is the civilization inwoven with slave and adjacent to free labor, is narrated without dogmatism and in matter-of-fact terms, whence the economist, the humanitarian, the philosopher, the Christian, the reasonable man may infer and elaborate the truth, and the duty that truth involves and demands.*

More desultory in scope, but not less interesting as the genuine report of calm observation, are Bryant's "Letters of a Traveller," which are fresh, agreeable, and authentic local descriptions and comments, superior in literary execution, and therefore valuable as permanent records in the literature of home travel.†

An important department of American Travels, and for scientific and historical objects invaluable, is the record of Government expeditions for military or exploring purposes, from the famous enterprises of Lewis and Clark to those of Simcoe, Stansbury, Kendall, Emory, Long, Marcy, Pike, Fremont, Bartlett, and others. Every new State and Territory has found its intelligent explorer. The vast deserts and the Rocky Mountains, the Great Salt Lake, Oregon, the Camanche hunting grounds, Texas, the far Western aboriginal tribes, the climate, soil, topography, &c., of the most remote and uncivilized regions of the continent, have been thus examined and reported, and the narratives are often animated by graphic and picturesque scenes, or made impressive by adventure, hardship, and intrepidity. Another remarkable class of books is the long list of those devoted to California, written and published within the last ten years, whereby the life, aspect, condition, scenery, resources, and prospects of that region are as familiar to readers in the old States as if they had explored the new El Dorado.

* "The Cotton Kingdom, a Traveller's Observations on Cotton and Slavery in the American Slave States," based upon three former volumes of Journeys and Investigations by the same author, by Frederic Law Olmsted, 2 vols. 12mo., with a colored statistical map of the Cotton Kingdom and its Dependencies.

† "Letters of a Traveller in Europe and America," New York, 12mo.— A discriminating critic observes of this work: "Mr. Bryant's style in these Letters is an admirable model of descriptive prose. Without any appearance of labor, it is finished with an exquisite grace. The genial love of nature and the lurking tendency to humor which it everywhere betrays, prevent its severe simplicity from running into harduess, and give it freshness and occasional glow in spite of its prevailing propriety and reserve."

The incidental records of American travel, such as may be found in the letters, diaries, and memoirs of our own civic leaders and military or political heroes, are not the least characteristic or suggestive As a specimen, let us refer to the notes of our peerless Chief in New England, when on his Presidential tour.

Here is a glimpse of Connecticut as it appeared to the practical eye of Washington in 1789. In his Diary, he says, under date of October 16th of that year: " About seven o'clock we left the widow Haviland's, and, after passing Horse Neck, six miles distant from Rye, the road through which is hilly and immensely stony, and trying to wheels and carriages, we breakfasted at Stamford, which is six miles farther, at one Webb's—a tolerable good house. In this town are an Episcopal church and a meeting house. At Norwalk, which is ten miles farther, we made a halt to feed our horses. To the lower end of this town sea vessels come, and at the other end are mills, stores, and an Episcopal and Presbyterian church. From hence to Fairfield, where we dined and lodged, is twelve miles, and part of it very rough road, but not equal to Horse Neck. The superb landscape, however, which is to be seen from the meeting house of the latter, is a rich regalia. We found all the farmers busily employed in gathering, grinding, and expressing the juice of their apples. The average crop of wheat, they say, is about fifteen bushels to the acre, often twenty, and from that to twenty-five. The destructive evidences of British cruelty are yet visible both at Norwalk and Fairfield, as there are the chimneys of many burnt houses standing yet. The principal export from Norwalk and Fairfield is horses and cattle, salted beef and pork, lumber and Indian corn for the West Indies, and, in a small degree, wheat and flour."

" Commenced my journey," he writes[*] on the 15th of October, 1789, " about nine o'clock, for Boston and the Eastern States." He did not reach that city until noon of the

---

[*] " Diary from the 1st of October, 1789, until the 10th of March, 1790," printed by the Bradford Club from the original manuscripts, New York, 1858.

23d; and it is curious to read of the frequent halts for meals, to feed the horses, or to pass the night, on a route we are accustomed to pass over in as many hours as days were then employed. Washington makes agricultural and topographical notes, and in many respects we recognize the same traits of industry, and identify the face of the country; while in others the contrast is remarkable.

He notes a linen manufacture at New Haven, white mulberry "to feed silkworms" at Wallingford, and remarks that the silk culture, "except the weaving, is the work of private families, without interference with other business, and is likely to turn out a beneficial amusement."

At Hartford, Colonel Wadsworth showed him the woollen factory, and specimens of broadcloth. "I ordered a suit," he writes, "and of the serges a whole piece, to make breeches for my servants." Continuing his journey, he observes "the whole road from Hartford to Springfield is level and good, except being too sandy in places, and the fields enclosed with posts and rails, there not being much stone." He is met often by mounted escorts of gentlemen, is entertained by the local officials, and receives addresses from the towns. Of his impressions of the State, we may form an idea by the casual entries in his brief diary: "There is great equality in the people of this State—few or no opulent men, and no poor; great similitude in their buildings, the general fashion of which is a chimney always of stone or brick, and door in the middle, with a staircase fronting the latter, and running up the side of the former—two flush stones with a very good show of sash and glass windows; the size generally is from thirty to forty feet in length, and from twenty to thirty in width, exclusive of a back shed, which seems to be added as the family increases. The farms, by the contiguity of the houses, are small, not averaging more than a hundred acres. They are worked chiefly by oxen, which have no other food than hay."

At Portsmouth he "went in a boat to view the harbor. Having lines, we proceeded to the fishing banks and fished for cod, and only caught two. Dined at Mr. Langdon's, and drank tea there with a large party of ladies. There are some good houses here, but, in general, they are indifferent, and almost entirely of wood. On wondering at this, as the country is full of stone and good clay for bricks, I was told that, on account of the fogs and damps, they deemed them wholesomer."

At Exeter, he writes, "a jealousy subsists between this town, where the legislature alternately sits, and Portsmouth; which, had I known it in time, would have made it necessary to have accepted an invitation to a public dinner."

"In Haverhill is a duck manufactory upon a small but ingenious scale."

At Boston he went to an oratorio, and was entertained at Faneuil Hall, "dined in a large company at Mr. Bowdoin's, and went to an assembly in the evening, where "there were upward of a hundred ladies. Their appearance was elegant, and many of them very handsome."

Another attractive branch of this subject may be found in commemorative addresses—a peculiar and prolific occasion of local reminiscences and comparisons in America. Compare, for instance, the descriptions of New York by Mrs. Knight, Brissot, or Wansey, with those of Dr. Francis[*] or General Dix[†] in their historical discourses; or the pictures of Albany by Mrs. Grant and Kalm, with the recollections thereof in his boyhood so genially imparted by the late Judge Kent;[‡] or Irving's epistolary account of his first voyage up the Hudson with his last trip to the Lakes, and we have the most complete historical contrasts and local transitions, and realize by what means and methods the vast social and economical changes have taken place.

[*] "Old New York," a Discourse delivered before the New York Historical Society, by John W. Francis, M. D., LL. D., in commemoration of the Fifty-third Anniversary, New York, 1857.

[†] "The City of New York, its Growth, Destiny, and Duties," a Lecture by John A. Dix, before the New York Historical Society, New York, 1853.

[‡] "An Address Delivered before the Young Men's Association of Albany, February 7, 1854," by William Kent, New York, 1854.

Of the countless books of Western travel and adventure, one of the most spirited and authentic is Mrs. Kirkland's "New Home: Who'll Follow?" to which were subsequently added her "Forest Life" and "Western Clearings." The "delightful humor and keen observation" of the former work made it an established favorite as a true reflection of life in the West at its initiatory stage. As a picture of travel in the same region, Washington Irving's "Tour on the Prairies" is the most finished and suggestive. 'It is an unpretending account, comprehending a period of about four weeks, of travelling and hunting excursions upon the vast Western plains. The local features of this interesting region have been displayed to us in several works of fiction, of which it has formed the scene; and more formal illustrations of the extensive domain denominated *The West*, and its denizens, have been repeatedly presented to the public. But in this volume one of the most extraordinary and attractive portions of the great subject is discussed, not as the subsidiary part of a romantic story, nor yet in the desultory style of epistolary composition, but in the deliberate, connected form of a retrospective narration. When we say that the "Tour on the Prairies" is rife with the characteristics of its author, no ordinary eulogium is bestowed. His graphic power is manifest throughout. The boundless prairies stretch out illimitably to the fancy, as the eye scans his descriptions. The athletic figures of the riflemen, the gayly arrayed Indians, the heavy buffalo and the graceful deer, pass in strong relief and startling contrast before us. We are stirred by the bustle of the camp at dawn, and soothed by its quiet, or delighted with its picturesque aspect under the shadow of night. The imagination revels amid the green oak clumps and verdant pea vines, the expanded plains and the glancing river, the forest aisles and the silent stars. Nor is this all. Our hearts thrill at the vivid representations of a primitive and excursive existence; we involuntarily yearn, as we read, for the genial activity and the perfect exposure to the influences of nature in all her free magnificence, of a woodland and adventurous life ; the morning strain of the bugle, the excitement of the chase, the delicious repast, the forest gossiping, the sweet repose beneath the canopy of heaven—how inviting, as depicted by such a pencil!

Nor has the author failed to invigorate and render doubly attractive these descriptive drawings, with the peculiar light and shade of his own rich humor, and the mellow softness of his ready sympathy. A less skilful draughtsman would, perhaps, in the account of the preparations for departure (Chapter III.), have spoken of the hunters, the fires, and the steeds ; but who, except Geoffrey Crayon, would have been so quaintly mindful of the little dog, and the manner in which he regarded the operations of the farrier ? How inimitably the Bee Hunt is portrayed !—and what have we of the kind so racy as the account of the Republic of Prairie Dogs, unless it be that of the Rookery in Bracebridge Hall ? What expressive portraits are the delineations of our rover's companions ! How consistently drawn throughout, and in what fine contrast, are the reserved and saturnine Beatte, and the vain-glorious, sprightly, and versatile Tonish ! A golden vein of vivacious yet chaste comparison—that beautiful yet rarely well-managed species of wit—and a wholesome and pleasing sprinkling of moral comment—that delicate and often most efficacious medium of useful impressions—intertwine and vivify the main narrative. Something, too, of that fine pathos which enriches his earlier productions, enhances the value of this. He tells us, indeed, with commendable honesty, of his new appetite for destruction, which the game of the prairie excited ; but we cannot fear for the tenderness of a heart that sympathizes so readily with suffering, and yields so gracefully to kindly impulses. He gazes upon the noble courser of the wilds, and wishes that his freedom may be perpetuated ; he recognizes the touching instinct which leads the wounded elk to turn aside and die in retiracy ; he reciprocates the attachment of the beast which sustains him, and, more than all, can minister even to the foibles of a fellow being, rather than mar the transient reign of human pleasure.'

A candid and earnest inquirer, one who seeks to understand the facts and phases of nature, society, and life, past
and present, in North America, will find that native talent,
observation, and industry have done more to unfold and illustrate them than is generally known even by educated men.
Our literature includes not only ample historical materials and
contributions to natural history, but æsthetic and artistic
writings, elucidating local scenery and character; not only
economical and topographical books, but standard poems on
national themes, and many other generic illustrations of the
country and the people. No philosophical traveller, who aims
at a true knowledge of the country he explores, is satisfied
with a casual observation of its external features, but seeks
to realize its life and character, in history, biography, romance, art, and poetry.

The lives and writings of the remarkable men who originated and established the principles, while they illustrated
the spirit of America and her political aspirations, form the
most authentic and interesting sources of knowledge. Through
these the historical and social development of the country
may be not only understood, but felt as a conscious experience and vital power. The best modern statesmen have
sought and found therein auspicious inspiration — from
Brougham in the days of his liberal proclivities, to Cavour
at the summit of national success. The lives and writings
of Washington, Franklin, Otis, Marshall, Jay, Hamilton,
Adams, Jefferson, Morris, Quincy, Sullivan, and others of
the Revolutionary era; and, of a later, Livingston, Clinton,
Clay, Webster, Calhoun, Jackson,* and other civic leaders,

---

* "The Writings of George Washington," being his correspondence,
addresses, messages, and other papers, official and private, selected and published from the original manuscripts, with a Life of the Author, notes and
illustrations, by Jared Sparks, 12 vols. 8vo., Boston, 1855.—"'Far across the
ocean, if we may credit the Sibylline books, and after many ages, an extensive and rich continent will be discovered, and in it will arise a hero, wise and
brave, who, by his counsel and arms, will deliver his country from the slavery
by which she was oppressed. This shall he do under favorable auspices. And
oh! how much more adorable will he be than our Brutus and Camillus.' This

reveal the principles of our institutions in their normal, antagonistic, and practical relations. These men incarnate them, and their words illustrate and enforce what their example embodied. Representative men, their country's best aims and elemental force and instincts find adequate and memorable expression in their speeches, correspondence, controversies, policy, and character; and whosoever grasps and analyzes these, is alone equipped and authorized to comment intelligently on America as a political entity and a social experiment. "Let the people of the United States," writes Guizot, " ever hold in grateful remembrance the leading men of that generation which achieved their independence and founded their Government; influential by their property, talent, or character; faithful to ancient virtues, yet friendly to modern improvement; sensible to the splendid advantages

prediction was known to Accius the poet, who, in his 'Nyctegresia,' embellished it with the ornaments of poetry."—*Cicero, Frag. XV., Maii ed., p.* 52.

"The Life of George Washington," by Washington Irving, New York, 1860.

"The Works of Benjamin Franklin," with notes, and a Life of the Author, by Jared Sparks, in 10 vols. 8vo., Boston, 1856.

"Life and Works of John Adams," by his grandson, Charles Francis Adams, 9 vols. 8vo., Boston, 1851-'60.

"Works of Alexander Hamilton," comprising his correspondence and his official and political writings, 7 vols. 8vo., New York, 1851.

"The Life of Gouverneur Morris," with selections from his correspondence, &c., edited by Jared Sparks, 3 vols. 8vo., Boston, 1852.

"The Public Men of the Revolution," including events from the Peace of 1783 to the Peace of 1815, by William Sullivan, Philadelphia, 1847.

"Memoir of the Life of Josiah Quincy, Jr.," Boston, 1825.

"Life of John Jay, with Selections from his Correspondence," by William Jay, New York, 1833.

Tudor's "Life of Otis;" Amory's "Life of Sullivan;" Hunt's "Life of Livingston;" Wirt's "Life of Patrick Henry;" Austin's "Life of Gerry;" Wheaton's "Life of Pinckney;" Parton's "Life of Jackson;" Kennedy's "Life of Wirt;" The Naval Biographies of Cooper and Mackenzie; "Lives of American Merchants," edited by Freeman Hunt; "Life of Chief Justice Story," by his son; Sparks's series of American Biographies; the Lives of Schuyler, Rittenhouse, Fulton, Madison, Reed, Clay, Calhoun, &c.; and the historical and biographical contributions of William L. Stone, Brantz Mayer, George W. Greene, Frothingham, Headley, Moore, and others.

of civilization, and yet attached to simplicity of manners; high toned in their feelings, but of modest minds, at the same time ambitious and prudent in their impulses; men of rare endowments, who expected much from humanity, without presuming too much upon themselves." The later generation of statesmen elaborated the system and illustrated the principles of these peerless men; and the combined writings and memoirs of both constitute an essential and complete expression and indication of all the vital ideas and political sympathies of which America has been the free arena. To these personal data, so emphatic and illustrious, the philosophic inquirer will add the history of the country, whether unfolded with bold generalizations and effective rhetoric, and through extensive and minute research, as by Bancroft, tersely chronicled by Hildreth, drawn from personal observation by Ramsay, or treated in special phases by Curtis, Cooper, Dunlap, Lossing, Sparks, and others.*

The local histories, also, are in many instances full of important details and illustrative principles: such are Theodore Irving's "Conquest of Florida," Palfrey's "New England," Belknap's "New Hampshire," Williams's "Vermont," Arnold's "Rhode Island," Dwight's "Connecticut," Dr. Hawks's "North Carolina," Butler's "Kentucky," Drake's "Boston," Bolton's "Westchester County," and the contributions of the religious annals of the country in the history of Methodism

---

* Cooper's "Naval History of the United States;" Curtis's "History of the Constitution;" Parkman's "Conspiracy of Pontiac." "Dunlap's "History of the American Theatre, and of the Arts of Design in the United States." Lossing's "Field Book of the Revolution."

"Thirty Years' View; or, A History of the Workings of the American Government for Thirty Years, from 1820 to 1850," by Thomas H. Benton.

"The Writings of Thomas Jefferson," published from original manuscripts, by order of Congress, Washington, 1853, 9 vols. 8vo.

"The Works of Daniel Webster," Boston, 1857, 6 vols. 8vo.

"Correspondence of the American Revolution," edited by Sparks.

"Diplomacy of the Revolution," by W. H. Trescott.

"Correspondence and Speeches of Henry Clay," edited by C. Colton, New York, 3 vols. 8vo., 1851.

Upham's "Salem Witchcraft."

Thatcher's "Military Journal during the Revolution."

by Abel Stevens, of the Presbyterian Church by Hodge, of Universalism by Whittemore, of Episcopacy by Meade, Hawks, and Jarvis; and the history of manufactures, inventions, and educational institutions and public charities.

It is instructive to consult the county and town histories of the Eastern and Middle States, because they unfold in detail the process and method of municipal organization, the means of popular education, the initiation of manufacturing and commercial enterprise, and the religious and social arrangements, which have built up small and isolated communities into flourishing cities; and, if we compare the French and Spanish accounts of Florida and Louisiana with the American, a still more striking illustration is afforded of the practical superiority of free institutions. One of the latest historians of the latter State (where secession was so lately rampant) closes his narrative, in allusion to the foreign colonial rule, thus:

"There were none of those associations—not a link of that mystic chain connecting the present with the past—which produce an attachment to locality. It was not when a poor colony, and when given away like a farm, that she prospered. This miracle was to be the consequence of the apparition of a banner which was not in existence at the time, which was to be the labarum of the advent of liberty, the harbinger of the regeneration of nations, and which was to form so important an era in the history of mankind."*

Specific information is now attainable through a series of standard works of reference. Authentic statistical and official information in regard to North America may be gleaned from the *American Almanac,* Hunt's *Merchant's Magazine,* and Colton's "Atlas." The natural resources, geographical and political history, and remarkable public characters of each State and section are thoroughly chronicled in the "New American Cyclopædia," a work specially valuable for its scientific and biographical data. Putnam's "American Facts" is a copious and authentic work. The literary and

---

* Gayarré's "History of Louisiana."

educational history of the country is elaborately unfolded in Duyckinck's "Cyclopædia of American Literature."*

General literature offers a various and creditable catalogue of American works, wherein independence of investigation or originality of thought attests the impulse which free institutions give to private culture. In the department of pure literary labor, where faithful mastery of subjects for illustration must be sought afar, and with constant labor and care, the histories of Prescott, Ticknor, and Motley may be cited as of standard European interest and value. In juridical literature, Marshall, Kent, Story, Wheaton, Livingston, Webster, and other names are of established authority; and while, in the philosophy of our vernacular, Marsh, and, in its lexicography, Webster and Worcester, have achieved signal triumphs, the number and excellence of American educational manuals are proverbial. Of the political treatises, the

---

* Niles's "Weekly Register" commenced being published September 7, 1811, and ended June 27, 1849; making, in all, 76 volumes. The first 50 volumes were edited by Hezekiah Niles; vols. 51 to 57 were edited by William Ogden Niles. Jeremiah Hough bought out, and was editor to the end of vol. 73. The publication was then suspended for one year, and recommenced, and ended with the editorship of George Beattie, in 1849. This information I have from the celebrated bibliopolist of periodical literature, S. G. Deeth, late of Georgetown, D. C., who was the highest authority on subjects of this kind.—*Gowans' Catalogue.*

"American Facts, Notes, and Statistics relative to the Government, Resources, &c., of the United States," by George P. Putnam, 8vo., portrait of Washington, and map, London, 1845.

"American Almanac and Repository of Useful Knowledge," from 1830 to 1860, both inclusive, forming a complete set, paper covers, Boston, 1830–'60.
—"The abovenamed series of volumes forms the only consecutive annals of the United States for the last thirty-one years. They possess intrinsic value to all who would desire accurate information concerning the country during that period."

"National Almanac," Philadelphia, 1863–'4.

"The Census of the United States;" Reports of the Patent Office and Agricultural Bureau.

"New American Cyclopædia: A Popular Dictionary of General Knowledge," edited by George Ripley and Charles A. Dana, in 16 vols., New York, D. Appleton & Co., 1862.

"Cyclopædia of American Literature," by E. A. and G. L. Duyckinck, 2 vols., New York, Charles Scribner, 1855.

Federalist * has become a classic memorial of the foundation of the American Government. The prescience and perspicacity as well as comprehensiveness of the writers thereof have been signally demonstrated by the whole history of the Slaveholders' Rebellion; and the political discussion incident to its suppression.

The archives of American oratory contain, for the sagacious explorer, clear reflections of and genuine emanations from the life, the discipline, and the physical and moral conditions peculiar to the country. Indeed, to understand how democratic institutions act on individual minds, and in what light the duties of the citizen are viewed by select intelligences, the foreign inquirer should become familiar with the eloquence of Otis, Henry, Rutledge, Marshall, Adams, Clay, Ames, Hamilton, Webster, and Everett.

It requires no great effort of the imagination to behold in the distant future a literary apotheosis for the orations of Daniel Webster, at Bunker Hill, Plymouth, and in the Senate, akin to that which has rendered those of Cicero patriotic classics for all time. Even we of the present generation seem to hear the oracle of history as well as of eloquence, when we revert, in the midst of the base mutiny that rends the Republic, to the pregnant and prescient defence of the Union which identifies Webster's name and fame with the glory and love of his country.

Everett's Addresses, which form three substantial octavo volumes,† and will doubtless extend to four, constitute the most complete and eloquent record of the social and political development of our country. Their scope and value, in this regard, would have been more emphatically acknowledged but for the desultory association which identifies all spoken history and criticism with temporary occasions. Yet, when we consider that these discourses were studiously prepared to

---

* "The Federalist: A Collection of Essays written in favor of the New Constitution, as agreed upon by the Federal Convention, September 17, 1787."

† "Orations and Speeches on Various Occasions," 3 vols. 8vo., Boston, 1850.

celebrate anniversaries of settlements and battles, to do honor to national benefactors, to inaugurate great movements in education and charity, being thus equally commemorative of the past and indicative of the future, it is obvious that their subjects include the most salient facts and inferences of our origin, growth, and tendencies as a people, and bring attractively into view many local and personal incidents that otherwise would have been overlooked. Accordingly, apart from any rhetorical merit, we know of no single work which will convey to an intelligent foreigner, a better general idea of the memorable phases of our national development, and the principles whereby it has been inspired, sustained, modified, and characterized, than the orations and speeches of Edward Everett.*

Indeed, to specify the kind and degree of information and illustration which native writers have contributed, would require an elaborate critical essay. They form a mine of suggestive knowledge or subtile revelation to those who have the insight and sympathy to seek from original sources, the truth of history, nature, and character as regards this country. They are, to the mass of American Travels, what the finished picture is to the desultory series of offhand sketches from nature; or what the musical composition is to the casual airs or keynote of the *maestro*. However the authenticity of Cooper's aboriginal ideals may be questioned, or with whatever justice his nautical descriptions may be criticized, no true observer of nature, familiar with the scenes of his stories, can fail to recognize a minute and conscientious limner of local and natural features and facts in his pictures of the woods and waters of his native land. No American reader of sensibility and perception can ponder the poems of Bryant, in a foreign land, without a new, vivid, and grateful consciousness of the pure and truthful mirror his verse affords, not only to the forms, hues, and phenomena, but to the very spirit of

---

* A glance at the titles of these Addresses will indicate how completely they cover the entire range of American subjects—historical, educational, economical, and social.

American seasons and scenery. There is an undercurrent of pathos and psychology in the New England romances of Hawthorne, which seizes on the inmost soul of her primitive life, and philosophically explains the normal traits of her actual character. It has been objected to his writings, that, with all their artistic truth and delicacy, they are morbid in tone. This is the natural consequence of the element to which we refer. Analysis like his, implies going beneath the vital superficies to the inward function; and what such an experiment loses in art, it gains in metaphysical power. The "Blithedale Romance" illustrates the enthusiasm for reform and of transcendentalism in New England. "The House of the Seven Gables" and "Twice-Told Tales" contain the psychological essence of primitive New England life. In the "Scarlet Letter" there is a profound though indirect protest against the inhumanity of Puritanism, as it was developed in the old Bay State—a demonstration of the unchristian system and sentiment that fail to temper justice with mercy, and to recognize the blessed efficiency of forgiveness. No native writer has gone so near the latent significance of New England life, in its moral interest and historical relations.

Numerous, also, are the less finished and more casual but often striking and true glimpses of the primitive character or normal traits of life, manners, and natural influences in different sections and at various periods, which the published correspondence, the memoirs and reminiscences, and the literary efforts of our public men, scholars, and patriotic citizens, yield. The unartistic but deeply wrought romance of "Margaret," by Judd, is a kind of Balzac anatomy and analysis of a once singular human experience in the Eastern States. The exquisite and original illustrations with which this remarkable story inspired the pencil of Darley, are its best praise.

Many of the historical episodes, the transition eras, and much of the local character and scenery and life of the country, have been pictured with memorable truth and vividness by our romance writers. Irving and Paulding have thus illustrated New York colonial times, the legends and the picturesque scenes as well as social traits of the State; Simms those of the South; Kennedy has thus illustrated Virginia; Dr. Bird, Kentucky; Hoffman, the Valley of the Mohawk; Miss Sedgwick, primitive New England; Mrs. Stowe, Sargent, Trowbridge, and others, slavery; Flint, the Valley of the Mississippi; McConnell, Texas; Mayne Reid, frontier life; Major Winthrop, the Rocky Mountains; Miss Warner, Miss Chesebro', and others of their sex, the rural and characteristic life of the Eastern States; and we might indefinitely extend the catalogue. Nor should the peculiar veins of humor indigenous to the country be forgotten as characteristic of the people—its Western, Yankee, negro, and Dutch phases; nor the fact be ignored that, coincident with this and similar rude and extravagant development, we have the finished romances of Ware and Poe, and the refined critical and æsthetic writings of Dana, Hillhouse, Allston, Greenough, and Madame d'Ossoli, and the bold humanitarian speculations of Emerson, Dewey, James, Calvert, and others. Personal memoirs and reminiscences are a rich mine of facts and influences, whereby the true life and significance of America may be realized. Of the former, such biographies as those of the heroes of our history conserved in the series of Sparks;* such lives as those of Buckminster and Chief-Justice Parsons, of Irving and Prescott, indirectly exhibit the spirit of our institutions and society; while curious details thereof abound in such memoirs as Graydon's, and such recollections as Watson of Philadelphia, Manlius Sargent and Buckingham of Boston, and Dr. Francis of New York, and Thomas, Alden, Goodrich, Valentine, and the "Croakers," have recorded.†

---

* Sparks's "American Biography," containing the Lives of Alexander Wilson, Captain John Smith, John Stark, Brockden Brown, General Montgomery, and Ethan Allen, 2 vols. 12mo., Boston, 1834.

Sparks's "American Biography," first series, 10 vols., second series, 15 vols., in all, 25 vols. 12mo., Boston, 1834–'50.

† Watson's "Annals;" "Dealings with the Dead," by an Old Sexton; Buckingham's "Recollections of Editorial Life;" "Old New York," by J. W.

Such works preserve social incidents and vigorous chapters of individual experience, wherein the philosopher will discover salient evidences of what is peculiar to this land and life; and the poet may sometimes learn what were the conservative elements that moulded the mental and kept alive the emotional character, the traits of natural scenery, climate, and domestic love and duty, as well as the struggles, guides, and glamours through and by which here grew or were grafted whatsoever of originality redeem the social and civic history of the New World. Pamphlets, newspapers, and sermons, ballads, playbills, diaries and letters, schoolbooks, holidays, old houses, gardens, portraits, and costumes, to the eye of science and the heart of wisdom, each and all convey their lesson of character, history, and life.

We have spoken of Cooper in prose, and Bryant in verse, as standard authorities in the description and illustration of American scenery; but, throughout our native literature, the most graphic pictures of individual landscapes, of the seasons in the Western world, and the most glowing exhibition of the traits and triumphs of life, character, and history, may be found by the discerning and sympathetic reader. The spirit of reform, of labor, of freedom, and of faith, as well as the characteristics of nature as here developed, have been truly and melodiously recorded by Whittier and Holmes, by Dana and Pierpont, by Sprague and Street, by Longfellow and Lowell, by Drake, Percival, Halleck, and a score of other bards. Theology, as intensified or chastened by the social life and political institutions of the country, is elaborated in the writings of Jonathan Edwards, Cotton, Mayhew, Stiles, Dwight, Witherspoon, Emmons, White, Mason, Hopkins, Miller, Woods, Alexander, Breckenridge, Wayland,

---

Francis, M. D.; Thatcher's "Military Journal;" Thomas's "History of Printing in America;" Alden's "Collection of American Epitaphs;" "Recollections of a Lifetime," by S. G. Goodrich; "Manuals of the Common Council of New York," by D. T. Valentine; "The Croakers," by J. R. Drake and Fitz Greene Halleck (annotated), first complete edition, printed by the Bradford Club, New York, 1860.

Murray, Parks, Walker, Bethune, Chapin, Hodge, Bushnell, Bush, Channing, Dewey, Parker, and many other representative men; and its every dogma and modification through freedom, conservatism, and speculation, exhibited in the published discourses of these and other of the leading clergy of all denominations, whose biographies,* also, written by Dr. Sprague and others, incidentally reveal the most interesting and characteristic details of clerical and parish life as well as domestic traits. To appreciate intimately the picturesque, social, or traditional local features of the country, we have a group of authentic and graceful or vigorous and sympathetic writers, who have sketched the scenery and life of the land with memorable emphasis: Brown, Dennie, Tudor, Wirt, Irving, and Wilson have been succeeded by Audubon, Kennedy, Fay, Longfellow, Hoffman, Sands, Willis, Curtis, Mitchell, Street, Prime, Ellet, Poe, Neal, Elliot, Hammond, Lowell, Shelton, Milburn, Thorpe, Baldwin, Cozzens, Kettell, Bard, Mackie, Headley, Parkman, Mrs. Gilman, Starr King, Strothers, Taylor, Webber, the Countess d'Ossoli, Whitehead, Kimball, Holland, Lanman, Mrs. Childs, Thoreau, Higginson, Miss Cooper, Dr. Holmes, and many others.†

Perhaps there is no class of books more characteristic of the American mind than the numerous records of modern exploration and travel. Herein even British critics acknowledge a peculiar freshness and vigor; and this is chiefly owing to the independent point of view, the natural spirit of adventure, and facility of adaptation incident to the freedom, self-reliance, and elasticity of temper fostered by our institu-

---

* "Annals of the American Pulpit," by William B. Sprague, D. D., 9 vols. 8vo., New York, 1857.

† Among the graphic landscapes, portraits, and incidents thus eliminated from life and observation by these writers, we may mention, as significant and illustrative, the American papers in "The Sketch Book" and "Idle Man," "Kavanagh," "Letters from Under a Bridge," "Up the River," "Woods and Waters," "The Adirondack," "Rural Letters," "The Bee Hunter," "The Axe, Rifle, and Saddle Bags," "My Farm of Edgewood," "Wild Scenes of the Forest and Prairie," "Lotus Eating," "A Summer Tour to the Lakes," "The White Mountains," "At Home and Abroad," "Fireside Trav-

tions and social discipline. Europe kindles the enthusiasm, Central America excites the speculative hardihood, and the Arctic regions inspire the adventurous heroism of our countrymen. What they see they know how to describe, and what they feel they can express with courage and animation; so that, in the memorials of other lands, the native mind often reflects itself with singular force and fervor.* He would miss a great source of knowledge, who, intent upon seizing the true significance of American life and character, or even the influences of nature and government, of trade and travel, should ignore the journalism of the country, wherein the immediate currents of opinion, tendencies of society, and tone of feeling, both radical and conservative, reckless and disciplined, find crude and casual yet authentic utterance.

Freneau's ballads should not be thought beneath the notice of the candid investigator, nor even Barlow's "Hasty Pudding;" nor can the historical student safely neglect the aboriginal eloquence of Red Jacket and Tecumseh, nor the early periodical literature initiated by Dennie. He may consult with benefit the first scientific essays of Catesby, Ramsay, Williamson, Colden, and Mitchell; Espy and Redfield on

els," "Walden, or Life in the Woods," "A Week on the Concord and Merrimac Rivers," "The Moravian Settlement at Bethlehem, Pa.," "Carolina Sports," "Hunting Adventures in the Northern Wilds," "Excursions in Field and Forest," "Life in the Open Air," "At Home and Abroad," "Blackwater Chronicle," "Out-of-Door Papers," "Letters from New York," "Wild Sports of the South," "Rural Hours," "Letters from the Alleghany Mountains," "The Oregon Trail," "Poetry of Travel in New England," "Autocrat of the Breakfast Table," "From Cape Cod to the Tropics, " &c.

* Indirectly, the literature of America illustrates the original enterprise that, with free and bold aspiration, seeks new and laborious fields of research or creation: as instances of which, in the most diverse spheres, may be noted the translation of the great work of Laplace, by Bowditch, Dr. Robinson's "Biblical Researches in Palestine," Kane's "Arctic Expedition," Allibone's "Dictionary of Authors," that picturesque memorial of the Fur Trade, Irving's "Astoria," and Dr. Rush on the "Human Voice;" while the literature of Travel in our vernacular has been enriched by the contributions of Stephens, Brace, Fletcher, Wise, Melville, Mackenzie, Dana, Mayo, and Taylor.

Climatology; Hitchcock and Rogers on Geology; Barton, Nuttall, and Grey and Torrey on Botany; Davis, Squier, and others on the Mounds; Schoolcraft on the aborigines; Carey on economical subjects; the newspaper and diary literature, familiar letters, and controversial pamphlets, which more than highly finished productions bear the fresh stamp of civil and social life, and have been wisely collected by local and State associations, to facilitate inquiries into the past of America.*

Nor have our institutions and social tendencies lacked the highest native criticism. One of the most consistent, lucid, and able ethical authors in the language—William Ellery Channing—has left, in his writings,† the most eloquent protests and appeals, based on the application of religion and philosophy to American life, character, and politics. No writer has more perfectly demonstrated the absolute wrong and the inevitable consequences of slavery; and, at the same time, no social reformer has more justly appreciated the claims, difficulties, and duties of the slaveholder. We seek in vain among the most renowned foreign critics of our national character for a more unsparing, earnest, yet humane analyst. Channing rebuked emphatically "the bigotry of republicanism;" continually pointed out the inadequacy of government, in itself, to elevate and mould society; he warned his countrymen, in memorable terms, against the tyranny of public opinion, and advocated the rights, responsibilities, and mission of the individual. When slavery extension was sought through the annexation of Texas; when the repudiation of State debts drew obloquy upon the national honor; when popular vengeance burned a Roman

---

* Among the early pamphleteers were James Otis (1725–'83), Josiah Quincy, Jr. (1744–'75), John Dickinson (1732–1808); Joseph Galloway (1730–1803), a Tory writer; Richard Henry Lee (1732–'94), Arthur Lee (1740–'92), William Livingston (1723–'90), William Henry Drayton (1742–'99), John Adams (1735–1826), Thomas Jefferson (1743–1826), and Timothy Pickering (1748–1829).

† "Complete Works," with an Introduction, 6 vols. 12mo., Boston, 1849.
"Memoirs of, by W. H. Channing," 3 vols. 12mo., Boston, 1848, London, 1848.

Catholic convent, and sought to suppress journals that promulgated obnoxious views in religion and politics—this eloquent friend of humanity seized the opportunity to show how essential is the dependence of government, order, social progress, and peace upon Christianity; and how, in the last analysis, the individual citizen alone could sustain and conserve the freedom and the faith upon which human society rests. He referred great public questions to first principles; solved political problems by spiritual truths; recognized human rights as the foundation of civic rule; justice as the one vital element of government; and made his hearers and readers feel that the "forms of liberty do not constitute its essence." Were we to select a single illustration of the divine possibilities incident to free institutions,—liberty of conscience and of the press, the presence of nature in her most grand aspects of ocean, forest, and heavens, and an equal scope for social and personal development,—considering these national privileges in their influence upon intellectual development and religious aspirations,—we should point to the example, the influence, and the written thought of Channing; for therein we find the most unfettered expression of private conviction united to the deepest sense of God and humanity; the freshest expansion of freedom combined with the most profound consciousness of individual responsibility.

CHAPTER XI.

CONCLUSION.

For many years after the earlier records of travel in America, the local and social traits therein described lingered; so that those who look back half a century, find many familiar and endeared associations revived by these casual memorials of an antecedent period. Two principal agencies have caused the rapid transition in outward aspect and social conditions which make the present and the past offer so great a contrast even within the space of an average American life—immigration, and locomotive facilities. The first has, in a brief space, quadrupled the population of cities, and modified its character by a foreign element; and the second, by bringing the suburban and interior residents constantly to the seaboard, has gradually won them to traffic and city life. What was individual and characteristic, exclusive and local therein, becomes thus either changed or superseded. There is no longer the reign of coteries; individualities are lost in the crowd; natives of old descent are jostled aside in the thoroughfare; the few no longer form public opinion; distinctions are generalized; the days of the one great statesman, preacher, actor, doctor, merchant, social oracle, and paramount belle, when opinion, intercourse, and character were concentrated, localized, and absolute, have passed away; and the repose, the moderation, the economy, the geniality and dignity of the past are often lost in gregarious progress and prosperity. A venerable reminiscent may lead the curious stranger to some obscure gable-roofed house, a solitary and decayed tree, or border relic strangely conserved in the heart of a thriving metropolis, and descant on the time when these represented isolated centres of civilization. Standing in a busy mart, he may recall there the wilderness of his youth, and, before an old, dignified portrait by Copley, lament the fusion of social life and the bustle of modern pretension; or, dwelling on the details of an ancestral letter, argue that, if our fathers moved slower, they felt and thought more and realized life better than their descendants, however superior in general knowledge. Except for the purpose of literary art and historical study, however, the past is rarely appreciated and little known; hence the curious interest and value, as local illustrations, of some of these forgotten memorials of how places looked and people lived before the days of steam, telegraphs, and penny papers.

Sir Henry Holland, writes Lockhart to Prescott, "on his return from his rapid expedition, declares, except friends, he found everything so changed, that your country seemed to call for a visit once in five years." The truth is, that, owing to the transition process which has been going on here from the day that the first conflict occurred between European colonists and the savage inhabitants, to the departure of the last emigrant train from the civilized border to the passes of the Rocky Mountains; and owing, also, to the incessant influx of a foreign element in the older communities, to the results of popular education and of political excitements and vicissitudes, there is no country in the world in regard to which it is so difficult to generalize. Exceptions to every rule, modifications of every special feature and fact, oblige the candid philosopher to reconsider and qualify at every step.

One vast change alone in the conditions and prospects— political, social, and economical—of this continent, since the records of the early travellers, would require a volume to describe and discuss—the increase of territory and of immigration, with the liberal character of our naturalization laws. Whole communities now are nationally representative; each people finds its church, its *fêtes*, its newspaper, costume, and habits organized in America. Every convulsion or disaster abroad brings its community of exiles to our shores. After the French Revolution, nobles and people flocked hither; after the massacre at St. Domingo, the creoles who escaped found refuge here; famine sends thousands of Irish annually, and in the West is a vast and thrifty German population; Hungarians make wine in Ohio; Jenny Lind found her countrymen on the banks of the Delaware; an Italian regiment was organized in a few days, when New York summoned her citizens to the defence of the Union; and in that city, the tokens of every nationality are apparent—the French *table d'hôte*, the Italian *caffè*, the German beer garden, image venders from Genoa and organ grinders from Lucca, theatres, journals, churches, music, and manners peculiar to every people, from the Jewish synagogue to the Roman convent, from the prohibited cavatina to the local dish, from the foreign post-office clerk to the peculiar festival of saint or municipality, betoken the versatile and protected emigration.

It is when, with the horrors of Spielberg vivid to his fancy, such an observer beholds the industrious and cheerful Italian exile in America; when he notes the Teutonic crowd grouped round the German post-office window at Chicago, and thinks of the privations of the German peasant at home; when he watches the long ranks of well-fed and hilarious Celts, in procession on St. Patrick's Day in New York, and compares them with the squalid tenants of mud cabins in Ireland; when he listens to the unchecked eloquence of the Hungarian refugee, and thinks of the Austrian censors and *sbirri;* when he beholds Sisters of Charity thridding the crowd on some errand of love; placidly clad Friends flocking to yearly meeting; Fourier communities on the Western plains; here a cathedral, there a synagogue; in one spot a camp meeting, in another a Unitarian chapel; to-night a political caucus, to-morrow a lyceum lecture; here rows of carmen devouring the daily journal, there a German picnic; now a celebration of the birthday of Burns, wherein the songs and sympathies of Scotland are renewed, and now a Gallic ball, the anniversary *fête* of St. George, the complacent retrospections of Pilgrims' Day, or the rhetoric and roar of the Fourth of July;—it is when the free scope and the mutual respect, the perfect self-reliance and the undisturbed individuality of all these opposite demonstrations, indicative of an eclectic, tolerant, self-subsistent social order, combination, and utterance, pass before the senses and impress the thought, that we realize what has been done and is doing on this continent for man as such; and the unhallowed devotion to the immediate, the constant superficial excitements, the inharmonious code of manners, the lawlessness of border and the extravagance of metropolitan life, the feverish ambition, the license of the press—all the blots on the escutcheon of the Republic, grow insignificant before the sublime possibilities whereof probity and beneficence, tact and talent, high impulse and adventurous zeal may here take advantage.

An English statesman, on a visit to New York, expressed his surprise at the spirit of accommodation and the absence of violent language during a deadlock of vehicles in Broadway, whence his conveyance was only extricated after long delay. The fact made a strong impression, from its contrast to the brutal language and manners he had often witnessed, under like circumstances, in London. After reflecting on the subject, he attributed the self-control of the baffled carmen to self-respect. "They hope to rise in life," he said, "and, therefore, have a motive to restrain their temper and improve their character." There was much truth and sagacity in this reasoning. An artist fresh from Europe and the East observed that the expression of self-reliance was astonishing in the American physiognomy. These spontaneous remarks of two strangers, equally intelligent but of diverse experience—the one a social and the other an artistic philosopher—include the *rationale* of American civilization. The prospect of ameliorating his condition elevates man in his own esteem,

19*

while self-dependence gives him confidence; but the latter feeling is apt to make him indifferent to public duty: hence the gross municipal corruption and legislative abuses which are directly owing to neglect of the duties of the citizen. Not until there is a "rising of the people" in the cause of national reform, as earnest and unanimous as that which rallied to the national defence, may we hope to see those ameliorations, the need of which all acknowledge, to purify the elective franchise and the judicial corps, make the centripetal force in political affairs dominate the centrifugal, and bring the best men in capacity and honor to the highest positions.

To the eye and mind of an American, when disciplined by study and foreign observation, while the incongruities of our social and physical condition, as a nation, are often startling, the elastic temper, the unsubdued confidence of the national character, reconcile discrepancies and console for deficiencies, by the firm conviction that these are destined to yield to a civilization whose tendency is so diffusive. There are, indeed, enough signs of amelioration to encourage the least sanguine. Within a few years, the claims of genius and character, of taste and culture, have been more and more practically recognized. The refinements in domestic economy, the popularity of art, the prevalent love and cultivation of music, the free institutions for self-culture, the new appreciation of rural life, the tempered tone of religious controversy, the higher standard of taste and literature, and the more frequent study of the natural sciences, are obvious indications of progress in the right direction, since the severe comments upon American life and manners were partially justified by facts. Even the specific defects noted by travellers half a century ago, are essentially lessened or have quite disappeared.

A living and candid French writer alludes to the United States as "une terre plus séparée de nous par les nuages de nos préjugés que par les brouillards de l'Atlantique." Not a few of these prejudices had their origin in facts that no longer exist. It is almost impossible for a European to make due allowances for the changes that occur on this side of the water. But while some of the minor faults and dangers recorded by tourists are obsolete, the chief obstacles recognized by all thoughtful observers to our national welfare, are only so far diminished that they are more clearly apprehended and more candidly acknowledged. The crisis foretold as regards slavery, has arrived, and taken the form of an unprovoked rebellion against the Federal Government, whereby the national power and virtue have been confirmed and elicited. The double term of the Presidential office, the almost indiscriminate right of electoral suffrage, in connection with the vast emigration of ignorant and degraded natives of Europe, the facility in making and consequent recklessness in spending money, the extension of territory, the decadence in public spirit, the increase of unprincipled political adventurers, and the license of the press, have, each and all, as prophesied and anticipated, worked out an immeasurable amount of political and social evil. Irreverence and materialism have kept pace with success; abuses in official rule, neglect in civic duty, convulsions in finance, crises of political opinion and parties —a kind of mechanical, unaspiring, self-absorbed prosperity, have resulted from so many avenues to wealth thrown open to private enterprise, and such a passion for gain and office as the unparalleled opportunity inevitably breeds. Yet, withal, there have been and are redeeming elements, auspicious signs, hopeful auguries; and those who are least cognizant of these, should never forget that our social life and political system bring everything to the surface; and it is the average character of a vast nation, and not the acts of a few exclusive rulers, that the daily journals of the United States reveal. The Government is always behind and below what it represents; the facts of the hour that are patent, and taken as significant of the national life, are but partial exponents of private use, beauty, faith, freedom, progress, and peace, which eternal blessings the individual is more free to seek here and now, than under any institutions the record whereof is concealed in royal cabinets.

It has long been an accepted proposition, that the peculiar interest, importance, and moral significance of the United States in the family of nations, rests exclusively on a practical realization of the "greatest good of the greatest number;" in other words, Europe has represented the idea of culture and of society—America of material prosperity, the paradise of the masses, the one place on earth where nourishment and shelter can be had most certainly in exchange for labor: hence the manners of the country have been invariably criticized, and physical resources magnified; and hence, too, the cant whereby a few general facts are made to overshadow countless special details of life, of character, and of civilization. Never was there a populous land whose inhabitants were so uniformly judged *en masse*, or one about which the truth has been more generalized and less discriminated. We find it quite easy to imagine the far different conclusions to which an observant and perspicacious student of life in America might arrive, with ample opportunities and sympathetic insight. To such a mind, the individual of adequate endowments, born and bred or long resident here, would offer traits and triumphs of character or experience, directly resulting from the political, social, and natural circumstances of the country, which, to say the least, would impress him with the originality and possible superiority thereof in a psychological or ethnological view. To group, define, or analyze these peculiarities, would require not only an artist's insight and skill, but a much broader range than a traveller's hasty journal or a reviewer's flippant commentary. There is one branch of the subject, however, to which every thinking observer is irresistibly led—the remarkable diversities of tone and tact, of vigor and adaptation, of personal conviction and individual careers, which the life of the prairies and the mart, and the plantation, the seaboard, and the interior, the scholar of the East, the hunter of the West, the agriculturist of the South, and the manufacturer of the North, mould, foster, and train;

the rare and rich social combination thence eliminated; the occasional force and beauty, bravery and influence thus developed in a way and on a scale unknown to Europe: such possibilities and local tendencies being furthermore infinitely modified and tempered, intensified or diffused, by the extraordinary degree of personal freedom and range of speculation and belief, experiment and inquiry—religious, scientific, political, and economical;—perhaps not the least striking evidence whereof is to be found in the modification of national traits observed in foreigners who become Americanized—the sensitive and capricious native of Southern Europe, often attaining self-reliance and progressive energy; the English solidity of character becoming "touched to finer issues" by attrition with a more liberal social life and a less humid climate; and even Gallic vivacity reaching an unwonted practical and judicious equilibrium: for it is a curious fact, that the student of character can nowhere detect in solution so many of the influences of all climes and the idiosyncrasies of all nations, as in this grand rendezvous and arena—obnoxious, indeed, to the evils that attend extravagance, superfluity, incongruity, the wilfulness and the wantonness of gregarious prosperity; but none the less radiant and real with the hope and the health of abundant human elements, and the abeyance of caste, despotism, and conformity; so that, more and more, the great lesson of moral independence comes home to personal conviction. From early learning to work and think for themselves, and to feel for others, our people grow in the intimate conviction that here and now, if nowhere else in God's universe, men and women can, by the just exercise of their will and the wise use of their opportunities, live according to their individual wants, capacities, and belief; rise above circumstances; assert their individuality; cultivate their powers in faith and freedom; enjoy their gifts; and become, however situated, true and benign exemplars of manhood and womanhood. And in all these natural and civic agencies that excite and eliminate and intensify, ay, and often prematurely wear out and unwisely concentrate the energies and the life of humanity here, we behold an arena, a series of influences, a means and medium of experience and experiment, designed by Infinite Wisdom for a special purpose in the vast economy of the world; and before this conviction the pigmies of political prejudice and the venal critics of the hour sink into contempt.

In a broad view and with reference to humanity, as such, it is Opportunity that distinguishes and consecrates American institutions, nationality, nature, and life. No microscopic or egotistical interpretation can do justice to the country. A narrow heart, a conventional standard, are alike inapplicable to test communities, customs, resources, as here distributed and organized. Berkeley as a Christian, Washington as a patriotic and De Tocqueville as a political philosopher, recognized Opportunity as the great and benign distinction of America. The very word implies the possible and probable abuses, the periods of social transition, the incongruities, hazards, and defects inevitable to such a condition. Commerce, science, and freedom are the elements of our prosperity and character; and it is no Utopian creed, that, by the laws of modern civilization, they work together for good; but the dilettante and the epicurean, the rigid conservative, the exacting man of society, and the selfish man of the world, find their cherished instincts often offended, where the generous and wise, the noble and earnest soul is lost in "an idea dearer than self," when, with disinterested acumen and sympathy, regarding the spectacle of national development and personal success.

To the eye of a historical and ethical philosopher, no possible argument in favor of liberal institutions can be more impressive than the insane presumption which has led men of education and knowledge of the world to stir up and lead an insurrection to secure, in this age and on this continent, the perpetuity and political sanctity of human slavery. So desperate a moral experiment argues the irrationality as well as the inhumanity of "property in man" with trumpet-tongued emphasis. And this solemn lesson is enforced by the new revelation, brought about by civil war, of the actual influence of slavery upon character. The ignorance and recklessness of the "poor whites" became fanatical under the excitement to passion and greed, which the leaders fostered to betray and brutalize the "landless resolutes." Under no other circumstances, by no conceivable means, except through the unnatural and inhuman conditions of such a social disorganization, could a white population, in the nineteenth century, on a flourishing continent and under an actually free Government, be cajoled and maddened into hate, unprovoked by the slightest personal wrong, and exhibiting itself in blasphemy, theft, drunkenness, poisoning, base and cruel tricks, barbarities wholly unknown to modern civilized warfare; such as bayoneting the wounded, wantonly shooting prisoners, desecrating the dead to convert their bones into ghastly trophies, and leaving behind them, in every abandoned camp, letters malign in sentiment, vulgar in tone, and monstrous in orthography—patent evidences of the possible coexistence of the lowest barbarism and ostensible civilization, and the moral necessity of anticipating by war the suicidal crisis of a fatally diseased local society.

When the English replied to John Adams's defence of the American Constitution, their chief argument against it was, that, in war, the Executive had not adequate power. This supreme test has now been applied in a desperate civil conflict. An educated people have sustained the Government in extending its constitutional authority to meet the national exigency, without the least disturbance of that sense of public security and private rights essential to the integrity of our institutions. Nor is this all. The war for the Union has, in a few months, done more to solve the problem of free and slave labor, to do away with the superstitious dread of servile insurrection in case of partial freedom, to expose the fallacies of pro-slavery economists, to demonstrate the identity of prosperous industry with freedom, to mutually enlighten different populations, to make clear the line of demarcation between the patriot and the politician, to nationalize local sentiment, to make apparent the absolute resources of the country and the normal character of the people, and thus to vindicate free institutions, than all the partisan dissensions and peaceful speculation since the Declaration of Independence. Moreover, the war has developed original inventive talent in ordnance and camp equipage, afforded precisely the discipline our people so "disinclined to subordination" needed, won our self-indulgent young men from luxury to self-denial, evoked the generous instincts of the mercantile classes, called out the benign efficiency of woman, confirmed the popular faith, fused classes, made heroes, unmasked the selfish and treacherous, purified the social atmosphere, and, through disaster and hope deferred, conducted the nation to the highest and most Christian self-assertion and victory. The history of the Sanitary Commission, the improvements in military science, the letters of the rank and file of the Union army preserved in the local journals, the topographical revelations, personal prowess, vast extent of operations, new means and appliances, and momentous results, will afford the future historian not only unique materials, but fresh and surprising evidence of the elements of American civilization as exhibited through the fiery ordeal of civil war. The Proclamation* of the President of the United States at the close

---

* "Fellow citizens, we cannot escape history.

"We, of this Congress, will be remembered in spite of ourselves.

"No personal significance, or insignificance, can spare one or another of us.

"The fiery trial through which we pass, will light us down in honor or dishonor to the latest generation.

"We say that we are for the Union. The world will not forget that while we say this, we do know how to save the Union. The world knows we do know how to save it. We, even we here, hold the power and bear the responsibility.

"In giving freedom to the slave, we assure freedom to the free, honorable alike in what we give and what we preserve.

"We shall nobly save or meanly lose the last best hope of the earth.

"Other means may succeed. This could not fail.

"The way is plain—peaceful, generous, just; a way which, if followed, the world will ever applaud, and God must forever bless.

"ABRAHAM LINCOLN."

of the year 1862, betokens a new and advanced charter of American progress.

"Will anybody deny," asks John Bright, in a recent speech to his constituents, "that the Government at Washington, as regards its own people, is the strongest Government in the world at this hour? And for this simple reason, because it is based on the will of an instructed people. Look at its power. I am not now discussing why it is, or the cause which is developing this power; but power is the thing which men regard in these old countries, and which they ascribe mainly to European institutions. But look at the power which the United States have developed! They have brought more men into the field, they have built more ships for their navy, they have shown greater resources than any other nation in Europe at this moment is capable of. Look at the order which has prevailed at their elections, at which, as you see by the papers, 50,000, or 100,000, or 250,000 persons voted in a given State, with less disorder than you have seen lately in three of the smallest boroughs in England—Barnstable, Windsor, and Andover. Look at their industry. Notwithstanding this terrific struggle, their agriculture, their manufactures and commerce proceed with an uninterrupted success. They are ruled by a President chosen, it is true, not from some worn-out royal or noble blood, but from the people, and one whose truthfulness and spotless honor have gained him universal praise. And now the country that has been vilified through half the organs of the press in England during the last three years, and was pointed out, too, as an example to be shunned by many of your statesmen,—that country, now in mortal strife, affords a haven and a home for multitudes flying from the burdens and the neglect of the old Governments of Europe. And, when this mortal strife is over, when peace is restored, when slavery is destroyed, when the Union is cemented afresh—for I would say, in the language of one of our poets addressing his country,

> 'The grave's not dug where traitor hands shall lay,
> In fearful haste, thy murdered corse away'—

then Europe and England may learn that an instructed democracy is the surest foundation of government, and that education and freedom are the only sources of true greatness and true happiness among any people."

When the new scientific methods of historical writing are applied to the annals of our own country, some remarkable coincidences and a dramatic unity in the sequence of memorable events will illustrate the chronicle. To subdue the wilderness; to colonize with various nationalities a vast continent; to vindicate, by the ordeal of battle, the supremacy among them of the Anglo-Saxon element; to raise and purify this into political self-assertion, by establishing free institutions; under their auspicious influence to attain the greatest industrial development and territorial expansion; and, finally, in these latter days, to solve, by the terrible alternative of civil war, the vast and dark problem of slavery—this is the momentous series of circumstances whereby it has pleased God to educate this nation, and induce moral results fraught with the highest duties and hopes of humanity; and, deeply conscious thereof, we cannot but exclaim, with our national poet:

> "O country, marvel of the earth!
> O realm to sudden greatness grown!
> The age that gloried in thy birth,
> Shall it behold thee overthrown?
> Shall traitors lay thy greatness low?
> No! land of hope and blessing, no!"

INDEX.

INDEX.

ABUSE of America, English, 252.
Addison, writings of, compared with those of Washington Irving, 288.
Address of eminent Frenchmen to loyal Americans, 154.
Addresses, commemorative, 421.
Adriani, Count, 340; Washington's opinion of his book, 340.
Adventure, spirit of Americans for, 434.
Agassiz, on the priority of the formation of the American continent, 14.
Albany, sketch of society at, by Mrs. Grant, 172; Peter Kalm's picture of, in 1749, 296.
Alessandro, Pietro d', 342; his letters from Boston, 343; visits Cambridge, 349; the Boston Athenæum, 351.
Allouez, Father Claude, narrative of, 44.
Allston, Washington, on the affinity which should exist between the United States and England, 259.
Alyaco, Petrus de, "Imago Mundi," Washington Irving's remarks on, 23.
America, similarity of, to Italy in furnishing subjects of interest to authors, 2; general sameness of writings of travels in, 4; European writers of travels in, each interested in a different theme, 4; toleration in, the source of its attraction to foreign exiles, 7; natural features also interest, 7; early discoverers and explorers of, 13; its natural features conduce to the spread of civilization, 15; its antiquities compared with those of the Old World, 16; conjectures in regard to the primitive inhabitants of America, 17; claimed by the Welsh to have been discovered by Madoc in 1170, 18; early pictorial representations of manners and customs of its inhabitants, 23; the fifteenth and sixteenth centuries prolific in works on, 24; curious relics of annals of discovery in, 26; miscellaneous publications relating to, 33; English abuse of, 252; book collectors in, 317; deceptions practised upon travellers in, 341; self-respect of its people, 441.
American travellers and writers, 371.

Ampère, J. J., "Promenade en Amérique," 142; notes carelessness of Americans, 143; versatility of his descriptions, 144.
Anbury, Thomas, "Travels in the Interior of America," 186; description of Cambridge, Mass., 187; notices the defective teeth of Americans, 188; regrets that he cannot visit Boston, 188; anxiety to return to England, 188.
Antiquities, American, compared with those of the Old World, 16.
Ashe, Thomas, 202; his travels in America, 203; his peculiar opinions of Americans, 204.
Athenæum, the Boston, described by Pietro d'Alessandro, 350.

BACKWOODSMEN, American, Talleyrand's opinion of, 114.
Bancroft, George, visit of John G. Kohl to, at Newport, 324.
Barre, Col., on English of America before the Revolutionary war, 254.
Bartlett, John R., "Dictionary of Americanisms," 286; similarity between the provincialisms of New England and those of Great Britain, 286.
Bartram, John, 372; his botanical labors, 372; his travels, 374; Peter Collinson's opinion of him, 374; his close observance of nature, 376; description of Oswego, 377; appointed botanist and naturalist to the king of England, 378; explores Florida, 379; his home life, 380.
Bartram, William, 382; his study of nature, 384.
Beaumont, Gustave de, his "Marie," 139; women of America and France compared, 141.
Belknap, Dr., the foremost primitive local historian of America, 3; founder of the Massachusetts Historical Society, 3; his description of the White Mountains, 3.
Beltrami, J. C., "Pilgrimage in Europe and America," 342.
Benton, Thomas H., sketch of, 322.
Berkeley, Bishop G., 156; obtains a charter for erecting a college in Bermuda,

157; his letters, 157; Walpole and, 158; lines of, 159; marries and embarks for America, 159; his friendship for Smibert the painter, 161; his sacrifices, 161; arrives at Newport, R. I., 162; religious condition of Rhode Island in 1714, 162; his reception at Newport, 163; letter describing the town, 164; is delighted with American scenery, 165; his munificence to Yale College, 167; memorials of his residence in America, 169.
Biography, American, 424, 432.
Blackwood's Magazine, remarks of, on Harriet Martineau's book, 225; its ridicule of Yale College and New Englanders, 263.
Bonaparte, Joseph, resides in seclusion in New Jersey, 122.
Book collectors, American, 317.
Books of travel, diversity of treatment of, 4.
Boston, notes of Marquis de Chastellux on, 74; described by L'Abbé Robin in 1781, 76; its people, 77; commerce, 78; visit of Brissot de Warville to, 83; commercial intercourse of, in 1729, 166; John G. Kohl's impressions of, 313; book collectors of, 317; Luigi Castiglione's impressions of, 339; Pietro d'Alessandro's description of its people, 345.
Botany, promoters of the science of, in America, 372.
Botta, Carlo, 334.
Bradford, Governor, poetical description of New England, 33.
Breckinridge, Dr., on the necessity of the maintenance of the American Union, 277.
Bremer, Fredrika, her novels, 298; her reception in America, 298; her comparisons of Swedish and American scenery, 299; her curiosity, 299.
Bright, John, on the strength of the United States Government, 449.
Brillat-Savarin, " Physiologie du Gout," 125; wild-turkey shooting, 126; visit to the family of M. Bulow, 127.
Brissot de Warville, 82; visits Boston, 83; journeys to New York, 84; Philadelphia, 84; visits Washington at Mount Vernon, 85; Whittler's lines on, 86; his anti-slavery sympathies, 86; admiration of Americans, 87; sketch of New York city in 1788, 87; smoking in New York, 88.
Bristed, Rev. John, 205; his " America and her Resources," 205; opinion of *London Quarterly Review* on his work, 206.
British authors, writings of, compared with those of America, 288.
British colonists in America described by Charlevoix, 49.
British travellers and writers on America, 156; desirableness and feasibility of a compilation of their works, 215; miscellaneous works of, on America, 218, 219, 220, 222, 224, 229.
Brown, Charles Brockden, translates Volney's work on America, 97.
Browning, Elizabeth, on British illiberality, 290.
Bryant, William Cullen, his " Letters of a Traveller," 418; his poems, 430.

Bulow, M., visit of Brillat-Savarin to the family of, 127.
Burke, Edmund, " Account of the European Settlements in America," 181.
Burnaby, Rev. Andrew, 173; his description of Virginians, 173; visits Philadelphia, 174; New York, 174; opinion of Long Island, 175; visits Rhode Island, 175; opinion of its people, 175; his description of Bishop Berkeley's residence at Newport, 176; visits Boston and Cambridge, 177; strict observance of the Sabbath in New England, 178; his opinions in regard to the American colonies, 179.
Byrd, William, expeditions of, described in the Westover Manuscripts, 32.
Byron, 211; his apostrophe to America, 212.

CAMBRIDGE, Mass., described by Thomas Anbury, 187; Pietro d'Alessandro's visit to, 349.
Canonicut Island, Bishop Berkeley lands at, 162.
Capobianco, Raffaelle, 358; ridiculous statements of his book, 359.
Carli, Le Comte, " Lettres Americaines," 5.
Carlisle, Earl of, his lecture at Leeds on the United States, 231.
Carver, Capt. John, 287; his " Travels," 388.
Castiglione, Luigi, 338; his impressions of Boston, 339; visit to Mount Vernon, 330.
Catholic missionaries the pioneer writers of American travels, 37.
Channing, William Ellery, 436; his influence on free institutions in America, 437.
Charlevoix, P. F. X., travels in Canada and the Northwest, 47; his letters, 49; account of New England and other British provinces, 49; description of the Missouri and Mississippi, 50; review of the scene of his labors, 51; his " Histoire de la Nouvelle France," 57.
Chastellux, Marquis de, 58; a friend of Washington, 59; his " Voyages dans l'Amérique Septentrionale, 60;" romance of his style and comparisons, 60; opinions of his writings, 61; his " Travels " translated into English, 61; justness of his criticisms, 62; visits Providence, R. I., 63; Hartford, 64; sketch of Gov. Trumbull, 64; visits the Hudson Highlands, 65; interview with Washington and his officers, 65; visits Philadelphia, 66; Mrs. Bache, 66; Robert Morris, 66; social customs of Frenchmen and Quakers compared, 66; his description of Northern New York, 67; journey into Virginia, 68; describes Jefferson, 69; minuteness of his observation, 71; traits of different sections, 72; visits Portsmouth, N. H., 73; attends a ball at Boston, and describes the " prettiest of the women dancers," 74; other Boston celebrities, 74; takes leave of Washington at Newburgh, 74; his description of Washington, 75; translates Col. Hum-

INDEX.   455

phrey's "Address to the American Armies," 76.
Chateaubriand visits the United States, 118; visits Washington, 119; impressed with American scenery, 120.
Children, American, Anthony Trollope on the precocity of, 239.
Civilization, natural features of America conduce to the spread of, 15.
Cleveland, Morris, his visit to Ohio from New England in 1796, 400.
Clinton, De Witt, his " Letters of Hibernicus," 404 ; his exploration of Western New York, 405 ; impressed with the necessity and feasibility of a great canal, 408 ; realization of his project, 410.
Cobbett, William, 208 ; praises farm life in America, 209; his bluntness, egotism, and radicalism, 210 ; Heine's apostrophe to, 211.
Cobden, Richard, his opinion of the London *Times*, 291.
Collinson, Peter, his opinion of John Bartram, 374.
Columbus, Christopher, familiar with the writings of Petrus de Alyaco, 23.
Commemorative Addresses, 421.
Congress, Continental, Jacob Duché, chaplain of, 81.
Connecticut, a glimpse of, in Washington's Diary, in 1789, 419.
Cooper, J. Fenimore, his romances compared with those of Scott, 288 ; endeavors to censure and counsel, 413 ; Halleck's lines on, 414 ; accuracy of his descriptions, 430.
Cooper, Thomas, 197; his opinions of America, 198.
Coxe, Tench, his " View of the United States of America," 393.
Crevecœur H. St. John, settles in New York in 1754, 89 ; Hazlitt's opinion of his work, 89 ; his misfortunes, 90 ; his " Letters of an American Farmer," 90 ; taste for rural life, 92 ; birds, 92 ; his humanity rewarded, 93.

DABLON, Father, superior of the Ottawa Mission, 44.
Davis, John, 200 ; his " Travels in the United States," 201.
De Bry, " Voyages and Travels to America," 23.
Deceptions practised upon travellers in America, 341.
De Pradt, "L'Europe et l'Amérique," 149.
Dickens, Charles, 221; his remarks on American slavery, 221 ; ridicules English writers on America in " Pickwick," 264.
Domenech, Abbé Em., his " Seven Years' Residence in the Great American Deserts " ridiculed by a London journal, 6.
Douglass, Dr. William, his work on the " British Settlements in North America, 183 ; Adam Smith's opinion of him, 185.
Duché, Jacob, remarks of, on America before the Revolution, 81 ; treachery of, 81.
Duval, Jules, his opinion of the advantages of emigration, 283.

Dwight, Timothy, " Travels in New England and New York," 390 ; Robert Southey's opinion of his " Travels " in the *Quarterly Review*, 392.

EARLY discoverers and explorers of America, 13.
Early travellers, accounts of, most to be preferred, 1.
Eddis, William, " Letters from America," 186.
Education, Anthony Trollope's opinion of the American system of, 236.
Elliot, Rev. Jared, becomes acquainted with Bishop Berkeley, 167.
Emigrants, European, freedom of action enjoyed by, in America, 440.
English abuse of America, 252 ; their ignorance of America before the Revolution, 254.
English and French writers on the War for the Union contrasted, 153.
English, brutality of the, 281 ; their want of consideration for woman, 282; the debasement of their poor, 282 ; furnish frequent subjects for caricature, 284 ; their ridicule of Yankeeisms, 286 ; Mrs. Browning on the illiberality of the, 290 ; Voltaire's comparison of the, 290 ; change of feeling of Americans toward the, 291.
English periodicals, misrepresentations of, 260.
English publisher, venality of an, 260.
European Governments, facilities offered by, for the diffusion of knowledge relating to early explorations, 26 ; writers, northern, 293 ; French literature in, 293.
Everett, Edward, his opinion of Captain Basil Hall's book, 200 ; visit of John G. Kohl to, 318 ; his Addresses, 429.
Expeditions, U. S. Government, 418.
Eyma, Xavier, " Vie dans le Noveau Monde," 151.

FAUX, an English farmer, 222 ; his absurd calumnies, 223.
Fearon, Henry B., Sydney Smith's opinion of, 200.
Female writers, British, on America, 222.
Fiddler, Rev. Isaac, remarks of his " Observations," 201.
Fisch, Georges, " Les États Unis en 1861," 149 ; first impressions of New York, 150 ; opinion of H. W. Beecher, 151; religion, art, etc., 151.
Flint, Timothy, 401 ; his pictures of the West, 402 ; his " History and Geography of the Mississippi Valley," 403 ; opinion of the *London Quarterly* upon, 404.
Florida, a paradise for the naturalist, 379 ; explored by John Bartram, 379.
Force, Peter, writings and compilations of, 36 ; a collector of works relating to America, 318.
Foster, John R., translates Peter Kalm's " Travels in North America," 295.
French and Americans, cause of their affinity, 153.

French and English writers on the War for the Union contrasted, 153.
French economical works on America, 146.
French missionaries the initiators of travel literature in the New World, 24; explorations of, 37.
French Protestant clergy, books of, on United States, 149.
French travellers and writers, 58.
French writers on America, their superior candor, 269.
Frenchmen, American opinions of, described by L'Abbé Robin, 79; eminent, address of, to loyal Americans, 154.
Furstenwäther, Baron, first impressions on America, 303.

GALE, Ludwig, "My Emigration to the United States," 306.
Gasparin, Count de, his "Uprising of a Great People," 153.
Germans, interest of the, in the United States, 301; their literature on the United States," 302.
Goldsmith, Oliver, his ignorance of America, 254.
Gorges, Fernando, "America Painted to the Life," 28; his American enterprises, 29.
Gorges, Sir Ferdinand, remarks of Winthrop and Bancroft on, 29.
Government expeditions, U. S., 418.
Grant, Mrs., 170; her "Memoirs of an American Lady," 171; sketch of society at Albany, 172.
Grassi, Padre Giovanni, 341; his "Notes," 341; extravagant statements of, 341.
Grattan, Thos. Colley, "Civilized America," 229; his animadversions, 230.
Grund, Francis J., his books on America, 308; his opinion of the writings of Basil Hall and Hamilton, 309; business habits of Americans, 309; interests of the people connected with the Government, 310; necessity of concord between England and America, 310.
Gurowski, Adam, 300; his book on America, 300.

HAERNE, Le Chanoine de, "La Questione Américaine," 301.
Hakluyt, Richard, 24; his works, 25.
Hall, Capt. Basil, remarks of Edward Everett on his book, 200; criticized by *Blackwood's Magazine*, 200.
Hall, James, 411.
Halleck, Fitz-Greene, lines of, on Cooper, 414.
Hamilton, Capt. Thomas, "Men and Manners in America," 223; his prejudices, 223; appreciates natural beauty, 223.
Hawthorne, Nathaniel, his book reviewed by the London *Daily News*, 275; his hits at British tendency to stagnation, 275; his romances, 431.
Hazlitt, Wm., his opinion of Crevecœur's "Letters of an American Farmer," 89.
Heine apostrophizes Wm. Cobbett, 211; his estimate of English blockheads, 255; on the exultation of the English at dissensions in America, 267.

Hennepin, Louis, 39; explores the Mississippi, 40; returns to France, and in 1683 publishes his "Descriptions," 41.
Henry, Alexander, his "Travels and Adventures," commended by Chancellor Kent, 185.
Historical romances, American writers of, 431.
Histories, local, 426; general, 428.
Hodgson, Adam, 217; Jared Sparks's opinion of his book, 218.
Hoffman, Charles Fenno, his "Winter in the West," 416; his geniality and versatility, 416.
Holland, Sir Henry, on the mutability of everything in America, 439.
Honyman, Rev. James, receives a letter from Berkeley, 162.
Humboldt, Alexander Von, remarks of Prescott on, 19; remarks of, on America, 303.

ILLINOIS, early history of, 52; natural features of, 53; commercial facilities of, 54; rapid increase of population in, 54; Jesuit missionaries in, 55; Father Marest's account of, 56.
Imlay, Gilbert, 390.
Immigration, 440.
"Inciquin the Jesuit's Letters," 394.
Ingersoll, Charles J., 395.
Inns, number of, in America, 216; Priscilla Wakefield's description of, 216.
Irving, Washington, remarks on the "Imago Mundi" of Petrus de Alyaco, 23; extract from a letter from Moore to, 211; accounts for the abuse of English writers of travel in the United States, 258; his writings compared with those of Addison, 288.
Italian travellers in America, 334.
Italy and America alike interesting to authors, 2.

JANSON, C. W., "The Stranger in America," 218.
Jefferson, Thomas, visit of Marquis de Chastellux to, 69.
Jenks, Rev. Wm., D. D., account of Madoc's Voyage to America in 1170, 18.
Jesuits, the, in Illinois, 55.
Jews, a number of, in Rhode Island, 168.
Johnson, Rev. Samuel, becomes acquainted with Bishop Berkeley, 167.
Josselyn, John, "New England's Rarities Discovered," 32.
Judd, Sylvester, his "Margaret," 431.
Juridical literature, 428.

KALM, Peter, 295; his works on America, 295; notes of his diary on Philadelphia, 295; his picture of Albany in 1749, 296; visit to Niagara Falls, 297.
Kay, Joseph, "Social Condition and Education of the People in England," 283.
Kemble, Mrs., on the affinity between the Americans and the French, 153; John G. Kohl's opinion of, 316.
Kendall, E. A., "Travels through the Northern Parts of the United States," 206.

INDEX. 457

Kent, Chancellor, commends "Travels and Adventures of Alexander Henry," 185.
Kirkland, Mrs. C. M., her books on the West, 422.
Knight, Madame, her "Private Journal," 385; her journey from Boston to New York, 386.
Kohl, J. G., "History of Discovery in America from Columbus to Franklin," 30; sketch of his writings, 311; his impressions of Boston, 313; sketch of Mrs. Kemble, 316; Edward Everett, 318; Prescott, 320; John Lothrop Motley, 321; Thomas H. Benton, 322; visit to Newport, 324; Bancroft, 324; Sumner, 325; Southern hate of New England, 326.

LABOULAYE, Edouard, "Paris dans l'Amérique, 153.
Lafayette, on the necessity of the perpetuation of the American Union, 11; his love of the people and institutions of America, 148.
La Salle embarks for Canada in 1675, with Father Hennepin, 39; explores the great lakes, 39; gives the name to Louisiana, 40.
Lauzun, Duke de, charmed with the society at Newport, 147.
Law, writers on American, 428.
Lecomte, Col. Ferdinand, "The War in the United States," 300.
Lederer, John, the first explorer of the Alleghanies, 32.
Ledyard, John, 387.
Lenox, James, a collector of books and documents relating to America, 318.
Libraries, American private, ignorance of British writers concerning, 274.
Lieber, Dr. Francis, 305; his "The Stranger in America," 305.
Lincoln, Abraham, Proclamation of, 448.
Literature, American, considered beneath contempt by British writers fifty years ago, 287; claimed to be made up of imitations of British authors, 287.
Literature, juridical, 428.
London Quarterly Review, its opinion of Rev. John Bristed's "America and her Resources," 206.
Lowell, factories of, compared with those of Manchester, Eng., by Anthony Trollope, 237.

MADOC, Rev. Wm. Jenks's account of his voyage to America in 1170, 18.
Marbois, 388; his "Notes on Virginia," 389.
Marest, Father, travels in Illinois, 56.
Marquette and Joliet, explorations of, 45; death of Father Marquette, 45.
Martineau, Harriet, 224; her fairness as a writer, 224; *Blackwood's* opinion of her book, 225.
Mather, Cotton, "Magnalia Christi Americana," 7, 33.
McSparron, Rev. James, letters of, 170.
Meier, K., "To the Sacramento," 300.
Ménard, Father Réne, plans an expedition in search of, the Mississippi in 1660, 44.

Michaux, Dr. F. A., visits the country west of the Alleghanies in 1802, 121; his descriptions of natural productions, 121; passion of Western people for spirituous liquors, 122.
Michelet, his opinion of America, 265.
Montalembert, discourse in the French Academy on America, 10.
Moore, Thomas, projects emigrating to America, 211; extract of letter from, to Washington Irving, 211; arrives at Norfolk, Va., 213; meets Jefferson at Washington, 213; his remarks on New York scenery, 213; his prejudices regarding America, 214.
Morris, Robert, description of, by Marquis de Chastellux, 66.
Motley, John Lothrop, John G. Kohl's sketch of, 321.
Mount Vernon, visit of Luigi Castiglione to, 339.
Murat, Achille, settles in Tallahassee, Fla., 122; his work on the United States, 123; his pro-slavery ideas, 124.

NATURAL features of America conduce to the spread of civilization, 15.
Naturalists, interest of America to, 295.
Neal, John, writes articles on America for *Blackwood's Magazine*, 396.
New England, religious character of her primitive annals, 24; strict observance of the Sabbath in, 178; Southern hate of, 326.
Newfoundland, fisheries of, long the only attraction to European adventure, 21.
New Netherlands, Van der Dock's account of, in 1659, 27.
Newport, R. I., its society attractive to French officers, 148; Bishop Berkeley arrives at, 163; Berkeley's discription of, 164; Dr Burnaby's remarks on the commerce of, 175; sketch of, by John G. Kohl, 324.
New World, the effects of its discovery and settlement upon maritime progress and interests, 22.
New York Bay, Verrazzano's description of, 338.
New York, Northern, described by Marquis de Chastellux, 67; sketch of, by Brissot in 1788, 87; varied nationalities represented in, 440.
Niagara Falls, visit of Peter Kalm to, 297.
North America, continent of, its extent and area, 15; its climate, soil, and productions adapted to the tastes and wants of European emigrants, 15; its productions confounded with those of South America by ignorant Europeans, 22; a refuge from persecution in early colonial times, 193.
North American Review, remarks of the, on Rev. Isaac Fiddler's "Observations," 201; exposes the ignorance of British writers on America, 262.

OLMSTED, Frederick Law, his travels in the South, 417.
Opportunity the characteristic distinction of America, 446.

20

Orators, American, 429.
Oswego, John Bartram's description of, 377.

PALMETTO tree, description of, by Priscilla Wakefield, 216.
Paulding, James K., "Letters from the South," 398; description of Virginia and its people, 399; his "John Bull in America," 400.
Peabody, George, his gift to the London working class, 280.
Pinchin, Mr., one of the first settlers of Springfield, Mass., 29.
Pianni, Lieut.-Col. Ferri, 365; his impressions on the patriotism of the American people, 366; visits the Union and Rebel armies, 369; pleased with Boston and its society, 370.
Poets, American, 433.
Political treatises, American, 428.
Portsmouth, N. H., visit of Marquis de Chastellux to, 73.
Prentice, Archibald, "A Tour in the United States," 245; his appreciation of American character, 246; compares American to Scotch scenery, 246; American dislike to "John Bull," 247.
Prescott, William H., sketch of, by John G. Kohl, 320.
Press, the Paris, on the War for the Union, 152; the British, its general unfairness on the American question, 244; the British, blinded by self-love in discussing American institutions, 280.
Primitive inhabitants of America, conjectures in regard to the, 17.
Providence, R. I., sketch of, by Marquis de Chastellux, 62.
Purchas, Rev. Samuel, 25.

QUAKERS, prevalence of in Rhode Island, 168.

RAFN, Carl Christain, claims the discovery of America by the Scandinavians in the tenth century, 13; his "Northern Antiquities," 294.
Raumer, Freidrich von, "America and the American People," 304.
Raynal, the Abbé, writings of, on America, 107.
Rebellion, the Slaveholders', literature arising from, 8; Anthony Trollope's view of, 242.
Reference, American works of, 427.
Religious Annals of America, 426.
Religious sects in America, writers on, 426.
Revue des Deux Mondes, the, on French disinterestedness, 272.
Rhode Island, Bishop Berkeley settles in, 168; religious toleration in, 168; prevalence of Quakers in, 168; Jews in, 168; Dr. Burnaby's opinion of the people of, 175; Major Robert Rogers's opinion of, 181.
Ritter, Prof. Carl, "Geographical Studies," 15.
Robin, L'Abbé, describes Boston in 1781, 76; customs of its people, 77; its commerce, 78; American ideas of Frenchmen, 79.

Robinson, Mrs. (Talvi), 329.
Rochambeau, Count, arrives at Newport, R. I., in 1780, 111; his "Mémoires," 111; opinion of American women, 112; description of a settlement, 112; church and state in America, 113; popular respect for law, 113; is impressed with the patriotism of the people, 114.
Rochefoucault, Duke de La, visits America, 94; his minuteness of detail, 95; traits of American character, 96.
Rogers, Major Robert, 181; his opinion of people of Rhode Island, 181.
Romances, American historical, 431.
Rupplus, Otto, the novels of, on the United States, 310.
Rush, Richard, on the fall of the naval supremacy of Great Britain, 255.

SABBATH, strict observance of the, in New England, 178.
Salvatore Abbate e Migliori, 302.
San Domingo, connection of Columbus with, 20.
Saxe-Weimar-Eisenach, Bernhard, Duke of, his "Travels in North America," 304.
Scenery and local features of America, writers on the, 434.
Schaff, Dr. Philip, 330; his "Sketch of the Political, Social, and Religious Character of the United States," 330; respect for law in America, 332; relation of America to Europe, 333.
Schultz, Christian, "Travels," 306; his description of locomotive facilities in the United States in 1807-'8, 306.
Science, American writers on the various branches of, 435.
Scotch writers on America, 245.
Seatsfield, Charles, novels of, on the United States, 310.
Sects, religious, writers on, in America, 426.
Segur, Count, arrives in America in 1783, 115; becomes attached to the Quakers of Philadelphia, 116; is favorably impressed with the American people, 116; dines with Washington, 116; prophetic significance of his observations on the future of America, 117; his remarks on embarking for the West Indies, 117.
Sicily, ignorance of its people concerning America, 361.
Slavery, American, Dickens's remarks on, 201; its debasing and brutalizing influence, 447.
Smibert, the painter, embarks for America with Bishop Berkeley, 160; paints portraits of Berkeley and his family, 160; Horace Walpole's opinion of, 160; his contributions to art in New England, 160; Berkeley's lasting regard for, 161; notices identity of race between Narraganset Indians and Siberian Tartars, 167.
Smith, Captain John, his explorations in America, 27; his writings on America, 28.
Smith, Sydney, his opinion of Henry B. Fearon, 200.
Smythe, J. F. D., his "Tour in the United

States of America, 188; his opinion of Washington, 191; views of Americans, 192.
Smythe, Prof., remarks on the collections of Hakluyt and Purchas, 26.
Society, Northern European writers on, in the United States, 307.
Southern hate of New England, 326.
Southey, Robert, his opinion of Timothy Dwight's "Travels," 392.
Spanish and Portuguese the pioneers in voyaging westward, 21.
Springfield, Mass., account of the first settlement of, 29; its appearance in 1645, 30.
Statistical works, American, 427.
Stirling, James, "Letters from the Slave States," 247; respect and affection due from England to America, 250.
Sumner, Charles, visited by John G. Kohl, 325.
Sweden, writers of, on America, 293; colony of, on the Delaware, 297.

TALLEYRAND, his opinion of American backwoodsmen, 114.
Theology, writers on, in America, 433.
Times, the London, its inimical spirit toward America, 291; Cobden's opinion of, 291.
Tocqueville, Alexis De, sent to America in 1830, 129; his "Democracy in America," 130; his philosophical view of American institutions, 132; his death, 134; notices a similarity of American tastes and habits, whether in the city or the wilderness, 136; his idea of State sovereignty, 138; considers the probable future supremacy of America and Russia over each half of the globe, 139; on English selfishness, 268; remarks on religion in America, 270; English opinion of his writings on America, 272.
Toleration in America the source of its attraction to foreign exiles, 7.
Travel, books of, enduring in interest, 1; general sameness of writings of, in America, 4; miscellaneous French works of, on America, 146, 147.
Trollope, Anthony, 232; his "North America," 232; his candor as a writer, 232; his ignorance of previous writings on America, 234; his egotism, 234; impressed with the beauty of American scenery, 236; education and labor in the United States and England contrasted, 236; dislikes "Young America," 238; American women met in public conveyances, 239; spoiled children, 239; versatility of the Americans, 240; mania of Americans for travel, 241; opinion of the rebellion, 241.
Trollope, Mrs., 225; her "Domestic Manners of the Americans," 225; her powers of observation, 225; superficiality of her judgment, 226; is pleased with American scenery, 228; her want of discrimination, 228.
Tudor, William, "Letters from the Eastern States," 412.
Turrel, Jane, "An Invitation to the Country," 33.

UNION, the war for the, changes of opinion wrought by, 447; its influence on society, 448.
United States, the earliest descriptions and associations connected with its territory tinctured with tradition, 19; extent of the, 276; John Bright on the strength of the Government of the, 449.

VAN DER DOCK'S account of New Netherlands in 1659, 27.
Verrazzano, 338; his description of New York Bay in 1524, 338.
Virginia, the name given to the Jamestown colony, 21; provincial egotism of, 30; journey of Marquis de Chastellux into, 68; the people of, described by Rev. Andrew Burnaby, 173; number of early descriptions of, 397; its associations, 397.
Volney, C. F., work of, on America, 97; his early passion for travel, 98; a victim of the French Revolution, 99; his philosophy, 100; difficulties as an emigrant, 101; his death, 101; review of his life and writings, 102; recollections of by Dr. Francis of New York, 105; his visit to Warrentown, 105; scientific vein of his writings, 106.
Voltaire, his comparison of the English, 290.

WAKEFIELD, Priscilla, her compilation from the works of early writers on America, 215; description of the Palmetto Royal, 216; number of inns met with in America, and independence of innkeepers, 216.
Walpole, Horace, his opinion of Bishop Berkeley's scheme, 158; his sketch of Smibert, the painter, 160.
Walsh, Robert, 395; his "Appeal," 395.
Wansey, Henry, 194; his "Excursion to the United States," 194; breakfasts with Washington at Philadelphia, 194; his impressions of Washington, 194; remarks the general contentment of the people, 195; journeys through New England, 195; meets distinguished persons at New York, 196.
Washington, George, first interview of Marquis de Chastellux with, 65; takes leave of De Chastellux at Newburgh, 74; described by De Chastellux, 75; visited by Brissot de Warville at Mount Vernon, 85; J. F. D. Smythe's opinion of, 191; breakfasts with Henry Wansey, 194; his opinion of Count Adriani's book, 340; a glimpse of Connecticut, 419; visits Boston, 421.
Webster, Daniel, imperishability of the record of his eloquence, 429.
Weld, Isaac, "Travels in America," 207.
Welsh, the, claim to be early explorers of America, 17.
Western travel and adventure, books of, 422.
Wheaton, Henry, "History of the Northmen," 19.
White, Rev. James, on British prejudices, 266.

Wied, Prince Maximilian von, "Journey through America," 305.
Williams, Roger, liberal spirit of, 168.
Wilson, Alexander, 199; his "American Ornithology," 199.
Winterbotham, his authorities in compiling his "View of the United States," 3.
Winthrop, John, journal of, 31; on the debasement of the poor in England, 282.
Wirt, Wm., "Letters of a British Spy," 412.
Women, American, Anthony Trollope's remarks on, 239.

Wood, William, "New England Prospect," 32.

YALE College, gifts of Bishop Berkeley to, 167.

ZENGER, John P., printer of the New York *Weekly Journal*, narrative of his trial for libel, 7.
Zimmerman, E. A. W., "France and the Free States of North America," 306.

www.ingramcontent.com/pod-product-compliance
Lightning Source LLC
Chambersburg PA
CBHW022105300426
44117CB00007B/600